Dad's Best Memories and Recollections

by Charles J. Humber

◆ FriesenPress

Suite 300 - 990 Fort St
Victoria, BC, Canada, V8V 3K2
www.friesenpress.com

Copyright © 2016 by Charles J. Humber
First Edition — 2016

Design Services provided by
deasbook.com

Cover photo credits:
Front cover: Erik Shennette
Back cover: Kristy Shennette

CANADIAN CATALOGUING IN PUBLICATION DATA
978-0-9948968-0-3
MAIN ENTRY UNDER TITLE
Dad's Best Memories and Recollections

All rights reserved.

No part of this publication may be reproduced in any form, or by any means, electronic or mechanical, including photocopying, recording, or any information browsing, storage, or retrieval system, without permission in writing from FriesenPress.

ISBN
978-1-4602-8336-3 (Hardcover)
978-1-4602-8337-0 (Paperback)
978-1-4602-8338-7 (eBook)

1. Biography and Autobiography
2. Biography and Autobiography, Personal Memoir
3. Biography and Autobiography, Cultural Heritage

Distributed to the trade by The Ingram Book Company

*D*edicated

to my wife Gayle

and our four children:
Kristan Laura Humber
Karyn Anna Humber
Charlie William Humber
Scott Nicholas Humber

and our eight grandchildren:
Christopher James Shennette
Bradley Jarvis Shennette
Mitchell Gary Shennette
Charlie Henry Humber
Gordon Peter Humber
Caroline Emily Humber
Madelyn Nicole Humber
Austin Nicholas Humber

Acknowledgements

The last several years have been rather hectic times in my household where most of the writing for **Dad's Best Memories and Recollections** took place. Now that the project is coming to a close, I'd be remiss not to acknowledge those individuals, present or past, who have contributed to my ambitious publication efforts. Truly, they've made my literary saga possible.

One of these is a former colleague at Heirloom Publishing Inc. where for fifteen years Angela Dea Cappelli, as President, and I, as Publisher, worked diligently together to publish the nationally acclaimed seven-volume Canada Heirloom Series. She not only designed and "redesigned" **Dad's Best Memories and Recollections**, but has earnestly proof-read each story and has made sure that all the illustrations were properly cropped, placed in sequence and accompanied by correct captions. Her discriminating eye has made sure that subtle design balance and illustration deportment throughout this project was pleasing and professional.

From my parents, now long gone, I learned to be reflective and old-fashioned, loyal and considerate, characteristics that turned me into a very, reflective, sentimental person. As I write these remarks, I cannot help but recall one of my very favourite lines of poetry, namely, "I am a part of all that I have met." This line taken from Alfred Lord Tennyson's "Ulysses" has, over the years, engaged me to understand in a most meaningful way the thrilling journey we all take as we pass through this life and into the next. My life has, for sure, been most rewarding and has generated for me extraordinary memories, 125 of which I've now recorded in this volume for those who follow me. I trust that my four children and eight grandchildren will every so often pick up this volume and peruse it and reflect that the individual who shared his memories with them will cause them each to reflect that their own lives, too, are full of wonder. They just have to take time out, be reflective and recall those memories we have shared together....

It would also be a terrible mistake not to recall that my loving wife, Gayle, has consistently encouraged my endeavours to record our cherished past times together. They all began after we first met in Fairbanks, Alaska, 1960. She was teaching at Ladd Air Force Base and I was a foreign student at the University of Alaska. Over many hectic years since, Gay has supported my various literary urges, especially these last three years during which time I have chaotically left both our Mississauga home and Muskoka cottage in total disarray. These two residences regularly have displayed scattered papers and various print matter of all kinds, thousands of photographs, stacks and stacks of various files and calling cards, and manila envelopes filled with ephemera in virtually every room of our two residences. In many ways, she has been the backbone of my publishing endeavours and has unconditionally supported my ambitious efforts to produce my ninth overall book, this one, in particular, recording my 125 "Best Memories."

Not to acknowledge these immense contributions would be great negligence and disservice. And so I take this time as I finalize this project to thank them for their ongoing and overall efforts in making **Dad's Best Memories and Recollections** a treasured, future heirloom…

Introduction

If we live a reasonably long life, I suggest, in our sunset years, that we tend to become reflective and sentimental. As I approach my eightieth birthday, I honestly can say that I do not have many regrets. If anything, the negative impacts that I've endured were long ago turned into lessons. Sometimes a baseball player strikes out in the first inning. But he or she has several more at bats in the game! That last at bat could be a game-winner, a walk-off home run! In no way am I comparing this last book of mine to a game-winning home run but it is a base hit and hopefully captures many highlights of my life. It is now my pleasure sharing them with you.

When I was publisher of the CANADA Heirloom Series (1985-2001), three books of that seven-volume series, namely, **PATHFINDERS, WAYFARERS** and **VISIONARIES**, each profiled the achievements of 125 Canadians whose individual accomplishments impacted the world stage with lasting positive consequences. Thus it was that I felt 125 stories of my best memories would continue in the same vein permitting me to share a portion of my enriched life with those who have come to know me and perhaps some who have never known or heard of me.

This sharing has very little to do with any self-importance or ego although I must admit that had I an inferiority complex this book would probably never have got off the ground. Whatever, my wish is to express that my journey through life has indeed had some interesting chapters that I feel are uplifting, inspirational and educational.... For my own children and grandchildren and those who follow me into a post-Obama world, I did think it would be interesting for my readership to learn that this politically incorrect father, grandfather and uncle did have an enriched life. I do want to share with them what it was like to grow up in post-World War II America, what it was like to be a door-to-door salesman in the 1950s and what it was like to hitch-hike three thousand miles to attend university in Alaska. I just felt that telling stories about what it was like to interact with some of the world's best-known celebrities, to hunt and find rare examples of Canadiana, or to discover family roots, might just help some to discover their own inner joys. The best memories I now share have each shaped my personality. It was also meaningful for me to demonstrate that people, famous or the not so famous, are not much different from any of us. A few of my vignettes attempt to show what it was like to travel to Jerusalem, London, Hawaii, and San Francisco, worldly places, that, over time, will undergo major cultural changes. Thus, many of these vignettes are meaningful time capsules capturing local colour for posterity. It was also a great pleasure for me to reminisce how I connected with individuals such as President Harry Truman, JFK's father, Joe Kennedy, Prime Minister Brian Mulroney, The Rt. Hon. Roland Michener, Her Majesty The Queen, hockey moguls, Hartland Molson and Steve Stavros, plus Jack Dempsey and Mickey Rooney, as well as Prime Minister Jean Chretien, Frankie Laine and some 100 others. How I acquired Thomas Alva Edison's rocking horse is as great a memory for me as telling what it was like to drive, in 1945, from Toronto to Boston in a Model A Ford or, indeed, what it was like, at fourteen, to spend New Year's eve in the boondocks of New Hampshire or, at twelve years, to attend in 1948 a one-room school.

Whether you have even remotely heard of me, **Dad's Best Memories** will, I hope, inspire you to duplicate something similar so that your own offspring will understand from whence you or they came.... In many respects I feel that this volume is my tombstone, a monument to my life. You may pass by it with a cold eye or you may be inspired to undertake to write your own book with your own 125 stories. I encourage you to do so, to let your offspring know that you, too, had a life, that you loved and pumped blood, and that your life, too, had meaning....

Table of Contents

Dedication	iii
Acknowledgements	iv
Introduction	v
Table of Contents	vi-vii
Memories I	viii
Last Professional Baseball Game of the 20th Century	9
His Holiness Pope John Paul II	10
Harry Truman	11
A Canadian Champion in the Family	12
Carl Millard	14
H. L. Mencken	15
Judge John Ross Matheson	16
Chain of Office, 1982-1984	17
Uncle Bill Donaldson	18
Major-General Richard Rohmer	19
California, Here We Come	20
Jack Dempsey	24
Mickey Rooney	25
Toronto Blue Jays Meet John Graves Simcoe, 1980	26
H.R.H. Prince Andrew and Okill Stuart	28
Frankie Laine	29
One-Room School House	30
Travelling in a 1930 Model A Ford, Part I	32
Travelling in a 1930 Model A Ford, Part II	34
Mrs. Pattison of Cohasset	36
Alice Morse	38
Joseph Patrick Kennedy	39
Pine Vista: Our "Castle in the Wilderness"	40
Hitchhiking to Alaska, 1960	42
H. Northrop Frye	44
Two Lords: Roy and Ken Thomson	46
Venturing to the Maritimes, 1983	48
Orange and Athol, Massachusetts	52
Les Trevor	53
Cornelius Biddle, Crimean War Veteran	54
Uncle Lester Prosser	56
Thomas Alva Edison Rocking Horse	58
Her Majesty Queen Elizabeth II	59
Trip to Israel, 1984	60
Allan Walters, M.D.	62
Mortlach, Saskatchewan	64
Gio Batta Garlatti	66
Historic Emigh House	67
Historic Road Signs	68
Summer, 1948, Part I	70
Summer, 1948, Part II	72
Howard Pain	74
Sir Isaac Brock	76
Aunt Marie Jarvis	77
Steve Stavro	78
My First Driver's License, 1957	79
Prime Minister Brian Mulroney	80
Franc Joubin	82
Run Free Now – Go Play with the Angels	84
Gordon Ball	88
June Schweyer	89
John W. Fisher, "Mr. Canada"	90
Lt. Col. James A. Rolen	92
My Romanov Connection	94
James K. Irving	95
James C. Floyd	96
Aunt Lillian Maude Jarvis Wolf	98
Prof. J.M.S. Careless	99
Café Trieste, San Francisco	100
Hugh P. MacMillan	101
Honest Ed Mirvish	102

Senator Hartland de Montarville Molson	103	H. C. Burleigh, M.D.	164
Governor General D. Roland Michener	104	100th Anniversary Dinner UELAC	165
David Macdonald Stewart	106	Maurice Strong	166
Grandparenting	108	Louis Mayzel	168
J. C. Potter	112	C. Miller Fisher, M. D.	170
Group Captain J. C. Bauer	114	Col. Strome Galloway	171
Double Trouble, October 17, 1973	116	The Grobb Cupboard	172
Lord Mayor Wilbert Dick	118	Deltiology	174
Grandmother Humber's 100th Birthday	119	My Belfast Connection	176
Stan Barrett	120	Isle of Wight, 2002	178
John Kenneth Galbraith	122	The Big Chute	180
Dr. Wilfred G. Bigelow	124	Aloha Hawaii	182
Rick and Bruce Humber	126	Dad and Kik's Trip to New England, 2014	184
Charles W. Dunn	128	Visiting Britannia, 2001	186
Prime Minister Jean Chrétien	129	50th Wedding Anniversary, August 22, 1984	188
Bill McNeil	130	Brian and Betty: Very Best of the Very Best	190
Wayne Getty	132	Goderich, a Last Hurrah	192
Fields Corner Reunions, MacTier, 2009 & 2010	134	Les Donaldson, Dean of Antiques	194
Oriskany	136	The William Morris Chair	196
Calvin Katz	138	Dunn Court, Dorchester	198
Two War Memorial Dedications	140	University of Alaska, 1960-1961	200
John W. Holmes	142	University of Wisconsin, 1967-1970	202
New Year's Eve, 1951	144	Newfoundland, "Whadda ya'at b'y"	204
Christmas Letter, 2008	146	Percé on the Rocks	206
C.A. Humber's Tool Chest	148	Launching **LOYAL SHE REMAINS**, 1984	208
G. Blair Laing	150	**Family Sleuthing** Revisited, 2006	210
Sir William Campbell House	152	Writers I Have Known	214
Bert Case Diltz	154	Wally R. Kent, M.D.	216
Ted Williams	155	R.G. LeTourneau	218
Max Storey, Auctioneer	156	Open-Heart Surgery at Ninety-Five Years	219
The Sunshine State Beckons	158	Premier E. C. Drury	220
Farr's Mills	162	Memories II	221
Mr. Speaker, Steve Peters	163	Index of Surnames	222

Grandparents get first peek at first granddaughter, Caroline Emily Humber, 2006.

Flanking Gay and Charlie Humber are two sisters, Anna and Priscilla, with their respective husbands, namely, Jim Rolen and Chuck Hurlbut, Gravenhurst, 2007.

Four Humber siblings dressed in UEL period costumes, 1983, in New Brunswick.

Left: Two California families, Gay's brother and sister with their spouses, visit **Pine Vista** in Muskoka, 2009. **Right:** Former students flank their former teacher after watching movie **Black Mass.** Left to Right: Dave Battison, Frank Carnovale, John Turco, Chazzz, Steve Pecar, Tullio Capone and Joe Provato.

Last Professional Baseball Game of the 20th Century

Being a baseball fan ever since my family moved to Boston from Toronto, 1945, I loved listening, first, on the radio, then watching, on television, the two professional baseball teams playing out of Boston, namely, the Braves of the National League, and the Red Sox, of the American League. Who could ever forget Curt Gowdy broadcasting the Red Sox games on TV at the same time sipping Ballantine Ale in his broadcast booth from the first to the ninth inning! As a youth, it was just wonderful to follow such Braves as Alvin Dark, Eddie Stanky and Tommy Holmes, and it was just as devastating when the Braves lost the World Series, 1948, in spite of the fact that the two best pitchers in all of professional baseball at the time, Warren Spahn and Johnny Sain ("Spahn and Sain and pray for rain"), were the backbone of the team. I remember going one night, sometime in the late 1940s, to Braves Field (which today is the home field for the Boston University baseball team) and watching Johnny Mize of the New York Giants hit a towering homerun right over the scoreboard in dead center field. I also remember one particular evening in Cohasset, Massachusetts. I was working, during the summer of 1953, as a lobster cook at Hugo's Lighthouse. Because the owner of the Boston Braves, Lou Perini, had decided to move "my" team to Milwaukee that same year, I made sure that the lobster he ordered was only semi-cooked. He probably had poor taste buds as I never heard one way or the other whether he enjoyed his lobster half-cooked! As for the Red Sox, the heartbreak team in both 1948 and 1949 lost out winning the pennant on the very last game of both seasons. But Ted Williams, "the splendid splinter," was the backbone of the Red Sox in my early teenage years. His home run in 1946 still stands out as the longest ever hit at Fenway Park. If you go to Fenway Park early enough before a Red Sox game, you can see one red seat in the stadium located in the right center field stands amid the other seats all of them colored green. That's where his homer went a swat over 502 feet! I also remember skipping school on "Ted Williams Day", April 30, 1952. I was there to watch him hit a home run to win the game, 5-3, on the very day before he re-entered the service as a bomber pilot in Korea.

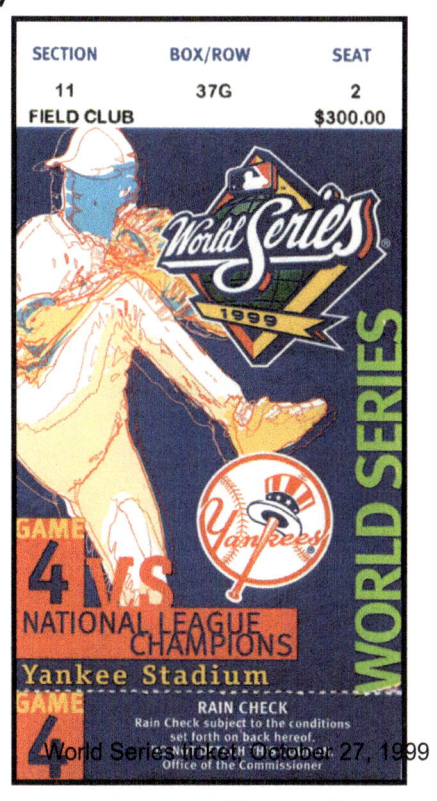

Over many years, I have remained a stanch baseball fan but have shifted my allegiance from Boston to the Toronto Blue Jays. I was absolutely thrilled when the Blue Jays won back-to-back World Series in 1992 and 1993. And sometimes, as my sons Charlie and Scott grew up, or a generation later when my grandsons were at the right age, I took these guys to a variety of baseball parks, including old Cominsky Park and Wrigley Field in Chicago, Briggs Stadium in Detroit, stadiums in Cleveland, Baltimore, Philadelphia, New York, including both Yankee and Shea stadiums, the Giants ballpark in San Francisco, even the Tropicana stadium in Tampa Bay.

But the highlight of all these treks to various stadiums over the years occurred on October 27, 1999, when the New York Yankees were playing the Atlanta Braves for the World Series. The Yankees were up three games to none. If they won the game that my son, Charlie, and I attended, not only would the Yankees win the World Series but we would be able to claim forever to have watched the last professional game of baseball played in the twentieth century! Of course, the Yankees and Roger Clemens did win! The atmosphere that memorable night was absolutely over the top. Charlie somehow, through his business connections, had secured a pair of three hundred dollar tickets about ten rows up on the first base side of the iconic old stadium. New York Mayor Rudy Giuliani was sitting several rows in front of us. Billionaire Donald Trump was sitting behind us. The atmosphere of some 60,000 fans was like midway madness. After the game, as we walked to the subway, the happy-go-lucky crowds were in jubilation. People were selling souvenirs, dancing, yelling, drinking, kissing, smoking, you name it.... It was all there amidst all the traffic jams. The team of Derek Jeter, Mariano Rivera, and Roger Clemens had won! Frank Sinatra's song **New York, New York** was blaring everywhere. It was all so very magical. Someone even died from cardiac arrest on the very subway car we travelled back to Charlie's apartment!

What a night to remember! For sure, this night was one of life's memorable memories....

World Series Ticket, October 27, 1999

Dad's Best Memories and Recollections

His Holiness Pope John Paul II

The Ontario Bicentennial of 1984 was a remarkable year of success in generating unprecedented heritage awareness and historical perspective. Two world figures visited the province during this year of celebration. These figures were Her Majesty The Queen and His Holiness Pope John Paul II.

LOYAL SHE REMAINS, the 600-page book I had co-edited for the bicentennial distribution, was receiving so much media exposure that it was very difficult for the Government of Ontario not to recognize its significance as an all-Canadian publication and a coffee-table book destined to become a family keepsake. Every Ministry in the Bill Davis government committed to buying multiple copies for ceremonial presentations throughout the year. Upon examining this volume, government authorities also found major references in **LOYAL SHE REMAINS** that met the needs of the government, especially the references to the Martyrs' Shrine in Midland where the Pope was going to visit the sacred sanctuary where eight Jesuit priests were martyred in the 1600s. When it was decided that the official gift to His Holiness the Pope would be a leather-bound copy of this book, announcements were made in multiple media outlets including a front-page story in **The Toronto Star.** In part the paper with the largest circulation in Canada said, "Ontario's official gift to the Pope will be a special edition of **LOYAL SHE REMAINS**, a lavish pictorial history of Ontario prepared for the provincial bicentennial by the United Empire Loyalists' Association of Canada.... The book is to be given to the Pope tomorrow evening at a thanksgiving ceremony at the Metro Convention Centre for more than 1000 special volunteers who organized the papal visit." The Premier, the Hon. Bill Davis, sent a special invitation letter to my residence inviting me to attend the ceremony which took place in the mid-afternoon on September 14, 1984. It was an honor to stand just several feet right in front of the decorated platform which the Pontiff stood on when the premier welcomed the Pope to Toronto and presented **LOYAL SHE REMAINS** to His Holiness. The Pope then turned to his audience, recognizing that a great many people present were likely absent from their regular employment just to be present for this occasion. With a brilliant sense of humor, he turned to the people in front of him, raised his hands and said, with broken English and a twinkle in his eyes, something very similar to, "Many of you here at this moment have likely come here without permission. I take this liberty, therefore, to absolve you collectively of the sin you have committed." The smile on his face spoke volumes. And while the crowd clapped, Bill Davis looked through the audience, briefly caught my eye right at the edge of the platform and nodded his head in recognition. It was a thrilling day for many reasons, especially for a high school teacher on leave of absence who left the Metro Convention Center that day back in 1984 completely satisfied, if not overwhelmed, as the immediate past President of the UEL Association of Canada and as the co-editor of **LOYAL SHE REMAINS,** the first book he had ever worked on and which had become such a resounding success in generating unprecedented heritage awareness.

THE POPE IN CANADA
A2/ TORONTO STAR, FRIDAY, SEPTEMBER 14, 1984

History book gift for Pope

Ontario's official gift to the Pope will be a special edition of *Loyal She Remains*, a lavish pictorial history of Ontario prepared for the provincial bicentennial by the United Empire Loyalists' Association of Canada.

"We're very honored," said Charles Humber, the book's co-editor, who had asked Walter Borosa, the province's protocol chief, to give John Paul II a copy during his visit.

But it was only a couple of weeks ago that Borosa told him that Premier William Davis wanted to make the 700-page volume Ontario's official gift to the Pontiff.

The Queen is to receive No. 1 of a limited edition of the book when she visits later this month, but the Pope will receive an unnumbered "exclusive" edition, Humber said.

The book is to be presented to the Pope tomorrow evening at a thanksgiving ceremony at the Metro Convention Centre for more than 1,000 special volunteers who organized the papal visit.

Excerpts from *Loyal She Remains* were published in 10 weekly instalments in The Star over the summer.

His Holiness Pope John Paul II accepts from Ontario Premier Bill Davis a copy of **LOYAL SHE REMAINS** at the Toronto Convention Centre, September 14, 1984.

Dad's Best Memories and Recollections

Harry S. Truman

Harry S. Truman, 33rd President of the United States, gave official approval for the fortress bomber, **Enola Gay,** to drop the Atomic Bomb on Hiroshima, Japan, August 6, 1945, then, three days later, on Nagasaki, thus bringing World War II to an end. A Missourian, who took office after the death of President Franklin D. Roosevelt, April 12, 1945, also approved the first test of the hydrogen bomb, "Ivey Mike", in 1952. President Truman was a very down-to-earth man. After surviving eight years as President, the former President, in retirement, was vacationing in New England during the summer of 1953 and ventured to Hugo's Lighthouse, a well-known seafood restaurant in Cohasset, just to the south of Boston. During that summer, I worked as a lobster cook in a kitchen nook that was situated near the front entrance of Hugo's Lighthouse. **Holiday Magazine,** on a yearly basis, always included Hugo's Lighthouse as one of the top ten restaurants in the United States during the 1950s.

The ex-President, affable smile on his face, walked over to the lobster pool where I was working and he pointed to a particular crustacean in the pool he desired for his supper. I picked up the ungarnished lobster from the cold running water of the circulating pool and took the lobster's big front claws, and used the same claws to balance the lobster up-side-down on its head. This was performed on the border of the lobster pool that was made of granite stone. To make the lobster stand on its head, so to speak, I quickly rubbed, with my knuckles, the back of the lobster which always resulted in the lobster reacting as if it were being electrically shocked. Immediately, the lobster began to flip its tail back and forth rather furiously.

The former President stood there in amazement at this show, looked at me through his rimless glasses, and said with a chuckle: "Well, I'll be god-dammed". He then left the "performance" for the reserved table set aside for him and his party. His table setting romantically overlooked Cohasset's beautiful harbor and the historic Minot Ledge Lighthouse off in the distance. From the outset I knew the guest was Harry Truman but took the whole happenstance in stride. Seventeen years old at the time, I tossed his lobster into a steam pot and prepared the two-pounder for the former President.... I think this took place in July but it might have happened in early August, 1953. This milestone episode in my life took place more than sixty years ago. It really is hard to believe that so much time has elapsed since my one and only encounter took place with a former President of the United States of America.

Top: Interior of Hugo's lighthouse illustrated on a 1940s postcard.
Bottom: the affable Harry S. Truman in retirement, circa 1954.

Dad's Best Memories and Recollections

A Canadian Champion in the Family

With Manitoba's provincial capitol building in the background, Karyn Anna Humber took time out from her busy track schedule in March, 1988, to visit with her father some of Winnipeg's historical landmarks. Little did we know, at the time, that her track and field team from York University would go on to win the all-Canadian Woman's Indoor Track and Field Championships.

Ever since my youngest daughter, Karyn, was a tyke, she strove to be at the head of the line in just about everything. For example, I'd take her to the Santa Claus Parade in downtown Toronto and plunk her down by the curb-side to assure her that she'd get a good place to view Santa and the parade. As the sidewalks filled up and the parade was imminent, other children began pushing. Using the strong-willed DNA she inherited from both parents, Karyn tenaciously held on to her "principality." She became spunky, using elbows, feet and self-reliance to keep her ground. No question about it, Karyn always held her stake with gusto in such situations, a trait that has been her key to a successful life, especially her long and successful track career.

While passing through grade school, Karyn blossomed as a runner even against older kids. This was particularly true in MacTier when Karyn, before she was ten years, ran in open events, year after year, out-performing students several ages above her. Some parents resented Karyn running against their offspring even though their children were a grade or so ahead of her. Once she entered high school, it became apparent that Karyn's drive to excel in all her races became a hallmark trait. As she entered her senior year, she clearly established herself as a top performer in the 400-metre hurdles. At the finals of OFSSA (Ontario Federation of School Athletic Associations), in 1985, she qualified for the provincial finals in the 400-metre hurdles running against Donalda Duprey who would, in short time, garner international recognition by winning two NCAA Championships at Louisiana State University. Duprey also represented Canada at the Barcelona Olympics, 1992. While Karyn came in second to Duprey in that 1985 OFSSA final, the two of them initiated good-spirited rivalries that lasted for years.

After graduating from high school, Karyn gained admittance to three top schools in Ontario: York University, the University of Western Ontario, and the University of Toronto. Instead of choosing to attend one of these schools, Karyn accepted a full-ride Track and Field Scholarship to Illinois State University in Normal, Illinois, a two-hour drive south of Chicago. I remember driving her there for the 1985-86 school year. I was a very proud father knowing that her running skills had clinched a full athletic scholarship and that she was heading off to an American university much like her father had done twenty-six years earlier. But her school year at ISU did not work out to her advantage. After developing a nasty hamstring injury, Karyn was coerced into competing for the Red Birds against her will. Her ability to run competitively was therefore seriously compromised. She felt that she had no choice but to leave Illinois State University and start over again at Toronto's York University which took place that fall, 1986.

After sitting out a year of track, Karyn re-gained her track and field eligibility and began competing for York University. During the 1987-1988 indoor track season, while Karyn was sprinting and hurdling for York University, the Canadian Interuniversity Association of Universities (CIAU), today the Canadian Interuniversity Sport (CIS), held its Indoor Canadian Track and Field Championship in Winnipeg. As publisher of Heirloom Publishing, 1988, I decided to initiate a business trip to Winnipeg while the city was hosting and the CIAU was running this all-Canadian championship track meet. My trip turned out to be, for sure, most memorable!

What I did not realize when I flew to Winnipeg that cold March, 1988, was that the York University women's track team consisted of just five participants. I was totally mesmerized watching these five women compete and win the Canadian University Women's Track and Field Championship for York

Dad's Best Memories and Recollections

University, Canada's equivalent to the annual NCAA championships held each year in the United States. It was truly an unprecedented accomplishment! Also amazing is the fact that the five members of this team did not participate in all the meet's events! In fact, when examining the schedule, the five members competed in just eight events, including the women's 4X200 and the 4X400 relay teams. Karyn ran the third leg of each of these two gold medal relay events handing the baton to France Gareau who had anchored, four years earlier, her Canadian team to a silver medal in the 4X100 relay at the Los Angeles 1984 Olympics. Witnessing Karyn's women's track team win the 1988 Canadian Indoor Track and Field Championship has remained an awesome memory for me over the last twenty-seven years.

At the Ontario Secondary Schools Track and Field Finals, 1985, Karyn, representing Leaside High School, Toronto, second left, gets off to a good start against her nemesis, Donalda Duprey, of Saugeen, far left, who finished first to Karyn's overall second place finish at Etobicoke Centennial Stadium.

Above: York University's Women's Track Team won the indoor Canadian Interuniversity Athletic Union (CIAU) Championship in Winnipeg, 1988. The team had only five members! This view depicts the Canadian University Women's Track and Field Champions: left to right, Karyn Humber, Coach Sue Wise, France Gareau, Lesa Mayes, Hester Westenburg, and Andrea Hastick. **Right:** Karyn's certificate honouring her as a member of the "All Canadian Team" that won the Canadian Indoor Track and Field Championship in Winnipeg in 1988.

13

Dad's Best Memories and Recollections

MILLARDAIR INCORP. | Carl Millard

I will always remember the time I stopped by to see Carl Millard's only son, Wayne, at the Millardair Hangar up on Derry Road East in Malton (Mississauga, Ontario). I believe my visit took place in 2008. What prompted me to reflect on our get-together was to learn that all the news outlets in Toronto in early 2014 were reporting that Wayne's son, Dellen, had just been formally charged with the murder not only of his father, Wayne, but at least one other person. What a shame! What a waste of talent! Dellen's grandfather, Carl Millard, was such a wonderful man and good friend. He passed away in 2006 at age ninety-three. When he was in his mid-80s, I remember this living legend standing in front of me in his Malton office and inducing me to check out his abdomen with my fist. I couldn't give him my best punch for any money but this former captain with Trans Canada Airlines, forerunner of Air Canada, was rock hard. And what a life he had! It is difficult, in 2014, to realize that Carl's grandson, Dellen, has recently and formally been charged with two murders, and suspected in still one other. These indictments include the suspected murder of Carl Millard's only son, Wayne!

Carl was one of my uncle Lester Prosser's buddies in the 1940s and '50s. They had both been bush pilots! Carl had also become a friend, especially after he was profiled, in 1991, on page 439 of **ALLEGIANCE, The Ontario Story**, volume III of the ongoing CANADA Heirloom Series. Lester and Carl often flew missions together back in the 1940s. It was uncle Lester who commissioned Carl to fly to British Columbia way back in the early-1950s to bring back containers filled with a special clay excavated from an isolated Indian Reservation somewhere in central British Columbia. My uncle was intent on manufacturing a powdered clay-compound, a medicinal product that he had registered as Peloid Clay. It was going to be marketed as a miracle cure for arthritis. When Lester tragically died, 1958, the clay project never got off the ground with the result that the clay was still stored in a collection of various-sized containers nearly fifty years later in one of several Millardair Hangars. This was as late as 2009 when Carl's son, Wayne, as president of Millardair, was still storing the product not knowing what to do with it. Today, at one time, Carl told me that he had flown more air miles than anyone except for two other individuals. I believe they were not Canadian. Carl flew a recorded 44,000 air hours. Because the average person works a forty-hour week, this means the average employee works some 2000 hours per year. In Carl's case, one could argue that Carl flew the equivalent of twenty years of full-time work, mainly aboard a fleet of piston-pumping DC3s or DC4s or as pilot in his Piper Apache, his Cessna 172, his magnificent twin-engine Beechcraft or at the "wheel" of his Citation Jet. I'm pleased Heirloom Publishing profiled him for posterity in **Allegiance**. Carl's bungalow in the old town of Meadowvale still stands at the southeast corner of Derry Rd. West and the old Second Line. He was a fascinating memorable character....

Dad's Best Memories and Recollections

H. L. Mencken

Often rebelling against the educational elitists of my day as well as the corrupt public school system that unquestionably promoted mediocrity, I embraced and adhered to very much what H.L. Mencken taught and wrote about nearly three-quarters of a century ago. He was, for sure, an obstinate rebel much like I have been throughout most of my life.... H. L. Mencken (1880-1956) claimed that:

> The aim of public education is not to spread enlightenment at all; it is to reduce as many individuals as possible to the same safe level, to breed and train a standardized citizenry, and to put down dissent and originality. That is its aim in the United States whatever the pretensions of politicians, pedagogues and other such mountebanks.

As far as I'm concerned, this quotation reflects the malaise that has insipidly generated today's American culture. Please read this quotation again. Take it in and absorb it and come to grips with the real enemy at large in America and give some thought to Mencken's belief that democracy, for the most part, is a system in which inferior men dominate their superiors. I studied the writings of H.L. Mencken (1880-1956) at both Temple University (1959-1962) and the University of Wisconsin (1967-1970). This erudite **Baltimore Sun** columnist was a journalist, essayist, editor, satirist, critic, and scholar of American literature, especially Mark Twain and Ayn Rand. As well, Mencken touted Joseph Conrad's **Heart of Darkness** as one of the world's great novels. He is still regarded (and often marginalized) as one of America's greatest thinkers, an eminent intellect of the first half of the 20th century. Ironically, he is just about universally scorned today because he just does not fit the formula promoted by America's so-called elite educators, both in classrooms and in the political arenas in Washington. The conscious teaching of mediocrity is today's educational mantra. It is a platform that I personally fought against throughout my twenty years of high school teaching, a career that included four and one-half years at T.L. Kennedy Secondary School (Mississauga), one year at Streetsville Secondary School (Mississauga), seven and one-half years at Lawrence Park Collegiate Institute (Toronto), and six years at Oakwood Collegiate Institute (Toronto). Most of my students accepted my passion and my personal fight against an educational establishment that promoted and advocated mediocrity. As young people growing up, each of my four children often looked at me as if I were some sort of oddity because my motivational efforts were so often unconventional. But today I feel safe in saying they have all grown up feeling pretty confident about themselves. My wonderful wife, Gay, who was a much better mother than I was a father, did everything she could, along with me, to make sure each of our children would not embrace or accept mediocrity. We also trusted that their inner instincts would lead them to understand that most people only rise up the proverbial social or business ladder until they reach their level of incompetence. To understand this Peter Principle should be a paramount plank of everyone's social platform. It has enabled each of our children to become strong-willed individuals, each refusing to accept mediocrity as a life goal and, avoiding, at all cost, the concept that people are quite comfortable and content to remain at their level of incompetence.

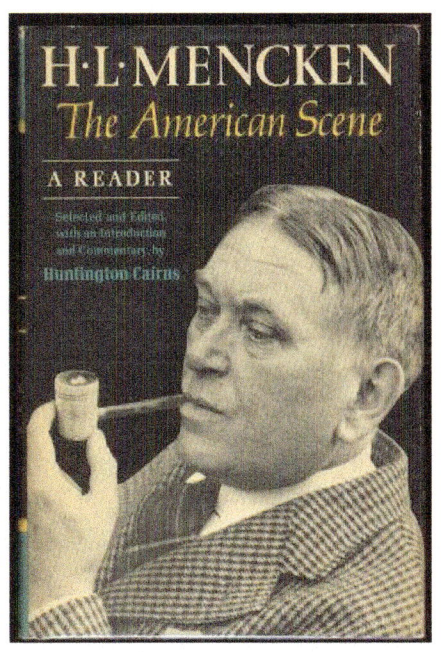

The selected works of H.L. Mencken was first published in 1965, nine years after his death in 1956.

Judge John Ross Matheson

It was sometime in the early 1990s. It was actually a crucial time in that if I were ticketed just one more demerit point to my total accumulation of 14, my driver's license would automatically have been suspended. I was driving to Ottawa from Toronto. I had an appointment with Prime Minister Brian Mulroney and was travelling pretty fast along Highway 7 through Peterborough to Ottawa. My appointment with the Prime Minister was at 3:00 p.m. As I was approaching Perth, Ontario, at about noon, I passed a slow-moving car and was caught speeding just outside Perth. The police officer was pleasant. He approached my car, asked for and took my car license and ownership and returned to his vehicle. I was very annoyed for two reasons. First I was going to lose my driver's license. Second, my timing to see the P.M. was very tight. In fact, I thought I might even be late. So, after about one minute, I got out of my car, counted to ten and took a deep breath and went back to the officer sitting in his cruiser and making out my ticket. I asked him if I could talk to him from his back seat. He indicated it was okay. Sitting down I asked the officer if he was from Perth. He said he certainly was "... all my life!" I then asked him if he knew Judge John Matheson. Indeed the officer did and wanted to know if I knew the Judge.... Realizing that the officer had taken my bait, I replied that the Judge used "... to work for me", a statement that very much took the officer by surprise, going as far to ask me how well I knew the Judge, a very prominent former Canadian Member of Parliament (MP) and a Judge who designed, back in 1964, the Canadian flag, the one with the red maple leaf. The Judge was also a very prominent citizen of Perth, living in a very distinguished heritage home on the main street. My statement about Judge Matheson totally caught the officer by surprise, so much so that he picked up his phone and called the home of Judge Matheson and asked His Honor directly if he knew a certain "Mr. Charles Humber". The two of them, both the Judge and the officer, had a little chit chat that I could tell was going quite well. Little did the officer know that when I was serving as the National President of the United Empire Loyalists' Association of Canada, 1982-1984, that Judge Matheson served as one of my four honorary Vice-Presidents. After the officer's conversation with the Judge, the officer turned to me and said that the Judge spoke highly of me. At the same time he ripped up my ticket and urged me to drive safely to Ottawa and wished me good luck with the Prime Minister. Now, then, I ask you, have you ever heard of a better way of talking your way out of a speeding ticket? Needless to say, I met up with the Prime Minister, had my photo taken with him and unfortunately, when I published **FAMILY SLEUTHING**, 2006, I used a photo of myself with Prime Minister Chrétien, whom I later met several years later, in my own chapter of that book, instead of the one that was taken with me and Prime Minister Mulroney about three hours after my incident with the officer on Highway #7 just outside Perth, Ontario.

Given credit for designing the "new" Canadian flag, the one with the red maple leaf, Judge John Matheson (1917-2013), a former member of the Canadian House of Commons, was a distinguished United Empire Loyalist descendant who served as an Honourary Vice-President under Charles J. Humber's term as President of UELAC, 1982-1984.

Dad's Best Memories and Recollecions

Chain of Office, 1982-1984

The two photos at the bottom of this page were taken on May 29, 1982. The person standing in the middle of the first photograph, bottom left, is The Hon. Robert F. Nixon, UE., formally the Official Opposition Leader of the Liberal Party for the Province of Ontario – on three different occasions! Mr. Nixon, with polish, graciously was the keynote speaker at the 1982 Annual Convention of the United Empire Loyalists' Association of Canada, a gala event hosted by the Grand River Branch. The setting was the University of Waterloo. The Hon. Robert Nixon, in this view, is shaking hands with Dr. Gordon Leggett, a retired dentist and a World War II veteran and the person who gave me, in 1980, Field Marshall Hermann Goering's ceremonial armband. When looking at this photo one can see Charles J. Humber to the far left. To the far right in the same photograph, still wearing his Chain of Office, is the President of the United Empire Loyalists' Association of Canada, 1980-1982, the late John Eaman of the London Branch of the UEL Association. President of the Grand River Branch, Mrs. Doris Marcellus, stands next to the incoming President.

The second photo, bottom right, timely reveals immediate past UELAC president preparing to present the President's Chain of Office to the new UELAC President, Charles J. Humber, who would serve as the twenty-fourth National President of the Association, 1982-1984. The forthcoming two-year term included two impressive bicentennial conventions. One took place in the Maritime provinces of both New Brunswick (Fredericton and Saint John) and Nova Scotia (Shelburne), 1983; the second was celebrated at Queen's University, Kingston, Ontario, 1984, the year Her Majesty The Queen came to the trillium province and dedicated the Loyalist Parkway outside Kingston. It was on this Parkway that Her Majesty officially received **LOYAL SHE REMAINS**, the 600-page volume published in 1984 by the United Empire Loyalists' Association.

My entire family – my wife, Gay, and our four children, Kristan, Karyn, Charles Jr. and Scott Nicholas – thoroughly supported my two-year term as National President of the UELAC even though the demands on the family during that tumultuous term of office were often overwhelming involving a great deal of personal and family sacrifice. But the two-year term was a great presidency and very rewarding. It was an interval that opened for me a new door to a new profession, namely, publishing books about Canada's rich culture, history and heritage, after teaching high school English since 1962.

Dad's Best Memories and Recollections

Bill Donaldson

At one time I had eight uncles, two on my father's side and six on my mother's side of the family. My uncle Bill Donaldson was my favorite uncle. He married my father's youngest sister, aunt Edie. It should be noted that I never had an uncle who was not nice, friendly or wonderful, but uncle Bill was very special. In some respects, uncle Bill was a second father. My father, Charles M. Humber, was Uncle Bill's best man when Bill and Edie were married back in 1929, at the outset of the Great Depression. So there was always a close relationship between my mom and dad and my uncle Bill and his very dear wife, my aunt Edie. In fact, it was Uncle Bill who bent over backwards for Gay and me to buy the family cottage on Stewart Lake in MacTier, Muskoka, back in 1969. His terms were wonderful and it was a no-brainer to buy the property from him. He had originally bought the cottage property back in 1955 from Carl Riva, one of the most astute hucksters in MacTier. The cost for the property was $1000.00. One of Bill's nephews, Ted Donaldson, built the original cottage for Uncle Bill in 1956. When Gay and I bought the cottage for $12,500.00 in 1969, it came at the same time we also bought our home at 61 Westhumber Blvd., in Rexdale, on the outskirts of greater Toronto. So we were pretty tight for money at the time, that's for sure. As the years went by, Uncle Bill remained very close to us. He and Aunt Edith had three sons: Chuck, dying in 1953 as the result of cerebral palsy, Phillip, dying in a car accident in 1963, and Dave, Bill and Edie's middle son, remaining to this day my closest cousin. Dear Aunt Edie died in 1970, the same year we clinched the deal for the cottage. So, uncle Bill was, emotionally, a rather vulnerable man at the time he sold us our summer haven in Muskoka. Uncle Bill was also very much attached to our four children, Kristy, Karyn and twins, Charlie and Scott. In fact, he loved them all very much and frequently returned with us to the cottage to watch the family grow up and to enjoy the 500 foot lake-frontage property he started to develop back in the mid-1950s.

As Bill aged, he had a wish to visit Nesquehoning in northwest Pennsylvania where my parents, Evelyn and Charles, were living. In other words, he wanted to see them one more time before he gave up the ghost. So, I agreed to drive him to Nesquehoning where Dad was the preacher of the first Baptist Church there, 1968-1973. I'm not sure of the year, but it was in the early 1970s. Bill was thus about seventy-two or seventy-three. I was in my late thirties. Our three-day visit was more than pleasant and the drive down and back afforded me an opportunity to pump information from my uncle about his youth and his adult life. It was so fascinating to learn about his young life in Fort Qu'Appelle, Saskatchewan, where he was born, 1901, about his father, Alexander, whose huge farmlands fed Gen. Frederick Middleton's army, 1885, before the famous Canadian General led his Armed Forces to Batoche, Saskatchewan to defeat Louis Riel.

On our way back from Nesquehoning to Hamilton, Ontario, where uncle Bill was living, he indicated to me on Highway 20 just outside Buffalo that he was in desperate need to go to the bathroom. There was an antique shop in the town we were then driving through. So I stopped and while I was perusing the various antiques, Uncle Bill got permission to use the proprietor's personal bathroom. As the shop did not have much to offer in antiques, I was anxious to get back on the road. But uncle Bill's visit to the bathroom was a seriously long one. Ten minutes went by! Then finally he came out. He looked worn out and was sheepish and said to me hurriedly, "Let's get going". We left the shop, hustled into the car where he said to me with a wicked smile, "Get going, because that bathroom is going to blow up any minute!" Then he yelped with laughter. I couldn't help but bellow chuckles out loud. Neither could he! Obviously, I learned a great deal about my favorite uncle on that memorable trip!

My favourite uncle William James Donaldson, 1901-1991

Dad's Best Memories and Recollections

Major-General Richard Rohmer

Most people from Canada have heard of or visited Toronto's famous Roy Thompson Hall. This concert hall is where The Canadian Opera Company stages many of its fine performances. The Roy Thompson Hall also is where The Toronto International Film Festival showcases many of the about-to-be-discovered films at this world-famous annual festival staged each September. The famous landmark was designed by Vancouver's erudite architect, Arthur Erickson. It officially opened in the fall of 1982. For the first year or so, there were no public forums other than The Canadian Opera Company or The Toronto Symphony Orchestra of any kind performing in the circular design of the Hall, with its sloping and curvilinear glass exterior, that is, until the OSSTF (The Ontario Secondary Secondary Teachers' Federation) conducted its 1983 annual meeting. Because the OSSTF was slow in booking a keynote speaker for their annual convention, I was approached by the Federation's Executive who thought that this high school teacher of English with his U.E. Loyalist background might know of an appropriate Cicero for the upcoming year. Since 1984 was Ontario's Bicentennial, which saluted, among other matters, the Loyalists who came to Canada following the American Revolution, 1784, the OSSTF executive committee thought that maybe some well-known personality could address the annual conference and talk about the importance of the upcoming 1984 Ontario Bicentennial. I thought about what admired Canadian personality to approach then decided on contacting Canada's only living General, Richard H. Rohmer, wondering if he might consider addressing the convention. No one person had ever formally addressed any meeting of any kind at the Roy Thompson Hall, at least up to this time. Since I personally knew the General, I made contact with him and indicated that he would be the very first person ever to address any professional gathering of any kind at the Roy Thompson Hall. Needless to say, the General was very pleased with the invitation and was extremely honored to be the first "celebrity" to speak at the Roy Thompson Hall. When the time came, the Federation asked me if I would consider introducing the General to the packed house. I jumped at the opportunity. In preparation for the upcoming event, the General and I went out to lunch at the Park Plaza Hotel in downtown Toronto where he essentially told me various stories about himself, including his own loyalist connections and, of course, his involvement in World War II which included his first encounter with General George Patton. Indeed, I had enough material to write his full biography. Finally the day came. There was so much to say, so many interesting stories about this very interesting General to convey to the large gathering of high school teachers.... The General was also a well-known Toronto lawyer, a successful writer and novelist in addition to being a World War II veteran as well as one of Canada's most decorated veterans. Needless to say, I had difficulty narrowing my topic. Thus, when I finally introduced the General to the some 2000 secondary school teachers in attendance, my introduction was so long that I can unabashedly claim that it was not the General who was the first person to address an audience from the stage of the Roy Thompson Hall but yours truly who must have taken at least ten minutes to introduce the General. No question about it, I took away from the General his opportunity of being the first person to address a convention gathering of any kind at Roy Thompson Hall! The General, as the second person to address an audience at the Roy Thompson Hall, was upstaged by the very person who introduced him....

Major-General Richard Rohmer and Charles J. Humber greet each other at Fort York in Toronto in the late 1970s.

Dad's Best Memories and Recollections

1964 and 1981

Long before I was born, July 14, 1936, Al Jolson was a celebrity. His popularity surfaced in the 1920s, continued throughout the 1930s and was strong during World War II. When Hollywood produced **The Al Jolson Story** (1946), his celebrity status was etched in fame. His most popular song from the roaring twenties to this 1946 movie was "California, Here I Come." People crooned this magnetic melody everywhere, aiming to imitate Jolson's versatile tenor's voice shading into light baritone. At twenty-eight, I finally initiated my first trip to the Golden State. It was 1964. Gay and I had not yet been married three years. As excited as I was in preparing for our two-month odyssey, Gay, a native Californian, was actually returning "home" because she was born there in 1939. Our trip was more memorable because our first-born, Kristy, not yet four months, was making the trip with us in our brand new 1964 Ford Galaxy.

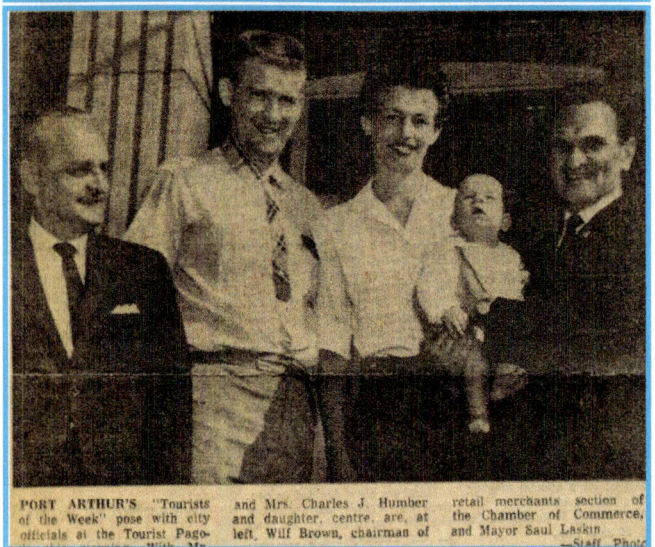

We left Cooksville (now Mississauga), Ontario, at the end of June. As we travelled across Canada, one of our first key stops was visiting the twin cities of Port Arthur and Fort William. While there, Port Arthur Mayor Saul Laskin, brother of Bora Laskin, Chief Justice of Canada's Supreme Court, selected us as "Tourists of the Week" following our visit to the Chamber of Commerce. Set up in a hotel for two days, we were royally treated to the very best that the future city of Thunder Bay offered. This also included a babysitter. While crossing the prairies, we camped in provincial parks. We also enjoyed a three-day stay in Calgary visiting with my good friend from my Brampton High School days, Wayne Getty, and his family. After visiting Stanley Park Zoo in Vancouver and watching adorable year-old polar bears play in the zoo's grotto, our time table made us hurry south to Washington State where we passed through Seattle, the site of the 1962 World's Fair. Here we saw the forerunner to Toronto's CN Tower, Seattle's Space Needle, an impressive landmark. We followed Highway 1. It hugs the west-coast much of the way to Sacramento where we rendezvoused with Dee and Tom Birch, Gay's sister and brother-in-law, as well as Gay's mother BJ Jenkins plus

Top: Lucille Ball and Desi Arnaz poster promoting their upcoming **I Love Lucy** TV season, 1955. **Centre:** Newspaper article from Port Arthur **News-Chronicle,** July, 1964, reporting that Charles J. Humber and his family had been selected as the Tourists of the Week. Mayor Saul Laskin, far right, is holding four-month old Kristy. **Bottom:** View of popular Polar Bear Grotto, Stanley Park Zoo, Vancouver, where we watched adorable "teddy bears" at play, July, 1964.

Dad's Best Memories and Recollections

Gay's brother, John. The drive from Vancouver to Sacramento took less than thirty hours meaning that we did not get much chance to "hug" those magnificent Redwood trees that guard the California coast. As we passed by these behemoths, we marvelled at their immense trunks and towering heights. After visiting San Mateo, Gay's birth place just south of San Francisco, and meeting people from Gay's childhood days, like Eula Arthur and Bob McIver, a test pilot with United Airlines, Gay's mom journeyed with us as we drove south through Los Angeles and on to La Jolla, the Jewel of the Pacific. Gay's mom was still living in the same home on La Jolla Blvd. that Gay had left in 1960 when she went to teach in Fairbanks, Alaska. Kristy was such a good baby for the entire trip and loved her grandmother's care while her parents combed beaches, toured San Diego, visited Hotel del Coronado, travelled to Tijuana, Mexico, and watched the iconic comedian, Cantinflas, perform in the Tijuana Bull Ring. We spent quality time with Gay's teenage friends, Wendy and Lee Browning and Val and Cal Montgomery. One special occasion was visiting with Gay's maternal grandmother, Gertrude Evans (nee Reich), who earlier had been partially immobilized with a stroke. We also spent one quality evening with Gay's father, Ray, who drove down from Los Angeles for a day. The three of us, together, spent a most memorable evening dining on the skyline floor of San Diego's elaborate El Cortez Hotel.

Before long, summer's end was upon us. Bidding farewell to the Golden State and BJ was difficult. We briefly stopped in Los Angeles to see Gay's dad one more time – ironically a last time. It seemed that we had hardly encountered southern California, but, on reflection, we did explore extensively La Jolla Shores and Cove, Gay's favourite beaches as a teenager. It surely is one of the glorious places as a retreat and a place to swim anywhere in the world! This trip has become, for me, an unforgettable memory made possible by a most accommodating BJ who made her home our home for close to a month. Our trip back to Ontario took us through Las Vegas, another one of those places I had always wanted to see. We never had any car trouble the entire trip. But with no credit cards at the time, we were running short on cash. After crossing the border at Windsor, across from Detroit, Gay and I realized that Kristy had spent nearly half her life "on the road" during that memorable summer of 1964.

Although Gay and I visited California many times during the 1990s and 2000s, another seventeen years would slip by before we, now a family of six, made a second trip to the Gold Rush State. This was 1981. This second trip, perhaps our most memorable, took still another two months from our lives.

As we did in 1964, our family said goodbye to Ontario when the school year ended. Together we shouted, "California, here we come!" as we took off in our 1976 maroon-coloured Buick Station Wagon. We camped along the way and once again stopped in Calgary to visit with Wayne Getty and his family. We also travelled to Victoria, British Columbia, to seek out Humber relatives I had never met but who were descended from the brother of my great, great grandfather, David Hess Humber, born on the Isle of Wight, 1818 (see "Rick Humber" story elsewhere in this volume). We took the ferry from Victoria to Port Angeles, Washington State, and from there it was on to the San Francisco region, meeting up with Gay's relatives in Yuba City plus my sister Priscilla and her family living in Redwood City. I fondly remember

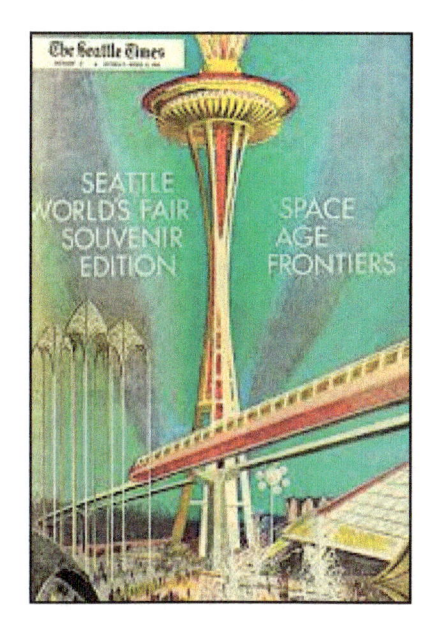

Top: Brochure depicting Seattle's famous Space Needle that we picked up on our California trip driving through Seattle, July, 1964.
Centre: El Cortez Hotel where Gay's Dad, Ray, joined Gay and me for a grand evening of dinner and tasty libations at the Skyline Room, atop this world famous hotel overlooking San Diego.
Bottom: Ray Jenkins, Gay's Dad, in Los Angeles, holding his grand-daughter, Kristy, as we prepare to make the long drive home to Canada in late August, 1964.

the bleary-eyed Hurlbut and Humber families getting up at 3:00 a.m., July 29, to watch on television the marriage of the Prince of Wales and Lady Diana Spencer. Before leaving San Francisco, Chuck and Priscilla took their guests to historic Cliff House, founded 1858, overlooking the Pacific Ocean. As a family we visited various sites in and about the tributaries and branches of the American River as we followed the various trails of 1849 Gold Rushers. Tom Birch was such a great guide. As well, we tripped through Sequoia National Park where Gay's brother, John, was a Forest Ranger during summer months. While we stayed at the Lodgepole Visitor Centre for two days, Gay's brother, John, became our personal Park Ranger. The very best of the very best National Park Guides, he took our entire family on glorious hiking trails, especially to Heather Lake. Eight-year old twin sons, Charlie and Scott, loved the wilderness wanderings with their uncle as did daughters Kristy and Karyn. We could not decide which trees we liked better: Redwoods or the Sequoia. Majestic species, at maturity they stand more than 300 feet. When learning the General Sherman tree's first limb is longer than any tree east of the Rocky Mountains, we were stunned to understand and see just how massive these 2000-year old trees are. Yet some people today are determined to cut them down!

While touring northern California that memorable 1981 summer, I had to return to Toronto to play the role of historical figure John Graves Simcoe for a CBC film being made at Fort George, Niagara-on-the-Lake. After flying back, our jam-packed Buick bid northern California farewell and off we headed to southern California via Monterey and John Steinbeck country. We did stop in Monterey for a day and visited the wonderful aquarium there before departing for Disneyland where we took in as many rides as possible for a full day before taking off for La Jolla and Gay's mom, BJ, who had moved into a detached townhouse on Eads Ave. While in San Diego, we visited Balboa Park, Sea World, the San Diego Zoo, multiple beaches, especially Pacific Beach, a playground conducive to so much fun for the kids as the big waves were perfect for body-surfing. We actually spent more time just relaxing in southern California, simply enjoying the warm weather and above all else the beaches. But as with all vacations, "parting is such sweet sorrow" and we had to bid farewell to La Jolla. As parents, we knew that this was likely the last time that the six of us would spend so much

Top: One of San Francisco's most famous landmarks is the Cliff House overlooking Seal Rocks and the Pacific Ocean. Chuck and Priscilla Hurlbut royally entertained the Humber family from Ontario there in 1981.

Centre: Mickey Mouse greets Charlie and Scott Humber at Disneyland, Anaheim, California, July, 1981.

Bottom: Gay and our four children, Kristy, Karyn, Charlie and Scott, take in the Grand Canyon during the Humber family's 1981 drive home from California to Toronto, Ontario.

Dad's Best Memories and Recollections

extended time vacationing together.

Journeying home meant stopping at tourist sites and gawking at natural monuments and geographical phenomena like the Grand Canyon. The magnificent Grand Canyon is a perfect wonder to behold. As well, Slide Rock State Park in Sedona afforded the entire family an opportunity to enjoy slipping and sliding down waterfalls lined with red limestone. A must stop was visiting Mesa Verde National Park. A Colorado World Heritage Site, this Park protects the best preserved Puebloan cliff-dwelling site anywhere. To note and observe Cliff Palace was as breathtaking and awesome as anything on our trip. As we continued our trek home we luckily avoided a flash flood in Colorado by some fifteen minutes. It was a thrilling experience, for sure, to witness rushing stream water rising so fast that cars tumbled up and down waterways much like fishing bobbers. One hilarious stop was walking across the Royal Gorge Suspension Bridge, a foot bridge located in eastern Colorado. At the time, in 1981, it was the tallest bridge, at 955 feet high, in the world. It was hilarious because the wind was so strong and it caused everyone's head of hair to turn into Medusa locks. Our last big stop was St. Louis, Missouri, on the west banks of the Mississippi River. Here we took time out to journey up and over the famous stainless steel arch, the symbolic gateway to "the wild west." At 630-feet in height, it is the world's tallest arch. Exhausted when we got home, with scads of memories to share, we were ready to head back to school.

Top: On the Humber family drive home from California, August, 1981, we all agreed that Mesa Verde National Park, in Colorado, where ancestral Pueblo first nation peoples lived in cliff dwellings between 700 and 1300 A.D., was a most memorable and intriguing stop.

Centre: View of Royal Gorge Bridge, Canon, Colorado, the tallest bridge in the world at the time the Humber family walked across it, August, 1981.

Bottom: The St. Louis Arch, symbolic gateway to the American West, elegantly stands on the shores of the Mississippi River. Six Humbers, on their way home from California, summer, 1981, toured this stainless steel arch and gasped at the glorious view it afforded us as we visited the apex of the arch, August, 1981.

Dad's Best Memories and Recollections

Jack Dempsey

Most people from my generation have heard the name Jack Dempsey. But when growing up some twenty years after the heavyweight champion retired from boxing, 1927, the very name "Jack Dempsey" powerfully resonated with monumental fame…. Known as the "Manassa Mauler" from Colorado, after Jack Dempsey retired as the former heavyweight champion of the world, he opened a restaurant in 1935 opposite Madison Square Garden, New York City. He then re-located his famous restaurant to Times Square a decade later, calling it appropriately Jack Dempsey's Restaurant. The famous tourist site operated on Broadway between 49th and 50th Streets until 1974 when its doors closed permanently. In his day, Jack Dempsey was a celebrity whose name was as famous as the iconic names of Joe Louis, Mohammed Ali or Rocky Marciano are today. In 1953, when I left home for the summer at the age of sixteen, I arrived in New York City with a guy by the name of Wally Donahue (whose distant cousin, Michael Donahue, nearly thirty years later, was unintentionally shot and killed by the notorious mobster, Whitey Bulger, in South Boston). While Wally and I were touring New York City, one of the first places we visited was Times Square and eventually the famous Jack Dempsey Restaurant. We both had small duffel bags and were a little scruffy looking. We decided that this was a good place to eat and upon entering the up-beat-looking restaurant, low and behold, we were approached at the front door by none other than Jack Dempsey who promptly welcomed us to his establishment. I think he instinctively knew we were not from New York City. He asked us how we were doing and we simply said that we just wanted to visit his restaurant and order a sandwich. He led us to a booth near the front door and saw to it that we had a waiter to serve us. When it came time to leave, he shook hands using the same hand that knocked out the likes of Jack Sharkey, Luis Firpo, Jess Willard and George Carpentier. They say that his fist could knock over a donkey with a six-inch punch. He gave us a restaurant menu with his signature prominently autographed on the cover. It was a pretty swanky restaurant opened mainly for the tourist trade. But Jack Dempsey, as host, was there as a greeter, not a bouncer. The boxing legend, famously quoted as saying "A champion is someone who gets up when he can't," was most gracious with two teenage vagabonds from Boston who were looking for some action in the Big Apple. We found it at Jack Dempsey's Restaurant back in 1953. Whatever happened to the autographed menu is not known.

In 1953, two Boston teenagers hitch-hiked to Times Square and wandered into Jack Dempsey's Reataurant and met the "Manassa Mauler".

"The Meeting Place of the World"
Jack Dempsey's Broadway Restaurant

Dad's Best Memories and Recollections

Mickey Rooney

Way back in 1953, when I was attending Boston Latin School, I worked part-time after school in downtown Boston at Paul's Shoes, 268 Washington Street, opposite where School Street ends. This small business establishment at the time specialized in selling Elevated Shoes. In other words, some people who were short in height sometimes wanted a pair of shoes that would discreetly "elevate" them some two or three inches. The shoes were manufactured in such a way that one was unable to detect the inflated height that the shoes offered prospective clients. Elevated Shoes were not the only kind of shoes sold in this specialty store, but one out of every five pairs of shoes sold overall in that small family business was footwear that helped make any individual overcome an inferiority complex. I was just a stock room employee, repackaging shoe boxes and replacing them back into their proper stalls lining the three impressive walls of the store. As I became more familiar with the store and the owner, once in a while Mr. Paul would let me serve customers, especially young people, gradually leading me to handle an entire sale. One day Mickey Rooney, the famous Hollywood actor, walked into the store. Five feet, three inches in stature, he was always smiling as he surveyed the plush interior of the premises and wondered if I could locate a pair of shoes that would add several inches to his overall height. The sale, if I were to consummate it, would have been my very first sale of Elevated Shoes. I sized up the famous actor's foot by measuring it with a special foot guide and went into the back room where I located two boxes of Oxford shoes that I thought the actor would like and brought them to where he was sitting. Needless to say, I was pretty awe-struck by the fact that I was waiting on "Andy Hardy", the boy Mickey Rooney played in fifteen films throughout the 1930s and 1940s. He also had co-starred with Spencer Tracy in **Boys Town** and with Judy Garland in **Babes in Arms.** He had been married to Ava Gardner in 1943 so I could not help but look at Mickey Rooney with wonder as the beautiful Ava Gardner was truly one of my all-time favorite actresses. I'll always remember how he clicked the heels of his shoes as he waltzed up to the showcase mirror to see how he looked. He winked at me as he bobble-headed back to his seat. He truly was funny in the store. I did not ring him up after he agreed to purchase a pair of shoes (Mr. Paul completed the transaction), but the famous actor went out of his way to shake my hands upon departure. His hands were bigger than mine! As he left the store, with his wrapped shoe box under his left arm, he nodded goodbye and departed out the front door. Some forty-two years later I noticed that he was performing in Toronto, at age seventy-five, in **Crazy for You.** I was tempted to attend just to see if I could accost him and ask him if he remembered me at Paul's Shoes back in 1953....

Mickey Rooney died in 2007 at age 93.

Top right: Mr. Bramson Paul's business card which I have kept over all these years.
Bottom right: 1930s postcard capturing Mickey Rooney's house in Encino, California.

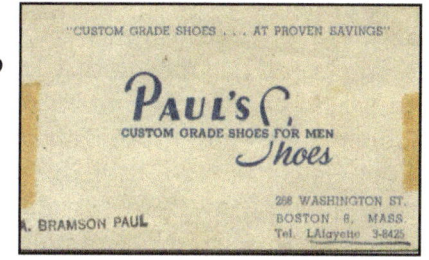

Dad's Best Memories and Recollections

Toronto Blue Jays Meet John Graves Simcoe, 1980

When the Toronto Blue Jays played their first game, June 3, 1989, at the SkyDome (renamed the Rogers Centre), Jimmy Key threw out the first pitch to Ernie Whitt. Twenty-five years later, to the day, this historic event was repeated when the Blue Jays were playing the St Louis Cardinals. Jimmy Key and Ernie Whitt, the famous Blue Jays battery from their World Series days, did it all over again. Their repeat performance, June 6, 2014, made me recall another time when, in my alter ego as John Graves Simcoe, I also threw out the ceremonial first pitch at a Blue Jays' game. This was on August 3, 1980. The catcher was the same Ernie Whitt. The "historic" event took place on Simcoe Day, first Monday of each August when the City of Toronto honors John Graves Simcoe, founder of the Town of York, Upper Canada's capital, in 1793, and renamed Toronto, March 6, 1834.

In 1980 I was a Director of the John Graves Foundation, an agency of the Province of Ontario. The late John W. Fisher, formerly Canada's Centennial Commissioner, 1967, was the Chairman of the Foundation at the time. He came up with the idea that perhaps the Foundation should find someone to dress up as John Graves Simcoe and throw out the first pitch at a Blue Jays game. The Chairman approached me about the idea, wondering if I would consider throwing out the ceremonial first pitch, that is, if the professional baseball team liked the idea. As one of the Foundation's handful of Directors, I approached Paul Beeston, on behalf of the Foundation. At the time he was Vice President, Business Operations, for the Toronto Blue Jays (later, President of Major League Baseball, 1997-2002). After making the Foundation's proposal for Simcoe Day, 1980, Mr. Beeston was very supportive, especially when I proposed that John Graves Simcoe would be ushered into Toronto's Exhibition Stadium, located in those days on the grounds of the Canadian National Exhibition, by a horse-drawn Brewster Drag Coach, formerly owned by Sir Henry Pellatt, builder of Toronto's famous tourist attraction, **Casa Loma**. At the time, the Brewster Coach was owned by Dr. Wally Kent of Mississauga. My *aide-de-camp* was Terry Poulos, one of my former students at Lawrence Park Collegiate Institute in Toronto.

Simcoe Day came, August 3, 1980. The Coach, pulled by four wonderful hackneys, made it all the way from left field to the pitcher's mound with the Governor and his aid inside. Before "Simcoe" threw out the first pitch to legendary Blue Jays catcher, Ernie Whitt, Paul Godfrey, Metropolitan Toronto Chairman, briefly spoke to the crowd about the importance of Gov. Simcoe to the City. He clearly emphasized that the City welcomed Gov. Simcoe to the great city that His Honour had founded 187 years earlier. After making "a pitch for history", I joined the Rt. Hon. Roland Michener, former Governor General of Canada

Designed and printed by the John Graves Simcoe Foundation, this four-page educational brochure was distributed to the crowd that came to the Blue Jays game, August 3, 1980, to watch His Honour, John Graves Simcoe, throw out the first pitch.

Dad's Best Memories and Recollections

26

as well as a John Graves Simcoe Board member, in the stands behind home plate. There we watched the rest of the game with all of my family. It certainly was a rewarding experience for John Graves Simcoe, as the home team beat the American "invaders", the California Angels, 3-1, a performance that made Upper Canada's first Lt. Gov. very happy. The ushers at the stadium who handed out brochures to the incoming thousands of fans were former students of mine at Toronto's Oakwood Collegiate, the high school where I was teaching at the time, that is, except for two ushers. These were my two daughters, Kristy and Karyn, students at Lawrence Park C.I. To this day, I can still hear Ernie Whitt say to me after the ceremonial first pitch was thrown directly into his glove, "That throw almost burned a hole in my glove!" With the huge billboard blazing "Welcome Governor Simcoe," we both chuckled as we walked back to the dugout....

It is hard to believe as I write this anecdote that some thirty-five years have come and gone since that ceremonial first pitch. What a memory!

Charles J. Humber, aka John Graves Simcoe, makes a "pitch for history" as he throws the opening pitch at a Toronto Blue Jays game, August 3, 1980. The sign in the upper right corner welcomes Governor Simcoe.

Ernie Whitt, all-time favourite catcher for the Toronto Blue Jays, congratulates Charlie Humber after the Governor threw the opening pitch - a pitch that "almost burned a hole in the catcher's mitt."

Dad's Best Memories and Recollections

H.R.H. Prince Andrew and Okill Stuart

The success of **LOYAL SHE REMAINS: The Ontario Story,** a 600-page, highly illustrated volume published by the United Empire Loyalists' Association of Canada, 1984, commemorated Ontario's two hundredth anniversary. At the time, I began an agenda to leave teaching and enter into the publishing world by co-founding Heirloom Publishing Inc. in 1985. By 1986, I and three partners set out on a very ambitious endeavor, namely, to produce a series of books celebrating Canada's rich culture, history, and heritage. After publishing the first two volumes of the upbeat CANADA Heirloom Series, **CANADA From Sea Unto Sea** (1986, rev. 1988), Volume I, and **CANADA's Native Peoples** (1988) Volume II, Heirloom decided on publishing Volume III of this same series named **ALLEGIANCE: The Ontario Story.** Honoring the founding, in 1791, of the province of Upper Canada by Lt. Col. John Graves Simcoe, Heirloom Publishing felt that **ALLEGIANCE** had enough credibility to entice Premier Bob Rae to write the Introduction, to persuade Lt. Gov. Lincoln Alexander to write the Preface; and to convince Dan Hill, a pioneer in Black Studies, to dedicate **ALLEGIANCE** to John Graves Simcoe whose legislation in 1793 promoted the abolition of slavery throughout the province. Additionally, Heirloom decided to approach His Royal Highness, Prince Andrew, Duke of York, to write a very special introductory message for **ALLEGIANCE**. I felt that Prince Andrew was a good candidate for this endeavor in that he had lived in the Province in 1978 while attending Lakefield College School, proudly claiming, at the time, that "Ontario was his home away from home."

Okill Stuart and HRH the Duke of Edinburgh, two former classmates at Gordonstoun School, in Scotland, 1937. Photo taken at Balmoral Castle, Scotland, 2004

Instead of going through Government House in Ottawa, I directly approached Prince Andrew. I wrote to Prince Andrew at Buckingham Palace, requesting that His Royal Highness accept Heirloom's invitation. I also supplied the Prince with suggestions for his message. After six months came and went, the Prince had yet to provide us with a response. We were getting concerned as the production of **ALLEGIANCE** was progressing nicely. I also happened to learn that Prince Philip, the Duke of Edinburgh, husband of Her Majesty Queen Elizabeth II, and father of Andrew, was visiting Montreal near this time and that my good friend, Okill Stuart, of Montreal, was going to have lunch with the Prince in Lennoxville, Quebec. So I contacted Okill, stating the scenario and he told me with certainty that he would follow through with my request and do his best for me. I knew that Prince Philip had gone to school with Okill in Scotland in 1937, but was not too sure of their close friendship. Nevertheless, within two weeks Heirloom received a package directly from the United Kingdom. Upon opening it, we found Prince Andrew's special introduction on Buckingham Palace letterhead, signed by him, and accompanied by a wonderful official photograph. When I called Okill Stuart, who was born in St. Lambert, Quebec, the same place where I was born, he informed me what had happened when he and the Duke of Edinburgh had a private luncheon get-together. He told me that when he brought up the topic for discussion, Prince Philip was seemingly annoyed that his son, Prince Andrew, had not responded to "Mr. Humber's invitation", exclaiming that matters would be taken care of when he returned to the UK. I have often wondered if Prince Philip remembered me back in 1984, Ontario's year of Bicentennial Celebrations, when Gay and I were presented to Her Majesty outside Kingston, Ontario, on the newly opened Loyalist Parkway. At the time I was privileged to give Her Majesty, on behalf the United Empire Loyalists' Association of Canada as well as the citizens of Ontario, a special limited edition of **LOYAL SHE REMAINS.** Whether or not my friend Okill Stuart who was President, UELAC, 1994-1996, was instrumental in convincing Prince Philip to intercede on my behalf is irrelevant. Nevertheless, as William Congreve suggested in his play **The Way of the World,** it's not what you know, not who you know, but who knows you that oftentimes gets one to the next step.

Prince Andrew visits his *alma mater*, Lakefield College School, during Alumni Days, September, 1992.

Dad's Best Memories and Recollections

Frankie Laine

Frankie Laine songs in the late 1940s and early 1950s were almost always number 1 on the Billboard Charts. Winners such as "That Lucky Old Sun"(1949), "Jezebel"(1951), "High Noon" (1952) and "I Believe" (1953) were iconic. His first hits can be traced back to the late 1930s. His last official public appearance occurred when he sang "That's My Desire"(1947), his all-time greatest hit, on a national PBS show in 2005. Back in the early 1950s, one of my close friends in Dorchester was a guy named Jackie Flaherty. We were in South Boston after attending a Boston Red Sox game in either 1952 or 1953 and decided to crash the best known nightclub in Boston, a place called Blinstrubs, located at the corner of Broadway and D Street. When Laine, the star attraction, came to one of his blockbuster hits, "Mule Train", he stopped at a crucial place in that thunderous song and asked someone in the audience to screech out his most stridulous line from that song, namely, "Yeah, yeah." Full of *braggadocio*, I volunteered, and the song was started again, full blast from the orchestra, and at the appropriate time, the son of Al Capone's barber, pointed his finger at me and I bellowed the famous slurring, high-pitched "Yeah, yeah!" He thought my performance was so good that he had me vocalize each time he came to that section of the song that demanded a performance of looking ridiculous and so I bellowed from my contorted mouth the utterly stupid "Yeah, Yeah" flourish that he required to complement his overwhelming voice.

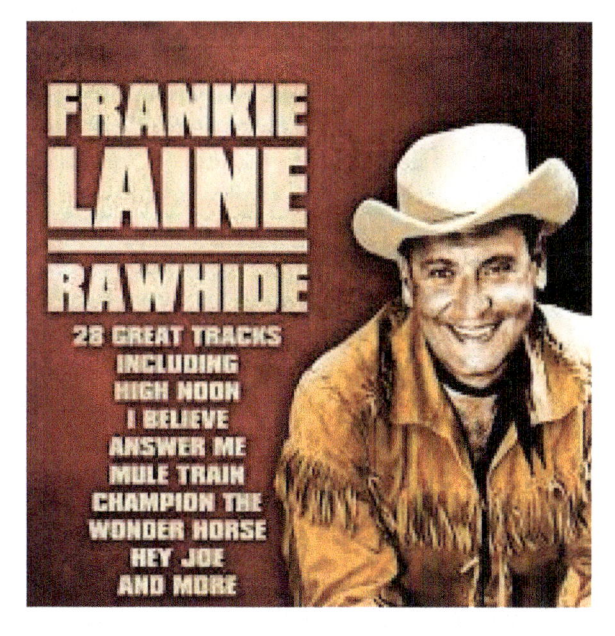

It was a lot of fun. But the story does not end there. About twenty years later, precisely January 8, 1969, Mr. Steel Tonsils, as he was sometimes called, was performing at the Beverly Hills Motor Hotel, in Downsview, Toronto. I and my friend, Alan Emerson, who lived in Weston, dressed up and went to hear the legendary Frankie Laine. At half time, Frankie Laine was in the foyer of the hotel theatre enjoying a cigarette when I accosted him, reminding him that I had attended one of his famous gigs at 'Blinnie's" back in the 1950s. Well, he was taken aback when I reminisced with him about what happened that crazy night in South Boston and how he induced me to perform with him. And the amazing thing was that he actually remembered the occasion to perfection when I helped him out with that "Mule Train" song. "Old Leather Lungs" even gave me his autograph and was legitimately pleased to remember me way back in the early 1950s when he was approaching the height of his career and I was just a sixteen year-old misfit!

Frankie Laine died at 92 years in 2007.

Above left: Frankie Laine's autograph he gave me in 1969 when I reminded him of our first encounter at Blinstrub's in the early 1950s.
Left: Arthur Godfrey referred to Blinstrub's as "Blinnie's"

Dad's Best Memories and Recollections

One-Room School House

1948 was a rather tough year for the Humber family living as foreigners or aliens in Boston, Massachusetts. My Father had graduated from Harvard University in 1947 while strictly on a visa that permitted him to enter the U.S.A., in 1945, solely as a student. Unable to earn much of a living, it must have been tough going for Dad to cope with a family of six while attending university full time. Exactly when Dad applied to immigration authorities to extend his stay following his graduation is not known. But the fact remains that Dad was unable to get either a temporary or permanent extension of his student visa. This fact disrupted our entire family with the consequences that the six of us had no choice but to leave behind our second and third floor tenement flats at 1145 Dorchester Ave (the whole tenement block burned down in the early 1970s). We packed up whatever we could in the old 1930 Model A Ford, and returned to Canada with no place to go except to a sparsely furnished empty cottage, named for **Hiawatha**, the founder of the Six Nations Confederacy, on the north shore of Lake Erie, south of Hagersville, Ontario. It was a cottage, moreover, without running water, no electricity, and a domicile not insulated for cold weather. We arrived at the cottage in mid-April. The winter snow had just melted. One of the priorities was to get two of the four Humber siblings admitted as students in a public school. Re-applying for visa privileges to return to Boston as permanent resident aliens was in the works. It was a matter of time how long the process would take. In post-World War II America, there was not much understanding of such words as "convenience", "rush", "priority" or "hardship". So, it was off to school for both Anna and me (our twin brother and sister, Paul and Priscilla, were too young to start school that Spring) with the hopes that sooner than later we would return to our schools on Meeting House Hill in Dorchester by summer's end.

The school we enrolled in consisted of one large classroom. It was a red brick, country school about one mile from our cottage which was located on the north shore of Lake Erie at a place called Woodlawn Beach. Rain or shine, cold or warm weather, off we went each morning carrying lunches wrapped in newspaper. Our dirt-road trek was fun but time-consuming. We had no refrigerator at the cottage but we did have an ice chest. The only store offering food amenities was Bagely's, a country store that offered very limited supplies. We got milk each day from the Murphy farm that was located midway between the school and the cottage. On the way home from school, it was my responsibility to pick up and bring "home" fresh milk in sterilized bottles from cows that were milked by either Elmo Murphy or his wife Sylvia. Eventually, I also participated in milking cows.

By the fall, the four Humber kids were all attending the school known as SS #2 Walpole. The one-room school was locally known as the McGaw School. After it closed in 1965, it was turned into the Wilson Pugsley MacDonald Museum, named after one of its former students who had lived just up the road in Cheapside. He was well-known as one of Canada's leading poets during the first quarter of the 20th century. In fact, Albert Einstein called MacDonald "the greatest thing I have found in Canada." This one-room, gabled-roofed, ringing-bell schoolhouse was enhanced with two backhouse three-seaters, separated by a wooden planked wall, one for girls, the other for boys. But the main feature was its teacher, an eighteen-year old young man whose father had been a Brethren in Christ preacher. He lived just down the road from the school in the town of Cheapside. His name was Morris Sider and, as a fledgling teacher, he taught grades one to eight to about forty students including the four Humber kids, two in the first row, one in the third row and one, myself, in the back seat of the fourth row. This is where I spent most of my time as a grade-six student in a one-room schoolhouse between April and November, 1948. Morris Sider was a strict teacher who often played baseball during recess with his students. He eventually moved to Pennsylvania where he, for nearly forty years, was Professor of History at Messiah College.

After a long glorious summer on the shores of Lake Erie singing to such hit songs as "Zip-a-Dee-Doo-Dah" or "I'm Over-Looking a Four-Leaf Clover" or Arthur Godfrey's "Too Fat Polka", and after starting school again at the McGaw School in the fall of that year, we finally were granted our respective visas and returned to Boston in our old Model A Ford very early that November to continue with our education at America's oldest public school, founded, 1639, by Cotton Mather's grandfather, Richard Mather. It was quite a spell of time, those six months away from our Dorchester home. While we were gone, Sir Laurence Olivier appeared on the cover of **Life Magazine**, Babe Ruth died, and the Cleveland Indians beat the Boston Braves in the World Series, a real heartbreaker for me who followed the World Series via the **Hamilton Spectator** at Bagley's General Store. As I said, 1948 was a rather rough year – but – a memorable one!

Left: Charles J. Humber stands in front of the one-room school house.
Above: Interior of McGaw School, now a museum.
Below: McGaw School Student Photograph, September, 1948. E. Morris Sider, standing far right, was the teacher. He went on to teach for forty years at Messiah College in Pennsylvania. Four Humber children attended McGaw school. Seen in first row, far right, sitting, is Charles J. Humber. In second row, third from right, is Anna Humber. In third row are twins Paul and Priscilla Humber, fourth from left and far right repectively. The McGaw School closed in 1965 and, led by Rev. Earl Sider and his wife, May, parents of Mr. Morris Sider, (standing right) the school has been maintained ever since as a museum. On June 3, 1965, it re-opened as the Wilson Pugsley MacDonald Memorial School Museum. My uncle Percy Schweyer attended the school pre WWI.

Travelling in a 1930 Model A Ford, Part I

Stopping along Highway 20 in Upper New York State, October, 1945, was not uncommon for the Humber family. In this view Rev. Charles M. Humber stands at rear of Model A Ford with 3-year-old twins, Paul and Priscilla. Sister Anna peers outside window while Charles Humber Jr. gazes through the car's rear-view window. Evelyn Humber took this photo after a flat tire was fixed.

In 1938, when Rev. Charles M. Humber, my father, was called to be the new pastor of Hagersville Baptist Church, just south of Hamilton, Ontario, he had recently purchased a second-hand car from his brother-in-law, Perce Schweyer, who was working for Kett Motors also of Hagersville. The eight-year old car, a 1930 Model A Ford, would remain in the family for twelve more years, going back and forth to Boston a half dozen times starting in 1945 immediately after World War II. Dad's Model A was a two-door vehicle with a double back seat. One got to the back seat by folding down the single front passenger seat and flipping it forward towards the dashboard. A foot pedal-starter for the driver was located on the rising floor above the gas pedal. The dashboard was very sparse. There was a gas gauge, a temperature gauge, a speedometer, and a dial choke enabling the driver to feed greater amounts of gas to a hard-to-start engine. The car horn looked like a small round black overcoat button located in the center of the steering wheel. Front seat windows were manually controlled with a crank. Back seat windows rolled up or down. The windshield was adjustable in that it could open from the bottom during hot, humid summer days allowing for fresh air to flow. There was no side-view mirror, no radio, and no glove compartment. Windshield wipers had no washer fluid. The seat covers were a heavy cloth, much like twisted tweed. The headlights were metal, bulbous fixtures rimmed with chrome and balanced on both sides of the radiator. Both headlights were controlled from the inside by a simple pull-out, push-in plug. I do not recall there being high or low beams. The outside roof was like pastry-spread tar. In hot weather it was sticky. The inside cover for the car's ceiling was a herring-bone, gray-colored cloth that tended to sag a bit. There was a rear window but it was small. In those days, driving was more of an adventure than a pleasure. One had to be alert all the time even though one rarely went over fifty miles per hour.

This Model A Ford was our Conestoga Wagon as we trekked to Boston in mid-October, 1945, from what is today, Pickering, Ontario, just east of Toronto. There was a full-day auction sale, September 22, 1945, on the property where we had been staying in a rural Toronto suburb called Rosebank. Our passports were not totally ready as we prepared to cross the border into Buffalo, New York. So we journeyed back to St. Catharines where Dad's sister, Fern Schweyer and Percy, her husband, lived with their family and stayed for a couple of days before returning to the border at Buffalo and successfully re-entering the United States on Dad's student's visa.

Dad's Best Memories and Recollections

One has to understand, that before we left Canada for the United States, Dad had arranged to build a two-layer shelving unit above the driver's running board on the outside of the car. It was plugged with all sorts of cardboard and wooden boxes, various pots and pans and the odd suitcase. In other words, this meant, when the driver, namely, Dad, had to get out of the car, he caused his wife Evelyn, my mother, sitting in the passenger seat to get out first. This always meant that mother with her three-year old twins, Paul and Priscilla, had to get out of the car, rain or shine, before Dad could exit. The gear shift plus the emergency brake, both of which were located between the two front seats, were laden with various pillows and sundry blankets enabling one of the twins to sit on top of the squished down pillows smothering the top of the emergency brake and the partially covered stick shift. The other twin sat on his/her Mother's lap. This must have been very arduous for both parents in that Dad was unable to work the gear shift with ease and Mother always had to be in charge of two lively three-year olds fussing and moving about. Obviously, in those days, there were no seatbelts.

The back seat was just as crammed as the front seats. Sister Anna and I were crunched together with boxes, suitcases, and a variety of things like food packages and extra clothing for everyone. These items were always flopping on top of us and not just because the car swerved. On the roof of the Model A, father had arranged for a double bed mattress to be used as the foundation for other things such as a table roped down with its legs poking skyward. At the rear of the Model A was the spare tire, plus a variety of other items like pots and pans, suitcases, and a variety of household items, all held together with ropes of all colors, widths and brands. No question about it, we must have looked like those people in that famous John Steinbeck novel, **The Grapes of Wrath**. The trip to Boston took three nights and four days, arriving in Boston in the midst of a gloomy Fall night with Dorchester Avenue street lights streaming sepulchre-yellow beams across the sidewalks and peering into dark hallways of the various tenement buildings in our new neighborhood. All these were ominous beginnings to ten years of a fascinating family life that awaited an immigrant family of six settling in Boston on a student visa enabling Dad to attend Harvard University.

Before the Humber family moved from Rosebank, Ontario to Boston, Massachussets, October, 1945, Rev. Charles M. Humber advertised an auction sale of household chattels on front lawn of our property. Not mentioned in the contents list was the large grizzly bear rug, complete with stuffed head, that originally had come through the hands of my great-grandfather, Charles A. Humber of Goderich, Ontario. It had been stolen, much to my father's chagrin!

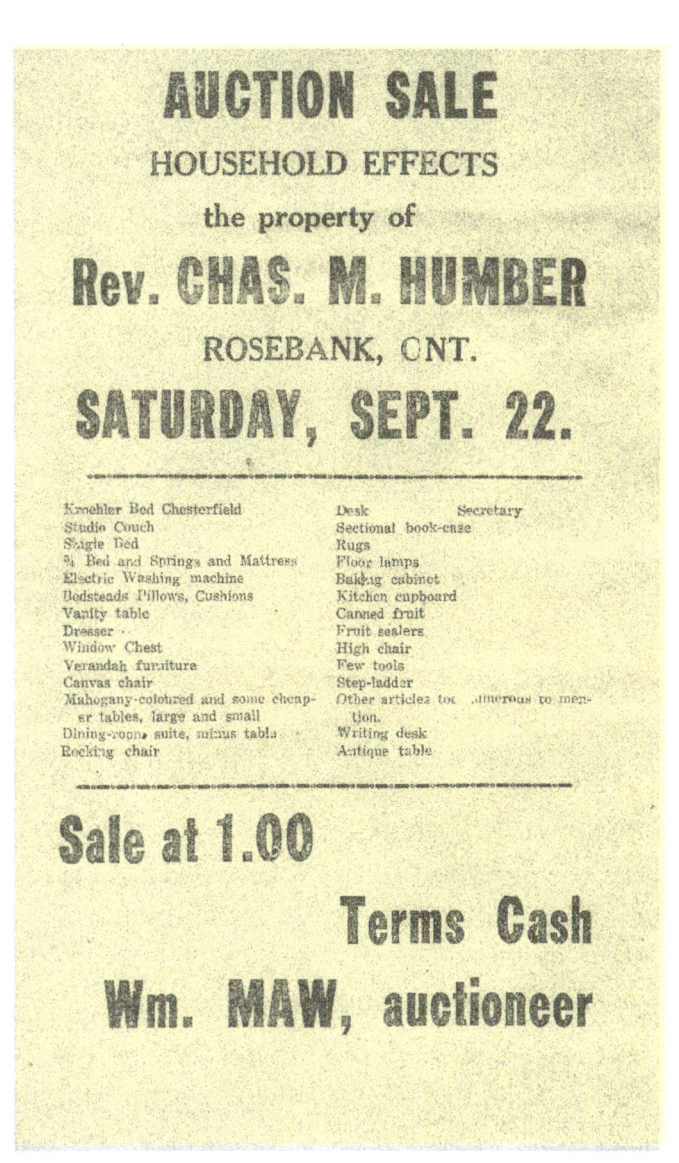

AUCTION SALE

HOUSEHOLD EFFECTS

the property of

Rev. CHAS. M. HUMBER

ROSEBANK, ONT.

SATURDAY, SEPT. 22.

Kroehler Bed Chesterfield	Desk Secretary
Studio Couch	Sectional book-case
Single Bed	Rugs
¾ Bed and Springs and Mattress	Floor lamps
Electric Washing machine	Baking cabinet
Bedsteads Pillows, Cushions	Kitchen cupboard
Vanity table	Canned fruit
Dresser	Fruit sealers
Window Chest	High chair
Verandah furniture	Few tools
Canvas chair	Step-ladder
Mahogany-coloured and some cheaper tables, large and small	Other articles too numerous to mention.
Dining-room suite, minus table	Writing desk
Rocking chair	Antique table

Sale at 1.00

Terms Cash

Wm. MAW, auctioneer

Travelling in a 1930 Model A Ford, Part 2

Humber family experiences in driving back and forth between Canada and Boston, 1945 to 1951, have made good grist for campfire stories over the years. Our first Boston trip took four days and three nights. One night on our inaugural trip to Boston we slept in the old Model A, stopping because it was raining so hard. The windshield wipers just couldn't handle the down pour. Somewhere in upper New York State, Dad noticed a desolate laneway in the bleakness of that dark night. It led to a barn with a wide open doorway. To avoid the wicked storm, Dad decided to drive right into the barn but because the roof of the 1930 Ford had a table with its legs poking upward, he was unable to proceed into the barn's interior. When we awoke in the wee hours of that morning, we discovered, to our dismay, that had the Model A gone another two or three feet, the car, with all of us in it, would have plunged one complete story through decrepit plank flooring. Mother praised the Lord that morning, knowing that He was guiding our journey and was watching over us. With immense relief, we all gave thanks. While Dad was backing up that early morning, leaving behind a potential tragedy, brother Paul exclaimed: "I wanna go to Bosson, I wanna go to Bosson...." as if everything was just hunky-dory. It turns out that the barn we had "lodged" in was abandoned. We also noticed that the farm house, near the barn, was derelict and empty. "No Trespassing" signs were nowhere to be seen....

The journey in October, 1945, through Upper New York State and western Massachusetts was startlingly beautiful. The deciduous trees were aflame with God's paintbrush. Since the New York Turnpike had not yet been built, we drove New York State's equivalent to Route 66, namely, Highway 20, a route that, to this day, still goes up and down hills and through historic villages. I'll always remember a particular billboard sign as we approached one quaint, historic town. In big lettering, it declared "Deal with Honest Crooks", a clever wordplay on the proprietor's surname. I particularly remember the sign because Richard Crooks, at the time, was one of Mother's favorite Metropolitan opera singers and, as a nine-year old, I wondered if the two surnames had some connection. Then, of course, there were the Burma Shave signs which had many moral lessons for drivers. One points a finger at speedy drivers: **HARDLY A DRIVER / IS NOW ALIVE / WHO PASSED ON HILLS / AT 75 / BURMA-SHAVE!** Another attacked the inebriated: **CAR IN DITCH / DRIVER IN TREE / MOON WAS FULL / SO WAS HE / BURMA-SHAVE!** Another of these clever signs was directed at drowsy drivers: **DROVE TOO LONG / DRIVER SNOOZING / WHAT HAPPENED NEXT / IS NOT AMUSING /BURMA-SHAVE!** These unique advertising signs appeared, 1926-1963, along all major highways across the United States, especially during the post-World War II years. Each sign, six or seven feet off the ground, stood upright along various pastures, each separated by some hundred feet. The lettering was white with a cranberry-colored background. Very few hotels were evident on Route 20, at least outside the towns. For the most part there were also few motels as they had not yet become plentiful as commercial enterprises. Rather the roadways were dotted with little cabins, always located on the outskirts of towns. They constituted eight or ten cabins, side by side. Some were even quaint log cabins. However, Dad found it far more economical to sleep in the car – or – on one occasion, to slip into a country church, late at night. Each of us slept on a church pew for several hours, then, in stealth, hurried off into the wee morning hours.

Burma-Shave signs dotted American Highways during the 1940s and 1950s.

But it was the tire trouble I remember the most about our Boston trips and not just in 1945. All road tires in those days had inner tubes. Because of World War II, there was an extreme shortage of rubber of any kind. So treaded tires not only were very expensive and hard to buy but the

Dad's Best Memories and Recollections

inner tubes for those tires were virtually impossible to purchase. Anyone driving a car knew that if he had a flat tire, his only choice was to fix it on the spot. So, when we had a flat tire, Dad jacked up the corner of the car where the tire was flat. Then he unbolted the tire from the axle and separated the outer tire from the inner tube with a crowbar.

To repair the deflated inner tube, Dad had to hand-pump the flat inner tube, hoping to discover a hissing hole. Once the leak was discovered, a tin can full of rubber patches were at hand along with a tube of special glue which Dad applied to the hissing hole. Before the application of the glue, the rubber tire had to be scraped to a coarse surface. This way, the patch would stick better to the inner tube. After putting the half-deflated rubber tube back into the outer tire, air was hand-pumped into the tire while using a gauge to determine the correct tire pressure. This whole exercise took at least one half hour. Needless to say, working on flat tires was frustrating. Once the rim of the tire was fastened to the axle, we restarted our journey, that is, until the next flat tire. Depending on the heat of the day, we probably averaged three or four flat tires per day. By journey's end, all four inner tubes looked as if they had measles because the rubber patches that were attached to the four inner tubes made the tires all look as if they were sick. One major problem Dad had to confront was that the old glue just did not stick very well. As well, the inner tubes that Dad used were likely deteriorating much like old elastic or rubber bands do. As Dad's unofficial tire helper, I rarely heard Dad say anything negative. He just did his work. After each tire episode, Mom would get a wet rag and clean our hands and faces before we, once again, set off on our way. After one tire episode, we were driving along the highway, when I noticed a tire on the other side of the road moving in the same direction just as fast as our car. It was bumping along the combined fields and skipping fences as if it was racing our car. When I pointed out this phenomenon to Dad, he immediately realized that it was the back tire of the Model A that somehow had come off the axle, had scurried across the road and onto a field and was galloping parallel to our Model A Ford. In other words, our Ford was driving strictly on three wheels. Dad, realizing this was a dangerous situation, gently slowed down the old car to a stop in such away as not to scrape the underside of the car. We came to a quiet halt. The car leaned to the ground. Dad got out of the car, hunted down the tire, brought it back to the car, jacked up the car and re-attached the wheel, this time bolting it firmly to the car's axle. Where he got new bolts for the job I do not know but he fastened the tire rim to the axle and, once again, Mother gave thanks to the Lord for taking care of our family. I thought that what had happened was no big deal, but, upon reflection, I just knew that somebody up there was watching over us. Brother Paul once again chimed, "I wanna go to Bosson...."

In those post-World War II years, gas was expensive at twenty to twenty-two cents a gallon. One way of saving gas through the hilly countryside was, after reaching the crest of a hill or mountain, Dad would turn off the Model A's ignition and glide down the hill with the motor turned off. This going down the hill with no motor on would sometimes last for several miles. Once we bottomed out, Dad would switch on the ignition and the car's motor would kick in with a little jump. And off we would go to the next hill crest and repeat our decent into the next valley. We probably coasted with the motor turned off some fifty or sixty miles on those long trips, an activity that generated considerable savings for a family with very little money. It was also fun to coast over the roads and highways as if we were on a roller coaster or up in an airplane. Sometimes we would go over a small hill and, as a family unit, we would all cheer "Up and over! Wheeee!" Those were the days....

Priscilla and Paul, 3-year-old twins, sit on the running board of the old Model A Ford on their venture trip to Boston, October, 1945.

Mrs. Pattison of Cohasset

The summer of 1953 was the best summer of my teenaged years. I was carefree and seventeen. This was the first time I had left home for any extended period. It was also the summer when Joseph Stalin died, when the Korean War ended, when Julius and Ethel Rosenberg were executed for espionage, and when Christine Jorgenson underwent the first successful sex change. I rented a room in Cohasset, Massachusetts, after landing a job at Hugo's Lighthouse, one of America's premier eating establishments in the early 1950s, at least according to such periodicals as **Holiday Magazine.** Today the restaurant is called Atlanticus. My residence in Cohasset was 19 Parker Avenue just a short walk from where I worked. My landlords were a wonderful couple, Mr. and Mrs. Harry A. Pattison, originally from Fields Corner, Dorchester, ironically the same area where I had been growing up. Mr. and Mrs. Pattison charged five dollars each per week for the four rapscallions boarding at the Pattison home, all of us from Fields Corner. I loved paying my rent with lobster and tenderloin steaks that I was able to get at Hugo's Lighthouse for next to nothing. Mrs. Pattison used to let us move about her house and listen to the popular songs of the day on her tall wooden floor radio. Roy Hamilton singing "Ebb Tide", or Tony Bennett singing "Rags to Riches", or Perry Como singing "Don't Let the Stars Get in Your Eyes", all hit songs during that fabulous summer, all sounded so good on that tall wooden floor radio with its big lit-up dial. When the summer ended, I returned home to Dorchester, started school and carried on as usual. In fact, I basically lost contact with Mrs. Pattison until I returned to Cohasset in 1964 when Gay and I, now living in Cooksville, Ontario, were travelling through Massachusetts. I was showing Gay all the various places I had contact with in my misspent youth. I drove right up to Mrs. Pattison's front door on Parker Avenue and sure enough, when I knocked on the door, the elderly Mrs. Pattison came to the door and was so glad to see me and meet my wife, Gay, especially after a long ten year absence. We were invited into the same living room where I and Billy Barry and others like Donnie Gillis, Ralphy Minichiello, Franny Fitzgerald and Dickie Rose, all from Fields Corner, used to stay and listen to all those wonderful hit songs. Eventually, I told Mrs. Pattison that Gay and I had ventured to Hyannis Port, prior to visiting Cohasset, to see the Kennedy compound but were unfortunately unable to get anywhere near the late John F. Kennedy family homestead because of police barricades and various road blocks. Nearly a year had come and gone since the late President's assassination in Dallas and there was still so much police protection and privacy issues protecting the property that it was impossible to see anything associated with the so-called Kennedy dynasty. Upon hearing our plight, Mrs. Pattison, whose husband had passed away several years earlier, said to us, "Well, let me call Rose Kennedy and I'll arrange for you to drop in for a visit." I was flabbergasted. How would she be able to do this? Her response was simple. She told me that way back in the 1920s, when Joe and Rose Kennedy lived at the end of Parker Avenue, she used to babysit for the Kennedys, including Joe Jr. and

Typical postcard from the 1950s illustrating the three restaurants that Mr. John Carzis, a Greek immigrant, owned form 1940-1979 in Cohassett. Hugo's Lighthouse is illustration at bottom.

Dad's Best Memories and Recollections

Jack, the future President. In fact she took me to a particular place on her living room wall and showed both Gay and me the official invitation that she and her husband had personally received to attend John F. Kennedy's Inaugural Ball following JFK's election to the Presidency in 1960. What Mrs. Pattison did not tell me was that Joe Kennedy and his family left Cohasset because they were Catholics and were not accepted in the staunch Protestant community. The final straw came when Joe Kennedy was turned down for membership in the Cohasset Country Club. He was not going to have his children subjected to further slights of Brahmins who had migrated from Boston to the south shore. Consequently, Joe moved his upwardly mobile family to Riverdale, New York. But by 1928, Joe and Rose Kennedy and their family had purchased a summer home in Hyannis Port about sixty miles from Cohasset. It became known as the Kennedy compound. This is where the last Kennedy, Senator Ted Kennedy, died in 2009.

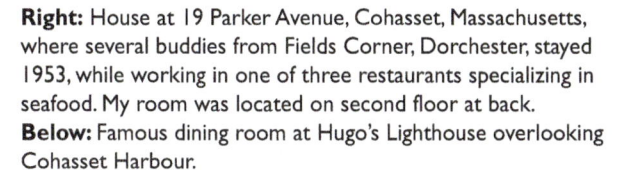

Right: House at 19 Parker Avenue, Cohasset, Massachusetts, where several buddies from Fields Corner, Dorchester, stayed 1953, while working in one of three restaurants specializing in seafood. My room was located on second floor at back.
Below: Famous dining room at Hugo's Lighthouse overlooking Cohasset Harbour.

Dad's Best Memories and Recollections

Alice Morse

When my father was the pastor of Bethany Baptist Church, on the border between Dorchester and Roxbury, Massachusetts, 1948-1951, I became a member of Boy Scout Troop 4 there under the leadership of Mr. Albert Chamillard. Because of his leadership, Troop 4 was on the lookout for ways to serve the community, in particular, assisting the elderly members of Bethany. Dad was one of those devoted preachers who weekly visited the sick and elderly. He also encouraged the Troop to visit many of the church elders, including one particular member, Alice Morse. She lived at 8 Folsom Street, just a few blocks from Bethany Baptist located on West Cottage Street, and just one block south of Dudley Street. One spring day in 1951, Dad encouraged the Troop to spend a Saturday cleaning up Mrs. Morse's outdoor property. At the time Mrs. Morse was in her early 90s, meaning that she was born at the outbreak of the Civil War. One blustery spring morning, some five or six of the Troop showed up to rake leaves, pick up debris, sweep her porch and fix the fence separating her property from her neighbor's property line. She sat in her enclosed porch and watched us work and offered drinks and kind words and loving looks. When it was all over, the Troop left but I remained behind at her encouragement. She also knew I was the pastor's son. Anyway, she volunteered to tell me that she had boarders in her house living on the second floor. They had been living above her for over fifty years. Then she told me that she had, at one time, been diagnosed with tuberculosis and that her parents isolated her in an unheated back room of the house which they had built for her. She recuperated (I think her husband had left her after she became inflicted) and, at the time of my visit, had lived in this house at 8 Folsom since the 1860s.

One thing she wanted to make sure I learned from her was that one of her neighbors was America's first national sporting hero. John L. Sullivan was his name. In my Boston days, there was not anyone who had not heard of John L. Sullivan! Born in Roxbury, 1858, about the same time as Alice Morse, he was known as the "Boston Strong Boy." He was the last of the bareknuckle fighters to hold the heavyweight title, and the first to hold the heavyweight title using gloves. Mrs. Morse made sure I knew all this information! In 1889, she claimed, the Boston Strong Boy fought and won a bareknuckle bout that lasted 75 rounds. Overall, John L. Sullivan fought 450 bouts and was the first sporting figure of any sport in America to earn more than one million dollars. Mrs. Morse told me that she used to watch him pass her house strutting and blustering with the biggest handle bar moustache on any male figure she had ever seen. He did not walk, she said, but instead swaggered – all with a walking stick which he flipped back and forth under his arm to look important. With his Derby hat perking, he would tip his hat "Hello" as he passed her by but rarely said a word to her. Mrs. Morse told me this story, I feel, because it probably was one of the highlights of her life, namely, to live on the same street with a man with super star power, a man's man, so to speak, who could "lick anybody in the house". Mrs. Morse then gave me a couple of trinkets which she had picked up on some of her world travels, sea shells and a couple of books.

She was a very dear woman with a gentle look and throughout my life I still carry her smiling face in my memory bank. I wish I had a photo of her to share. All I have today is a book she signed to my father. My daughter Kristy and I visited the outside of her house on Folsom Street in November, 2014, and took a photo of what looks like, today, an Alfred Hitchcock setting for one of his horror movies.

Heavyweight boxing champion, John L. Sullivan, lived next door to Alice Morse in Roxbury. Photo far right is the home of Alice Morse in 2014.

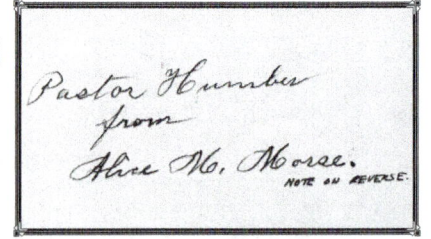

Dad's Best Memories and Recollections

Joseph Patrick Kennedy

After we moved as a family of six from Toronto to Boston, 1945, I had never heard such terms as Boston Brahmins, Irish Famine, Boston Commons, Tremont Temple, Scollay Square, Quincy Market or Meeting House Hill. Moreover, I soon found out after we moved to 1145 Dorchester Avenue, in the heart of Dorchester, still another world emerged, namely, that our family seemed to be the only Protestants in our entire neighborhood of Savin Hill and its environs of Fields Corner and Uphams Corner. Dad had rented the top two floors of a typical three-story tenement building that is so characteristic of Dorchester, South Boston, Roxbury, the

Ambassador Joseph P. Kennedy in his heyday.

South End and still other neighborhoods of Boston to this day. We struggled at 1145 "Dot" Ave. on very little income while Dad went to Harvard University, 1945-1947. In order to put some change into my pocket, I used to deliver **The Boston Record**, a daily paper that came out in the early evening. Each Sunday, I used to shine shoes on the portable shoeshine box that my friend Wee Wee O'Neil loaned me. On one of those Sundays in 1946, I stationed my shoeshine box two or three stores down from the old Fields Corner Theatre on Adams Street. I stood in front of a small variety store that specialized in selling newspapers, magazines, and tobacco. The painted sign on my box indicated that shoe shines were ten cents. One Sunday afternoon, I felt lucky as I was the only one with a shoe shine box in front of the store. As usual, several guys in their zoot suits were smoking their cigarettes or cigars and passing the time away in front of the variety store. Fields Corner was always a very busy place on a Sunday afternoon. One such Sunday in the fall of 1946 a four-door black Lincoln limousine pulled up in front of me and my shoebox. On the sidewalk outside the storefront, locals were smoking their Camel, Lucky Strike or Chesterfield cigarettes. Three very stiff-looking guys got out of the car, all dressed in rather long overcoats with felt collars. Each was wearing a silk scarf and a Homburg or Derby hat typically worn in those days. Two of the guys went into the store and the third approached me and wanted a shoe shine. He stood with his back to the storefront, put a foot up on my shoe-stand, the traditional cue to begin shoe shining. At about the time I finished, the other two guys came out, seemingly in a good mood. I indicated that I was done. The man whose shoes I had just polished gave me two quarters. This was a huge tip! I was almost speechless. The three companions then got into their limo and drove off. One individual standing in front of the store and who watched my shoe-shine job from beginning to end, said, "Hey, Humba, did you know who that was?" I just shook my shoulders indicating that I had no idea whose shoes I had just shined. He said, "That was Honey Fitz's son-in-law!" I had no idea who Honey Fitz was. But I was told that Honey Fitz used to be the Mayor of Boston and that his daughter Rose Fitzgerald had married this guy who just happened to be Joseph Kennedy. Later on in life I connected this same individual as the father of the future President of the United States, John Fitzgerald Kennedy, and as the bloke from Boston who made countless millions in booze during the Prohibition days, interacting with the Chicago boys known as "The Outfit". I suppose I'll never know what Joe Kennedy was doing in Fields Corner that fall of 1946. But as I look back, what took place that day has registered with me as one of the more unique things that ever happened to me. And the tip was glorious. No wonder I've always had a soft spot in my heart for the Kennedy family.... What a memory!

Period postcard illustrating John F. Fitzgerald, Mayor of Boston, 1906-1908 and 1910-1914.

Dad's Best Memories and Recollections

Pine Vista, our "Castle in the Wilderness"

In 1955 my Uncle Bill Donaldson discovered property for sale on Stewart Lake in MacTier, Ontario, some 150 miles from Hamilton from where he and his wife of some twenty-six years, my father's sister, my dear Aunt Edie, had lived most of their married life. Totally undeveloped on a very primitive bush trajectory called, at the time, Riva Road, the property Uncle Bill bought from Mr. Carl Riva for $1000.00 had beauty accentuated by 500 feet of water frontage, including a small blueberry-laden peninsula. It turns out that Carl Riva's stretch of land was located at the northern end of Stewart Lake and extended southeast for about one half mile along the lake's shoreline. He was in the process of sub-dividing this property into some twenty-five lots. He raised two sons, Calvin and Wayne, in an old house located on the first lot. He kept the last lot in this stretch of land for himself. In 2015, his son Calvin and Helen Healey live in this year-round house, just a few lots from **Pine Vista**.

Most of the people who purchased the Carl Riva lots were not from MacTier or even the general area. Many were from the Hamilton area. After Uncle Bill purchased his cottage property, his nephew, Ted Donaldson, from Bass Lake, was commissioned to build a twenty by thirty foot wooden structure with three open concept bedrooms not including a small back porch of one hundred square feet. The cottage was crudely built, much of it second hand wood probably taken from the CP Railway yards in MacTier. It was built to rest on seasoned cedar stumps that would last only fifteen years. In those early years, I used to visit my Aunt and Uncle when I was working in the late 1950s for the **Toronto Telegram** canvassing for new delivery customers in the Muskoka area. I remember my grandmother Lizzie Humber visiting the cottage property when she was in her 80s. Of course, I always visited after my mother and father had driven up from Pennsylvania to spend their vacation with relatives. I'd only stay for a brief spell, perhaps for lunch, as bedroom quarters in the cottage were very limited. Dad's mother was usually up at the cottage at the same time with Uncle Bill and Aunt Edie as well as Aunt Fern, Dad's oldest sister. After Aunt Edie passed away, 1970, Uncle Bill sold his cottage property to Gay and me for $12,500.00. He continued to come up on his own to watch the trees he and Aunt Edie had planted, including one each to commemorate their two sons they prematurely lost: one named Chuck, who died in 1953, and the second one, Philip, who died in a car accident, 1963. Uncle Bill also enjoyed watching our own four children grow up. He so loved the family cottage activity, often threatening, with a smirk, to cut off either Charlie or Scott's fingers if they were caught picking their noses! His visits lasted about ten years until he went into a Hamilton senior's home, circa 1985.

Eventually, we replaced the original cedar posts holding up the cottage with a different set of posts. The guy from Bass Lake who finished the job explained that if we had waited one more year to complete the job we would have found our cottage slipping into Stewart Lake by the next spring. We added to the cottage a front porch that included an enlarged bathroom. Also added was a new bedroom on the other side of the back porch. Over the years we have entertained many guests. My brother Paul and his wife, Prudence, even spent their honeymoon here in 1966, four years before Uncle Bill sold us the cottage. The cottage is also the place where my Mom and Dad celebrated their 50th wedding anniversary in 1984. More than fifty relatives joined the celebration dinner at the Foot's Bay Community Centre just outside MacTier. All of my siblings have visited the cottage on numerous occasions. Priscilla and her husband, Chuck Hurlbut, drove all the way from Texas, in 2007, after we completely rebuilt the cottage. Anna, my older sister, has made several trips to the cottage, once with

Doorway to the front porch at **Pine Vista,** built 2005.

Dad's Best Memories and Recollections

her husband, Jim Rolen, all the way from Florida, at the time, pulling his remarkable boat, a **Mark Twain**. They also came from Alexandria, Virginia for an extended stay in 2007. Gay's only sister, Dee, and her husband, Tom Birch, from California, have visited the cottage twice for extended stays over the years. So, too, have John, Gay's only brother, plus his wife, Alice. They first came from California on several occasions for extended cottage visits. When they moved to Hawaii in 2006, they chose to travel a long way to visit the Humber clan in MacTier. As our four children, Kristy, Karyn, Charlie Jr., and Scott, grew up, graduated from high school, attended university and got married, Gay and I have kept up the cottage property over our fading years by landscaping and adding trees. I estimate that over the years each member of the family, collectively, has ceremonially planted some 130 trees, mainly white pine with some red pine, a number of hemlock and one tamarack tree, several cedar and balsam trees but no oak or maple trees as there was no need to plant them. They plant themselves!

By 2004, Gay and I, after selling one key antique in our collection, decided on tearing out the front porch that we had added shortly after we purchased the cottage, in 1970, and erecting a post and beam, story-and-one-half addition to the old cottage. When finished, it was not quite twice the size of the original cottage. Costing us some $150,000.00 dollars, the builder, a twenty-eight year old buck from MacTier named Mike Healey, had a constant love affair with wood that attracted me to commission him to be our builder. He spent his winter erecting our dream cottage, completed in 2005. The posts and beams used were harvested thirty minutes from the cottage we now call **Pine Vista**. Several years later, 2011, we sold still another antique and added a new roof line to the old cottage to match the new roof line of the grand addition. With a few minor adjustments, such as getting Calvin Riva, Carl's son, to engineer the stone steps to the lake from the back porch or getting Paul Ignani, my unofficial "property manager" to oversee cottage problems that continue to surface, our cottage property is pretty much completed as we like it. As well, my terrific son-in-law, Eric Shennette, has wonderfully assisted me in ongoing landscaping projects such as building the bunkie and stone fences and pruning trees. Whatever happens to the beautiful "castle in the wilderness" that we have built is up to our four children. They all love the property. In fact, there has never been a year in which all four children, independent of each other, have not visited the cottage. After all, wherever they walk on the property they retrace their own steps when they were pre-schoolers. And now they watch their own children falling in love with Muskoka much in the same way they did. In other words, our eight grandchildren are taking over from where their own parents left off. The cottage has been our heaven on earth for well over forty-five years, and three times longer than my Uncle Bill owned it.

Above left: As you come down the driveway to **Pine Vista**, you park your car and you stand in front of a "castle in the wilderness". **Above centre:** My consummate son-in-law, Eric Shennette, has been my right-hand man at **Pine Vista**. I could not ask for a better "Mr. Everything!" Here he is in his kayak adoring his family pet, Tanner. **Above right:** Two guys celebrate the completion of **Pine Vista:** Charlie Humber and post-and-beam builder Mike Healey of MacTier, Ontario. **Right:** the Lake side of **Pine Vista** has a deck with an electric awning, which, in this view, is not extended.

Dad's Best Memories and Recollections

Hitchhiking to Alaska, 1960

As I entered the Yukon Territory, my driver stopped his Cadillac (parked beyond the sign) and took this photo, September, 1960.

Up into the 1960s, hitching a ride was a popular way of getting around. John Steinbeck wrote about it in **The Grapes of Wrath.** Jack Kerouac explored hitchhiking in his 1960 classic, **On the Road.** For the most part, people who hitched rides did so because they had no car. For instance, during the summer of 1957, following my graduation from Brampton District High School, I got a summer job at J.M. Dent and Sons located near the intersection of Leslie and Lawrence Ave., in Toronto, just south of the new 401 Highway. Because I had no car, I had to hitchhike, daily, from my residence to work and back, a round trip of approximately thirty miles. Never once was I late for my job and never once was I late for my aunt Lefa Prosser's fabulous suppers at L and L Farms, in the town of Meadowvale, Ontario.

After completing three semesters at Temple University in Philadelphia, between January, 1959, and June, 1960, I considered doing something that everybody else thought was absolutely crazy. I had just received approval for a one-year transfer from Temple University to the University of Alaska, in Fairbanks. My only way of getting there was by hitching the entire distance from the junction of Highway 7 and Highway 400, north of Toronto, a distance of some 3000 miles. So, on the last day of August, 1960, a high school friend, Doreen Wiggins, drove me to that highway junction. After I bade her farewell, I just took it for granted that I would be in Fairbanks within ten days. Carrying a single duffle bag plus a sleeping bag (and a knife strapped to my ankle), my cross country route took me through Timmins and Kapuskasing in northern Ontario, all the way to Port Arthur and Fort William on Highway 11, and on up through Kenora in extreme western Ontario until I crossed into Manitoba. At night, I usually slept just off the highway right near the sound of tractor trailer mufflers rolling by me on the Trans-Canada Highway. I'll always remember waking up my first morning in Manitoba. It was going to be my third day "on the road." When I woke up, I was staring at expansive prairie lands. The fields, full of brilliant wheat, glistened with gold in the early morning sun. This first experience with the Canadian prairies was a memory I've never forgotten.

As I passed the outskirts of Portage la Prairie, about an hour or so west of Winnipeg, it dawned on me that I had two great uncles, Frank and Oliver Humber, uncles of my grandfather Charles Herbert Humber, who had pioneered this prairie town back in the late 1890s and early 1900s. Entering the next province, Saskatchewan, I saw signs pointing to Fort Qu'Appelle and reflected that my favorite uncle, Bill Donaldson, was born there the same year Queen Victoria died, 1901. The flatlands of the prairie always fooled me. What looked like a town some five to ten miles down the road turned out to be twenty or more miles into the horizon. Undulating roads on the TransCanada Highway were rare. Rather, they were as straight as the two foul lines at Fenway Park, running parallel either to the Canadian Pacific or the Canadian National Railway tracks. I can remember passing by the town of Mortlach, Saskatchewan, where still another distant uncle of mine, W.T. Scott, was the town's mayor at the time his wife succumbed to the Spanish Flu Epidemic in 1918. On and on I travelled, sometimes in a car for only thirty or forty miles, sometimes in a tractor trailer for a hundred miles. As I headed to Lethbridge, Alberta, where my good friend Wayne Getty and his family were living, I eventually took my first glimpse of the Rocky Mountains. Although they appeared to be a short distance away, they were lurking well over 50 miles to the West in front of me.

I stayed overnight in Lethbridge where Wayne's father had a connection with a radio station that reported there was a young man hitchhiking to Alaska and encouraged anyone needing a passenger to call him. We had one call. It was from two girls who wanted a man to join them on their trip to Alaska. I decided that this was not a good idea. Accordingly Wayne and his mother drove me

Dad's Best Memories and Recollections

on a Saturday afternoon to the suburbs of Edmonton where we said goodbye. The traffic flowing west from Edmonton was pretty good. I caught a ride to Whitecourt. Soon thereafter I caught another ride to just south of Grande Prairie, another two hours or so before Dawson Creek, Mile 0 of the 1500-mile Alaska Highway. In that it was now approaching midnight, I asked if the place where my driver would drop me off was at some major intersection. He replied that there would be an intersection at the drop-off and a gasoline station on the corner. But when we got to the corner, we realized that it was early Sunday morning when all stores were closed. As he drove off, I watched his rear lights disappear into the night. I was left standing alone in pitch blackness. It was after three o'clock in the morning. I literally could not see the palm of my hand in front of my face. After an hour of standing in the pitch darkness, I saw this huge "thing" way up in the sky. It was a brilliant white light, like a glistening diamond, and was slowly moving across the sky. I wondered what it possibly could be. Later I learned that it was a weather balloon, some forty stories high, travelling some thirty or so miles above me. It truly was the only thing that made me think I was not alone in the world. A ride came at about six that early Sunday morning. It was a trucker who gave me a lift to Dawson Creek. He dropped me off at a restaurant where I ordered breakfast then waited outside the restaurant for my next ride. I had made a very crude sign that said "University of Alaska." About an hour went by and a brand new Cadillac drove into the restaurant's parking lot. The car had Alaska license plates. Out of the car emerged a young guy, my age. He went into the same restaurant where I had breakfasted, had his breakfast, and while returning to his car, I approached him about a ride. He hesitated. But I suspected he could not say "no". He relented, informing me that he also was a student at the U. of A. and was travelling to Anchorage before heading for Fairbanks. He was driving the Cadillac from Seattle to Anchorage where his uncle had a GM dealership. So off we headed north on the Alaska Highway. It took us two days to drive to Tok Junction, about one half hour inside Alaska. This was the first main junction in Alaska where cars turn off to travel to Anchorage or go straight ahead to Fairbanks. It was also a border crossing where one's identity was handed over to immigration officials for inspection. Although we did not become close friends on campus we did see each other every once in a while and enjoyed a laugh over how we met.

    On the tenth day of my journey, I was less than thirty miles from Fairbanks, home of the University of Alaska. The car that stopped to pick me up was coming from Eielson Air Force Base. It turned out that the driver of the vehicle, after he saw my "University of Alaska" sign, abruptly stopped to pick me up. It was the newly-appointed President of the University! What a stroke of luck. When Dr. William R. Wood told me on the way to the university campus that all the campus residences were filled up, I must have had a very discouraging look. But he said not to worry because the administration had arranged with Ladd Air Force Base to put all new students over twenty-one years into a Civilian Bachelor's Quarters (CBQ) located conveniently on the base and that travel to the campus was less than ten minutes away by bus service provided by the university. He pointed out that the university had attracted more students than usual and indicated that we would be getting a very good food deal in that all fifty registered students staying at the base (today known as Fort Wainwright) would be able to purchase what civilians on the base pay when ordering meals at the Civilian Club. It was here that I would meet Gayle Jenkins. We were married in just over a year's time! While explaining all this information to me, Dr. Woods not only drove me to the campus where I was registered as a foreign student, but delivered me to where a big red wooden box that had been shipped to me from Orillia, Ontario, was awaiting me at the campus post office. Only years later have I realized what an epic journey I had made. It truly is one of the great memories I have, knowing, as well, that such an epic odyssey could not be repeated today....

Duffle bag and sign, my hitch-hiking companions from Toronto to Fairbanks, Alaska, 1960.

Dad's Best Memories and Recollections

H. Northrop Frye

Lionized thinker, globally-renowned literary critic and intellectul beacon, H. Northrup Frye (1912-1991), according to American literary critic Harold Bloom was "the foremost living student of western literature".

Reader's Digest used to publish a monthly story called "The Most Unforgettable Character I Ever Met." Had I the chance to write such a story, I would have told the story of Northrop Frye, certainly one of the most unforgettable persons I ever met. He was the memorable English professor at Victoria College, University of Toronto, from 1939 until he died in 1991. I first heard of the intellectual beacon when I was a student at Brampton District High School, 1956-1958. My English teacher there for two years was J. C. Potter, another one of those most unforgettable individuals who entered my life. I would say that because of Jim Potter, more than anyone else, I became an English high school teacher. Mr. Potter used to mention, sometimes emphasize, Northrop Frye in his grade twelve and thirteen English classes. I suppose this was partially because he studied under Frye when he himself attended Victoria College. His proselytizing, if that is what it was, did not register with me as being important at the time, but when I started my own high school teaching career at Thomas L. Kennedy Secondary School, in Cooksville, Ontario, 1962, several of my colleagues in the English department there had also studied under Northrop Frye and were incorporating Frye's literary theories in their own teaching of English literature. I liked what I heard and saw back in those early days of my teaching career. Then, when I left T. L. Kennedy to pursue graduate studies at the University of Wisconsin, January, 1967, I once again discovered that Northrop Frye was just as big a name there as he was at University of Toronto. I was impressed because Frye was a Canadian academic revered by several of my world-renowned American professors, including Drs. A. B. Chambers, Ricardo Quintana, Mark Eccles and John C. Shawcross. As part of my graduate work at Wisconsin, I returned to Toronto in September, 1968, to take a special seminar at the University of Toronto that Northrop Frye was offering to graduate students. It was overwhelming to be in the presence of this globally-renowned literary critic. He would walk into class with, perhaps, one or two texts and several pieces of chalk which he constantly used to fill up the blackboard with diagrams illustrating the two worlds he felt the human race was constantly struggling with, namely, the innocent world we lost in the Garden of Eden and the world of experience and sin into which we have fallen. I began to understand more clearly what another world-famous Canadian academic, Marshall McLuhan, had metaphorically said about Frye, namely, that Frye "...is not struggling to find his place in the sun because he is the sun."

After Frye published **The Anatomy of Criticism** (1957), one of America's most distinguished literary critics, Harold Bloom, claimed that Frye "was the foremost living teacher of Western Literature." Frye felt that the foundation for teaching western literature was learning as much as possible about Greek and Roman mythology in addition to the Bible. He felt that these two disciplines should sink to the bottom of one's brain upon which everything else is built. According to Frye, this is the necessary formula for anyone or everyone to have to be a competent literary critic. He taught that literary criticism was a discipline, that it is a "coherent field of study which trains the imagination quite as systematically and efficiently as the sciences train the reason." The paper I wrote for Frye the year I studied under him investigated the imagery of John Keats and although I only got a B+, his comments were invaluable and encouraged me to follow in his footsteps as I continued to teach high school English. Over the next fourteen years, each fall, I spent six weeks with my grade thirteen students going over Northrop Frye's sixty-page volume called **The Educated Imagination** (1963). In other words, my students, each week, mastered ten pages of Frye's famous little book which emphasized that "all societies indoctrinate its membership with its own mythology." Many of my students went on to the University of Toronto and gravitated to Frye's course entitled "Bible and Mythology." For about five years in the 1970s I visited with my former teacher in his special office at Victoria College and latterly at Massey College. He would offer me a glass of sherry and reflect on what I had been teaching until he got around to telling me that each year he gets a few of my former students, all of whom he dubbed as "small Fryes." He was certainly not parading himself as a puppeteer. But somehow the lionized thinker was getting some satisfaction that he was having a positive influence on the next generation and that his students were recognizing that "Poetry was the gold standard for our use of words".

In the year 2000 Canada Post Corporation honored H. Northrop Frye with a postage stamp some eight years after he passed away, January 23, 1991. He was not just remarkably stirring and solemnly impressive. He was marvelously memorable and radioactively recollective....

Many accomplished authors, columnists and famous historians were solicited by Heirloom Publishing over the years to write chapters in the 7-volume series of books published between 1986 and 2000. Unfortunately, when I approached professor Frye to write a chapter documenting Canadian literature, he politely declined because he "was running out of time". This letter reveals his honesty and sincerity. Fortunately, Dr. Clara Thomas took his place and over several years wrote numerous chapters for Heirloom, including one celebrating Canadian Literature in **CANADA From Sea unto Sea**.

UNIVERSITY PROFESSOR

UNIVERSITY OF TORONTO

MASSEY COLLEGE
4 DEVONSHIRE PLACE
TORONTO, ONTARIO
M5S 2E1

February 4, 1985.

Mr. Charles Humber,
43 Lawrence Crescent,
Toronto,
Ontario
M4N 1N3

Dear Mr. Humber,

I am very sorry that on looking over my writing schedule I find that I have committed myself quite recklessly and cannot find any extra space. Unlike the Ontario book, a book on Canada would need an article which deals with French as well as English literature. That is why I suggested Clara Thomas and Doug Jones: the latter is at the University of Sherbrooke, and has an unusually comprehensive knowledge of French-Canadian literature. I myself have not been able to keep up with other than bits and ends of it.

Yours sincerely,

Northrop Frye

NF:jw

Two Lords: Roy and Ken Thomson

Lord Roy Thomson (1894-1976)

Lord Kenneth Thomson (1924-2006)

    Before Roy Thomson Hall, home of the Canadian Opera Company, officially opened in downtown Toronto, 1982, the complex was dubbed the New Massey Hall. Because the family of the late Roy Thomson agreed to donate the monies needed to complete construction of this ultra-modern concert hall, it was named after one of the 20th century's greatest newspaper moguls. According to **Forbes Magazine**, Roy Thomson, the First Baron of Fleet Street, was one of the world's ten richest men when he died in 1976. He controlled over 200 newspapers in Canada, Great Britain and the United States including **The Sunday Times, The London Times, The Scotsman,** in Edinburgh, and numerous media outlets in Canada, including **The Globe and Mail.**

    When I was a first-year teacher at T.L. Kennedy Secondary School, in Cooksville, Ontario, my only encounter with Lord Thomson occurred in September, 1962. This high school, where I began my career as an English teacher, was located in a crossroads community that became part of Canada's sixth largest municipality, the City of Mississauga, in 1974. As do most schools, T.L. Kennedy offered a special evening in September when parents could meet the various teachers of their children. Parents would gather in the homeroom class at the beginning of the evening's Parents-Teachers Night, then follow a typical day, in ten minute segments, which lasted between 7:00 and 9:30 p.m. Subject teachers would outline their respective courses of study to parents who often, on these occasions, sat at their child's desk. My responsibility, as the homeroom teacher, was to outline the schedule for the evening and provide maps of the school's various hallways leading to a gamut of classrooms. After the school bell rang, parents would follow their child's typical school schedule. This ten-minute rotation of various classrooms afforded everyone to get to know one another. It was good public relations and opened the door to teacher/parent communication. At the end of my introductory remarks to my home room parents, and following the school bell, anxious parents began leaving my classroom. At the same time, this elderly gentleman approached me and pointed his finger at me and said that he would very much appreciate if I would remain in my homeroom following the evening events because he wanted to have "a little chat." I had no idea who he was but was more than willing to oblige his request. When the mini-school day was over at 9:30 p.m., sure enough this gentleman, wearing an overcoat and carrying a black Derby hat, strode over to my desk where I was awaiting him or any other parent that might wish to see me after 9:30 p.m. He did not introduce himself but immediately stated that he really appreciated my talk at the beginning of the evening and was also keenly aware that I was a first-year teacher. He said something like, "Mr. Humber, you should really consider leaving this teaching profession because there are greater opportunities out there in the real world for you. You've got a significant presence that is so necessary for success in the business world." This is not an exact quote but it is very close to what he said to me

Dad's Best Memories and Recollections

some fifty years ago. He then indicated who he was, namely, a newspaper man, and that he was always on the lookout for young men who could speak with charm, elucidate information with confidence and have overall charisma." He did not offer me a job but I really think that this grandfather of one of my students would have made some kind of offer had I shown him any interest.... He then abruptly left and The First Baron of Fleet Street, Lord Thomson, wished me well....

Years later, in 1995 I had the opportunity to meet with Ken Thomson, Roy Thomson's only son, whom I had come to know since the early 1980s. In fact, at the Toronto Hilton Harbor Castle, October 2, 1984, more than ten years earlier, when the Province of Ontario, under the leadership of Premier Bill Davis officially hosted Her Majesty The Queen with a gala Bicentennial Dinner, Ken Thomson and I sat next to each other as we toasted Her Majesty before the Bicentennial dinner was served. Also known as the Second Baron of Fleet Street, Ken was regally sitting in his special office in the 25-story Thomson Building on Queen Street West, across from Toronto's "new" City Hall. I had arranged to meet with him to discuss his father's vignette, "The Paper Chaser," that I had commissioned for publication in Volume V of the CANADA Heirloom Series, a volume named **WAYFARERS: Canadian Achievers** (pages 178-181). Ken sat at his desk on a slight podium and read his father's four-page illustrated story, while looking down upon me sitting in front of his desk. Upon finishing the story, and, with an undisguised smile, this Second Baron of Fleet Street gave approval of the story declaring it was well written except for one paragraph that he felt was unneessary. This was the one which described his father sleeping on the couch of Viola and George MacMillan when Roy was preparing to purchase the Timmins' first radio station **CKGB** in the early 1930s as well as **The Timmins Press.** He also bought 100 books at a pre-publication price for his holding company, The Woodbridge Company Limited. It was then that I took liberty to tell him about how his father approached me in my classroom some twenty-five years earlier. Upon hearing the story, Ken calmly replied: "Well, father was always looking for talent and when he saw talent not being maximized, he was sometimes annoyed or frustrated."

When Ken Thomson died in 2006, he was the world's ninth wealthiest man at 20 billion dollars....

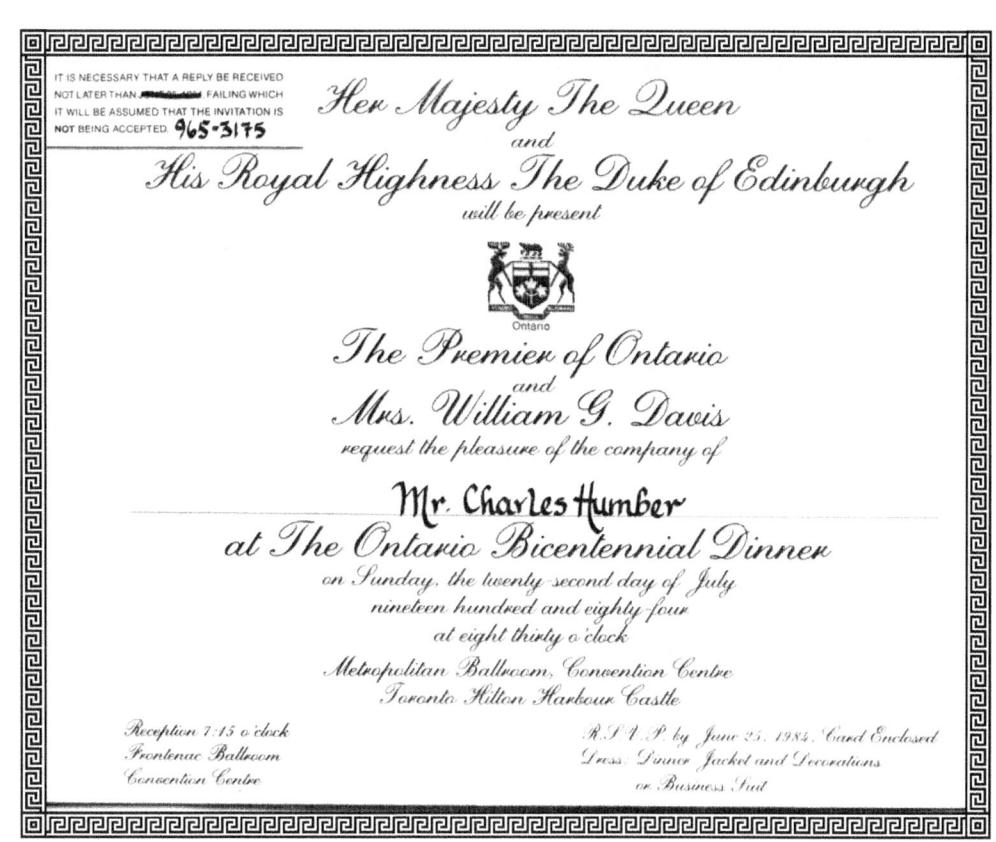

Ken Thomson and I sat next to each other at the Ontario Bicentennial Dinner, October 2, 1984, honouring the presence of Her Majesty The Queen and His Royal Highness the Duke of Edinborough at the Toronto Hilton Harbour Castle.

Venturing to the Maritimes, 1983

In June, 1983, our family drove to New Brunswick and Nova Scotia for the annual UEL Convention. As the National President of The United Empire Loyalists' Association of Canada (UELAC), I was completing the first half of my two-year term. The two provinces were co-hosting the nine-day affair in which some 300 descendants of Loyalists were assembling to give important recognition to their forefathers who had re-settled along Canada's east coast two hundred years earlier. Expelled from the new republic, 40,000 banished loyalists arrived by boat, in 1783, to what then was British North America and today constitutes Nova Scotia and New Brunswick. For sure, our family of six greatly anticipated the 1983 Maritime Bicentennial.

New Brunswick Convention activity, six days, included sessions in Fredericton, St. Andrews by-the-Sea and Saint John followed by three more days of Convention activity in Shelburne, Nova Scotia. When the Bicentennial Convention ended, July 3, our family of six drove in our 1976 Buick station wagon to Halifax and bid goodbye to daughter Kristy who flew home to her Toronto job. After touring Halifax, we took the Cabot Trail to Fortress Louisbourg. And while heading home, via Quebec City, we visited the Giant Angus MacAskill Museum in St. Ann's, Cheticamp, where Acadian culture still flourishes, and Hartland, New Brunswick, where the world's longest covered bridge crosses the Saint John River. In passing through Inverness County, I recalled how my friends, Donnie and Allan Gillis, from Boston, had parents who had come from this Scottish region. For sure, our four children got more education on this trip than any week of school.

The 1983 Convention in the Maritimes provided amazing chances to connect with Loyalist descendants and to visit historic Loyalist landmarks. For sure the week was most memorable....

It gave me a great pleasure on Sunday, June 26th, day two of the Convention, to read the Bible lesson from the pulpit of Fredericton's stunning Gothic Revival Christ Church Cathedral, an historic place of worship consecrated in 1853. The congregation, filled with four bus-loads of UE Loyalist descendants, exuberantly sang timeless hymns such as "Faith of our Fathers." The previous day, Saturday evening, more than three hundred Loyalist descendants assembled in the Lady Dunn Dining Hall on the campus of the University of New Brunswick. This event initiated the nine-day Convention. The evening dinner was highlighted with fresh fiddleheads, a delicacy often

LOYALISTS' DECENDANTS MEET — The 1983 bicentennial of the landing in the Maritimes of United Empire Loyalists was celebrated during the weekend with the a convention of Loyalists' descendants. Attending were, back row, left to right: Karyn Humber; C. Fred Everett, president of the Fredericton branch of the United Empire Loyalists Association of Canada; Charles Humber Sr., Toronto, Dominion President, UELAC; Kristy Humber. Front row, from left to right: Charles Humber Jr. and Scott Humber.

Fredericton's daily paper, **The Daily Gleaner,** gave a detailed report, June 27, 1983, of the UELAC's Bicentennial Convention which began with the gala Saturday night dinner on the University of New Brunswick campus. In this view, the President of the UELAC stands with his four children in period costume along side Fred Everett, President, the Fredericton Branch. of the Association.

The 1983 Bicentennial Convention's fourth day took UE Loyalists to a buffet picnic on the front lawn of **The Algonquin** in St. Andrews by-the-Sea.

Dad's Best Memories and Recollections

48

missed in other Canadian regions but a savoured delicacy in New Brunswick. Many Loyalist costumes provided authentic air to the gala banquet. On Monday, June 27, a Loyalist brigade journeyed to King's Landing, a recreated Loyalist Village just north of Fredericton. While there we visited the ancestral home of my mentor, John W. Fisher, a Sackville, New Brunswick, old boy. A car and bus parade travelled to St. Andrew's by-the-Sea on Tuesday, June 28. To observe the Bay of Fundy at low tide on the way was so fascinating. Docked boats sitting at the bottom of estuaries awaited the tide to elevate them upwards some fifteen feet! **The Algonquin,** a prized hotel built in 1889, is the oldest seaside community resort in Canada. Located prominently in St. Andrews by-the-Sea, the resort's front lawn, upon our arrival, was decorated with cloth-covered picnic tables awaiting 300 Convention-bound Loyalist descendants looking forward to fresh lobster, tasty shrimp and savory scallops, plus an array of fresh fruit. Bouquet flowers decorated each picnic table. The Loyalist descendants were not disappointed with the food, especially ten-year old twin brothers, Charlie Jr. and Scott Humber, who joyously feasted on Maritime seafood.

The gala banquet in Saint John, July 29, was the highlight of the week in New Brunswick. But before all the Loyalists congregated at Saint John's Trade and Convention Centre for a gala evening of festivities, I personally took time out to meander over to Trinity Anglican Church on Charlotte Street. Founded in 1783, the Church's nave displays a very historic Royal Coat of Arms. Pruned from Boston's Old State House by Loyalist Edward Winslow during the evacuation of British forces, it found its way to Halifax, then to Saint John, where it has been a Trinity Church fixture ever since. The Royal Arms, formally on display in Boston's State House during the Reign of George I, was so stunning to see on display and preserved in this famous Canadian Church.

The head table of the Convention banquet, June 29, included Lt. Gov. of New Brunswick, Dr. George Stanley as well as Mayor Elsie Wayne of Saint John. After bringing regards to the UEL membership, I was privileged to read bicentennial greetings from a list of very distinguished personalities. These included tidings from Her Majesty Queen Elizabeth II, Governor General Ed Schreyer, Canadian Prime Minister Pierre Elliott Trudeau, Premier Richard Hatfield of New Brunswick, and Premier John M. Buchanan of Nova Scotia. These impressive salutations all recognized the importance of the United Empire Loyalists to Canada. They set a good tone for the Lt. Governor, a much beloved historian, who was the keynote speaker of the evening.

We departed the Delta Brunswick Inn in downtown Saint John, Thursday, June 30, and boarded the vessel **Princess of Acadia** on its three-hour trip across the Bay of Fundy to Digby, Nova Scotia. Here the town and its mayor welcomed our "Loyalist flotilla" with a prepared luncheon. After driving to Shelburne for the last stage of the Bicentennial Convention, my family and I drove to our destination just north of Shelburne where a lovely residence on the waterfront, owned by a member of the Loyalist Branch in Shelburne, had been conveniently set aside for the National President and his family. In fact, in the kitchen were instructions how to go about preparing lobsters for outdoor cooking. The lobsters, already pre-cooked, were in the refrigerator. You can bet your bottom dollar that no arthropod was wasted on the beach. Other highlights of the trip included the

A rare 1901 postcard view of the Royal Coat of Arms (1714). The armorial was retrieved from Boston's famous State House during the American Revolution and brought to Saint John by evacuated Loyalists where it has been on permanent display in the historic nave of Trinity Anglican Church for over two hundred years. A bust of Queen Victoria celebrating Her Majesty Queen Victoria's Golden Jubilee (1887) rests atop the Royal Coat of Arms.

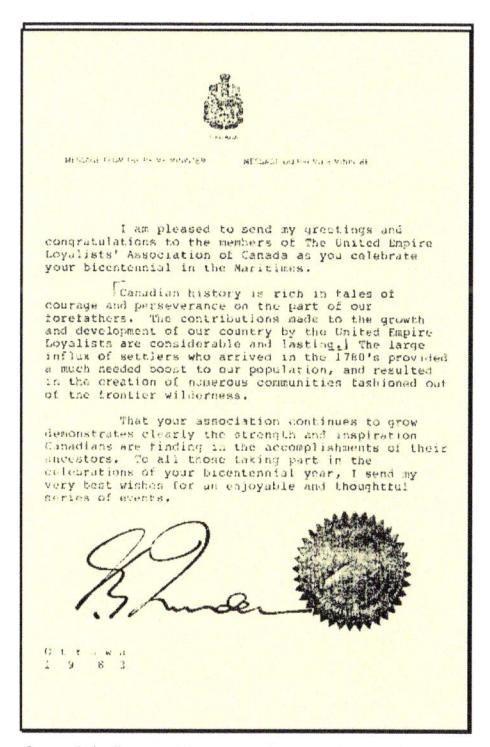

Canada's Prime Minister Pierre Elliott Trudeau sent a salutary message to the 1983 UEL Convention gathered in Saint John, June 29, 1983.

Dad's Best Memories and Recollections

Banquet and Ball held at the Shelburne Royal Canadian Legion Hall, on Dominion Day, July 1st. While Gay and I sat at the head table, our four children were assembled at a table directly in front of us. When they were served their steamed red lobsters they were unsure how to attack them. It was fun to watch Loyalist descendants demonstrating how to eat lobster. Eventually, they learned quickly and enjoyed their dulcet seafood dinner.

The next two days were highlighted with re-enactments of the 1783 Loyalist landing, Loyalist landmark tours and plays performed on the water front. To visit the old Dory Shop where Sidney Mahaney, in his 87th year, worked as an 18th century boat-maker was memorable.

Although we visited the famous **Bluenose II** in Halifax Harbour and toured Halifax Citadel and its historic Citadel Clock that has kept time overlooking Halifax Harbour since 1803, we were anxious to get on our way and visit Fortress of Louisbourg in northeastern Nova Scotia. Spending a day there is not enough time but we did so thoroughly enjoy touring this very early 18th century fortress that cost the King of France so much money. In fact, historians claim that the King used to look out his castle widow in Paris and scan the horizon believing that his fortress would grandiosely emerge above the horizon from across the Atlantic Ocean.

Stopping in Quebec City on the way home gave us an opportunity to visit a remarkable French city, walk its narrow streets, take the ferry from Lévis to Quebec City and walk the Dufferin Terrace, all affording the kids a chance to experience what it was like to visit a French city. Ironically, Charlie and Scott would return to Quebec City, 1987, and play there in the famous International Pee Wee Hockey Tournament in Le Colisée, home of Quebec Nordiques.

Our family's two-week trek to Canada's Maritimes, to say the least, was most memorable.

Top Left: The road sign along the highway by-passing Shelburne, Nova Scotia, clearly identifies the area as Loyalist countryside. **Bottom**: Shelburne, Nova Scotia, is but one of many jurisdictions in Canada's Maritimes where UE Loyalists landed after being expelled, in 1783, from the newly created Republic of the United States. Two hundred years later Canada's Maritime provinces experienced many re-enactments of Loyalist activity. This view reveals an enthusiastic crowd witnessing the re-creation of the Loyalist 1783 landing in Shelburne's protective harbour, July 2, 1983. This event attracted hundreds of UE Loyalist descendants to watch the re-enactment. **Top right:** For three days the UEL Association of Canada conducted its 1983 nine-day convention in Shelburne, Nova Scotia. Sitting in close proximity to the head table where their parents were seated are twins Charlie and Scott sitting opposite each other. Next to Scott is his oldest sister, Kristy, while Karyn, youngest sister, sits next to Charlie Jr. They are waiting to consume their first-ever lobster!

Dad's Best Memories and Recollections

Left top: Fortress of Louisbourg along the Cabot Trail in Cape Breton, Nova Scotia, is one of the most expensive restoration projects in all of North America. Built during the Reign of Louis XV, the Fortress was destroyed by the British during the 1760s. Here twins Charlie and Scott Humber march alongside the Drum and Fife Corps at the Fortress Louisbourg.

Left centre: Our Maritime trip took us to various destinations including the **Bluenose II** moored in the Harbour of Halifax. The iconic vessel has been illustrated on the Canadian dime since 1937. It has been reproduced on stamps and is officially part of the design of Nova Scotia licence plates today.

Left bottom: On our trip back to Toronto we stopped in Hartland, New Brunswick, so that the family could see the longest covered bridge in the world. Opened in 1901, it stretches 1,282 feet across the Saint John River.

Above right: I thought it was a neat idea to visit the Angus Macaskill Museum in St. Ann's, Cape Breton. Giant Macaskill stood 7'9" tall and was considered the tallest man in the world at the time he died in 1863. The twins, Scott and Charlie, plus Karyn flank the scale replica of the giant.

Dad's Best Memories and Recollections

Orange and Athol, Massachusetts

CJH's letter addressed to his three siblings in 2014 following a trip to New England:

Dear sibs (Anna, Paul and Priscilla):

After Father left Boston's Bethany Baptist Church, 1952, one year before he graduated with his doctoral degree from Boston University, he anticipated a teaching profession at such schools as Gordon College. While awaiting a call, he secured odd jobs such as painting the interior of houses, but he also travelled to such towns as Orange, Massachusetts, as well as the next town, Athol, in addition to Fitchburg and Melrose, where he preached part-time. Dad rarely drove to these faraway destinations. Rather, he took, by train, the many trips from downtown Boston to his various pulpits. I have in my family archives Dad's old Massachusetts road map. There is a black crayon mark drawing a line between Boston and Orange with Dad's writing under the marked line that says "Maybe fifty Train Trips". This was quite a commute in those days. It is not known if he left on a Saturday, stayed overnight in Orange, then returned to Dorchester following his Sunday preaching engagement. The round trip was about 180 miles. A one-way ride from Dorchester to Orange was likely two-plus hours by car back in the 1950s.

In June, 2014, sixty or so years after the fact, Gay and I travelled to Massachusetts. We decided to travel the same road Mom and Dad took back in the 1940s when they were driving back and forth between Boston and Ontario (1945, 1948, 1949, 1950, and 1951). These trips in the old Model A Ford took place before there was any Mass or New York Turnpikes. So, Gay and I took the old Highway 20 route in Upper New York State and when we got to the northeast corner of Massachusetts, near Williamstown, we drove the magnificent Mohawk Trail which meanders through the Berkshire Mountains peaking across northwestern Massachusetts. We even travelled up Mount Greylock (which is just off the Mohawk Trail to the south), something our parents did in the late 1940s. Mount Greylock is the tallest mountain in Massachusetts. It was fascinating to consider that Dad and Mom and their four children drove up that mountain in the old Model A Ford. I remember the trip ever so well, especially the famous Hairpin Turn on the Mohawk Trail....

The Mohawk Trail leads to the town of Orange. Gay and I spent some time there talking to a fine gentleman who had been a postal carrier in Orange for many years. Naturally, he did not remember Dad who had been a supply preacher in this town sixty years earlier, but he did tell Gay and me a little about the Orange Baptist Church, founded 1870. Located in the downtown section of Orange, he indicated that the church had closed down many years ago and had amalgamated with the Athol Baptist Church, located in the next town east of Orange. Today, the old Orange Baptist Church building still exists, but now as a yoga studio called The White Elephant. The lovely old wooden church steeple is long gone, destroyed, years ago, by a hurricane. Nevertheless, the white-painted clapboard building still looks good. We then drove to Athol and saw the lovely Athol-Orange Baptist Church. It is a beautiful structure located in the heart of Athol. This is the church that amalgamated with the Orange Baptist Church and, as I understand, there are still members of the old Orange Baptist Church who are now current members of the Athol-Orange Baptist Church.

It wouldn't surprise me if our father helped solidify, back in the 1950s, the dwindling membership of the Orange Baptist Church. He was the Interim Pastor there from October 1953 until June 1954. Soon after he left, the Orange Church congregation merged with the Athol Baptist Church. In 2014, seventy children are enrolled in the Athol-Orange Baptist Church Sunday School. This church is one of the most vibrant places of worship serving the region today. This reflection I cherish, knowing, that during hard times, our wonderful Father continued to serve his Master faithfully.

Love, Brother Charlie

Dr. Humber In Farewell Sermon

ORANGE — Dr. Charles Humber of Dorchester, who has occupied the pulpit of the First Baptist Church Sunday mornings for several months, will preach a farewell sermon Sunday at 10:45 a.m.

Mr. Humber has been instrumental in getting church calendars started again, has attended to some pastoral duties while in town Sundays and has been of much help. The supply for June 20 will be announced by Miss Reta Holland, church clerk.

Engaged for the first three Sundays in August is Rev. Harry Krieble of Springfield, Ill., who will be vacationing in West Wardsboro, Vt. He has been invited upon the request of several and will also work in the parish.

Above right: Greenfield Recorder-Gazette announces Doctor C.M. Humber's "farewell sermon" June, 1954. **Left:** Orange Massachusetts Baptist Church before it amalgamated with Athol Baptist Church.

Dad's Best Memories and Recollections

Les Trevor

When my father attended the University of Toronto as a first-year Chemical Engineering student in the mid-1920s, he had yet to turn eighteen years. As a freshman, rather than going into "student residence", he chose to board at 612 Spadina Ave., just off campus, a so-called boarding house that was, unfortunately, torn down sometime in the 1940s or early 1950s. One of his roommates in this so-called student residence was an interesting chap by the name of Les Trevor. I can recall Dad fondly mentioning Les Trevor's name in Dorchester, Massachusetts, when I was growing up in Boston. In fact, sister Anna, in the late 2000s, retrieved for me, from my brother, Paul, a water color painting, about 5" X 8", rendered by Les Trevor that had been in my brother's possession following my father's passing in 1988. The painting itself was one of two Trevor paintings that Dad kept over the years, both of which were displayed in our living room at 1145 Dorchester Ave. The painting is entitled "Adieu -- Adieu Kind Friend". The water color setting, in the style of the "Group of Seven", is that of a male figure, in the background, walking toward the horizon down a pathway with his suitcase in one hand and a walking cane in the other hand. Dad, in his youthful university days, used a walking cane. This was a very Victorian thing to do, namely, to walk or strut -- with a walking cane. In the foreground of this water color is a man wiping away tears from his cheeks. To me, the two characters in this painting, signed "Trevor", are definitely Les Trevor and Dad, Dad being the one walking into the sunset, so to speak. I would say that this water color was rendered in 1930 at the very time Dad was either leaving the U. of T. campus in the spring of 1930, or was heading off to Columbia University later that summer. In researching the Trevor family, I have found that Les Trevor became some administrative official at the Ontario College of Art (OCA) at the same time when my good friend, Howard Pain, attended that school (In 1978, Howard wrote and designed the classic book on antiques, **The Heritage of Upper Canadian Furniture**). Certainly Les Trevor was a teacher or instructor at this school as Howard believes that he had him as a teacher when he himself went to that art school in Toronto during the early 1960s. Of interest, it was at this first university residence on Spadina Ave. that Dad may have run into a woman whose attempts to seduce him failed. The seductress may even have been his land lady. I tried to wiggle this story from Dad over the years. He neither denied or said the story was true. Additionally, I got to know Les Trevor's brother, Clifford, who was a prominent antique dealer and hustler back in the 1970s at a store on Gerrard Street called The Serendipity. It turned out that because he was good friends with an antique picker I knew, Mitch Cadeau, one who tragically died in a car accident in the early 1970s, we hit it off as friends. I remember buying something from this Clifford Trevor and when he saw my name on my cheque he indicated that he used to know a "Charlie Humber". I indicated that it likely was my father he knew when Dad was an engineering student at U of T. He chortled and had a grin on his face that suggested that the two of them, along with Cliff's brother, Les, and still others, had some good old-fashioned times together back in the good old days when they were university students in the mid-1920s. It was at this time, when, as a freshman, Dad got the little blue tattoo on his upper shoulder. It is no wonder that my father, a "babe in the woods" from Goderich, would fail his first year of engineering studies! His membership in the Delta Kappa Epsilon fraternity probably didn't help either. Some of this background is found in a book entitled **Still Hunting: a Memoir,** by Martin Hunter. Turn to page 24 of this book, published, 2013, and read on for a couple of pages. You will get a certain feeling about what kind of man Les Trevor was. Is it any wonder that Dad wrote his Columbia University Master's Degree thesis, 1931, on prostitution?

Les Trevor's farewell gift to my father, Charles M. Humber, 1930 depicts the departure of two friends following their undergraduate days at the University of Toronto.

Cornelius Biddle, Crimean War Veteran

My grandmother, Lizzie Humber, born, 1875, often visited our family when we left Boston for the summer and vacationed, 1948-1951, at **Hiawatha Cottage** overlooking the northern shores of Lake Erie just south of Hagersville, Ontario. Gram would sit under two hickory trees flanked or linked together by a weathered plank seat, about two inches thick, ten inches wide and some six feet long. Over many years, the two trees grew in such a way that the plank became wedged between them. It was virtually impossible to disengage the "bench" which Grandmother loved sitting on. Many hours during those halcyon summers she would beckon me to come and sit on the grass near her where she would tell me stories about her beloved father, Cornelius Biddle. The Lake Erie waves rolling up on the shores behind us during these story-telling times offered a pleasant background and atmosphere. Needless to say, I got to know a lot about this great grandfather of mine who had died some eighteen years before my birth. He surely was loved and admired by his daughter who also became, in 1906, the mother of my own father. Bimp, as my great-grandfather was known in family circles, was born, 1833, in Gloucestershire, England, the same year Great Britain abolished slavery. Grandmother always enjoyed talking about her father. She stressed he was only four feet eleven inches tall when he joined, at age fourteen, the British Royal Navy. She had his discharge papers to prove it. She enjoyed talking about how her father trained aboard the most famous ship of all-time, HMS **Victory.** Of course, being only twelve or thirteen at the time grandmother first told me stories about Bimp, I was not aware of or knew anything about the heroic figure Lord Nelson or that this famous Viscount captained the HMS **Victory** and was tragically killed aboard it during the Napoleonic Wars at the Battle of Trafalgar, 1805. Often stressing that her father fought throughout the Crimean War, 1853-1856, I must confess, at the time, I had barely heard of that war. I had heard of Florence Nightingale and the famous poem, "The Charge of the Light Brigade", which I doubt any teenager today has heard of. My father often quoted from this long poem about the Crimean War, one he had memorized as a boy, thanks, I presume, to his mother. Grandmother even knew about the three war ships her father served on, namely, the 46-gun frigate, HMS **Arrogant,** the 70-gun ship-of-the-line, HMS **Cumberland,** and the 20-gun corvette, HMS **Cossack.** Each served with great distinction during the Crimean War. As I grew older, I always thought of the Crimean War as a war fought in the Black Sea arena where the Crimea juts out as a jagged peninsula into the northern shores of that huge body of water. Recently, the Crimea has come back into world news because Vladimir Putin, Russia's President, recently "repatriated" this geographical jurisdiction, taking it, without a shot fired, from the Ukraine, 2014. This news recently has prompted me to investigate exactly where my great-grandfather fought during the Crimean War. I was astonished to learn that when he served as midshipman during this 19th century "world war", he did so *not* in the Black Sea arena at all, but totally in the Baltic Sea, off the coasts of Finland, Latvia and Russia. While researching this information, the presence of my great-grandfather was, for sure, hovering over

Above: Cornelius Biddle's medals include the "Baltic, 1854-1855", presented to him by Queen Victoria before he immigrated to Canada. A second medal is the Fenian Raid Medal, 1866.

Left: Cornelius Biddle trained aboard HMS **Victory,** now dry-docked in Portsmouth, England, and preserved as a museum ship.

Dad's Best Memories and Recollections

me. For the first time in my generation as well as, perhaps, the previous generation, we can now say that Cornelius Biddle did not serve in the Black Sea during the Crimean War but fought exclusively in such memorable Crimean War sea battles as (1) Bomarsund, a fortress island in the Baltic Sea between Sweden and Norway, (2) the Battle of Gogland, an island off the coast of Finland which had its batteries silenced, (3) at Sveaborg, a harbor island off the city of Helsinki, and (4) at Courland, where a sea fortress was blockaded off the coast of Latvia. To me, these discoveries, gone undetected by my generation and likely my father's generation, were a huge discovery in sleuthing family history, and, to say the least, very satisfying....

    Before my great-grandfather came to Canada, 1856, as a seasoned war veteran, Her Majesty, Queen Victoria, personally awarded him the Crimean Medal, which to this day, remains in the hands of the great-grandson of Cornelius Biddle, namely, David Biddle of Port Rowan. When my great-grandfather died, 1918, his obituary, as reported in the local Port Rowan newspaper, stated that he was "the last known veteran of the Crimean War to die." A prominent stained glass window in the local Baptist Church, Port Rowan, memorializes both my great-grandfather, Crimean War veteran, Cornelius Biddle, and his wife, Elizabeth Fry, born also in Gloucestershire, England. She came to Canada in 1861. Both had settled in the Port Rowan area of southwestern Ontario; both lie buried next to each other in Bayview Cemetery, Port Rowan. The memories I have of my great-grandfather may not be direct, but they are, nonetheless, very real and generate goose bumps whenever he comes to mind.

Both sides of rug-mat, 24 inches X 40 inches rendered by Cornelius Biddle, 1916, two years before he died at age 85. The rug reveals my great-grandfather's love of country and family.

Dad's Best Memories and Recollections

Uncle Lester Prosser

It was in 1956 when I re-entered Canada from my formative years in Boston and took up residence in the town of Brampton, Ontario. There I enrolled in Brampton District High School (BDHS) for grades twelve and thirteen. Brampton was my destination because I had three pairs of aunts and uncles, the Gordon Jarvis, the Lester Prosser and the Adam Elliot families, as well as my grandmother Mabel Jarvis, all of whom lived close by in two lovely homes situated on a 100-acre farm located on the Third Line West, now known as Creditview Road. The property, which was known as L & L Farms, was less than ten minutes from Brampton. While completing my high school matriculation and working at part time jobs in Brampton over this two-year period, on weekends, I often ended up at the farm, staying in the 1840 McClure farmhouse where Uncle Lester and Aunt Lefa lived with Lester's daughter, Doris, along with my grandmother Jarvis. I was made to feel part of the family. After I got my car license, I was permitted to drive the 1948 Packard, one of a half dozen cars that L & L Farms owned. This was usually on the weekends enabling me to take out my girlfriend Doreen Wiggins.

Uncle Lester, as I early came to learn, was a gold-mining huckster out in British Columbia. He had his own airplane license and often would fly back and forth in his British Columbia-based Stinson aircraft to his various mining sites in British Columbia. He also took relatives for aircraft rides in his Cessna Model 195, many who came to the Brampton area from far away distances. The "tourist" flights skimmed over Brampton and Lester's farm. After I finished my high school education in June, 1958, I applied to Temple University in Philadelphia where the rest of my family had been living since 1955. Although I received my admission to Temple in time to start university that September, my student visa was not ready, meaning that I had to wait a full term to begin my freshman year that coming January, 1959. I thus moved to L & L Farms on a part time basis during the summer of 1958 while working as a door-to-door salesman for the Toronto Telegram. The job took me from Barrie all the way to Kapuskasing in the far north and all the way to Sault Ste. Marie to the west. This lucrative door-knocking job, with friends Wayne Getty and Stan Barrett, lasted throughout the summer months. Once summer was over, Wayne headed for Alberta and both Stan and I landed jobs that fall with Eaton's Department store in downtown Toronto. L & L Farms became my permanent base that fall of 1958.

One day in October, 1958, when my aunts Lefa and Lucille, along with their mother, my grandmother, Mabel Jarvis, were visiting relatives in Ohio, my uncle Adam Elliot, aunt Lucille's husband, met a police vehicle in the long driveway that led to the two residences of L & L Farms. After a brief discussion, my uncle Adam gravely got into his own car, a 1956 Buick, and followed the police car into the town of Meadowvale. About an hour later, he returned to the farm house and those present there that day were told that my uncle Lester had been tragically killed in a car accident outside the city of Lethbridge, in the foothills of Alberta. I was really shaken as I originally had been asked to drive my uncle Lester out west on that ill-fated trip. Because of his recent heart attack, Lester was forbidden by doctors from flying his Ontario-based Cessna. It was he who suggested that I should drive him out west. Aunt Lefa literally stamped her foot down on this idea. This was on the back porch of the farm

Levi Alfred Prosser (1900-1953), better known as Lester, was a gold-mining prospector, pioneering pilot, gentleman farmer, father to Doris and husband to my dear aunt, Lefa Scott Jarvis Prosser.

house. She vehemently said directly to her husband, my uncle, that she would not allow me to drive him out to British Columbia. The reason was not clear as to why she was so adamant. But, as far as Lefa was concerned, her nephew was not going to drive Lester to British Columbia! So – Lester drove on his own!

The tragic car accident, Uncle Adam was told, is alleged to have occurred on a road when a dog darted out in front of Lester's 1956 yellow, two-door, Cadillac DeVille convertible. The police report claimed he swerved to miss the dog with the consequence that he went over a cliff. It is alleged that Lester was found dazed by his car some time after the accident and died of heart failure in hospital. It was at least one week before the funeral and burial services took place in Brampton. I was one of six pall bearers along with several of Lester's mining friends who came from as far away as Texas and British Columbia to attend the funeral. My good friend Stan Barrett's father, Ray, was also a pallbearer.

But the story does not end with Lester's funeral. In fact, a rather completely different story surfaced forty years later, circa 1996, when I was having lunch with the legendary Franc Joubin, the famous geologist who discovered the world's largest-known uranium mine in Elliot Lake in northern Ontario. (See Joubin's story elsewhere in this volume.) A world-renowned miner who worked for the United Nations in underdeveloped countries and discovered world-significant mines on six continents, he shocked me when he quietly told me a story about my uncle Lester Prosser after he learned that I was his nephew. He stated quite categorically that Lester, when he finally made it to Lethbridge that October of 1958, got into a plane he either rented or borrowed and flew it into the side of a mountain, thus taking his life. I've had several persons check out the story and this Franc Joubin version of my uncle's death seems hard to prove especially considering the autopsy report. But Franc knew everyone in the Canadian mining world! He had no reason, forty years after the fact, to make up a story like the one he told me about my uncle Lester Prosser. In fact, he thought my uncle Lester was a standup guy, having worked with him on various projects since the late 1940s. This story has no happy ending but it is dramatically interesting. When I left the farm that December, 1958, to attend Temple University, I did return to Lefa and Lester Prosser's beautiful farm for a brief spell during the summer of 1959, mainly to pay further respects to my dear aunt Lefa and to visit my grandmother Jarvis. Needless to say, it was a sad reunion with my aunt Lefa. But life goes on. Soon Lefa sold the farm. I believe the year was 1961. It was sold to Cadillac Development Properties and became the nucleus for the new Town of Meadowvale, now, in 2015, a community of some 125,000 people.

Left: Lefa and Lester Prosser with dog Spike, L&L Farms, Meadowvale, Ontario, 1948.
Right: Lester and Lefa ready to "dig for gold" at Wayside Mines, Gun Lake, British Columbia, May 17, 1946.

Dad's Best Memories and Recollections

Thomas Alva Edison Rocking Horse

When researching **Family Sleuthing**, published, 2006, I interviewed a second cousin. I had not seen him for at least sixty-five years. But when William Elliott asked out of the clear blue sky, "Did you ever find the rocking horse?" I was taken by surprise and realized I had more research to do. Most people who know me also know that I've chased antiques as a collector for nearly fifty years. When the idea surfaced that there was an antique rocking horse somewhere in the family, the hunt was on. Billy Elliott was the son of Frank Elliott, the oldest son of Rev. Fred Elliott, who married, in 1900, my great aunt Fannie (Biddle) Elliott, my grandmother Lizzie Humber's oldest sister. Thus, my father and Billy Elliott were second cousins. This family background can be found on pages 136-143 of **Family Sleuthing**.

Billy Elliott, born, 1931, also informed me that his family once possessed the family rocking horse when he was a tyke and that the rocking horse had been handed down through to his grandfather, Rev. Fred Elliott, and his family. He also told me that his father's grandfather, the Rev. Isaac Elliott, was Thomas Alva Edison's first cousin, and that Thomas Alva Edison, born in Milan, Ohio, 1847, used to visit Vienna, Ontario, in his early years where he spent many summer months visiting his relatives, especially his grandparents, Samuel and Nancy (nee Elliott) Edison, pioneer settlers in Vienna, Elgin County, in southwestern Ontario. In fact, the Vienna Edison homestead, built in 1816, was moved, in 1933, to the Henry Ford Museum complex, Greenfield Village, just outside Detroit.

So, the hunt continued for a rocking horse that could very well be traced to the greatest inventor of all time, Thomas Alva Edison (whose family pronounced its surname as if it sounded like "Eedison"). Before publishing **Family Sleuthing** I frantically looked everywhere in my massive collection of thousands of old family photographs for a photo of family members with a rocking horse. For some reason, I just knew it existed. After days of searching through numerous boxes, I found this little photo, no more than two inches square. Three relatives were either sitting on the rocking horse or standing by it. These were my twin brother and sister, Paul and Priscilla, plus their cousin Philip Donaldson, my cousin Dave's youngest brother who was tragically killed in a car accident back in 1963. The date of the photo was circa 1948. I knew that since we never owned the rocking horse that this photo was likely taken at the Donaldson residence at 114 Longwood Road, Hamilton. Calling my cousin Dave Donaldson, in Dundas, Ontario, he told me rather matter-of-factly that, yes, it did belong to his family, and that, yes, his parents had loaned it many years ago to distant relatives and that, yes, when it was returned to them some thirty years later it was in several pieces and that it had been painted silver (Sing "Hi Ho Silver" as in The Lone Ranger). Well, when I travelled to Dave's lovely home at 738 Governor's Road we found the relic in pieces in the loft of his barn. We gently lowered it through his hayloft and put it in my van. This was about 2004. In turn, I took the rocking horse, in four pieces, to my good friend, Joe Garlatti, a ninth generation cabinet maker from Udine in northeastern Italy. He lovingly restored it. Within the year, and very unfortunately, after restoring the rocking horse, Joe passed on. But his work lives on in a fabulous rocking horse that Thomas Alva Edison used as a young boy when he and his family returned to visit grandparents each summer in Canada West (Ontario). This was way back in the 1850s. The horse, today, looks down on all visitors from the rafters of the Humber post and beam cottage, **Pine Vista**, up in MacTier, Ontario. The relic not only reminds me of my family but of one of the world's greatest inventors who used it back in the 1850s pretending he was a cowboy. The photo referred to is found on page 360 of **Family Sleuthing**.

Upper left: Twins Priscilla and Paul Humber with cousin Phil Donalson on Edison's old rocking horse, circa 1948. **Above:** Edison's rocking horse at cottage in Muskoka.

Dad's Best Memories and Recollections

Her Majesty Queen Elizabeth II

Throughout my two-year term as the President of The United Empire Loyalists' Association of Canada, 1982-1984, I worked as the Co-Editor of a book called **LOYAL SHE REMAINS,** a quasi-UEL publication venture that was launched in the Spring of 1984. This 600-page volume not only commemorated the Ontario Bicentennial of that year but also the coming to future Ontario of those refugee loyalists who staunchly had remained loyal to the British Crown throughout the struggle for American independence, 1776-1781. The Government of Ontario assured its citizens that 1984 would be a big year of provincial celebrations with over 800 communities across the province initiating active bicentennial celebrations. There was a personal connection between the Ontario Government and myself during the celebrations of that year in that Premier William Davis had graduated from Brampton District High School several years before I did. So we mutually knew of each other as Brampton Old Boys. I would thus suspect that **LOYAL SHE REMAINS** was chosen as the official gift to both Her Majesty The Queen and His Holiness the Pope that year, partially because of my hometown relationship with the Premier but more so, I presume, because it was such a classic book, a publication that would officially sell some 50,000 copies, ten times a Canadian best seller.

On the Loyalist Parkway, Amherstview, Ontario, September 27, 1984, Deputy Margaret Birch presents Charles and Gayle Humber to Her Majesty The Queen, a most memorable occasion.

I well remember speaking with Walter Borosa, Chief of Protocol for the Ontario Government back in 1984 before the Royal Visit. He said to me, prior to Her Majesty's visit, in Amherstview, a small community along the Loyalist Parkway just west of Kingston, Ontario, that there would be a line-up of some forty people greeting The Queen and that Her Majesty had less than forty minutes to shake hands with all those important people, all selected by government officials to be presented to Her Majesty. He also knew that I would be the only one in the line-up presenting Her Majesty with a gift and that I must refrain from saying anything to The Queen and from engaging Her in any conversation, that is, unless Her Majesty addressed me first. I concurred. On September 27, 1984, Gay and I were present at the end of a line of greeters anxiously awaiting the Royal Visit. A leather bound copy of **LOYAL SHE REMAINS,** encased in a specially crafted wooden box, was sitting on a table in front of me. This encased book was the official presentation to The Queen. Upon Her arrival, Her Majesty greeted admirers down the long line of well-dressed well-wishers. After an introduction by Deputy Premier Margaret Birch, Her Majesty greeted me with, "How do you do, Mr. Humber." With Walter Borosa standing just several feet from The Queen, right beside Prince Philip, I could also see out of the corner of my eye that Premier Bill Davis was smiling at a fellow Bramptonian greeting The Queen. But when Her Majesty asked me the question: "Mr. Humber, would you kindly explain the title of this book?" all the officials rolled their eyes upwards as they knew, just knew, that all that was needed for me to engage in conversation with the Queen was for Her Majesty to ask me a simple question! But I refrained as much as I could and said, "Your Majesty, I'm honored that you would ask such a question. The title of the volume you are being presented means exactly what it says, namely, that we, as a province, were loyal to the British Crown when the province was created and today, two hundred years later, the province remains loyal to the Crown". The Queen responded with a warm personal smile and said, "Thank you, Mr. Humber" and we shook hands. The party was over in a few minutes but the occasion was most memorable with my four children, Kristy, Karyn, Charlie Jr. and Scott, watching in the background and my wife, Gay, demonstrating queenly aplomb after her introduction to Her Majesty. We drove all the way home to Toronto soaking up what had just happened and have never forgotten the occasion ever since. For a short time after the presentation, Gay found a chuckling way to jostle a few colleagues at the school where she taught, including her principal, by putting on the very gloves that were used to shake the hands of Queen Elizabeth II, wondering if those at her school would like to shake the hands of a colleague who shook hands with Her Majesty Queen Elizabeth II on September 27, 1984.

Dad's Best Memories and Recollections

Trip to Israel, 1984

Three times I've crossed the Atlantic Ocean. The first was in 1984 to Israel. The only direct flight available for that prospective trip overseas was aboard El Al Airlines, a flight from Montreal directly to Ben Gurion Airport, Tel Aviv. How this trip came about is truly magical. It started following my mentor John W. Fisher's passing away, 1981. Shortly after his funeral, the John W. Fisher Society was formed by a series of close friends who wished to perpetuate the legacy of Canada's 1967 Centennial Commissioner known as "Mr. Canada." One of the original Directors was real estate developer, Louis Mayzel, a refugee from Poland. After he came to Canada he became wealthy and was a financial supporter of "Mr. Canada." In the mid-1990s I can recall meeting with Albert Reichmann, of Olympia and York fame, in the downtown office building that he built, 1975, called First Canadian Place, still the tallest building in Canada, 2015. He was the individual who, with several brothers, developed Canary Wharf in London, England, as well as the World Financial Center in Manhattan. He told me in his plush office, basically a miniature synagogue, that Louie Mayzel was a good business man who understood that real estate was, perhaps, the best way to generate wealth. I guess that was true because during Louis Mayzel's hay-day, he once owned real estate at three corners of Adelaide and University Avenue in downtown Toronto. After three years of perpetuating John's legacy, two Board members of the Society, Louie Mayzel and yours truly, now President, discussed what John Fisher would have done to celebrate the 1984 Ontario Bicentennial. Playing the role of John Fisher with Louie, I privately asked him how many rose gardens he owned in the world-famous Wohl Rose Park just outside Israel's Knesset (Parliament). Louie was not sure how many, but indicated he did own more than a few. I then made a proposal to him. I wondered if he would consider deeding one of his rose gardens to the Province of Ontario. By doing so, I suggested, he not only would be allocating a small plot of land to the Province of Ontario but would be enabling, symbolically, the province that we cherish, during the 1984 Bicentennial, to demonstrate that it cared enough about Israel to be associated with a small plot of land in that country. Louie's reaction was amazing. He said, "If you can make this happen then I will take you to Israel." Well, after several months of negotiations with the Province, the Office of Premier Bill Davis accepted Louie's proposal and agreed to send an official to Israel to accept the good will from Louis Mayzel. An impressive ceremony would take place on December 7, 1984, conducted just outside the Knesset.

The trip took place December 4-9, 1984. Teddy Kollek, Mayor of Jerusalem, 1967-1993, participated in the transaction ceremony and Canadian Ambassador Vernon George Turner added to the ceremonial aplomb. Deputy Premier Margaret Birch genuinely demonstrated appreciation for the rose garden on behalf of Premier Bill Davis and presented a copy of **LOYAL SHE REMAINS** to the esteemed Mayor, a man often touted as "the greatest builder of Jerusalem since Herod."

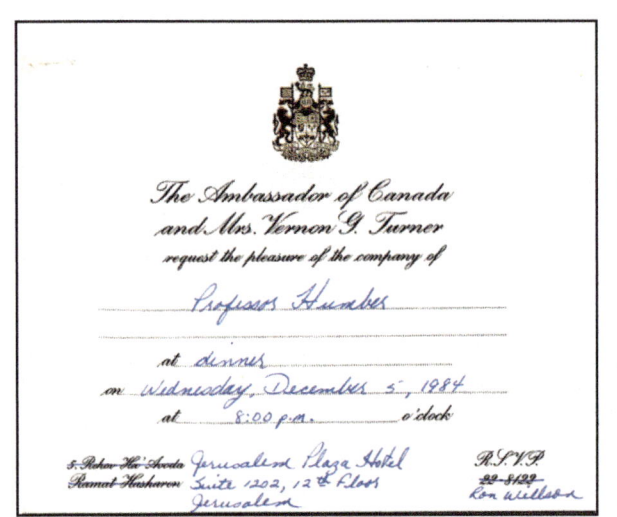

Top: Invitation to dinner, December 5, 1984, with Canada's Ambassador to Israel. **Bottom:** Louie Mayzel, left, and Charles Humber look on as Deputy Ontario Premier Margaret Birch presents Jerusalem Mayor Teddy Kollek with **LOYAL SHE REMAINS** in a ceremony on the outside grounds of the Knesset, December 7, 1984.

As part of a five-member team, Mrs. Birch flew to Israel, along with her aid, Naomi Goldie, in addition to Rabbi Jacob M. Kirshenblatt and, of course, Louis Mayzel. It was such a privilege to be Louie's guest. Rabbi Kirshenblatt, a co-founder of the Beth Shalom Synagogue in Toronto as well as one of Louie Mayzel's closest friends, was thrilled to tag along at the ripe age of eighty years.

Our Israeli trip was the most memorable of my life, at least up to that time. Our party stayed at the Laromme Jerusalem, touted as the best hotel in Israel. Rooms were $400.00 per night back in 1984! A six-door limo, known locally as a "cheroot," picked up our party each day, circa 7:00 a.m., and drove us to different places all over Israel. Our chauffeur for the duration of our trip was Beni Bitter, the Mayor's personal chauffeur. A well-known war hero, Beni was part of the Israeli forces who stormed the Air France **Airbus** in Entebbe, Uganda, 1976, that had been hijacked, and flown to Idi Amin's Uganda where 105 Jewish passengers were held hostage. All hijackers were eventually killed and all hostages, except for three, were saved. One trooper was killed, Yonatan Netanyahu, the brother of present-day Israeli President, Benjamin Netanyahu. Beni Bitter never once talked about his Entebbe Operation experience with the Canadian entourage. Our first stop after our arrival on December 4, 1984, was on the "Road to Jericho" where the cheroot stopped and Beni showed us the ancient home of the Good Samaritan as portrayed in the Bible. Bedouins with camels walked the undulating hillside above the dwelling. It was such a fantastic landscape and we had not really yet begun the day's journey! Over the next five days we travelled to the Golan Heights and the Sea of Galilee. We went to Mount Masada, to various Roman ruins such as the ancient city of Bet She'an, to the Red Sea, to where the Dead Sea Scrolls were found, to Jericho, to Bethlehem, to the Wailing Walls of Jerusalem, to the Mount of Olives, to Gilo where Rachel is buried, to the exact place where Lazarus rose from the dead and to the Knesset where so many of Marc Chagall's paintings are prominently on display in the hallowed hallways. Finally we went to the Yad Vashem, the Holocaust Museum in Jerusalem, where arrangements had been made for me to present to the curator of this famous museum the ceremonial Nazi arm band formerly belonging to Field Marshall Hermann Goering. The serial number attached to the armband clearly identified its authenticity as belonging to the one who was second in command of the Third Reich and founder of the Gestapo. It has now been on permanent display at this world famous museum for the last thirty years. When the trip was over, December 9, my Israel experience has indelibly remained with and haunted me. These recollections to this day are tattooed on my brain.

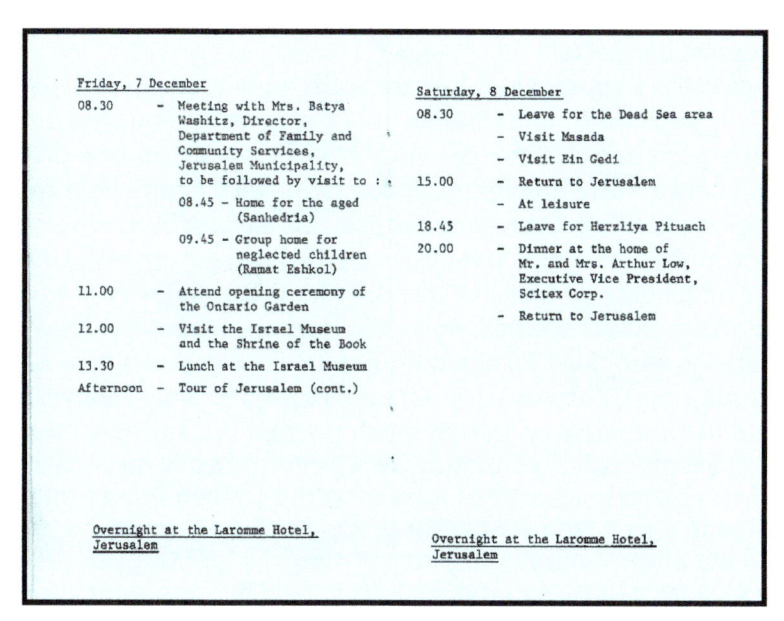

Far Left: Each member of Louis Mayzel's party was given a 16-page booklet outlining our fantastic itinerary in Israel.
Left: 2-page spread of booklet detailing our December 7 and 8, 1984 itinerary.

Allan Walters, M.D.

Born the same year as my father, 1906, Dr. J. Allan Walters, who passed away in 1986, entered this world in Napanee, Ontario, not far from where several of our mutual loyalist ancestors settled, including the Amey and Clark families, both of whom arrived in Canada as refugees from the American Revolution, 1783-84. Dr. Walters was a much-respected psychiatrist who graduated, 1930, from the University of Toronto, the year my own father graduated in Chemical Engineering from the same university. Dr. Walters served, with distinction, during World War II as a Major in the Canadian Armed Forces. He was a much-respected Psychiatrist in both Great Britain and Canada during his professional years. He was also the former Head of Psychiatric Services at the Toronto General Hospital and was a Professor of Psychiatry, University of Toronto, for many years. He was known as a specialist in "psychogenic regional pain syndrome, a.k.a., hysterical pain, concerning localized, specific physical pain arising in part or entirely through psyche."

Dr. Allan Walters was also very passionate about history, especially history associated with his United Empire Loyalist forefathers who settled the Bay of Quinte area just to the west of Kingston, Ontario. He was a long-time member of Toronto's Governor Simcoe Branch of the UEL Association of Canada. He was an active member when I became branch President in 1976, and over the years regularly pulled me aside to give me sound advice. After six years of serving on the national executive of the UEL Association, and shortly before I was about to be inducted as National President, 1982-1984, I was invited by Dr. Walters to his very lovely home in Rosedale, a plush section of Toronto where ostentatious Victorian houses are an elite enclave of the city. His wife had recently passed on so he lived in his very lovely home by himself. He had a housekeeper to assist him in his home and when he invited me to come for an evening of conversation, 1982, the visit included a delightful dinner set up in front of his stone-faced fireplace. We enjoyed a most delicious dinner on a classic Pembroke table placed on a Persian rug from the British Empire period. 18th century Chippendale chairs flanked the setting. All flatwear was sterling. Dishes were vintage Flow Blue. The four-course dinner was luxurious as was the vintage wine. Dr. Walters wanted to wish me on this occasion the very best before my taking the office of National President. Most of the evening was politely spent in guiding my term in the right direction, giving me advice that I would never get anywhere else!

Dr. Walters approached history from a unique point of view, namely, a psychiatrist's perspective. He fully seemed to understand the causes of the American Revolution. He volunteered to tell me that the population of the colonies in 1775 consisted of a diverse population, barely three million people. Most were immigrant Protestants with deep roots in Europe. These were Quakers, Congregationalists, Presbyterians, Baptists, Lutherans, Dutch Reformed, Huguenots, Mennonites, Brethern, Amish, Moravians, Swedes and still others. Roman Catholics, at the time, were a Christian minority. The Church of England was not the great majority it had in its homeland but its presence still wielded significant political power in Puritan-controlled New England. Most of the Protestant denominations who filled up the colonies were sent there by a British government that really did not welcome non-Conformists in Great Britain and thus sent many Christian denominations to the new world for colonization where much needed tax revenue could be generated.

Dr. Walters explained that those who remained loyal to Great Britain during the revolutionary years did so not so much out of fidelity to the Crown but as thanks to a country who gave them a new chance in a new land where these freedom seekers could put their fingers into the soil of their farms and say after hundreds of years of religious persecution in Europe that the land they stood on was theirs -- thanks be to God. They certainly did not want to lose their farmlands. Nevertheless, they deliberately chose to remain loyal to the Crown rather than support an uprising led by a corps of elites who, in their isolation from England, thought they could take advantage of a weak monarchy by taking complete possession of the far away colonies and creating a Republic. According to Dr.

Walters, our loyalist forefathers, when their cause was lost and they were consequently expelled from the Republic, they came to Canada as political refugees, the losers of a promising empire. According to Dr. Allan Walters, the entire concept of losing their farmlands and losing out to the revolutionaries who successfully had hijacked, from the British Crown, thirteen colonies in 1781, all generated a bruising trauma that has systematically and negatively impacted on the seven or eight generations who have followed their expelled forefathers ever since. Dr. Walters wanted me to understand fully that the loyalists, psychologically, were immense losers and have, psychologically, felt guilty about their losses ever since. He thus forewarned me that I should be careful about being too successful as President of the UEL Association because the UE Loyalists, since they had lost so much over two hundred years ago, cannot understand or accept any success of a loyalist descendant today because they see themselves, collectively, as perpetual losers. I presume that if Dr. Walters were alive today he would claim that this complex trauma suffered in the past was now indelibly lodged in the DNA of those descended from UE Loyalists. It is no wonder that descendants of UE Loyalists across Canada today are often divisive, negative and reluctant to embrace success of any kind. Today's history books are filled with misleading stories about UE Loyalists. They usually suggest they were all British and upper crust, a major distortion of the truth. Certainly, Dr. J. Allan Walters made it possible for me to better understand why Loyalist history is so poorly taught in our schools. The psychological impact that the American Revolution had on those people who lost an empire and came to Canada as losers in a war of ideology is still pathetically embedded in the succeeding generations with the consequence that Canadians today barely understand who they are.

Ironically, in 1984, at Queen's University, Kingston, Ontario, when the Bicentennial Service Awards were presented by Senator Eugene Forsey and Col. The Hon. John R. Matheson, two Honorary Vice Presidents of The United Empire Loyalists' Association of Canada, two of the ten recipients receiving their medals, were Dr. Allan Walters and immediate Past-President, Charles J. Humber.

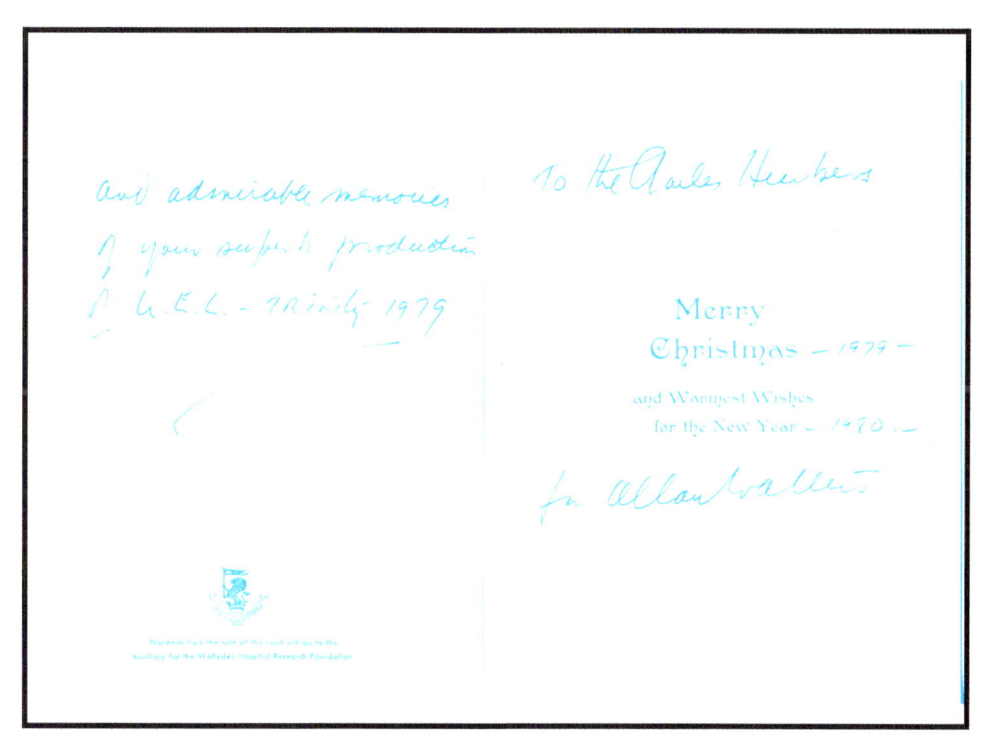

A Christmas card sent by Dr. Allan Walters to Charles J. Humber, President, Gov. Simcoe Branch, UELAC, for the superb hosting of the annual get-together at Trinity College, University of Toronto, 1979.

Mortlach, Saskatchewan

William Thomas Scott (1879-1959) and Geraldine Ostrander (1883-1918) and their seven children.

William Thomas Scott (1879-1959) was my maternal grandmother Mabel (nee Scott) Jarvis' youngest brother. He was known as "Uncle Will" or "WT" even by his siblings. After W.T. married local girl, Geraldine Ostrander, 1905, age twenty-five, they moved from Milford, Ontario to Mortlach, a booming Saskatchewan prairie town. Because my mother, Evelyn, was born, 1907, it is hard to understand how this uncle became her overall favorite of thirteen uncles in that she was born after he moved to Saskatchewan. Uncle Will became the father of seven children while residing in Mortlach before his wife tragically died, November 10, 1918, a victim of the Spanish flu epidemic that ravaged North America that year. As a result, a despondent Will Scott with his seven children returned "home" to Milford, Ontario. There he farmed out his seven children to various family members, including my grandmother's family living in Black River Bridge just down the road from Milford. All of this enabled Uncle Will to look for and find work. After several struggling years, he found employment, eventually moving his entire family to Ashtabula, Ohio, where he married Lucy Atkinson, a widow with two children of her own.

During my two year-stay, on and off, at L & L Farms in Brampton, 1956-58, I can anecdotally recall my grandmother Jarvis telling me wondrous stories while knitting in the sunroom of my Uncle Lester and Aunt Lefa Prosser's circa 1840 home, a farmhouse located on Creditview Road between Churchville and Meadowvale northwest of Toronto. Many stories focused on her youngest brother, Uncle Will, and the personal struggles he endured both before and following his wife's untimely death. One enlarged photo in grandmother's photographic album was that of Geraldine Ostrander's gravestone in Mortlach. More than anything, Gram felt the loss of Will's wife, Geraldine, was the most tragic happening ever associated with her family.

After publishing **FAMILY SLEUTHING**, 2006, I decided to travel to California by car via British Columbia. This plan enabled me to drop off books along the way and to meet people I had never seen or met but who had pre-ordered copies of this family history book. One place I visited was the small town of Mortlach, just off the Trans Canada Highway in southern Saskatchewan. I veered off the highway to familiarize myself with the town where great Uncle Will Scott lived, 1905-1919. I spent most of the day there. It was impossible not to notice the historic grain elevators. At one time they lined the Canadian National and Canadian Pacific Railway tracks all across the Canadian prairies. Uncle Will would have witnessed most of the grain elevators built in this town. Each of Mortlach's grain elevators, in 2006, looked decrepit and appeared ready for the wrecking ball. They looked like huge grave stones silhouetted on the horizon. Soon I learned that the small town was born, 1905, the same year that Will and Geraldine Scott arrived by railway as a newly married couple. After locating the town library, I approached a librarian and inquired who could best help me with information about my relatives Will and Geraldine Scott. Coincidentally, the Mortlach Historical Society was meeting in a separate room. The librarian took liberty to interrupt the meeting and to introduce me to the several elderly citizens gathered for a Board meeting. They kindly listened to my story that I had been and was still researching the W.T. Scott family tree. They went through multiple records and spent the next hour or so confirming most of what I already knew or suspected. Nevertheless, they happily retrieved documents, photographs, and various newspaper clippings all confirming that one of my mother's favorite uncles was much more than a town citizen. In fact they produced such evidence to show that he was elected Mortlach's first Overseer (town Mayor) in 1911, that he served on the town's Council for five years, that he represented Mortlach when the brand new Provincial Legislative Building in Saskatoon was officially opened by Canada's Governor General (1911-1916), H.R.H., the Duke of Connaught, October 12, 1912. They also showed me photos of the Scott home where Geraldine succumbed to the terrible Spanish Flu epidemic of 1918 which killed some 50 million people worldwide. He was also the Manager of the local Beaver Lumber, created nationally in 1906, and which became a chain of some 140 lumber supply stores across Canada until it was bought out in the year 2000 by Home Hardware. One large photograph in the library reveals a substantial photo of Will Scott as Skip of the champion Mortlach curling team, circa 1915. The photo reveals that the fingers of his left hand were all missing because of a Beaver Lumber accident that occurred at the mill he ran as manager sometime before 1918. Obviously, that handicap did not stop him from curling…..

When Aunt Lefa hosted a family reunion at L & L Farms, 1957, I remember great Uncle Will came from Ohio. I think it was the only time I ever saw him. Though he himself is but a vague memory, my trip to Mortlach in 2006 will always pleasantly haunt me, especially after visiting the gravesite where my great Uncle Will's wife lies buried. Her impressive tombstone can actually be seen from the Trans Canada Highway which countless thousands daily travel. They probably never notice her gravestone erected by a despondent W.T. Scott. "WT" passed away, in 1959, in Ashtabula, Ohio, some forty-one years after Geraldine's death. His descendants today live across North America. They are probably vaguely aware of the tragic circumstances that happened to this family in 1918 but are likely unaware of the fragile roots they planted there more than 100 years ago. It is also most satisfying to realize that at least one member of my great Uncle Will's family lived in prosperity after his youngest daughter, Helen, married a Mr. Robert Morrison, the mastermind behind the first mass-produced molded fiberglass auto body that made the 1953 Corvette car an iconic collectible.

Geraldine Scott monument in Mortlach, Saskatchewan. The Spanish flu epidemic of 1918 took the lives of some 20 million North Americans.

W.T. Scott, bottom row, second from right, sits next to Curling Trophy, circa 1915, Mortlach, Saskatchewan

Dad's Best Memories and Recollections

Gio (Joe) Batta Garlatti

One of my closest friends throughout the last quarter of the 20th century was antique dealer Gio (Joe) Batta Garlatti from Markham, Ontario. He was, for sure, one of the finest pure artisans of his day. Born in Italy, 1935, Joe, as he became known, immigrated to his new homeland, 1956, from one of twenty regions in Italy, a jurisdiction called Friuli in northeast Italy bounded by Austria and Slovenia. Joe's region was known for its wineries. He often reminisced over glasses of home-made wine he shared with me from his own wine cellar, stating each time how he missed Friuli wine. He so enjoyed teaching me how to sip and taste wine. The exact area of Friuli from where Joe immigrated is known as Udine and, for centuries, this jurisdiction has been regionally renowned, and beyond, for its carved furniture, wooden sculptures, artistic ceramics, mosaics, wrought iron, copper artisanship and stringed instruments. This is the heritage Joe's DNA brought to Canada. Upon his arrival, he worked with Markham legend, John Lunau, a descendant of the William Berczy settlers who helped build Yonge Street for John Graves Simcoe in the mid-1790s. The founder of the Markham District Historical Museum, 1971, John, with co-worker, Joe Garlatti, became good friends. Joe helped John move and re-build the very first of many historic buildings, a log structure that was moved to the Markham Museum grounds.

I first met Joe Garlatti and his wife Angela at a C.A.D.A. antique show in the early 1970s. I quickly learned that he was the very best in taking any piece of furniture needing repair and magically restoring it. It made no difference to Joe whether it was a table, a cupboard or a blanket box. Bringing each antique back to its original glory was what he always achieved. He literally was a genius with his massive collection of antique tools. One could take the furniture he restored and examine his work and swear that his repair was invisible. Over the years, Joe restored many pieces from The Charles and Gayle Humber Collection. Many have been long dispatched, but they are memorialized in Howard Pain's illustrious work, **The Heritage of Upper Canadian Furniture** (see plates 30, 95, 183, 540, 603, 642, 672, 696, 884, 904, 928, 931, 1051, 1059, 1091, 1106 and 1150, all furnishings restored by Joe Garlatti before Howard Pain photographed and illustrated them in his famous book published in 1978). Those antiques still part of our collection, in 2015, and also restored by Joe and illustrated in Howard Pain's "bible", are plates 62, 124, 149, 164, 253, 513, 890, 989, and 1330.

In 1984, when **LOYAL SHE REMAINS** was selected as the official gift from the people of Ontario to her majesty Queen Elizabeth II, I asked Joe to make a special box with Chippendale-styled feet (ogee) to hold a special encased edition of this publication. A brass plate, crafted by Joe and affixed to the inside of the lid commemorated the occasion. He also duplicated the same box for me, a special gift which, someday, I trust, will be handed down to a family member as a treasured family heirloom.

In the early spring of 2007, I brought to Joe a mid-19th century rocking horse I had acquired from cousin, Dave Donaldson. It had descended through our family for several generations via the family of Thomas Alva Edison. It was in four pieces. Joe was not feeling up to par but I pleaded with him to restore the vintage rocking horse. He told me after, I picked it up, May, 2007, he had laboured to remove the ugly second coat of silver paint. The restoration was remarkable. Today it rests on a beam up at the Humber cottage in Muskoka commemorating Joe's last commissioned work if not his last work for anyone. When I picked up the rocking horse, we shared a glass of wine upstairs in his lovely home, a house he had built a decade earlier near Coppins Corners just east of Markham. I wondered when Joe poured me a glass of his home-made wine if it might be the last time we would share such a moment. Ironically, Gio Batta "Joe" Garlatti passed on less than three months later, July 13, 2007.

When the province of Ontario selected **LOYAL SHE REMAINS** as the official gift to Her Majesty The Queen, I commissioned Joe Garlatti to craft the wooden box encasing this book. Joe stands in the background finishing up the second box he made for C.J. Humber.

Dad's Best Memories and Recollections

Historic Emigh House

As I matured into my thirties, I knew virtually nothing about Nicholas Emigh, my great, great, great grandfather. I do have a letter written by great aunt Agnes Clark (Humber) Cassels, written back in the 1940s, that claimed the Emigh or Amey family were U.E. Loyalists who came to Canada after the American Revolution and had left a cache of coins in a water well somewhere in Dutchess County, near Poughkeepsie, on the Hudson River in New York State. Through Dr. H. C. Burleigh (1893-1980) of Bath, Ontario, a local genealogist whose papers were willed to Queen's University following his death, I learned a great deal about the Amey family. As a family doctor for many years, and as a local historian who recorded the history of nearly 1000 families in the county of Lennox and Addington, Dr. Burleigh published a book about Kingston, Ontario, 1973. I inveigled him to sign a copy called **Forgotten Leaves of Local History, Kingston.** It is part of the ever expanding Humber Library today. Dr. Burleigh led me to several important people who entered my life in the 1970s and who led me to discover the Emigh stone house outside Poughkeepsie.

One individual was Ibra Conners of Ottawa. Another was Ada Johnston from Bath, both of whom were distant relatives and both of whom sent me photos of this historic home. I have kept all their letters in the family archives. They whetted my appetite so much so that I drove in 1973 to Clove Valley, near Verbank, the setting in New York State where the Emigh house has stood since 1740 amid some 5000 acres of land that belonged to a prestigious hunt club. The property virtually had no driveway leading to the house. Gay was pregnant with our twins, Kristy was nine years and Karyn not quite seven. Nevertheless we all trudged through overgrown fields and came to the abandoned house which some say was a safe haven for the underground railroad in the early 19th century. History books say that the first white child in Dutchess County was born there. On the impressive chimney are embossed the initials "NE" with the date of 1740. The restored house today is nationally registered on a list of heritage homes in America. The Emigh family records are inconclusive but suggest that the Emigh family were of Dutch descent. They came to the American colonies around 1710. But I have seen records suggesting that Emighs came as early as the 1670s. When the revolutionary war broke out in 1775, two Emigh brothers, one being Nicholas Emigh, were living in the Saratoga area of upper New York State. I've visited the Emigh house near Poughkeepisee three times over the years, once finding two pairs of original hinges from the house. One set is a pair of elongated tulip hinges; the other a pair of HL hinges. They are, for sure, original to the house. Both pairs hang high on a beam at our MacTier cottage overlooking the harvest table that Gordon Ball made for me in 2005. The last time I visited the restored Emigh home was in 2003 following son Scott and Molly's wedding, June 6, 2003. Not only did daughter Karyn accompany me to the site, but meeting me there was my sister, Priscilla Hurlbut, who also had been at Scott's wedding and was returning home to Sweetwater, Texas with family friend, Ed Brink.

As an anecdote, when I was teaching at Toronto's Lawrence Park Collegiate Institute, 1969-1977, I taught a grade thirteen student named Jane Millson. She was the granddaughter of the founder of Canada's General Motors, Col. Sam MacLaughlin. I commissioned Jane to paint the Emigh house with its surrounding landscape. Her rendering of this heritage house was copied from one of the several photographs that either Ibra Connors or Ada Johnston had sent me in the early 1970s. The painting was commissioned in 1973, the year after Jane's famous grandfather died. Jane Millson's painting has hung on the walls of our various dining rooms ever since 1973. It will be passed on to future generations reinforcing our family history.....

Far left: Painting of the historic 1740 Emigh House rendered by former student Jane Millson.

Left: The original "HL" hinges from the 1740 Emigh House now hanging in Humber cottage in MacTier, Ontario.

Dad's Best Memories and Recollections

Road Signs

Over the years I've discovered a number of roads signs that indicate a few of my ancestors left an indelible mark in their communities and were honored with "road signs" for their contributions. The first of these road signs is located in Stratford, Ontario. My dad's cousin, Helen (Humber) Sinclair, showed me an article taken from **The Stratford Beacon-Herald.** It revealed how her father was honored posthumously with a street sign. Located in the industrial section of Stratford, Humber Street was named after my grandfather's brother, Maitland Alexander Humber, who began his career with the Grand Trunk Railway in Goderich, Ontario, then moved to Stratford where he continued working for the same railway for the next forty years. He retired from Canadian National Railway in 1942. In Stratford, Mait was called "The Father of the Apprenticeship System." He organized hundreds of young men to work in the various GTR/CNR shops learning the railway trades. To keep his apprentices happy, Mait founded baseball and hockey teams to keep young men active in spare time both during summer months and winter seasons. His most famous "old boy" was Howie Morenz who went to fame with the Montreal Maroons and the Montreal Canadiens. My great uncle Mait was also founding President, 1914, of the first professional baseball league in Canada. It was named the Western Ontario Baseball League (WOBL). He was a prominent curler, as well, who skipped Stratford to winning the Ontario Tankard in 1930. Mason Mait Humber was also past Master of Lodge No. 332. Mait was, for sure, a serious contributor to his community.

Humber Street in Stratford, Ontario, named for Maitland Alexander Humber. Three Shennette boys, great-uncle Mait's great, great nephews, stand beneath the Humber St. road sign. Left to right: Bradley, Christopher and Mitchell.

Back in the late 1990s, I got to know another Humber "cousin", this time in Peterborough, Ontario. Allan Humber was the great grandson of Orenzo Humber who came to Canada, at age four, from the Isle of Wight with my great grandfather Charles Austin Humber. Orenzo was one of the contractors whose company poured the cement for the world-famous Peterborough Lift Lock back in the early 1900s. He also built homes along Peterborough's Water Street. It was in one of the Orenzo-built homes that I first met Allan Humber who was proud of his Humber surname but knew very little about his family history except that he had a special book he inherited formerly owned by David Hess Humber, my great, great grandfather, who brought his family to Canada in 1848. In getting to know Allan, who died in 2004, he told me that there was a street, Humber Road, in

Road in Peterborough, Ontario, named for Allan Humber, great-grandson of Orenzo Humber, brother of C.A. Humber.

Dad's Best Memories and Recollections

68

Humber Close named for H.H. Humber of Red Deer Alberta.

Peterborough named after him. He said he worked for a construction firm that had built the subdivision in Peterborough close to Little Lake Cemetery where most of the Orenzo Humber family lie buried, including Allan.

Two other jurisdictions in Canada incorporate Humber road signs. One is in Red Deer, Alberta; the other is located in Victoria, British Columbia. The Red Deer road sign is named after Henry H. Humber, one of my grandfather's four brothers. He was an optician and jeweler who went to the Northwest Territories in 1903, two years before Alberta became a province, then permanently settled in Red Deer, 1905, where eventually he built the Humber Block, which partially stands to this day in the center of the city. "Uncle Hank", as Henry was known by a young Roly Michener growing up in Red Deer, was best friends with Red Deer Mayor Edward Michener, father of Roland Michener. Roly later became Canada's Governor General, 1967-1974. The road sign in Red Deer, which I discovered in 2006, is called Humber Close. Nearby is Michener Close. Two "close" friends virtually inseparable at death....

The other road sign in Canada directly linked to the Humber family surname is located in Victoria, British Columbia. I discovered it for the first time in 2006 when I visited with Rick Humber, son of Bruce Humber who ran second leg on Canada's 400-metre relay team at the 1936 Berlin Olympics. A noted sprinter across North America, Bruce, in his prime, ran against the great Jessie Owens more than twenty times. He was also the coach of the Helsinki-bound Canadian Olympic Track and Field team in 1952. Humber Road is directly across from Bruce's former house in Victoria. The homes on Humber Road are all worth several million dollars or more per home.

There is at least one more road marker in Canada associated with the family. This sign is in Prince Edward County. Located in the historic village of Milford is a small body of water called Milford Pond. Scott's Mill, located along the edge of this pond is, today, an historic site managed by the Regional Conservation Authority. It is named after my great grandfather, W.B. Scott, a co-founder of Emporia State University in Kansas back in the 1860s. This was before he migrated back to Milford and re-established himself as a miller. Today, the body of water in Milford is affectionately called Scott's Mill Pond by locals. Officially, the pond is named Milford Pond. It is flanked on one side by Scott's Mill Road North where the Scott's Mill still stands today.

When William B. Scott married MaryAnn Farr, 1869, he must have known he was marrying into a large family of Farrs who had settled in the 19th century in Weston and Woodbridge, Ontario, jusrisdictions associated with Metro Toronto. Today, in Etobicoke, there is a Farr Avenue and in Woodbridge there is a William Farr Lane as well as an Ellerby Square. Like the Scotts, Ellerbys intermarried with the Farrs.

Road sign, Victoria, British Columbia, named for Bruce Humber, 1936 Olympian.

69

Dad's Best Memories and Recollections

Summer 1948, Part I

Hiawatha cottage was built by Mr. Van Loon, circa 1920. He is seen standing at the rear porch. The cottage was used by the Humber family, summers 1939-1942 and summers 1948-1951. The cottage on Lake Erie was owned by Hagersville Baptist Church into the 1970s.

For pre-teenagers, summers usually mean two months of freedom. For the four Humber kids living in Boston, the summer of 1948 was six months of sheer joy, freedom and happiness. Because of visa problems, the Humber family was required to leave Boston in April of that year and literally moved into **Hiawatha** cottage, a two story, three-bedroom summer home with an expansive sunroom encompassing a pair of ceiling-hanging, double-seated settee swings. **Hiawatha** was situated along the north shore of Lake Erie at a place called Woodlawn Beach located in Walpole Township, Haldimand County, Ontario, south of Cheapside, west of Selkirk and east of Jarvis. Shared with readers elsewhere in this volume are vignettes about our family's trips back and forth between Boston and Canada in the old Model A Ford as well as the story of how the four Humber siblings attended a one-room school in 1948.

But what we experienced during that enchanted summer has yet to be explored or recorded. What happened during the summer of 1948 was magical, whimsical, glorious and joyful....

Hiawatha presided over an eroding embankment of very hard clay some twenty feet high that loomed over Lake Erie and gawked at the United States on the fuliginous horizon some twenty or so miles away. As young kids, we could wade and wander out into the lake, perhaps the length of a football field, before the lake dropped suddenly. There were five different sandbars to cross before it was too dangerous to proceed any further. On the grassy lawn above the eroding cliff, directly in front of the cottage, were two huge hickory trees bridged by a thick slab of wood wedged between them. A pastime was sitting on this bench watching waves crash on the shoreline with clouds floating overhead and graceful seagulls calling each other. All was soothing and wondrous....

Behind **Hiawatha** was a dirt road separating another row of cottages that backed onto the Sandusk Creek, a slow-moving river gilded with thick, expansive marsh fields, lily pads, wavering bulrush and embankments of slippery flagstone covered with moss. The river glided eastwardly to the Wheeler fleet of fishing boats stationed near the river's mouth, about one half mile away from where I would, almost on a daily basis, fish and observe snapping turtles, ducks, blue heron, loons, muskrat and a variety of marsh birds, especially red-winged blackbirds. The Wheeler fishing fleet was pier-docked at the mouth of the Sandusk Creek with two kinds of boats. The first were entirely covered with a wooden structure with large openings at the back and the sides. They travelled in the wee morning hours to Long Point, perhaps twenty miles away. Stationary gill nets with round cork floats awaited them in deep water. The series of gill nets, loaded with white fish, were pulled up and unfurled into the boat's openings with the fish ending up in multiple containers filled with ice. Another kind of boat used by Wheeler's Fishery were flat bottom metal boats that would, in the early morning hours, go out a half mile or so from the shoreline, pull up alongside a thirty-foot square pond net held up by wooden posts lodged into the bottom of the lake. One side of the net was pulled up to the edge of the open boat. The entrapped fish that were stranded in the net were unfurled into the open boat. Most fish were blue pickerel, now extinct, with some bass, catfish and even the odd lake trout. The foul smell of dead fish was feculent and if one went out in the rough early morning water, the smell of dead fish

Photo taken of Charlie and Anna Humber, summer, 1940, in front of **Hiawatha** cottage. The hickory trees fell into the lake in the 1960s along with the slab wooden bench.

Dad's Best Memories and Recollections

along with an upset stomach usually affected guests on board to grope for the boat's rim and disgorge a morning breakfast.

The only time I ever heard a radio that summer was from the cars of various uncles parked in the driveway next to the cottage. I can still see uncles Adam Elliot and Joe Lindecker listening to John Cameron Swayze or Gabriel Heatter in uncle Adam's car radio. They listened as if it was a daily ritual. Other relatives visited. Newly wed aunt Lefa and her mining husband, Lester Prosser, with gold nuggets in his pockets, came. Every one of my uncle and aunts, on both sides of the family, at one time or another, came for visits in 1948. They rarely stayed overnight because facilities were very limited. There was no electricity. We always depended upon oil lamps or gas lamps from ceiling outlets. There were no flush toilets. There was no running water. Water came from an outdoor cistern. There was an outdoor backhouse in the garage. It had hornet nests and Eaton catalogues for toilet paper. During early summer months, mayflies would come by the thousands and dot the entire cottage, especially where it was painted white. At night, fireflies loomed everywhere. Next door neighbors, the Whitelaw boys from Springfield, Massachusetts, helped us chase and catch them and put them in glass jars. There was an ice box in mom's kitchen which was replenished routinely by the Bagley store delivery truck. This store, just down the road about ten cottages away, had a big dance floor and the juke box was always playing songs such as Vaughan Monroe's "Clear Water", Dinah Shore's "Buttons and Bows", and still other songs such as "There's a Tree in the Meadow". These songs were always played on 76rpm records. When I went down to the store to get something for Mom, I often read **The Hamilton Spectator,** anxiously following the Boston Braves who were heading to the World Series that year. Many times I picked wild mushrooms from the lawns of cottages dotting the shore line. Mom would cook them up to go with the fish I and sometimes Paul caught in the Sandusk. Wild strawberries and blueberries grew everywhere in fields, especially in the field down the back road where three World War II Spitfires were abandoned across from the Bagley store.

Perhaps the greatest joy of the summer for me was fishing with a ten-foot long bamboo pole. As a twelve-year old, I would often fish from early morning to supper time with Mother never worrying where I was. But I always brought back fish on a string, usually perch and catfish, including channel catfish, and the odd pike which were pretty big and made for an entire meal. On Sundays we would often drive to Selkirk or Rainham Centre to listen to Rev. Rich deliver two-hour sermons. Dad would exclaim, "Ha, Ha, that's rich!" punning on the Rev.'s surname and the minister's crippling, long sermons. Often, during the summer months, we would stop at Elmo Murphy's farm along the Cheapside Road and fill up two quarts of old-fashioned glass bottles with warm milk fresh from their cows. Murphy's also had a mink farm. Rows of cages with hundreds of mink were lined up inside a barn. I loved to tease the nasty rascals. I poked them and teased them with sticks. They would have loved to gnaw off my fingers. At night it was not unusual to watch the northern lights flicker in the skies. It was all Alice in Wonderland stuff, the entire summer. I've always claimed that 1948 was the most memorable summer of my life....And I still do....

The Wheeler fishing fleet located at Wheeler's Point at the mouth of the Sandusk Creek, south of Selkirk, Ontario, here circa 1945.

Left to right: Priscilla Hurlbut, Charles J. Humber and Anna Rolen, siblings, return to **Hiawatha** cottage, circa 2006, and sit at the same harvest table our family used daily sixty years earlier.

Dad's Best Memories and Recollections

Summer 1948, Part 2

The Cheapside Road Bridge crossed the Sandusk Creek and ended at Woodlawn Beach facing Lake Erie. Fishing from this bridge in the late 1940s was magic for a 12-year-old boy.

Almost each day during the summer of 1948 was a fishing day. Clearly, I was obsessed with fishing. Just about every evening would find me taking a flashlight out to the front lawn of the cottage and sneaking up on juicy dew worms that were soaking up ground moisture. Slippery as they were, once I had a can full of the slimy beggars, I was ready to get up early the next morning and find my way to one of three places along the Sandusk River where I enjoyed fishing the most.

The first of these places was almost directly behind **Hiawatha** cottage where there was an empty lot next to a summer house that almost looked abandoned. The owners, I was told, lived in the Brantford area and hardly ever came. A rickety wooden dock jutted out into the Sandusk Creek from behind their property. Mature trees hovered over the water making the lily obtruded water surface perfect for fishing. I always caught fish from this dock, usually small perch, sun fish, catfish and black bass, as locals called them, but correctly identified as largemouth bass. Rarely bigger than twelve inches, no matter what their size, they tasted delectable after I cleaned them up for Mom to cook.

A second place where I loved to fish was standing in the middle of the Cheapside Road Bridge about six feet above the Sandusk Creek. I'd just drop my line with a squiggly worm on my hook into the water. The water here was quite deep, perhaps just over my head, and was loaded with rock bass, perch, very big sun fish, and the odd black bass. I loved using a bobber and was fascinated watching it float gently away from the metal-framed bridge. I got used to what kind of fish were biting by the way my red and white bobber would react to how the fish took my hook-baited worm. It was magical to predict what kind of fish was nibbling at my bait. And every once in a while the bobber would not just create small rings of water spiraling away from its center but would completely plunge like magic beneath the dark water with one clear swump. That was the sign that a pike had taken the bait – or – better still, a channel catfish. Either species would just take my bait and move steadily toward branches of overhanging trees that caressed the creek or to where some fallen water-logged tree trunk rested along the edge of the river's bank. Sometimes the catfish was so strong that my line would break after I yanked it to pull in the fish. Inexperience in these matters caused heartache and often I was left disappointed. But I'd try again. Patience was my formula by summer's end. My battle with the daddy catfish of them all, "the big one", as my brother used to say, perhaps the size of Mom's rolling pin, finally ended. When I brought "the big one" home the same way a cat brings home a mouse, my mother was as proud as I was.

Of all the places along the Sandusk Creek where I enjoyed fishing the most was an enchanted area about a mile's walk from **Hiawatha**. I had to cross the Cheapside River Bridge and walk west along the river's bank lined with thistle bushes, ragweed, milkweed and wild rhubarb plants and disparate wild flowers, butter cups and daises, all dotting the grass lands of the old Evans family farm. The cow-chewed grass was dotted with both dried-out and new cow plops. The river with a flagstone bottom was never crystal clear. It hardly looked as if it was flowing and usually never got deeper than three or four feet, that is, until I got to the big bend in the river to a place called "The Deep Hole". This embroidered bend in the river

Dad's Best Memories and Recollections

was labeled so by Ralph Evans, one of my schoolmates at the old Wilson Pugsly MacDonald School House up the Cheapside Road. His father, who had fished the Deep Hole when he was a boy, along with Elmo Murphy of the next farm over, my father-figure that summer of 1948, referred to The Deep Hole as the place where the big fish of the Sandusk hid out.... It was one of the most empyrean places in the world to be as far as I was concerned. A big sandstone rock stood out by the water's edge where I could toss out my line and over and over again watch jack perch take my bait, sometimes using my red and white bobber, sometimes just tossing in my baited hook without any float and keeping eyes on the end of the line where it slithered into the water. When the string began to move, inch by inch, it was a tantalizing moment. All too often I would be too anxious and jerk the fish tugging at my line. The Deep Hole also offered the odd gar pike to spy on. Jumping carp were fascinating to watch as they flopped with a large splash on the surface of the water. There were snapping and sun turtles to watch. There were darning needles or dragon flies galore flying all over the place. I often thought I was the only one in the world to see this paradise except for the red-winged blackbirds, the mud hens, the blue herons, the bees buzzing from thistle bush to wild grape vine flowers, to wild elderberry blossoms and the bloom of buttercups and wild daisies. The deciduous trees were lofty and cast welcome shade. Some trees were blasted with age and harbored woodpeckers. This was an awesome place to be. The solitude was deafening....

    Years later, some thirty years later, in the mid-1970s, an antique dealer in the Niagara Peninsula area, Nick Trainer, came across a painting that had been picked from a farmhouse in the Selkirk area. He casually said that it was a painting of some small creek in Haldimand County called the Sandusk Creek. I looked at the 100-year old painting. It was a very eye-popping event. I was totally overcome with it. It revealed the exact same scene from the Deep Hole that I had experienced back in the late 1940s. I bought the painting without hesitation for $100.00 and it has been hanging in our house for the last forty years. I hope someday one of my grandkids gets it as an heirloom keepsake. For sure it has brought me daily memories....

Oil painting, circa 1890, depicting a Mennonite fishing in the Deep Hole, an area in the Sandusk Creek which yielded many yummy dinners.

Dad's Best Memories and Recollections

Howard Pain

There were hardly any publications about 18th or 19th Canadian antique furniture until Howard Pain's book. **Pre-Confederation Furniture of English Canada** published, 1967, by Don Stewart, had good intentions but did more damage to collectors than anything because it offered so much misinformation. When Henry and Barbara Dobson produced, 1974, their illustrated paperback called **The Early Furniture of Ontario and the Atlantic Provinces,** one could say that it was the first authentic reference book offering solutions to questions whether Canada's past was collectible. There were other books including Jean Palardy's French Canadian book and several books referencing furniture in both Nova Scotia and New Brunswick, but for the most part, there was just no reliable or extensive book about Ontario antiques until Pain's tome, **The Heritage of Upper Canadian Furniture,** was published in 1978. The prototype for Howard Pain's book in the United States was Wallace Nutting's **Furniture Treasury,** first published, 1928. Nutting's achievement had some 5000 illustrations. It may well have superseded Howard's 1350 illustration volume, but Howard's book was just as monumental. An astute collector with an eye for quality, Howard was a graphic designer whose annual reports for companies like Loblaws and Denison Mines achieved for him worthy status throughout Canada.

Heritage work began with blanket box

ANTIQUES
Hyla Wults Fox

When Howard Pain, a Toronto graphic designer, started to collect antiques 30 years ago, he could not have envisioned that his collection would one day be the basis for the most monumental work ever achieved on the subject.

Published in 1978, The Heritage of Upper Canadian Furniture brought the importance of our material heritage to the attention of the general public. It contained 548 pages, more than 1,200 black and white photographs, plus 250 color plates, and had a well written, extensively researched text.

This was a book that took years to put together. It did not just happen. "I started collecting when my wife and I were furnishing a house and we went to an auction sale and picked up something," recalled Pain. That first item was a blanket box, which, incidentally, the family still owns. It cost 50 cents.

He and a few friends used to wander into the handful of shops in Toronto. "I just began to pick things up; a piece here and another there."

Simply designed

Living in Markham was also a benefit to Pain. "I used to spend Saturdays going from auction to auction. At that time, it wasn't so much an interest in antiques, but rather in furniture that separated itself from the run-of-the-mill because it was simply designed and well made. There was something about it that was special.

"I had no idea what it was, but I began to place the earlier things into a special category, on the basis of the way they were made and designed."

Not surprisingly, this love for old things lured him into dealing. Ten years after he began collecting, Pain and a friend opened an antique shop in Unionville called the Woodshed Antiques. They gave it up after two years because they could not keep up with the work and they both had other full-time jobs.

After the shop closed, he went on buying and selling until the idea took shape about five years ago to do a book. "In the years prior to beginning the book I had developed an interest more than in the visual aspect of the objects. I began to be more interested in where the things had come from."

Traditional materials

Besides antiques, Pain loves old buildings. In a way they have been even more important to him than the old furniture. "They have been my first love. The buildings and the furniture are really so similar, in the way that they were conceived and in the techniques and the traditional materials used. For me, it has probably been a unit, all part of the whole thing."

He is now considering several other projects, including another book. In the meantime, he lives with and enjoys the things he has collected: A signed Ontario desk; a superb Canadian tall case clock that he repatriated from the United States three years ago, cupboards, Windsor chairs, and candlesticks which all somehow gracefully fit into his very new, contemporary, downtown Toronto home.

Furniture expert: Howard Pain, author of the Heritage of Upper Canadian Furniture, was simply shopping to furnish his home when he began collecting 30 years ago.

E22/ TORONTO STAR, SAT., NOVEMBER 28, 1981

Howard Pain's illustrious book was published, 1978, three years before this story appeared in the **Toronto Star.**

Howard probably spent ten years preparing for his tome. He concluded that if he was going to write a book with any substantial value he needed reliable historical background. He insisted on a better understanding of the various ethnic groups who migrated to 18th century Upper Canada bringing with them their trade skills from the old world. European Germans, for instance, who came to Waterloo Country, brought with them the craftsmanship they had been exposed to before they left their

Dad's Best Memories and Recollections

Furniture book is a Canadian classic

By Hyla Wufts Fox

Antiques

Howard Pain's book, The Heritage of Upper Canadian Furniture, is incredibly well written, well documented, and beautifully illustrated.

The work is geared, initially, to collectors of early Canadian artifacts, but, ultimately, it is important to historians and those interested in the early social development of Canada.

Who would have thought that a blanket box, purchased for 50 cents 25 years ago at a country auction in Markham, would have spurred Howard Pain on to such heights? But it did, obviously, and we are the benefactors.

The book is 9x12 inches, and contains 548 pages with 250 color plates, 1,207 black and white photographs and a full-color fold-out map.

Although the book has been available for only a week and a half, sales are astounding, especially at the list price of $49.95.

Nick Treanor, proprietor of Adam Haynes Antiques in St. Catharines and a dealer who specializes in the quality and kind of antiques featured in the Pain book, said in an interview:

"It has been universally well received and it ranks internationally with any of the world's classic antique books."

His only fear was that people would become so involved with the photographs that they would ignore the text, which contain some "exciting new contributions to our knowledge and understanding of early life in Canada."

The book takes as its basic premise the fact that Canada did not become a homogenized melting pot, but maintained a mosaic of cultures far longer than in the United States. As a result each group held onto many customs which were ultimately reflected in the furniture made and used.

So thorough is the research in this book that in order to learn about Wilno furniture — those pieces attributed to the early Polish settlers in Renfrew County — Pain travelled to Poland to visit the museums so he would be able to relate pieces there to the styles found in Ontario. He did the same with the furniture done by German, Irish, American and French immigrants.

Pain is a Toronto graphic designer. Although his wife and three daughters are all interested in antiques, none is as consumed as he. Twenty-five years ago, while looking for furniture to decorate a house, he became interested in antiques and since then has amassed an important collection and produced this mammoth work.

While Pain's book is a fabulous achievement, the publishing company, Van Nostrand Reinhold Ltd. (Canada), deserves to be congratulated, perhaps even more than the author. For it has shown its belief that the Canadian antiques market is sophisticated and big enough to support a book of this calibre.

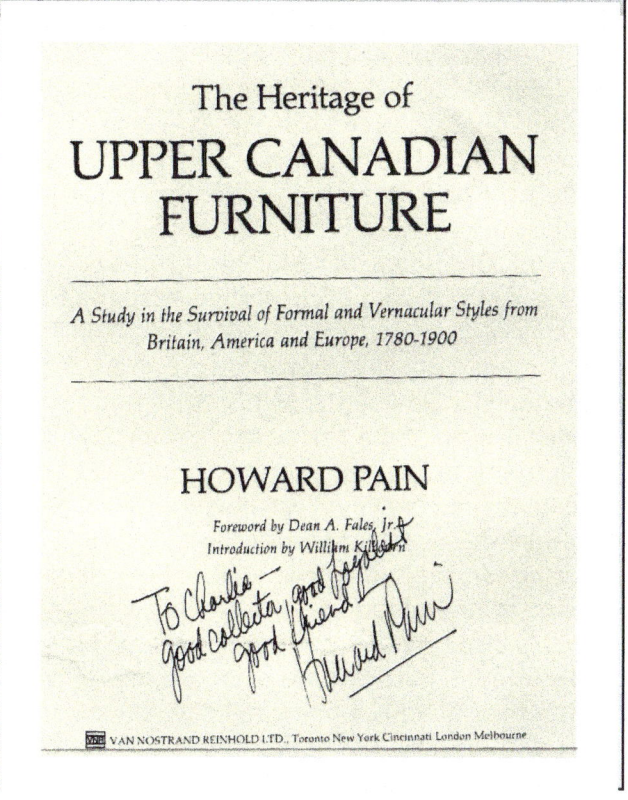

Above: Hyla Fox reviewed Howard Pain's book in the **Toronto Star** shortly after its 1978 publication.
Above right: Howard Pain signed the first edition of his 1978 publication to his friend "Charlie".

European homeland. Consequently, the furniture made in North America reflected a more continental style. The Germans who settled in Upper Canada from Pennsylvania, moreover, brought the skills and designs they had learned in eastern Pennsylvania where they had lived for at least a half century. Howard wanted verification of these suppositions. Likewise the Polish brought with them to the Ottawa Valley the styles they left behind in Poland. This was also true with the English, the Irish, the Scottish, the continental French, the Swiss, and so many more. Needing professional advice, especially about the first wave of settlers who pioneered the St Lawrence River and the shores of lakes Ontario and Erie, Howard sought out professional guidance from individuals who were not only collectors of Canadiana but understood the legacy of the UE Loyalists, the original founders of what we call Ontario today. Seeking my advice, over several years, we travelled together across the province and to the United States seeking out prototypical furniture in various regions reflected in the work of Upper Canadian craftsmen. I was able to lead Howard to many individual collections and various museums where early furniture associated with the original settlers of the province could be photographed. As well, the various chapters that he wrote about the original founders needed examination for reliability and authenticity. Consequentially, I introduced Howard to Murray Barkley, one of the most knowledgeable persons, especially about the first thirty years of social growth in Upper Canada. I will always remember driving to Conshohocken outside Philadelphia and introducing Howard to my mother and father as well as my sister Anna and her husband Jim Rolen and my brother Paul before visiting Landis Valley Museum near Lancaster. Always gracious, Howard had a knack of making people feel extremely comfortable. He was able to accomplish this demeanor with my family even though they did not understand very much about antiques. But Howard gave them all his time and charm and left with the immense good feeling that my folks were not only accommodating but genuinely interested in his project. It was a good memory. Today, Howard's book, after nearly forty years, is still considered the bible for Ontario antique collectors. People feel that I was privileged to get to know such an iconic person as Howard. I agree wholeheartedly with these sentiments.

Dad's Best Memories and Recollections

Sir Isaac Brock

A highlight year of my life was 1984. This was the year both Elizabeth II and Pope John Paul II visited Ontario and were presented copies of **LOYAL SHE REMAINS,** the publication I had co-edited to coincide with Ontario's Bicentennial celebrations (1784-1984). I also made a most memorable trip to Israel in 1984 shortly after my mother and father celebrated their 50th Wedding Anniversary up at our Muskoka cottage. Although these 1984 events were exciting and thrilling, there was also the success of **Trivial Pursuit**, an all-Canadian invented board game that sold over twenty million editions that same year, a feat that went unnoticed by most Canadians. A co-founder of **Trivial Pursuit**, Ed Werner, a former Colgate University hockey player, eventually became a lawyer and settled in the region of the Niagara Peninsula. The game made Ed Werner a very wealthy Canadian. He also became a notable collector of War of 1812 memorabilia, particularly items associated with Sir Isaac Brock. Ed Werner furthermore became friendly with antiquarian, Jon Jouppien, a heritage resource consultant. Jon successfully assisted Mr. Werner over many years to acquire historic items associated with Sir Isaac Brock. These included a lock of Brock's hair and historic ephemeral items with Brock's signature. By coincidence, Jon Jouppien and I happened to be friends that went back many years....

After Sir Issac Brock fell at the Battle of Queenston Heights, October 13, 1812, he was first buried at historic Fort George. Then he was buried a second time -- at the base of the original Brock monument built in 1824. After this monument was severely damaged in 1840 by malcontents who had ill feelings about the British, Sir Isaac Brock's remains were moved, again, and re-buried a third time in the Hamilton family cemetery in Queenston. When the new Brock Monument was re-built in 1853, Sir Isaac Brock's body was disinterred a third time and brought to the new grounds of the new monument, 185 feet high, commemorating the "The Hero of Canada". His remains were exposed for one day before re-burial so that the remaining former members of his 49th Regiment of Foot could file pass their former Commander-in-Chief and salute him one last time. Several wives of the officers, all in their seventies or eighties, stopped to cut locks of hair from Sir Isaac's scull and still another wife snipped a button from his burial jacket. Those who were present for the solemn march past claimed that Sir Isaac Brock's body "was in a perfect state of preservation". Many relics taken from the body of a man who had died in battle some 41 years earlier eventually ended up in the hands of collectors or institutions. One such place included the Canadian Women's Historical Society of Toronto. I was able to meet with several members of the Society's board before they closed shop in Toronto in the late 1980s. They were selling old posters, engravings, picture frames and much more from their collection. One particular item that caught my attention was a military button belonging to Sir Isaac Brock and which had been severed from his uniform back in 1853 during that final procession past his laid out body. The lettering "49th" was embossed on it. When it was offered to me, I did not bargain and gave the Society the asking price. Along with several other items that I purchased at their fire sale, I left their historic building, taking with me what I considered to be a small but precious bit of Canadian history.

When Jon Jouppien found out that I owned the button, it did not take very long for him to arrange for Ed Werner to meet with me at his magnificent estate just outside Niagara-on-the-Lake. After an hour or so with Mr. Werner, I consummated a button sale with the co-founder of **Trivial Pursuit**. I recognized that I had given up a very significant example of Canadian heritage but also recognized that Sir Isaac Brock's metal button that he wore at the Battle of Queenston Heights had found a better permanent home with one of the co-founders of **Trivial Pursuit**.

It is believed that this pewter button belonged to Major-General Isaac Brock when he commanded the 49th Regiment of Foot during the Battle of Queenston Heights, October 13, 1812.

Dad's Best Memories and Recollections

Aunt Marie Adelaide Louise Winslow Jarvis

My mother had six siblings, one brother and five sisters. My father had two siblings, two sisters and no brothers. Since each of my blood aunts and uncles were married, that means I had a total of eight uncles and eight aunts. The last of this generation to slip into eternity, including my mother and father, was my aunt Marie Jarvis who left this world, March 17, 2010, at age 101 years.

Aunt Marie Adelaide Louise Winslow was one of nine children born to immigrant parents from Ireland and the Isle of Wight. I probably knew my aunt Marie less than my other aunts. This was not because of anything other than circumstance as we just did not have the opportunity to connect over the years except at major family functions, like funerals, family reunions and happenstance. Nevertheless, I made an effort to stay in contact with both Marie and her husband, my uncle Gordon Jarvis. In fact, I used to go over to where they lived in a large condominium complex, in Mississauga, at the corner of Confederation Parkway and The Queensway West, diagonally across from the South Peel Hospital where my four children were born. My uncle Gordon liked to play snooker in the condo's game room and afterwards he would wonder out loud how a minister's son learned to play snooker so well. After our games, I would join both Gordon and Marie for coffee. Following Gordon's death, 1987, I used to visit Marie about once a year in her condo until Marie's son, John, my cousin, placed her in Pines Long Term Care Home in Bracebridge. When I was up at my cottage in MacTier I would every so often drop in to see Marie. She was usually asleep when I arrived and technically she was blind but when my aunt heard my voice in the background she always knew who it was by saying something like "How could one miss that voice!"

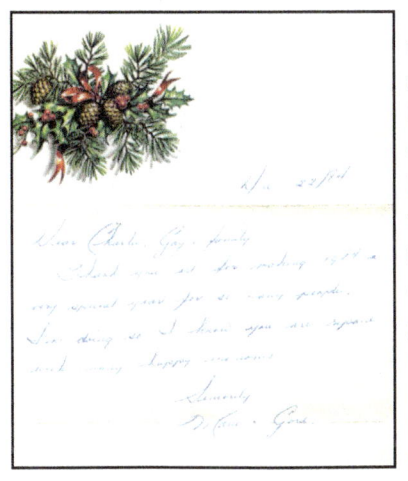

Aunt Marie Jarvis (1909-2010)

Aunt Marie had a special way of staying in contact with family

Gay and I went to visit Marie Jarvis in the fall of 2009. At the time, she was one hundred years old. One reason for my visit was to ask Marie one particular question. Being the last of her generation, Marie was the only possible one alive who just might recall whether one of her unmarried sister-in-laws had given birth to a baby girl way back in 1934. I did not think she would be able to answer my question, as she had not married my uncle Gordon until 1938, four years after Gordon's sister, Maude, had become an unmarried mother. Nevertheless, as the wife of Gordon, the brother of my aunt Maude who gave birth to a baby girl in October, 1934, I felt that perhaps Gordon might have known something about the secret birth of his sister's baby girl and over the years just might have confided in his wife, Marie, about what transpired way back in 1934 four years before they, Marie and Gordon, were married. When she answered, aunt Marie gave to me what I would call a definitive negative response: she matter-of-factly knew absolutely nothing about the birth. Thus the secret that my aunt Maude kept throughout all her years never reached any of her four children who were all so very shocked to learn that their mother had given birth to a baby daughter some four years before she married their father, my uncle Don Wolf. Shocked or surprised as they were, they each now had no choice but to embrace a half-sister named Eleanor Harle who had lived most of her married life in San Mateo, California, singing, in the same church choir for years with my sister Priscilla's husband's parents, and now desired, in 2008, to meet her four half siblings. As for Gordon and all his siblings, we will never know which ones, if any, knew the background story of my aunt Maude's secret birth in 1934. I can only conclude, as do each of my siblings as well as my cousin, Cynthia Ruble, Maude's oldest child, that those who did know about the secret birth kept Maude's 1934 motherhood to themselves and went to their respective graves keeping their secret to themselves.

Steve Stavro

One of the most interesting personalities during the last quarter of the twentieth century in Toronto was Steve Stavro. He made a prominent name for himself in various venues, from owning thoroughbred race horses to owning the Toronto Maple Leafs and a chain of grocery stores called Knob Hill Farms. He was instrumental in bringing the first professional soccer team to Toronto back in 1967. In fact, it was because of Steve's association with soccer fan John Fisher, Canada's 1967 Centennial Commissioner, that I became friends with Steve back in the 1980s near the same time I became President of the John Fisher Society following the unfortunate death of "Mr. Canada" in 1981. Steve and I became quite close as friends because of that soccer connection, so much so that he sponsored three of Heirloom Publishing's publications between 1988 and 1995, pumping more than $50,000.00 dollars into Volumes I, III, and IV of the CANADA Heirloom Series. His Knob Hill Farms were mega grocery stores that totalled nine in Metropolitan Toronto and when the Cambridge, Ontario store opened in 1991, it was billed as the largest grocery store in the world with 41,000 square feet. His ownership of both the Toronto Maple Leafs and the Toronto Raptors were his key pillars to establishing a lasting legacy. His interest in horses, as well, led him to win more than fifty stakes winners. In fact, two of his horses were named Canada's Horse of the Year. As well, the year he passed on, 2006, he was inducted into the Canadian Horse Racing Hall of Fame. Controversy followed him, however, after he closed the iconic Maple Leaf Gardens. The crown seat of the hockey world gave way to the prestigious Air Canada Centre. When it opened at the foot of Bay Street, 1999, it became the new home of both the National Hockey League's Maple Leafs and the National Basketball Association's Toronto Raptors.

One day, around 1986, I decided to have some fun and brought my twin sons, either twelve or thirteen years old at the time, to meet Steve Stavro whose office was on the second floor of an Eglinton Ave. complex near the Golden Mile Shopping Centre in east Toronto. When he found out that sons Charlie and Scott played hockey he took out a wad of hockey tickets, flipped through them and yanked out a pair of tickets for the upcoming game between the Toronto Maple Leafs and the Pittsburgh Penguins, saying to them as he slipped them into their hands, something like, "I bet you'd like to see Mario Lemieux play this Saturday night!" Their jaws dropped. Steve smiled, winked at me while they were getting over the shock of getting the tickets. He said something like "Now make sure you get your father to give you some spending money to buy hot dogs and some drinks at the game." The tickets were for a game at the old Maple Leaf Gardens, perhaps the last time my sons ever attended a game in the house that Conn Smythe built back in 1931.

When Steve died in 2006, it was estimated that he was worth 235 million dollars. Not bad for the son of an immigrant from Macedonia who liked to remind me that he was Alexander the Great reincarnated. Buried in Mount Pleasant Cemetery, Toronto, he lies beneath a 22-foot tall statue of Alexander the Great riding his steed with his sword hoisted high in the air.

At the opening of Cambridge Knob Hill Farms grocery store, left to right: Sally and Steve Stavro with Ontario's Lt. Gov. Lincoln Alexander and his wife Yvonne.

Dad's Best Memories and Recollections

My First Driver's License

When I was twenty-one I got my driver's license during the summer of 1957. I had been driving since 1953, back in my Boston days when I used to "borrow" my father's 1950 Mercury and drive off to the Quincy Quarries with the car filled with five or six guys from Fields Corner that I hung out with. When I moved to Brampton, Ontario, in 1956, I became good friends with a terrific guy by the name of Ross McKinney, a student at Brampton District High School where I also attended. Ross's father, Emerson, was co-owner of Flower Town Motors. Needless to say, Ross had access to a lot of nice cars in those days, including a magnificent 1957 Plymouth Fury which he often drove through Brampton with his girlfriend, Joyce Sommerville, in the front seat, and Doreen Wiggins and me in the back seat. This is the car with the biggest of the biggest rear fins. Not only was it a classy looking car, but it was a two-door, two-tone convertible. When we drove around Brampton in those "salad days", we literally were kings of the castle. One day during mid-week in late August, 1957 Ross suggested that I should get my driver's license. I said I was fine with his proposal but had no idea what was in store for me. Off we drove to the corner of Clarence Street and Main Street at the southern end of older Brampton. Ross was driving. The top of the Fury was down. The sun owned the sky. In we turned to this older looking house facing Hurontario. An old man was sitting by the side door of his house. He yelled out to Ross a friendly greeting as the two of us drove up the old man's driveway on the Clarence Street side of the brick house. Ross said something like I've brought you a close friend who wants to get his driver's license. The old man in an old hat said something like "What's his name?" Ross told him my name and pointed out that I lived across the street from him on Elizabeth Street South and that I was a friend of his family. The old man said, still sitting in his chair, "Well, Charlie, can you read the sign above the doorway across the way. What the old man was doing was pointing his finger to what looked like an old horse stable, leaning and all dilapidated, some 100 feet or so from where we were still sitting in the car. There was a sign above the stable's open doorway. It was an advertising sign, I think, for Valvoline Oil. I looked at it and, without even getting out of the car, told the old man what the sign said. His response has rung in my ears ever since. He said something like, "Anybody who can read a sign from that distance can drive a car" implying that there was no need for a driver's test. With a smile on his face, he got up from his chair, signed off the documents for my driver's license, and as we left, we drove off waving goodbye. I never knew that old man's name until 2014 when still another friend from my Brampton days, Pat McKitterick, told me over the phone about a guy by the name of Clark Bigham who lived at the corner of Clarence and Hurontario on the south side of Brampton. It occurred to me that this must be the same old man who wrote out my driver's license back in 1957. Pat assured me it was the same guy because this old man's daughter had married Pat McKitterick's father after Pat's mother, his father's first wife, died. In other words, this was Pat McKitterick's stepmother, the daughter of the man who issued my driver's license. Small world! The barn is long gone. So is Clark Bigham. But the memory I treasure about how I got my first driver's license will never leave me....

May Clark Bigham rest in peace.

Right: My first license with the surname misspelled. **Bottom right:** Ross McKinney getting ready to hit the road from 268 Main St. N. Brampton. **Bottom left:** Typical 1957 Plymouth Fury.

Dad's Best Memories and Recollections

Prime Minister Brian Mulroney

Before "Mr. Canada," John Fisher, a prominent CBC broadcaster in the 1940s and '50s, passed away, 1981, he had told me to keep my eye on Brian Mulroney, an upcoming Canadian politician destined to become Canada's Prime Minister. Within three years, the leader of the Progressive Conservative Party of Canada, the forerunner of today's Conservative Party, was Prime Minister Brian Mulroney. He served as Canada's 18th Prime Minister from 1983-1993. When I was preparing the first edition of **CANADA From Sea Unto Sea** for publication in 1986, I approached the Prime Minister's Office in Ottawa suggesting that The Right Honorable Brian Mulroney consider writing a special "Introduction" to Heirloom Publishing's forthcoming 600-page publication saluting Canada's rich culture, history and heritage. I mentioned to the Chief of Staff in the PM's office that Mr. Mulroney should be aware that the book was dedicated to John Wiggins Fisher, from New Brunswick, and that "Mr. Canada" was one of the men in the Prime minister's early life that had a positive influence on him. Shortly thereafter Heirloom Publishing received timely word that the Prime Minister would indeed be most pleased to write the "Introduction". I thought that this was thrilling. When the book first came out, 1986, and the erudite "Introduction" was printed front and center, I shared a photocopy of the PM's Introduction with the Prime Minister's office in Ottawa suggesting, at the same time, that perhaps I should make a trip to Ottawa and make a special presentation of the book to the Prime Minister. The PMO agreed that the idea was a good one and arrangements were made. The drive to Ottawa was an interesting one (see the vignette in this volume about Judge Matheson). I parked the car in the special designated parking space outside the Parliament grounds and made my way to the Prime Minister's office. This was going to be my first formal encounter with a national government leader in Ottawa so I was a little apprehensive as to what to expect. But the Prime Minister postured energetically from his office foyer and invited me inside to his inner sanctum while wearing his affable grin and commanding sophisticated deportment. We shook hands and before I had a chance to say a few words of how much this visitation meant to me he put me at ease. When I was getting ready to share with him a copy of the Canada book, he mentioned that he was quite impressed with the "Dedication" to John Fisher that I had earlier sent to his office. He then told me how he remembered John Fisher coming in the late 1940s to Baie Comeau, his boyhood home town on the north shore of the St. Lawrence River east of Quebec City. He emphasized that he was a little tyke in short pants. He said that he was mesmerized by John's booming voice and enjoyed the late Mr. Canada's stories so much. During our conversation he affectionately referred to John Fisher as "Mr. Canada". He said that when "Mr. Canada" addressed the crowd at the mill where his father worked, that John spoke French as well as

Prime Minister Brian Mulroney in his Parliament Hill office, 1991, meets with Reginald Stackhouse, MP, and Charles Humber, Publisher, Heirloom Publishing Inc.

Dad's Best Memories and Recollections

any polished Quebecois could. The PM said that to see an Anglophone speak such fluent French was jaw-dropping for him and that he never once thought of John as an anglophone after that but as a native French Canadian. Then the Prime Minister directed my attention to where many crayon drawings on paper were hanging all over his office walls, demonstrating how proud he was of his children who drew them for their father to hang in his Parliament Hill office. He said their art work is what inspired him on a day to day basis. When I presented him with a special leather bound copy of **CANADA From Sea Unto Sea,** the first words he said were: "Ahhhh, what a lovely looking book!" He then turned to the "Dedication" page, remarking that John Fisher was a rare Canadian who united the country like nobody else could. He did not turn pages in the book to find his own "Introduction" but did tell me that he very much appreciated being asked to write the introductory remarks for a book that was so appealing. He also asked if all the production work was done in Canada and when I told him even the paper was Canadian, he smiled with approval. We shook hands and he brought me to the doorway where I had entered, saying at the same time how much he appreciated my coming to see him.

> PRIME MINISTER · PREMIER MINISTRE
>
> OTTAWA, K1A 0A2
> October 29, 1986
>
> Dear Charles:
>
> Thank you for taking the time yesterday to present me with a copy of "Canada from Sea Unto Sea".
>
> This book is a valuable addition to the recorded history of our country.
>
> I want to take this opportunity to extend my congratulations to you and my personal best wishes for the success of this venture.
>
> Yours sincerely,
>
> Brian Mulroney
>
> Mr. Charles J. Humber
> Editor
> Canada from Sea Unto Sea
> The Loyalist Press Ltd.
> 2233 Argentia Road
> Suite 302
> Mississauga, Ontario
> L5N 2X7

After my visit to Ottawa, 1986, I received this letter from Prime Minister, Brian Mulroney, thanking me for taking time out to present him with a copy of **CANADA From Sea Unto Sea**, Volume 1 of the Canada Heirloom Series.

Before I realized it, the meeting was over. I felt that the whole affair was just awesome, that it was such a privilege to have done what I had just done. Shortly afterwards, the Office of Protocol in Ottawa contacted me in my Mississauga office and placed an order for one hundred books saying that the Prime Minister wanted to use the books ceremoniously as "cultural ambassadors." That was six thousand dollars in Heirloom's bank account! Now it was onward to more sales and six more additional volumes of the ongoing CANADA Heirloom Series.

Franc Joubin

Franc Joubin did not come into my life until 1989. My association with him came through D. MacCormick Smyth, a retired York University Professor of Administration. Del, as he liked to be called, had just completed, **Not for Gold Alone**, a publication in 1986 that celebrated the life of mine-hunter extraordinaire, Franc Joubin. When preparing **PATHFINDERS, Canadian Achievers,** Volume IV of the CANADA Heirloom Series, a publication celebrating the achievements of 125 Canadians, past and present, Del, who had graduated from Churchill College, Cambridge University, and became the first Dean of Atkinson College, York University, back in the 1960s, contacted me. He strongly suggested that one person who should be profiled in Heirloom Publishing's proposed list of 125 "pathfinders" was Franc Joubin. So I asked Del Smyth to have lunch with me and to discuss in much greater detail this man's life story and why it should be given space in **PATHFINDERS** at the expense of someone else. It soon became obvious over lunch that Franc Joubin's accomplishments were very overwhelming, so much so that I commissioned him, on the spot, to write an appropriate vignette about this fabulous mine hunter. Soon, I became friends with Franc Joubin, a man I came to admire, one who lived life on the edge of wonder. I discovered where he resided on Avenue Road, in mid-town Toronto, a bachelor's apartment following his wife's death. Franc never once told me that he owned or had an important stake in almost every condominium building along both sides of Avenue Road between Upper Canada College and St. Clair Avenue. Very humble and extremely polite, Franc was reluctant to talk about himself but loved to talk about mining and the places he had explored over nearly twenty years as a United Nations Mining Adviser. Wherever this treasure-hunter went, places like India, South America, Africa, the Middle East, Australia and behind the Iron Curtain, he discovered major mining sites, especially for third world countries that eventually would generate billions of dollars. His greatest discovery, however, was in Canada's northland where, in the early 1950s, Franc, backed by American art patron and well-known financial wizard, Joe Hirshhorn, made his most famous "strike" – Canada's largest uranium find that led to the establishment of Elliott Lake, near Blind River, a setting that was originally meant to be called Joubinville but, at Franc's insistence, the idea was rejected. Over the last sixty years it is estimated that Joubin's amazing discovery at Elliott Lake in 1953 has generated over 30 billion dollars in Canadian revenue.

After **PATHFINDERS** was published in 1994 highlighting Franc's amazing story, I used to meet with Franc in one of his condos either at 500 or 581 Avenue Rd. He would take me out to lunch and ask me questions as to how the publishing business was going. He knew it was a tough business to be in, especially in Canada, so every once in a while he would write a check to me for five or six or seven hundred dollars, saying that Heirloom probably does not pay me enough so he thought that a little bit here and there would help me out. Then during one luncheon, when mining magnate, Viola MacMillan, joined us for lunch, Franc discovered that I was the nephew of Lester Prosser. He became rather animated and told me stories about my uncle's activity in the mining world. He mentioned place names like Vananda on Vancouver Island, Pioneer Gold Mines, Sheep

Franc R. Joubin, shown here in the apartment of his good friend, Viola MacMillan, was truly one of the world's greatest mining explorationists, not only of his day but of all time.

Creek Mine, Minto, Wayside and Congress mines. He talked about Barkerville and Bralorne and Bridge River and surnames like Dr. Victor Dulmage and Grant McConachie. All of these names were thrown at me in conversation as if I knew them because they were all associated with my uncle Lester's mining forays. The stories were certainly fascinating including the one about the huge copper ore find that Lester discovered by mistake, didn't have the money to develop the find, and lost his claim. Franc said that Lester could have made millions had he had the financial backing. Then Franc let loose with a bombshell of a story about my uncle's death in October of 1958, stating quite categorically that my uncle did not accidentally die in a car accident in Alberta as was generally reported but took his own life by flying an airplane into the side of a mountain near Lethbridge, Alberta. To this day, all family still maintain that Lester died in a car accident trying to avoid a dog on a road at night in the mountains west of Lethbridge. But Franc Joubin had not heard that story. The only one he knew was that my uncle Lester was not physically well, owed money in the mining circles and decided that enough was enough and took his own life. Franc Joubin himself passed away in 1997 with McCormack Smyth giving the eulogy. I went to the funeral out of deep respect for a millionaire prospector, a very humble man, who brought Canada into the nuclear age.

Franc Joubin sometimes wrote letters, sometimes wrote notes, and with each correspondence expressed sincerity and gentility. He was a gentleman's gentleman who embraced learning as much as he enjoyed walking the shoreline of Arctic lakes.

FRANC. R. JOUBIN

489-6071

804-581 Avenue Road
Toronto, ON
M4V 2K4

December 16, 1991

Mr. Charles J. Humber
Editor-in-Chief
Heirloom Publishing Inc.
2233 Argentia Road, Ste. 304
Mississauga, ON
L5N 2X7

Dear Charles:

I regret exceedingly that I could not meet with you and Del McCormack Smyth on December 13, when you delivered to my office two of the first-born copies of "Allegiance - The Ontario Story". I had made an earlier day-long commitment to participate in a seminar at Seneca College for that day.

This Sunday I examined the volume with care. It is fascinating and the numerous pictures make it a pleasure to turn each page. I shall be spending about ten days out-of-town over Christmas and hope to have more quiet time to enjoy it - the only book I shall take along!

I did scan the contribution by Del (principally) and I, as a junior councillor. It reads well and is much improved, as is the entire book, by the historic photographs. I am somewhat embarrassed by the size of reproduction of my portrait but Viola, the "Queen Bee", squealed in pleasure at seeing hers!

All told, the volume is of impressive appearance. I am certain it will prove a delight and learning experience to a broad spectrum of readers.

With best wishes for its success.

Sincerely,

Franc R. Joubin

c.c. D. McCormack Smyth

Dad's Best Memories and Recollections

Run Free Now – Go Play with the Angels

Plaque in Gay's garden at cottage.

When I was fourteen and growing up in Boston, our family of six got our first dog. He was not a thoroughbred. Rather he was a mixture of several breeds, especially the Irish Setter pedigree. He was about one-year old when my Dad brought him home for Christmas, 1949. We named him Rusty because of his rust-coloured fur coat that had dominant white spots. Because we were living on busy Dorchester Avenue, in Boston, Rusty became as much a street dog as he was a house dog. The four Humber kids loved him dearly and often we would lie down next to him on the floor and cuddle him. Dad would do similarly saying all the while "the natha boy."

There was a two-year period when I didn't see Rusty. While I was living with my aunt Lefa Prosser at L & L Farms, Meadowvale, Ontario, summer, 1956, my family drove from Philadelphia, where they had been living since 1955. I remember, as if it were yesterday, Dad, in his 1947 or 1948 Mercury, driving down the laneway of the Farm. I was standing below the dam near the two barns at the end of the driveway. When Rusty got out of the car, he heard my whistle and tore after me with enthusiastic happiness in his soft brown eyes. He leaped into my arms as if to say, "Where have you been?" It was one of those precious moments in life that still haunts me. I was lucky to stay in touch with Rusty following that special reunion, especially after my home coming to enroll at Temple University, December, 1958. Rusty's last years were living with his family on 5853 Pentridge St., Philadelphia, spending glorious hours chasing muskrats along the banks of Cobbs Creek. The most vivid memory of Rusty I have is the flopping of his tail on the floor with a thump, thump, thump whenever he was greeted. The first of my several "natha boys," Rusty, the dog who loved to be loved, went to doggy heaven, summer, 1963, at fourteen years. At the time Gay and I were living in Cooksville, Ontario.

Gay and I got our first Golden Retriever, December, 1969. This was eight years after we were married. As a family of four, we had gone to the Fall Winter Fair at the Canadian National Exhibition in Toronto and fell in love with Golden Retrievers, a breed that was not well-known at the time. We were directed to breeder, Cliff MacDonald, in Schomberg. As we promised Kristy and Karyn during our Madison, Wisconsin days (1967-1969), our very first Golden Retriever, an adorable puppy, arrived in a cardboard box in time for Christmas, 1969. We called him Canuck. Once he grew up, he had the longest muscular hydrostat, especially after he played in the Humber Valley just across from where we lived at 61 Westhumber Blvd., in Rexdale. Canuck was slightly oversized. Tragically, he developed an epilepsy syndrome which deteriorated his health until we had no choice but to put him down. This was sometime in the spring of 1976. When I took him to the Humane Society, kissed him goodbye and left him, I don't think I ever remember bawling my eyes out so much as I drove home empty-handed without our beloved dog. He was the most handsome, perfect dog anyone could possibly own. It was devastating to lose Canuck way before his time, and we made a commitment

Rusty, part Irish Setter, was a rescued dog. He came as a Christmas present to the C. M. Humber family living in Boston, 1949. He loved to roam Boston's neighborhoods but faithfully returned to our tenement complex every day never forgetting that he was a much beloved family dog. Dying in Philadelphia, 1963, at age fourteen, he left all of us with wounded hearts.

This is Canuck.
He was a Christmas present in 1969 when the C. J. Humber family was living in Rexdale. Kristy and Karyn cherished him as a " brother." He loved cottage life and travelling. Here he is in Nesquehoning, Pennsylvania, circa 1972, on one of our family trips to see grandparents. Because of a severe epilepsy condition, he broke hearts when we lost him at seven years in 1976.

Dad's Best Memories and Recollections

to the girls that we would bring home another Golden.

Prior to our moving to Lawrence Park in North Toronto, March, 1978, we had acquired our second Golden Retriever. Again, Cliff Macdonald was the breeder. We didn't hesitate to name the puppy Canuck II. And what a great dog he was! All of us just adored him. The memories he has left us are very tender. Cottage recollections of Canuck II jumping from the cottage dock are indelibly imprinted and precious. He just loved swimming…. We'll all remember the time he caught a big water snake that had bit him on the nose. He was so irritated! He grabbed the snake from beneath the lake surface, flailing it back and forth and in so doing inadvertently released all sorts of snakelets. What a scene that was. Our dog was protecting us as much as Kristy and Karyn protected him when they took turns walking Canuck II, before school each day, rain or shine. But it was at the cottage where raucous Canuck II thrived, especially in the water. He went to play with the angels in 1989.

Canuck II was a great replacement dog for the first Canuck. He filled our hearts with love. He loved all four of the Humber children. In this view, Karyn and Charlie are teasing, with a frog, Canuck II up at the cottage, circa 1983. He left behind a mournful family when he left this world for doggy heaven at age thirteen years in 1989.

Our next two dogs were brothers: Torrey and Zachariah (Zacky). As brothers they not only tolerated each other but were inseparable always wanting to know what the other was doing. Torrey, essentially named after Torrey Pines near where Gay grew up in La Jolla, California, was dignified, princely, and a sophisticated dog whereas Zacky was a ball of fire, rambunctious, and so loyal. Torrey was the first of the brothers to depart, February 14, 2002, Valentine's Day. I was in Philadelphia where my mother was ironically undergoing a heart operation, the day before Valentine's Day. Happily, mother survived her ordeal at age ninety-four. But it was so tough coming home to a distraught Gay and a home that now only had the one dog. As a result, Whacky Zacky absorbed all the love that Torrey would have received plus all the traditional love he automatically got from us. But at the age of fourteen years, while on our way to the cottage, June 10, 2004, we had to let him go and took him to the vet for a final farewell. I was a total basket case as we drove north to the cottage to heal the holes in our respective hearts….

Torrey and Zachariah (Zack) were brothers, born, 1990. For the most part they were inseparable. Torrey went to be with the angels in 2002, aged twelve, and Zack out-lived his brother, giving up the ghost at age fourteen, 2004. The two dogs were beloved by just about anybody who saw them. Here, son Scott, in the late 1990s, is preparing to return home to Boston, leaving sad family pets behind. Torrey on the left and Zack to the right were used to the comings and goings of family and moped for days when they did not return.

And so life goes on and lo and behold we got our next Golden Retriever, Zebadiah (Zebby), born June 26, 2005. Zebby was the sweetest of all our dogs. All he wanted to do was please us. He certainly loved cuddling and would even try to snuggle closer if either of us wanted to give him a tad of love. One of his most endearing qualities was chasing rubber balls in the local park. He would crouch down and his penetrating eyes would focus on me or Gay, diligently waiting for us to fling his ball. And he would tear after it, tongue flapping, as if his life depended on his retrieving. Once he returned the ball he would patiently wait for the next toss and repeat this routine at least ten or fifteen times or, if possible, all day. What a dog! Unfortunately, Zebby, developed tumours and they spread throughout his body. He was so

Above: Photo taken Christmas 2012 at Karyn Humber's home in Brampton. The three Shennette brothers are each holding family pets. Bradley, left, is holding Kody, age three, his aunt Karyn's dog; Mitchell, centre, is holding Zebby (Zebediah), age seven years, his grandparents' dog, and Christopher is holding Tanner, the Shennette family pet, age eight years. Golden Retrievers are the glue that hold families together.
Below: Zebby (Zebediah) was so loveable. He loved to be cuddled and thrived in making one happy. He left this world too early, at age eight years, when cancer debilitated him. When he died in 2014, Gay and I had to go to Florida to get over the sadness that permeated our home. In this view, he rests on the stretcher of one of my favourite tables, a box-stretcher probably made in Pennsylvania in 1775 and brought to Canada in 1790s when Mennonite colonies settled the Niagara Peninsula.

tolerant of his affliction and conveyed to us that everything was going to be okay. One day Gay mournfully agreed that the dreadful day had come. Poor Zebby couldn't eat and had so many health difficulties. When Gay said her final goodbye to our loveable pet, I started to crack up. I led him to my Honda Pilot and drove to the vet's, Dr. Bob Smith's clinic. Two staff members were waiting at the back door when I arrived. When I was told that I had to sign some papers, I guided Zebby into the vet's sanctuary and let him wander the premises. He was anxious and uncomfortable as I signed the papers. How I hated to say goodbye to him. As I walked toward the back door, Zebby wanted to follow me. I bent down and gave him one last big hug and kiss, knowing that the two girls who were there to supervise the situation were as upset as I was as they also adored Zebby who had been under their care for nearly nine years. All the way home I wept uncontrollably. I was a total basket case again. I had to wait in the driveway before I could see Gay. The house became a funeral parlour. Shortly thereafter we travelled to Florida for five weeks which eased the trauma of our loss. Fortunately, our two daughters had dogs: Kristy and Erik Shennette and their three sons, with their very upbeat Tanner, a partial Golden Retriever, and Karyn with her beloved Kody, truly a re-incarnation of Torrey.

Then it happened during the summer of 2014. We got our seventh Golden Retriever (one other Golden, Cruiser, swallowed a stone before he turned one year and was tragically lost in 1993). This new family member has already recaptured all the best memories that our former six Goldens have left us with over a forty-six year period of owning Goldens. Wherever he goes, Colt is the life of the party. So affectionate, so alert, so smart, Colt is better than any medicine. Colt, I'm sure, will keep us going into our nineties or his rambunctiousness will send us early to our graves. Dogs may not be our whole lives, but they sure make our lives whole. They are all so unforgettable. and generate many happy memories....

Dad's Best Memories and Recollections

Great "family portrait" of four Goldens up at the cottage in MacTier, Thanksgiving, 1992. Left to right are Torrey (1990-2002), Cruiser, (1992-1992), brother Riley (1992-2004) and Zack, often called Wacky Zacky (1990-2004). View was taken at the point of the cottage property, with the old cottage in the background. A large portrait of same photo hangs above the kitchen table up at cottage.

Both Gay and I realized that once you have had a wonderful dog, a life without one is severely diminished. Thus within six months following Zebby going to play with angels, we acquired from breeder Carol Lee of Palgrave, yet another Golden Retriever, our seventh. This was in early August, 2014. We named him Colt. It's totally unfair to compare Goldens, but Colt is, without question, the most human of all our Goldens. He even sits down and talks to us. One thing is for sure: scratch this dog's back and you have a permanent job.

Dad's Best Memories and Recollections

Gordon Ball

Gordon Ball with the bench he made for the Humber cottage.

If anyone was "most unforgettable" it was Gordon Ball. A Brampton "Old Boy", he always looked about ten years older than he actually was. We first met at auction sales back in the early 1970s. They were held at the old Brampton Junior Farmers Building. Max Storey was the auctioneer and his bi-monthly sales were always held mid-week in the evenings primarily during the Fall/Winter months. Gordon Ball attended these sales dressed up in an old railway engineer's hat, wearing shoulder-strapped bib-overalls showcasing a typical old-fashioned flappy pocket. Rarely clean-shaven, Gordon usually wore a lackadaisical smile. His eyes always drooped. In my antique collecting days, I did not realize that the three hundred or so items that "the world's best auctioneer" sold each night at the Junior Farmers Building, probably half of the items were consigned by Gordon.

Gordon used to make trips to Scotland and Ireland once or twice a year. When he returned, at least one container followed him back to Canada loaded with 18th and 19th century porcelain, colored Victorian glassware, silver-plated ware, dishes of all kinds, some furniture and pottery jugs and various wooden items including small boxes, kitchenware, and clock shelves, many clocks, brass kettles, milking stools, medicine cupboards, various oil and fabulous Victorian banquet lamps and so much more. Gordon just sat back during the auction and watched the bidding, rarely blinking an eye. He never made a big deal of making money claiming that it was "just a dirty habit" that he indulged in. He and his parents lived on a multi-acre farm, south of Brampton, on the west side of Highway 10. Gordon sold the farm, after his parents died, for many hundreds of thousands of dollars back in the 1970s that gave way to the new 407 Highway. He eventually moved to a farm just east of Rockwood in the 1980s. The farm's stone house was a classic, mid-19th century, Victorian two-story dwelling. After moving to Rockwood, he decided he wanted a wife and went to the Philippines to get his mail-order bride. Before long, Florida, his wife, gave birth to two boys, Frank and Keith. Gordon built a saw mill on the Rockwood farm which served to cut his 150-year old pine trees located on still another farm he owned near Bancroft, Ontario. He erected at least four additional barns on his Rockwood property, built himself a fabulous log house which he never used, transferred a second log house to his property where he stored glassware and dishware. His stonehouse was filled with antique furniture primarily from Peel County. When Howard Pain was preparing his massive book on antiques in the 1970s, I led him to of some of Gordon's finer pieces of country furniture. Back in his Brampton days, in the 1960s and 1970s Gordon made trips to Quebec's Eastern Townships where he would fill truckloads of Quebec furniture, cupboards, armoires, *buffet bas*, wooden beds, on a monthly basis. In those early days, he called the clunky Quebec furniture "nothing but old lumber". He usually sold from his Brampton home to the public on Sunday afternoons. The laneway to his barn in Brampton was jammed with cars from all over southern Ontario. Following Gordon's move to Rockwood, he started making furniture for acquaintances and friends on a limited basis. He was an accomplished craftsman. He had piles of ten-foot high beautiful pine planks that he had cut from the massive pine trees on his Bancroft property. He did the work by himself, including the loading of the trees onto his truck. The plank boards he made from his sawmill were usually twenty inches wide and one inch thick. These pine slabs made forty-inch wide harvest tables at least six feet long. The table he crafted for me is up at the Humber cottage in MacTier. It is six and one half feet long with two drawers. He also made the full-backed, six foot long bench that we use daily at the cottage. It is the exact replica of a bench I tried to buy from Gordon for over forty years. Every time I went to his house I salivated over it so much so that he reproduced for me an exact copy. My grandchildren have been sitting on the armed bench facing the table Gordon made for most of their lives. I saw Gordon for the last time in January, 2011, when Dieter Sebastian and I paid him a visit. Dieter, like me, was always wondering when Gordon might sell one of his outstanding antiques populating his farmhouse. He indicated we should come back when the weather was warmer, perhaps within a month. But within the month he was killed in a tragic car accident while pulling out from his driveway on Highway 7 just east of Rockwood. A few of his close antique friends attended his funeral, namely, Bill Pinkney, Brian Reid, Don Colling as well as Dieter and me, old friends who knew that they were attending the funeral of a Canadian legend. It was fitting that Gordon was buried in his jean jacket and overalls wearing his railway hat. And he was clean-shaven!

Dad's Best Memories and Recollections

June Schweyer

My cousin June Schweyer was born February 1, 1927, making her my oldest cousin. Growing up in Haldimand County along the north shore of Lake Erie, she graduated from the Ontario College of Art, in Toronto, 1947. Her mother and father, plus her younger brother, Grant, used to vacation in Florida each winter, travelling to the St. Petersburg area where two of her mother Fern's uncles, Maitland Alexander Humber from Stratford, Ontario, and Dr. Albert Milton Humber from Detroit, Michigan, spent their winters enjoying the Derby Lane Greyhound Race Track. During one of those winters, circa 1948 or 1949, when June found time to vacation with her parents in Florida, she was introduced to a young man by the name of Warren Mendham. He was some eight years her senior. A veteran of World War II, Warren was the grandson of Dr. Albert Milton Humber, making Warren a second cousin to June. At the time, Warren was living in the St. Petersburg area as a veteran of World War II. After June and Warren met at some family levee, they developed a romantic relationship. It must have been frowned upon but not just because they were second cousins but also because June was Protestant and Warren was Roman Catholic. Besides, Warren was considerably older than twenty-year old June. Nevertheless, the relationship was such that when June and her parents returned to St. Catharines, following their extended stay in St. Petersburg, Warren, head-over-heels in love with June, drove in his new car all the way to St. Catharines, Ontario, carrying with him an engagement ring. After he proposed to June, she broke his heart by turning him down. As I write this vignette, June is eighty-eight years and Warren is nearly ninety-six years. Both are very much alive. Neither can recall for sure the year of his proposal. But this story was exceptionally expanded in the year 2011 when Warren Mendham flew to Toronto from his home in Fort Lauderdale, Florida, to meet me and Gay for the first time. Among other matters, he wanted to visit his old school, Toronto's De La Salle College, where he had briefly attended back in the 1930s. I had corresponded with Warren many times prior to meeting him. This alliance happened while I was preparing **FAMILY SLEUTHING** (2006), the 400-page hardcover book celebrating my family history. After Warren's arrival, I picked him up at the airport and took him to various places he frequented in Toronto as a young boy. I also introduced him to some of my own family. And, in addition to taking him to De La Salle College, I also pre-arranged with my cousin Dave Donaldson, who lived in Dundas, Ontario, to have Warren and June meet at a designated restaurant in June's hometown of Simcoe, Ontario. It was agreed that we would convene at a Simcoe restaurant that June frequented, and at a precise, designated time. And sure enough the surprise worked as planned. While June and Dave were sitting at a table, Warren and I walked into the restaurant and strolled to their table. June recognized Warren almost immediately. She started to weep and he, bright-eyed, was absolutely mesmerized. Please understand, the two of them had not seen each other or corresponded with each other for well over sixty years. Needless to say, it was a remarkable reunion. June was very polite when Warren indicated, perhaps with a quiver in his voice, that it was not too late, that they should unite and live happily ever after in Florida. We all chuckled, including June, at the suggestion realizing that anything is possible. At the moment we departed, the four of us recognized that what we had just experienced was an awesome moment that will live on as an incredible memory....

Cousins June and Warren are reunited after nearly 60 years at a Simcoe, Ontario, restaurant, 2011.

John W. Fisher, "Mr. Canada"

I was aware of the late John Fisher in the mid-1960s following his successful career as a "roving broadcaster" for the CBC. His "John Fisher Reports," broadcast, 1943-1955, generated more mail than anyone else in Canadian broadcasting history. "Mr. Canada", as he was dubbed, broadcast three fifteen-minute programs every week for nearly twelve years. He shared Canada's wonders with an audience who adored him. John became a special assistant to Canada's Prime Minister John Diefenbaker who appointed him, in 1963, to be Canada's 1967 Centennial Commissioner. I first met John Fisher in the early 1970s when he was Chairman, the John Graves Simcoe Foundation, a non-profit organization that maintained the Simcoe Chapel and family burial grounds in Honiton, Essex County, England. As Chairman, he asked me in 1979 if I would consider dressing up in a Queen's Rangers uniform, a replica of the one John Graves Simcoe would have worn during the American Revolution, and re-enact the Governor's historic trip from Lake Simcoe to Georgian Bay which was originally undertaken in 1793. I jumped at the chance and we got a re-enactment crew, led by Hugh MacMillan, of some forty voyageurs in 24- and 36-foot long reproduction canoes to paddle "the Governor" from Holland's Landing, Simcoe County, north of Toronto, all the way to Penetanguishene on Georgian Bay. John Fisher was the one who drew the crowds at each of many daily stops during the five-day-re-enactment trip. His booming voice thundered across the crowds that came to hear a Canadian legend perform magic. Perhaps the biggest crowd was at Big Chute on the Trent-Severn Waterway, near Port Severn, where "Mr. Canada" introduced John Graves Simcoe, a.k.a. Charles Humber, to a crowd, August 5, 1979, of some 5000 people. They had gathered in the wilderness to watch His Honor officially cut the ribbon to open the marine railway at Big Chute, near Port Severn. Touted as the largest marine railway in the world, it certainly is one of the most fascinating "portages" in all of North America.

Canada's Centennial Commissioner, John Fisher, was touted as "Mr. Canada" in a **Reader's Digest** article, December, 1967. The centennial logo is in the background.

After John Wiggins Fisher, UEL, passed away on February 14, 1981, I was elected President, 1984, of The John Fisher Society, a non-profit organization founded in 1981 by a group of John's friends to perpetuate his love for Canada. As editor and founding publisher of Heirloom Publishing, I took liberty, as a John Fisher Board Member, in 1988, to dedicate **CANADA From**

Chairman of The Ontario Heritage Foundation, The Hon. John H. White, accepts a cheque for $10,000.00 from Charles J. Humber, President of the John Fisher Society. A room in the building housing the Ontario Heritage Foundation will be called the John W. Fisher Room.

Dad's Best Memories and Recollections

Sea unto Sea, Volume I of the CANADA Heirloom Series, to John Fisher. How could I forget that wonderful 1979 re-enactment that we took together and how he inspired me with his electrifying voice to promote Canada's rich culture, history and heritage. In October, 1986, on behalf of The John Fisher Society, and five years after John's passing, I presented a cheque for $10,000.00 to the Ontario Heritage Centre at 10 Adelaide St. East. Receiving the cheque was the Hon. John H. White, Chairman, The Ontario Heritage Foundation, who was leading a fund-raising campaign to restore the historic centre in downtown Toronto. On stage with me that afternoon was Ontario Premier Bill Davis telling me stories about "Mr. Canada". A plaque acknowledging the gift from the Society hangs in the John Fisher Room of the Centre. In October, 1988, after John Fisher's personal library of some 1500 books had been donated to the library of his *alma mater*, R.C. Netherwood, in Rothesay, New Brunswick, a gala evening celebrating the occasion was held on the campus with Headmaster Paul Kitchen presiding. Two of John Fisher's siblings were present as well as several John Fisher Board members, including John Fisher Jr. In 1993, the Minister of Education, the Hon. Paul Duffie, on behalf of the Province of New Brunswick, agreed to distribute a copy of **CANADA from Sea unto Sea** to each school in the province where John Fisher was born. Many letters were sent to The John Fisher Society thanking the Society for the donation. It was such a pleasure to read several of these letters at the final meeting of the Board, February 14, 1984, especially the one that came from John Fisher's sister, Nora Tapley, Sackville, New Brunswick. We had done our best to keep the memory of an iconic Canadian alive. I'm sure John Fisher looked down on us and said, "Well done faithful friends." Canada Post over the years has contemplated honoring John Fisher with a commemorative stamp. Perhaps they will do this in 2017 when Canada celebrates its 150th anniversary as a nation.

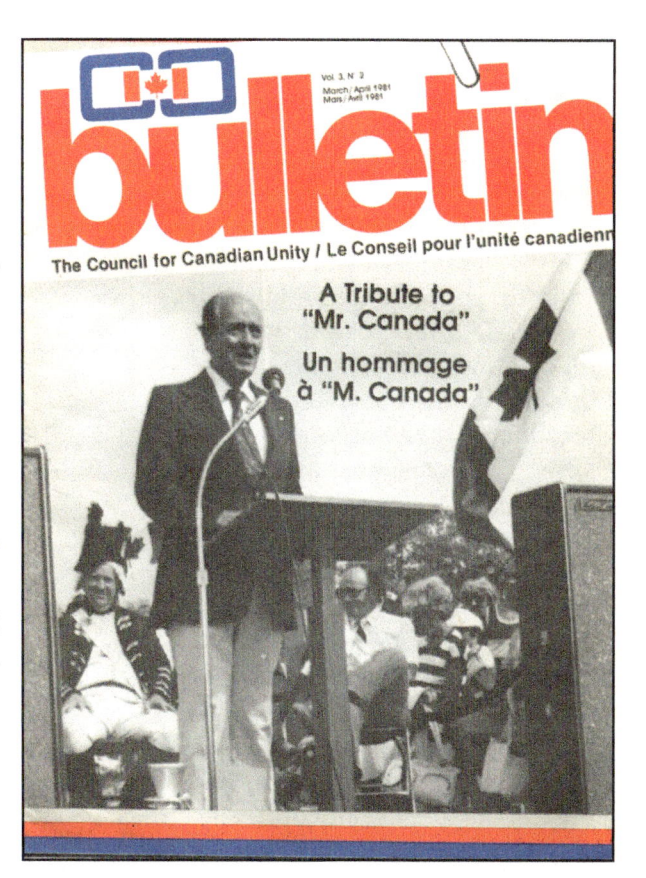

John W. Fisher, highlights cover of March/April issue of **Bulletin**, published six times a year by the Council for Canadian Unity. The image portrays "Mr. Canada" addressing a crowd at the Big Chute Marine Railway opening, Port Severn, August, 1979.

Final meeting of John Fisher Society, February 14, 1994, took place in the offices of Ontario Editorial Bureau (OEB), 500-10 Lower Spadina Ave., Toronto, with Charles J. Humber presiding as president. In this view, bottom row left to right sit Mrs. John Grimshaw, Ida Hewett, Nona McDonald Heaslip, and Dorothy Duncan. In rear stand Mrs. Vincent Egan, Charles Humber, Col. Michael Stevenson, Peter Breithaupt, John Fisher Jr., Elward Burnside, Lou Cahill, Len Wolsey, John Grimshaw, Vincent Egan and Bill McNeil. Missing is George Fisher. In the background hangs a portrait of John W. Fisher.

Dad's Best Memories and Recollections

Lt. Col. James A Rolen

When my sister Anna was united in marriage to mortgage banker and future computer consultant, James A. Rolen, she married a "bushwhacker", an affectionate name for people born in Missouri. Rev. Paul Humber, our brother, not only had introduced Anna to Jim but solemnized their wedding on October 14, 1974 at Spring Mill Baptist Church, Conshohocken, Pennsylvania. Five months following their wedding, my family in Canada finally met Jim as he and Anna plus his daughter, Linda, from an earlier marriage, drove to Canada to attend our grandmother Humber's 100th birthday party, celebrated on March 17, 1975, in St. Catharines, Ontario. What an affable, friendly brother-in-law Jim was right from the outset. Over the years, we would rendezvous at places such as our Muskoka cottage north of Toronto where Jim would trailer his **Mark Twain** boat from Florida for water-skiing activity on Stewart Lake. I'd visit their Miami home, or sometimes we'd connect at places like Providence, Rhode Island, to watch sons Charlie and Scott play hockey for Brown University's Division I hockey team. Sometimes we connected at son Charlie's home in San Francisco or visited with Jim and Anna in their Alexandria, Virginia, home following their move from Miami, 1992, or visited Philadelphia where brother Paul and his wife, Prudence, in their historic house, regulated the care of our parents. We also met at various family gatherings such as Uncle Joe and Aunt Ethelda Lindecker's 50th wedding anniversary, 1976, celebrated in Peterborough, Ontario, or at my mother and father's own 50th wedding anniversary at our cottage, in MacTier, 1984. It was a happy reunion each time we met. We last hosted Jim and Anna during the summer of 2007. After re-building our summer cottage, Gay and I wanted to celebrate the occasion. So Jim and Anna drove from Washington, D.C. to our Muskoka cottage to join sister Priscilla and Chuck Hurlbut from Texas. It was a wonderful week of comradeship, that's for sure. Then one day, in March, 2008, the unexpected happened: I received a telephone call from Anna vacationing with Jim in Scottsdale, Arizona, expressing deep concern and fear that she was "going to lose Jim". It caught me by total surprise. I had no idea about the severity of Jim's physical state. Tragically, two days later, March 20, 2008, my brother-in-law, who had served the USAF Reserves for forty years, succumbed to MRSA, Methicillin-resistant Staphylococcus aureus, a staph infection that is obstinately resistant to antibiotics.

Jim's second memorial service, some three months after his passing (a preliminary service took place at St. Barnabas Church on the Desert, Scottsdale, Arizona March 25, 2008), is a memory that is impossible to forget. Because Lt. Col. James A. Rolen was an officer in the United States Air Force Reserves, he had the right to a military funeral at Arlington National Cemetery joining such world figures as John F. Kennedy and William Howard Taft, former U.S. Presidents, as well as Audie Murphy, the most decorated soldier of World War II, Maj. Gen. George Patton, band leader, Glenn Miller, Joe Louis, and so many other luminaries. The memorial church service for Jim was conducted at the Old Post Chapel, Fort Myer. It is the ceremonial chapel for Arlington National Cemetery. One of the hymns sung at Jim's memorial service was "Amazing Grace".

Following the service, a military procession marched to drums and pipes up and down undulating hills to the covered Pavilion where an internment service would take place. Seven horses,

A reunion of Mother, Evelyn Humber, sharing a happy moment with eldest daughter, Anna and her husband, Jim Rolen, Philadelphia, 2001.

Dad's Best Memories and Recollections

pulling a caisson carrying Jim's American flag-draped urn, paraded with somber cadence to the Columbarium with its variety of sealed niches, one of which would hold Jim's urn. When the military procession reached the Pavilion where all guests gathered, my dear sister Anna took her seat, front and center, and watched as the military guard removed the flag from Jim's urn and folded it with meticulous precision. The leader of the parade corps, on his knees, presented the ceremonial flag to Anna, at the same time saying to her, "On behalf of the President of the United States and a grateful nation, please accept this flag as a symbol of our appreciation for your loved one's honorable and faithful service". This was followed with a gun salute that echoed throughout the burial grounds. The playing of taps and the committal service, at which time Jim's urn was sealed in a niche in the Wall, all served to remind each of us in attendance of our mortality and God's will. The bagpipes forlornly played as relatives and friends left the cemetery. We all gathered on the grounds of the Officers' Club at Fort Myer where guests, including my two sons, Charlie and Scott, plus grandson, Christopher, representing the Shennette family. They all assembled around cloth-covered tables lavished with a bouquet of foods from fish to meats to a gamut of desserts and drinks. Flowers adored the serving room. As we bade each other somber goodbyes, we realized that what we had witnessed on June 26, 2008, was a stirring funeral service that will remain with us as an impressive memory.... Several years later, Anna gave me the ceremonial flag presented to her at the funeral service feeling that my son Scott might like it as a keepsake. Gestures like that bind families together for generations.... The recollection I have is a comforting one in that Jim has found a better place where he is waiting for his beloved wife to join when it is God's will.....

A Celebration of the Life of

James Arnold Rolen

November 11th, 1938 – March 20th, 2008

Old Post Chapel, Ft. Myer
Thursday, June 26th, 2008
9:00 am

The ceremonial flag which draped Jim Rolen's urn following funeral ceremonies was folded and presented to Anna at Arlington National Cemetery, June 26, 2008.

Dad's Best Memories and Recollections

My Romanov Connection

When Gay and I first moved to Cooksville (now incorporated as part of the City of Mississauga), Ontario, 1962, I was well aware that Olga Alexandrovna (1882-1960) the younger sister of Tsar Nicholas II, had lived directly behind us at 2130 Camilla Road. Although the assassination of Tsar Nicholas II and his entire family at the hands of the Russian Bolsheviks, in 1918, was legendary, for those of us living in Cooksville, the name "Olga" resonated throughout the community long after she moved from Cooksville, in 1958, to east Toronto. She was frail at the time with only two years to live. Her wish was to spend her last days with Russian homeland friends.

Some forty years after her death, I was researching content for **CANADA at the Millennium** (2000), a hard cover book celebrating the diversified peoples who had chosen to immigrate to Canada during the twentieth century. Heirloom Publishing decided that this millennium publication would honor and celebrate fifty different ethnic groups, one being Russian. I learned from the Russian Embassy in Ottawa that it would be wise for me, when profiling personalities in the proposed Russian chapter, not to neglect recognizing a cross-section of both "white" and "red" Russians in my book. After my research, I concluded that I definitely wanted to profile Olga, the youngest child of Emperor Alexander III of Russia. My research led me to Galina Komarow, the daughter of Constantine Martemianoff and Zinaida Klugoff who had been dear friends of the Tsarist Romanov family prior to their execution in Russia. They were also white Russians who had fled the Bolsheviks, taking with them their one-year old daughter, Galina, to Europe, where they roamed as vagabonds for nearly twenty years. Eventually coming to Toronto, Galina established a hairdressing salon on Gerrard Street in east Toronto. Her business helped her take care of her parents living in the flat above her business. Although Olga was frail at the time when she moved in with them, 1958, she only wanted to be with compatriot friends when she died.

I contacted Galina by phone in 1999, asking her if she would help me profile Olga in my book. She was eighty-one years at the time she invited me to her apartment on Pacific Avenue near High Park in Toronto. Her living room walls were covered with paintings that Olga had rendered fifty years earlier. I sat at her decorated kitchen table that was accentuated with the finest china porcelain I had ever seen. Galina told me the gold-plated place settings were from the St Petersburg Palace where Tsar Nicholas had lived. The silverware was very heavy, almost clunky. She explained that these, too, came from the same palace and were used by the Romanov family, including Olga, before 1918 and afterwards in Canada. The cups and saucers from which we enjoyed an exquisite brand of tea were rimmed with solid gold. They too came from the Romanov family and had been with Olga over all these years and were left to the Martemianoffs when Olga died and in turn were left to Galina when her own parents died. Galina was such a delightful person. Her English was perfect. Before I left, I commented on the six-foot bird cage in the living room. The cockatoo inside was making all sorts of crazy sounds. I asked what the bird was fussing about. She replied that the bird, which had belonged to Olga some forty years earlier, was speaking in Russian and that it was unhappy we were speaking English. That in itself is a memory but eating from the very dishes that formerly belonged to Tsar Nicholas II (and Olga, the Tsar's younger sister) was certainly a memory I cherish and will never forget.

Grand Duchess Olga Alexandrovna 1882-1960

Grand Duchess Olga and Galina Komarow circa 1959, Toronto

Dad's Best Memories and Recollections

James K. Irving

Born in 1928, James (Jim) K. Irving, at eighty-six years, 2014, is the eldest son of the late Kenneth Colin Irving (1899-1992). "K.C.", as Jim's father was known, built the largest industrial complex in Canada's Maritime provinces. This industrial Caesar's three sons, combined, could be said today to be the wealthiest family in Canada. There are countless stories about K.C. Irving as a young man growing up in New Brunswick under the tutelage of his father, James Dargavel Irving. One of those stories involves his determination, at age twenty-five or so, to operate an Imperial Oil (Esso) gas station in his home town of Bouctouche. This was back around 1924. Owned by Standard Oil at the time, Imperial Oil was not willing to grant K.C. Irving a license to operate one of their stations so, as the legend

James (Jim) K. Irving (1928-   )

goes, he threatened to "put them out of business" in New Brunswick, his home province. Ninety years later, 2014, Irving Oil could be said to out-perform Esso in New Brunswick and as one drives through the New England states, one gets the distinct feeling that Irving is beginning to outperform Standard Oil everywhere. The Irving group of companies now owns and operates, 2014, some 900 gas stations in the eastern part of Canada and throughout the New England states and is still growing.... Esso may not have been run out of business in New Brunswick, but the Irving Group of Companies has given the American monolithic oil company a run for its money.

One day, back in 1988, I flew to Saint John, New Brunswick to meet with James K. Irving, now the company's statesman since his father's death in 1992. I was hoping he would, once again, support Heirloom Publishing's endeavors to promote Canada's rich culture, history and heritage. When I got to the Irving head office, his secretary led me to Mr. Irving's office where I took a seat and waited for "the man" to arrive. When he entered, he was wearing casual clothes as if he was going hunting or fishing somewhere. In actual fact Jim had been fishing and had flown in his private plane to Saint John for his appointment with me. He asked me how I got to New Brunswick from Ontario. I told him that I flew aboard Canadian Airlines International. He responded with a smile, "Then you flew over *our* property." Knowing that I was unsure what he meant by that statement, he smiled again and told me that the Irving Group of Companies actually had the forestry rights to most of northern Maine, and that to get to Saint John aboard Canadian Airlines International from Toronto, the route taken was always over Maine as opposed to Air Canada's route which never flew over Maine.

Our conversation was very cordial as we talked about John W. Fisher, better known across Canada as "Mr. Canada" and who was born in New Brunswick like Jim. He was impressed that we had dedicated our last publication to John Fisher and wanted to know how his company could help out our all-Canadian publishing house. I simply stated that it would be nice gesture if the Irving Group of Companies took out similar advertorial space as previously done. He said almost immediately that he would take two pages of space and had his secretary write out a check to Heirloom Publishing for $12,000.00 on the spot. He then suggested that I contact him when the book came out as he would like to buy a box of books. If I'm not mistaken, I believe we sold 100 volumes of **CANADA from sea unto sea** to Jim some six months later. I've always been impressed with the independence of the Irving family and the way they have provided countless jobs for people. Jim was a good example of how a company responds to its community. He certainly helped Heirloom who struggled to survive in the cutthroat publishing world without any direct government support. I cherished the occasion I had with Jim Irving and as a sign of gratitude, I sent him, upon my return to Toronto, a token gift of some fifty vintage Saint John post cards. His secretary later told me, via phone, that they were special and that Mr. Irving appreciated the gift. It was thrilling to learn that since 1957, under the guidance of Jim Irving, J.D. Irving Inc. has planted 900 million trees.

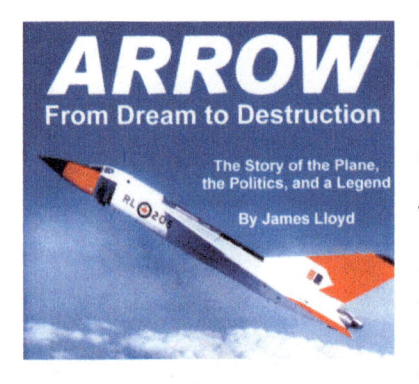

James C. Floyd

As I write this little story about one of the most innovative aeronautical engineers the world has produced, I am aware that James C. Floyd turned hundred years on October 20, 2014. Born in Manchester, England, by the time Jim was fifteen years old, 1929, as a destined-to-be world class designer of state-of-the-art aircraft, he was already working for A.V. Roe, certainly one of the most famous designers and builders of aircraft in Great Britain at the time. During the Second World War, Jim became Chief Project Engineer for the Lancaster bomber. The "Lanc", as it was affectionately known, became the most successful of all night bombers in Europe during World War II. In 1952 A.V. Roe enticed Jim Floyd to work for them in Canada where he became Chief Engineer in charge of all design, testing and research for this iconic British company in Malton, a community adjacent to the Toronto International Airport. He developed a growing team of experts in aeronautical engineering and they produced the CF-100 fighter jet, 700 of which flew for NATO and the RCAF during the Cold War. Jim's next project was overseeing the outstanding design of the Avro **Jetliner,** the first passenger jet servicing North America. Had it not been cancelled by the Canadian government in 1951, this fabulous aircraft would have been in a class all by itself in the very envious realm of aircraft manufacturing as various airlines and such individuals as Howard Hughes were lining up to purchase the **Jetliner,** in Mr. Hughes' case, thirty in number. But the Canadian government cancelled production of the **Jetliner** to re-focus on the development of an interceptor, an unexcelled fighter plane, once again, headed up by Jim's team of unsurpassed aeronautical engineers. When the Avro **Arrow** was finalized in 1958, it was able to fly twice the speed of sound and was far superior to any fighter plane in the world. In fact, after Prime Minister John Diefenbaker, in 1959, cancelled production of the **Arrow**, its capabilities remained unsurpassed for the next twenty years. Jim's frustration with the Canadian government was such that he returned to England and became consultant to the world famous **Concorde,** a joint venture between Great Britain and France. Ironically, it, too, was cancelled after several very successful years of trans-Atlantic flights, a one-way flight which took only three hours to complete.

    A legend in his time, Jim Floyd was retired and nearing eighty years when I finally met up with him in the mid-1990s. I rather felt a kinship with him before I ever met him as I remember hitch-hiking between Brampton and Meadowvale in 1958 and standing at the corner of Highway 10 and Derry Road West, just a couple of miles or so from Malton, and watching the **Arrow** streak overhead on practice flights. Its zoom was thrilling as it surged across the skies above me. Jim was such an iconic personality that I decided he should be profiled in the book I was editing and publishing called **WAYFARERS**. When the story was finalized, I asked Jim the question I had wanted to ask for some time: "Whatever happened to all those wonderful aeronautical engineers who were all displaced along with 10,000 employees of A.V. Roe when the Avro **Arrow** was cancelled?" Jim responded, "Would you like me to write that story for you? I could have it ready for your next book if you wish." Well, I jumped at the chance. And so Jim wrote me the fabulous, untold story. I called it "Canada's Gift to NASA", the story of how aerodynamicist, Jim Chamberlin, plus twenty-five wonderful aeronautical engineers, all of whom designed and helped build the Avro **Arrow** in Malton, Ontario, back in the 1950s, were recruited to Langley, Virginia, and were instrumental in designing for NASA the **Mercury Space Capsule**, the development of the **Gemini** and **Apollo** space projects along with the Lunar Module Eagle that put Neil Armstrong on the moon. This movement became known as the original "brain drain". It is an unknown story but very inspirational, one that should be taught to all Canadian students. You can read this story on pages 340-345 of **WAYFARERS** (1996), Volume V of the CANADA Heirloom Series. It is sub-titled "The Maple Leaf in Orbit".

Dad's Best Memories and Recollections

Left to right, in the offices of Heirloom Publishing: James C. Floyd, Charles J. Humber and Paul B. Dilworth, General Manager, Orenda Engines, manufacturer of the Iroquois Jet Engine that flew the Avro **Arrow.**

The Aerospace Heritage Foundation of Canada presented to Janusz Zurakowski, test pilot of legendary Avro **Arrow,** the first James Floyd award for outstanding contribution to Canadian aerospace, 1990. Left to right: James C. Floyd, Patron; David Onley President (future Lt. Governor of Ontario) and recipient J. Zurakowski.

Dad's Best Memories and Recollections

Aunt Lillian Maude Jarvis Wolf

My mother, Evelyn (Jarvis) Humber, had six siblings. Her closest sister by age was Lillian Maude (Jarvis) Wolf, born two days before Christmas, 1910. I do not remember ever visiting her at any of her homes where she and husband, Rev. Don, raised their four children, primarily because she lived in far-away places such as New York, Pennsylvania, Florida and North Carolina as I was growing up. But when she and her family travelled to the Toronto area to visit her mother, my Grandmother Jarvis, or visit siblings, or to attend family reunions, she was lively and affable as were her children, my four cousins, Cynthia, Jonathan, Timothy, and Lydia. Besides her family, my Aunt Maude's closest companions were Jesus Christ and the Bible. Together, they were the very foundation of her life.

When I was preparing **FAMILY SLEUTHING** (2006), a 440-page book celebrating my family history, a volume with sixty-five illustrated chapters, I came across an historic photo of my mother and father's wedding which took place at Knox College Chapel, University of Toronto, August 22, 1934. The photo (illustrated on page 245 of this tome) reveals my mother and father and their wedding party on the steps of the Chapel following their matrimonial ceremony. Various people are descending the stone front steps. One of those individuals is Marie Jarvis. She's to the far right of the photo looking quite debonair. She is glancing at my aunt Lefa, mother's Maid of Honor. I've always pondered why Maude was not mother's Maid of Honor because she and Maude were very close as sisters. Whereas Maude, at twenty-three, was but three years younger than my mother, Lefa, at only eighteen years, was some nine years younger so it was natural, at least from an historical perspective, that Maude might have been selected as mother's Maid of Honor....

The answer to this question as to why she was not chosen surfaced 75 years later. It was in December, 2008. I received a telephone call from my cousin Timothy Wolf, a Baptist minister serving in North Carolina. He told me that he had just received a telephone call from someone living in South Dakota claiming that her mother was Timothy's half-sister. Naturally, this statement was understandably quite shocking as Timothy had never heard anything remotely similar to this story while growing up. He thought that the telephone call from a woman claiming to live in South Dakota must be some kind of hoax. He gave me her name and her telephone number and asked me to call her and determine whether this telephone call was indeed fraudulent or just a prank. So, I called this person, named Gina Appel, and spoke to her for some forty minutes. There was no question that what she told me had a lot of common sense and much veracity. She claimed that her mother had spent a great part of her life wondering who her biological mother was. The internet, she claimed, led her to discover Maude's date of death, July 12, 2000. She dug deeper and found an obituary that listed Maude's children, including Tim. She then divulged all sorts of facts such as the exact date, October 22, 1934, when her mother was born in Erie, Pennsylvania, that her mother was originally named Kareen Jarvis, that the baby's mother, Lillian Maude Jarvis, was a Baptist from Toronto, that the baby was formally adopted on November 1, 1934, the same day the baby's mother, Maude, was released from the hospital, that the surname of the adopted parents was Keep, that the baby was raised in Erie and that her name was changed to Eleanor. Eventually Eleanor married insurance agent Don Harle and moved to San Mateo, California, where she raised her children. The name of Eleanor's biological father still remains a mystery.

I took all this information and relayed it to Tim's sister, Cynthia, living in Clemmons, North Carolina. I felt that she would be the one cousin able to accept this revelation about her mother and what had happened seventy-five years earlier. And I was right! It does appear that any of my relatives who knew about Maude's situation in 1934 went to their graves not divulging anything about an "uncomfortable truth". But all has seemingly worked out for the better. Cynthia has visited Eleanor in Reno, Nevada. Eleanor has made trips in which she has met each of her half-siblings, namely, Cynthia, Timothy and Jonathan. All feel that Eleanor looks exactly like her mother Maude. This observation includes my two sisters, Anna and Priscilla. It now would appear that we can better understand why Maude was not my mother's Maid of Honor, August 22, 1934....

Lillian Maude (Jarvis) Wolf (1910-2000)   Eleanor (Keep) Harle (1934 -   )

Dad's Best Memories and Recollections

Prof J.M.S. Careless

The debate is resolved: there are three kinds of historians, all serving significant and important roles in generating a better understanding of our historical past. The first of these is the academic historian. This is the one with a Ph.D. who, more often than not, and with taxpayers' money in the form of government grants, investigates what he or she deems to be of significance. Their books are rarely best sellers and usually cater to a select few of their peer group. Secondly, there is the "local historian", a key individual in our society who knows his/her little town or village or county, probably better than anyone else, and writes about what he or she intimately knows, telling anecdotal stories galore that tend to enhance if not glorify their respective communities. These prolific historians add color to their commentary and are not overly concerned if their history is somewhat exaggerated as long as the public gets the idea that history is both intriguing and exciting. Then there is the popular historian, the individual who attempts to appeal to the masses rather than a cortege of academics or a single community. Often they induce the media to get behind him (or her) by promoting their historical perspective with ads, book reviews, colorful commentary and advertorials -- all probably generated by their agents. Popularizers of history often see their works turned into television programs or even full-fledge movies. Of all the historians I have encountered over the years, by far the most erudite, if not most profoundly professional, was J.M.S. Careless (1919-2009), an academic with a flair for popularizing history with local color. He lived in North Toronto just several blocks away from where the Humber family used to live on Lawrence Crescent. After earning his doctoral degree at Harvard University, 1950, Professor Careless taught at the University of Toronto for four decades, heading up the History Department and creating a much-respected department un-excelled in Canada. He was much more than a teacher. He was a researcher, theorist, literary stylist and scholar. His personal interest in Canadian history had been stymied unwittingly by a gamut of historians whose collective interests, decade after decade, in military, political and economic history, totally submerged what J.M.S. Careless considered to be at the core of Canadian history, namely, cultural history. I surmised this and it was for this reason I became friends with Professor Careless and met with him periodically at his home to discuss what plans I had in store for publishing books about Canada. As a result of our get-togethers and following his discovery of **LOYAL SHE REMAINS,** the book I co-edited for the 1984 Ontario Bicentennial, Maurice, as I got to call him, became an integral part of the future books I would edit and publish over the next fifteen years for Heirloom Publishing. As I prepared this vignette, I decided to count exactly how many stories I had commissioned Maurice to write for Heirloom Publishing. The number is quite surprising. In addition to writing key chapters for both **CANADA from sea unto sea** and **ALLEGIANCE the Ontario Story,** Volumes I and III, respectively, of the CANADA Heirloom Series, Maurice wrote an additional forty biographical sketches for three additional volumes of the CANADA Heirloom Series entitled **PATHFINDERS, WAYFARERS**, and **VISIONARIES,** Volumes IV, V, VI of the CANADA Heirloom Series. Here he explored with his rich style and scholarship, such historical personalities as Northrop Frye, Marshall McLuhan, Lester B. Pearson, John Molson and Mary Ann Shadd, the first black publisher in North America....

One day I casually informed him in his University of Toronto office that the only two history courses I had ever taken was a year-course in American History as an undergraduate student at Temple University in Philadelphia, and a half-year course exploring the History of Alaska which I took when attending the University of Alaska, 1960-61. His response to my claim has stayed with me throughout these many years. He said that the main reason he enjoyed writing for Heirloom was because its publisher never took a course in Canadian history and therefore was never "corrupted" by all those professors who brainwashed their students, year after year, with dates, more dates and even more dates. He laughed, exclaiming that my fresh approach to Canadian history dovetailed with his, namely, that Canada's rich culture is just as intriguing as any good American story. Professor J.M.S. Careless left this world in 2009 at age 90 years....

Professor J.M.S.Careless (1919-2009)

Dad's Best Memories and Recollections

Caffe Trieste, San Francisco

Giovanni Giotta was born in old Yugoslavia in what today is known as Croatia. He immigrated to the United States from Trieste, Italy, in 1951, a political jurisdiction where he had developed a love affair with espresso and cappuccino. Papa Gianni, as he became known, brought his love for these iconic Italian drinks to the west coast of the United States long before Starbucks decided to follow suit. It was in North Beach, San Francisco, back in 1956, that he established his first Caffe Trieste at 601 Vallejo St. It became a mecca for hipsters, bohemians, *artistes*, and the many hundreds of flower children who flocked to San Francisco in the 1960s and "hung out" at places like Caffe Trieste. This pioneering establishment was a coffee palace for anyone associated with the so-called beat generation. What made this meeting place a landmark just a little different from others is that the background music was operatic. It was here that Allan Ginsberg publically read his famous poem *Howl*, the most famous of all poems to hook the beat generation. Here Jack Kerouac penned and read aloud many of his works including **On The Road,** perhaps the defining work of the post war Beat or Counter-Culture generation. It was here that Francis Ford Coppola wrote the screenplay for **The Godfather,** and would go on and produce a movie with the same title. Personalities such as Bill Cosby and Luciano Pavarotti checked out this place during their illustrious heydays.

In 2006, when I was visiting California and visiting my son Charlie and his family, I read in the **San Francisco Chronicle** about this pioneering coffee house and that it was going to celebrate its 50th anniversary while I was visiting the Golden Gate City. I decided to check out the place. The House of Beat was totally crowded with people in their sixties and seventies dressed up as if they were still living in the fifties and sixties, all covered with beads and head bands and long hair etc. The place was jammed with the faithful followers of Caffe Trieste. The walls were covered with all sorts of menus, posters, photographs and front-page stories from various newspapers. I must admit, it was very "cool" to be there. And when I had a chance, I was able to find the man himself -- Papa Gianni -- the founder, the man who "got the American people to like cappuccino" as he told me. I believe he was eighty-five. We dialogued for a decent spell of time especially after I told him one of my closest friends living in Canada was Joe Garlatti from outside Udine in the region of Friulano, Italy. Papa knew exactly what I meant when I said that people from that region of Italy were very special. He also knew that many people from where he emigrated had chosen to take "the boat" to Canada instead of the United States. When we parted, he did not just shake hands but gave me plump kisses on both my cheeks as well as an old-fashioned Italian hug. At that moment I almost felt I had been transformed into a flower child!

Charles J. Humber schmoozes with Giovanni Giotta, 2006, Caffe Trieste, San Francisco.

Dad's Best Memories and Recollections

Hugh P. MacMillan

I'm not sure when I first met Hugh P. MacMillan. Because we both were collectors of historical documents, vintage books, antiques, and various ephemera, and because we enjoyed travelling through the undulating dirt roads of Ontario admiring old farmhouses, barns and pioneering towns, whenever or wherever it was that we first met, we immediately connected as *confreres*. We both had fathers who were ministers; we both came from UEL stock; we both had Scottish ancestry; we both had four children; and we both just loved investigating and sharing our mutual interest in our country's rich heritage. Our first major interaction came when John Fisher, Chairman of The John Graves Simcoe Association, contacted Hugh, an individual who thrived on and who was in the habit of re-enacting North West Co. trade routes with a brigade of canoes and a gamut of young people wanting to participate in "living history". These excursions went as far away as Fort William (Thunder Bay), or up the Ottawa River, or along the shores of Lake Ontario on the New York State side.... Our first such venture together was following John Graves Simcoe's historic 1793 trip from Fort York (Toronto) to Georgian Bay, a landmark excursion that led to the construction of Yonge Street, which is, today, the longest thoroughfare in North America. We gathered at Holland Landing, north of Toronto, in 1977. I was dressed up in an authentic re-production uniform that Gov. Simcoe would have worn during the American Revolution. Hugh was all decked out as a classic voyageur ready to lead a canoe brigade. One freight canoe was 36 feet long. The indomitable Hugh MacMillan would lead the school of canoes taking Upper Canada's first Lt. Gov., in his regal splendour, on a five-day canoe trip from Holland Landing to Georgian Bay. Hugh was hyped up for the re-enactment that was followed by a CBC TV crew, all the media outlets, from Barrie to Orillia, from big Chute, at Port Severn, to Waubaushene, from Port McNichol to Midland and on to Penetanguishene on Georgian Bay. Better known as "Mr. Canada" during his broadcasting CBC days, John Fisher followed the parade of canoes by car. Our excursion throughout the entire trip was almost exclusively over water. We canoed such waterways as Lake Simcoe, such rivers as the Severn, and, of course, after officially re-opening the Big Chute Marine Railway at Port Severn, Georgian Bay. Mr. Canada commented to me that Hugh was such a natural leader for the trip. He said that Hugh must be a re-incarnation of one of those North West Company fur traders from the 18th century. Hugh even had an antique wooden barrel, perhaps three gallons in size, filled with whiskey that was concocted exactly as it was made around 1800 when the North West Company was competing with the Hudson Bay Company for furs. Hugh made each of us aboard the canoe he guided take an old burl cup that he provided. It was one similar to what the voyageurs would have used two hundred years earlier. We all filled the little burl dipper with his potent "whiskey" and were told to take still another swig of his patented formula from the old days. He would quote, at the same time, lines from a Robbie Burns poem: "O gude ale comes and gude ale goes/Gude ale keeps my heart aboon". Then he would chuckle and salute us with another Robbie Burns quote: "We'll take a cup of kindness yet for auld lang syne." He wore the same kilt and tattered plaid shirt the entire trip. He, with his scruffy beard and head band, certainly was a character to be photographed. But one should not let the looks of this stocky Scotsman fool you. This walking encyclopedia wore a kilt more than pants. He was a co-founder of the Glengarry Historical Society, the founder of Glengarry Pioneer Museum in Dunvegan, and the founder, 1962, of the Nor'Wester and Loyalist Museum in Williamstown. His autobiography, **The Adventures of a Paper Sleuth** (2004), explores all the exciting finds he made as Archives Liaison Officer for the Government of Ontario over a twenty-five year period, 1964-1989. Of course, his popular book also records the fabulous escapades he had with John Graves Simcoe, a.k.a., Charles Humber, in the late 1970s (see pages 53-54). My good friend Hugh P. MacMillan passed away at age eighty-eight in 2012.

Honest Ed Mirvish

At eighty-five years, Rabbi Jacob Mendel Kirshenblatt took me, in 1985, to see Ed Mirvish, Toronto's "patron of the arts." His wood-paneled head office was located on King St. West in a wonderful older theatre complex that he had saved from demolition in 1963 – the famous Royal Alexandra Theatre, built in 1907. Ed Mirvish became a legend in his time. He founded Honest Ed's Discount Store back in 1948 and turned it into one of the most successful retail stores and tourist attractions in Toronto. It was located on Bloor Street West near where my mother grew up on Markham Street. Ed was a specialist in the "lost leader" ploy claiming over the years that he was the inventor of "loss leaders". In fact, every Christmas he used to give away thousands of turkeys, understanding that one family turkey give-away was just the beginning of a family Christmas shopping spree. When he saved the Royal Alexandra Theatre from demolition, he told me that he just could not let a 1500-seat theatre, the oldest continuously operated theatre in North America, and named after the wife of King Edward VII, go to the wrecker's ball. It was just too wonderful a place, he said, to let it disappear from the Toronto skyline. He did the same thing with London's Old Vic Theatre in England, saving it from the wrecker's ball in 1982. Today, the Royal Alex is the only "royal theatre" in North America. My visit to Ed Mirvish in 1985 was the start of a friendship that lasted until he closed down Ed's Warehouse, circa 2000, a restaurant that appeared to have more Tiffany lamps than turkeys he gave out each Christmas. I used to patronize the restaurant each year especially when relatives visited Toronto from the United States, including my mother. Ed would greet us, and even escort us to our seats. Mother enjoyed chit-chatting with Ed about her "salad days" on Markham Street.

After my off-the-cuff presentation to Ed about taking out editorial space in the forthcoming **CANADA From Sea Unto Sea** (1986) publication, Ed agreed to purchase a one-page spread, thanks to the twisting of his arm by Rabbi Kirshenblatt. The cost was going to be $6500.00, but he squeezed out of me a discount of $500.00. He then had prepared for me twelve post-dated checks, each for $500.00. They were the oddest looking cheques I'd ever seen because on the face of each cheque was a printed cartoon of a basketball bouncing up and down with a hand conveniently above the ball. Next to the comical illustration was inscribed: "Honest to God, Ed's cheques don't bounce." After publication of the book, I watched Ed and his son, David, grow Ed Mirvish Enterprises into a massive entertainment empire with the building of the Princess of Wales Theatre (1993) and the total revamping of the Pantages Theatre, now called the Ed Mirvish Theatre, following Ed's death, 2007. But Ed would not let me forget that it was the "Royal Alex" that put him on the entertainment world map. As "the lion king" said, how could he let a theatre be demolished when such personalities as Mary Pickford, Fred Astaire, Mae West, John Barrymore, Ingrid Bergman, John Gielgud, and Orson Wells had performed there. And, he told me with a twinkle in his eye, "I just could not let this theatre be torn down when the rabbi father of Al Jolson, who performed at the Royal Alex before my time, circumcised me!" Ed did have an unique sense of humor....

David and Ed Mirvish in front of their empire of theatres and stores on King Street West, Toronto.

Left to right: Sister Anna Rolen, standing, Ed Mirvish, Mother Evelyn Humber and Charles J. Humber, in Ed's Warehouse Restaurant, 1984

Dad's Best Memories and Recollections

Hartland de Montarville Molson

As mentioned in another vignette, Group Captain A. J. Bauer drove me to Montreal in 1993 to meet with former Senator Hartland Molson. It was A.J. who suggested that we make the trip together, believing that the book I was preparing both as editor and publisher of Heirloom Publishing Inc. should be sponsored by Molson Breweries. He felt that Senator Hartland Molson, former president of Molson Breweries, might like the opportunity to be identified with **PATHFINDERS**, a publication destined to become a "cultural ambassador" especially since Prime Minister Jean Chretien was writing the "Introduction" to this latest volume of the CANADA Heirloom Series. As well, since the book was profiling Victoria Cross recipient Billy Bishop and because Senator Hartland Molson was the Patron of the Billy Bishop Museum in Owen Sound, Ontario, A. J. just felt there was good and appropriate reason for Mr. Molson to support this forthcoming publication. A.J.'s instinct would prove to be correct.

Former RCAF pilot during World War II, former hockey player, former football player at Royal Military College, former Track and Field star, former collegiate boxing finalist and former owner of the Montreal Canadiens, Senator Hartland Molson has his name engraved on the Stanley Cup six times.

Before we left on our trip, Senator Molson requested that I send him a brief biography of myself so that he could better understand who he was meeting with before I arrived. Since I was cited in the University of Toronto annual publication called **Canadian Who's Who,** I faxed the Senator the appropriate particulars from this publication hoping they would fulfil his curiosity.

At the time I met Senator Molson in his office, he was eighty-six years old and sitting behind his desk. I knew he was the former owner of the Montreal Canadiens and that he had his name engraved six times on the Stanley Cup. What I did not know was that he was a former RCAF pilot who, during World War II with the No. 1 Flight Squadron, had 62 missions during the Battle of Britain. I also did not realize that when he attended the Royal Military College in Kingston, Ontario, during the 1920s, he was a tremendous athlete. As a hockey player he went to the Memorial Cup Finals in 1926. He was a first-string football player at RMC. He also excelled in Track and Field and made it to the collegiate Boxing Finals twice. He was somewhat reserved but his chuckle gave him away and I could tell he liked a good joke. On the wall behind his desk was a substantial oil painting illustrating an ice surface behind a farm complex in the Eastern Townships of Quebec. The hockey players were all wearing either Montreal Canadiens sweaters or Toronto Maple Leafs jerseys. The referee was a priest. I fell in love with the painting and asked him if I could take a photo of it. My only regret when I took the photo was that I did not ask the Senator to stand beside it. Before we bade each other goodbyes, the Senator assured me that the firm would sponsor **PATHFINDERS** by taking out two pages of space. Well, did that ever make the trip worthwhile as that meant at least $12,000.00 in the Heirloom coffers. I assured Senator Molson that when we finally published **PATHFINDERS**, in 1994, that the story we were preparing on "Ice Hockey" would use the image behind his desk. He said something like "I like your style. You did not bother to ask me for permission." He then wished me well and told me that he would keep his eyes on my sons who were playing hockey at Brown University. That was the last time I saw the Senator. He passed on in 2002 at ninety-five years.

Painting hanging behind Senator Hartland Molson's desk in His Montreal office of Molson Breweries. The local priest is the referee. Onlookers kept warm by keeping the wood-stove going.

Dad's Best Memories and Recollections

Governor General D. Roland Michener

The Rt. Hon. D. Roland Michener (1900-1991) was a lawyer, Rhodes Scholar, Speaker, Canadian House of Commons (1957-1962), former High Commissioner to India, Ambassador to Nepal and Governor-General of Canada (1967-1974).

When I served as National President, The United Empire Loyalists' Association of Canada, 1982-84, one of several Honorary Vice Presidents at this time was former Governor General of Canada, the Right Honorable D. Roland Michener. Although we had known each other casually prior to my presidency, we became close friends during and following my presidency. Our friendship blossomed when I invited him to write the "Foreword" to **LOYAL SHE REMAINS**, a 600-page volume commemorating Ontario's 1984 Bicentennial. We met at least two or three times a year between the years 1982-1990, that is, until just before he passed away in 1991. We would rendezvous at places like the Albany Club where we discussed, among other matters, the 1984 Ontario Heritage Foundation Fun Run from Trenton to Picton, a marathon he would officially start on June 10, 1984. We often met at the Royal Military Institute, in Toronto, to discuss such matters as the content of his "Foreword" to **LOYAL SHE REMAINS** or to discuss the importance of John Graves Simcoe, Upper Canada's first Lt. Governor, or Mr. Michener's U.E. Loyalist ancestry. On each of these occasions, we shared good times together. The last time I saw Canada's 20th Governor General was at his gala 90th birthday party celebrated at Roy Thomson Hall, 1990. On one occasion we took time to walk over from the Military Institute to Mount Sinai Hospital to visit his wife, Norah, who was suffering from Alzheimer's. This was in 1986. Roly, as he wanted me to call him, seemingly was the only one in the world his wife recognized. And when he entered her hospital room, she was so delighted to see him.... Because there was nothing of substance he could share or discuss with her, he would motion, with a false gasp, for her to look out her window and see all the beautiful birds. When she looked to see them, Roly made motion for me to slip away from the room beside him. It was emotional for him to see her this way but he indicated that she would not remember our visit and that she would happily be occupied for some time looking for the birds. He felt that it was better to see her surprised and happy for that brief moment than for her to just look into space while he sat in her room and looked forlornly into her eyes. By tricking her, he felt, demonstrated an act of love and he practiced this routine several times a week. They had been married just under sixty years when she passed away in 1987.

My most memorable lunch with Roly took place in the late 1980s. He asked me if I had any relatives who formerly had lived in Red Deer, Alberta. My immediate response was "no". But then I recalled that my father had an uncle who once lived in Red Deer. Since this uncle died in 1933, I really hadn't given much thought that he was a relative of consequence. Then Roly asked me if this great uncle was known as "Hank", or "Uncle Hank" as Roly called him. I said that I did not recognize the name "Hank" but that I did have a great uncle named "Henry" who had lived in Red Deer. Roly immediately said that "Henry" had to be my great uncle "Henry Humber", stating that "Uncle Hank" was an endearing name the family called Henry Humber, and that "Uncle Hank" was one of Roly's father's best friends. Roly's father, Edward, was the Mayor of the Town of Red Deer and, latterly, became a Canadian Senator. Of course I did not know this but Red Deer, in 1904-1906, when Edward Michener was mayor, was a pioneering town. The downtown Humber Block would have been well-known by Red Deer citizens, including Roly and Roly's father, Edward.

As a sideline to this recollection, a well-known antique collector/dealer, Dieter Sebastian, a

Dad's Best Memories and Recollections

friend of mine for nearly thirty years, recently purchased a grandfather's clock originally belonging to the Michener family who had settled in Tintern, a Niagara Peninsula hamlet of some 50 people in the 1860s. Located near Beamsville, Ontario, Tintern, named after England's Tintern Abbey, was where the future Sen. Edward Michener, Roly's father, was born in 1869. Edward's own father, Jacob Michener, (1839-1921), therefore Roly's grandfather, came from a Quaker background whose family can be traced to William Penn, the founder of Pennsylvania in 1682. The first Michener coming to Canada was Roly's great grandfather, Joseph Michener, who migrated to Canada in 1818 and likely was the original owner of the grandfather's clock. Because the clock was crafted near this time, it is easy to speculate that this masterpiece was a matrimonial gift. Those who have seen this time keeper admit that it certainly is one the finest examples of a tall-case clock to have ever surfaced in Ontario. With a providence linking it to Canada's 20th Governor General, as a heritage piece it deserves recognition in someplace like the Museum of Civilization in Ottawa. The former Governor General, born in 1900, presumably never saw the clock although he might have been aware of it. For that matter, his father, Senator Edward Michener, probably did live with it during his early formative years in Tintern. But when he left Tintern to pursue his call to Methodism ministry in Alberta in the late 1890s, he likely had forgotten the clock. He certainly would not have remotely realized that someday this very fine example of Upper Canadian craftsmanship would have such historical significance, and not just because of its connection to Canada's 20th Governor General. This reflection has real significance for me because I had wanted to bid on this clock at an Anderson auction sale in Caledonia, Ontario, 1999, when it sold to a well-known antique dealer for more than $12,000.00....

Above: Governor-General D. Roland Michener talks to twins Scott and Charlie Humber about their Loyalist costumes while their proud father looks on....
Right: The Michener grandfather clock was found in the Niagara peninsula in the 1990s and re-surfaced at an auction sale in Haldimand County, 2000. It is now owned privately.

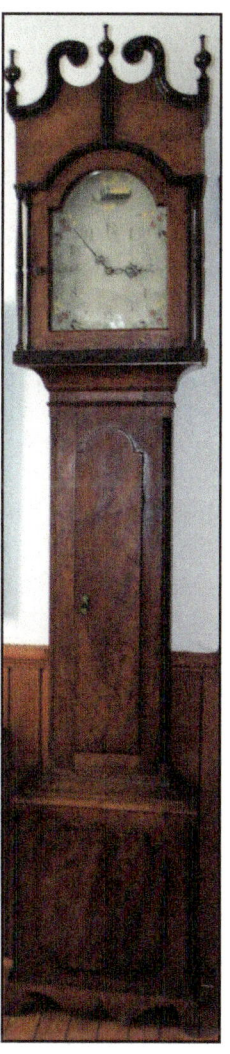

105 | Dad's Best Memories and Recollections

David Macdonald Stewart

David Macdonald Stewart (1920-1984)

One of the most influential persons in my life was the late David Macdonald Stewart (1920-1984). Before I met him, he had sold off, 1974, the Montreal-based family business, Macdonald Tobacco Company, to R.J. Reynolds of North Carolina. How much money the sale of this historic Canadian company generated for David Macdonald Stewart is not publicly known, but it is estimated to be no less than 250 million dollars. The proceeds of this money was converted into an endowment fund operated solely by the newly created Macdonald Stewart Foundation, a non-profit organization that set out to create museums, buy historic sites and restore them, and protect historic properties. The Macdonald Stewart Foundation, over the last forty years, has funded multiple worthwhile causes including hospitals in the Montreal area as well as in Quebec City. It supported McGill University's funding needs (over ten buildings on the McGill campus are named either Macdonald or Stewart) as well as purchasing and restoring Jacques Cartier's Home in St. Malo, France. It donated funds for the restoration of Fortress Louisbourg in Nova Scotia. It donated significant funds for the church in Brouage, France, where Samuel de Champlain worshipped. As Chairman of the Foundation, David Stewart founded a number of Societies, including the Lac St. Louis Historical Society, The Montreal Military and Maritime Museum on Ile-Ste-Helene in the St. Lawrence River, developed the Stewart Museum, and with his wife, Liliane, founded the Montreal Museum of Decorative Arts. On top of all these endeavors, he was Chancellor of the University of Prince Edward Island, he sat on various boards, including the University of Montreal and the Hotel Dieu Hospital; he was also the Honorary Col. of the Queen's York Rangers, whose roots go back to the American Revolution when John Graves Simcoe commanded this Loyalist regiment. He was also an Honorary Vice President of the UEL Association of Canada.

A memorable encounter I had with David took place in 1981. This occurred in October of that year when, as the Hon. Colonel of the Queen's York Rangers (First American Regiment), David invited a number of historical dignitaries, including Brig. Gen. Dr. George Bell, Vice-President of York University, and politicians, including the Hon. Dennis Timbrell, Minister of Health, and the Hon. John H. White, Chairman, the Ontario Heritage Foundation, to gather at the Canadian Forces Base in Downsview, and jump aboard an airplane that David had chartered to fly to Virginia where we all would take part in the 200th anniversary of the surrender of the British Army at Yorktown. Part of the activities was the unveiling of a plaque commemorating the Queen's York Rangers, commanded by John Graves Simcoe, near the battlefield site where British General Lord Cornwallis surrendered, October 19, 1781. This humiliating date brought an end to the American Revolution and freed the colonies from Great Britain. Whereas I was not a part of the international dignitaries sitting with President Ronald Reagan and other notables such as President Francois Mitterrand of France and representatives from Great Britain and Canada, David, who was part of this group, was thoughtful enough to solicit President Reagan, during all the activities transpiring at this time, to sign one of my official brochures. It was an exhilarating weekend, that's for sure. And the trip there and back all happened as the result of David's generosity, love of history and abiding friendship....

One of my most important encounters with David Macdonald Stewart occurred when I was dressed up as Col. John Graves Simcoe. I was giving a speech, October 21, 1980, at the Chateau Champlain Hotel, in Montreal, demonstrating how Quebec City celebrated its 1908 Tercentenary. Some two hundred images from my vintage postcard collection were used to illustrate my talk. David was in attendance and was so impressed with the presentation that he asked to borrow my slide show. Of course, I did not know why he wanted it but I happily loaned it to him. He soon presented the slide show to the Quebec City Council, urging the City to sponsor Jacques Cartier's 450th anniversary of laying claim to New France, suggesting a fleet of tall ships would sail from

Dad's Best Memories and Recollections

Cartier's hometown of St. Malo, France, to Quebec City. Quebec City went for David's presentation and, in 1984, the Tall Ships sailed across the Atlantic ocean to Quebec City. It entailed a massive celebration of the greatest collection of Tall Ships ever assembled in the 20th century. As well, the same Tall Ships sailed up the St. Lawrence River to Toronto and continued on to Detroit. It was an over the top celebration honoring Jacques Cartier and his discovery of New France. The result of loaning slides from my vintage postcard collection to David generated in him a desire to second me to the Macdonald Stewart Foundation. Beginning in 1983, he paid my salary for the next three years to the Toronto Board of Education, permitting me to build a commercial base strong enough for me and my three partners, Angela Dea Cappelli Clark and Bill and Phyllis Melbourne, to incorporate Heirloom Publishing Inc., an all-Canadian publishing house that would create the seven-volume CANADA Heirloom Series and still other books over the next twenty plus years before I decided to retire in 2006. In other words, David Macdonald Stewart, plus his wife, Liliane, made it possible for me to switch careers, from being a high school teacher for twenty years to being a publisher for over twenty years. It was a thrilling experience that the Stewarts gave me as I discovered the country with the red maple leaf through publishing books about Canada. Such a memory is awesome!

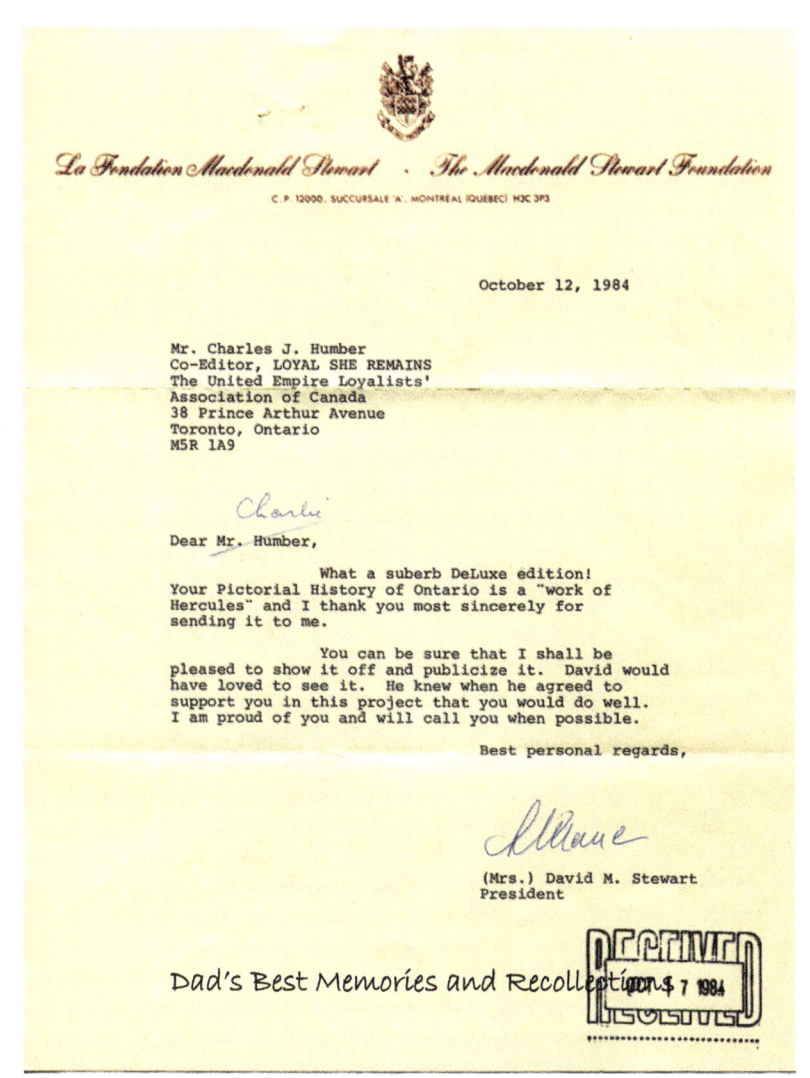

Above: Following the publication of **LOYAL SHE REMAINS**, 1984, Mrs. David Macdonald Stewart, President, The Macdonald Stewart Foundation, sent Charles J. Humber this lovely letter following the passing of his mentor, her husband.

Left: David Macdonald Stewart is flanked by Charles J. Humber and Mrs. John H. (Beatrice) White of London, Ontario, in Yorktown, Virginia, October, 1981.

Grandparenting

December 10, 1992, was not a typical winter's day in Toronto. My eldest daughter, Kristy (Kik), was driven by ambulance from the Toronto Star building, from where she was employed, to Mount Sinai Hospital. After learning she had gone into labor, I volunteered to pick up Erik, my son-in-law, at his Mississauga home. Together we drove through ice and snow to Mount Sinai where we anxiously awaited the birth of Erik's first-born and my very first grandchild. The premature tyke, upon entering this world, was named Christopher James Shennette, born shortly after Bill Clinton's election as 42nd U. S. President. Now nearing twenty-three years, Chris, a graduate of University of Western Ontario (B.A., 2015), is preparing for medical school, September, 2016.

My fondest memory of Chris, other than his birth, goes back to 2004. He was not yet twelve when the two of us went on a week's excursion to the U.S.A. Our junket included visiting my ninety-eight year old mother, Evelyn, Chris' great-grandmother, living in Philadelphia with my brother Paul, his wife, Prudy, plus Peter, their son. Peter joined Chris and me as we took in a NLB game at the new Citizens Bank Park, home of the Philadelphia Phillies for whom Jim Thome, a future Hall of Famer, played. Our next stop was New York City. We drove over the Verrazano Bridge, from Staten Island, through Brooklyn and Queens, to Shea Stadium. Son Charlie had arranged for us to pick up tickets at the Box Office and watch a game in the Fox News Sports Box. It was a treat to see Mike Piazza, future Hall of Famer for the Mets, face Astros pitcher, Andy Pettitte, still another future Hall of Famer. Following the game, we drove to and stayed in Old Greenwich, Connecticut, for an overnight, enjoying and admiring newly-born baby Charlie, son Charlie and Liz's first born. From Old Greenwich, we next travelled to Mystic Seaport, also in Connecticut, home of the world's largest maritime museum. Chris was fascinated with whaling boats there. Travelling on to Hingham, south of Boston, where son Scott and his wife, Molly, had just moved, Scott, Chris and I took in a game at Fenway Park, starring future Hall of Famer, slugger David Ortiz, plus White Sox pitcher Mark Buehrle, a future Hall of Famer as well as a future Toronto Blue Jays pitcher. The best overall memory of the entire trip was grandparenting Chris, teaching him how to be "beasty" while driving and eating take-out fried chicken!

Two years later, 2006, I grandparented another grandson, twelve-year old Bradley Jarvis Shennette with a "Huckleberry Finn" trip to Florida. Because Gay and I had rented a condo near Clearwater, I thought an excursion to the Sunshine State might generate great memories for Erik and Kik's second son, duplicating his older brother's east coast trip with me two years earlier.

On our way to Florida, we stopped at an off-the-road restaurant in Georgia, south of Hilton Head. Here Brad or-

My oldest grandchild, at eleven years, Christopher Shennette, found out what it was like to travel as a vagabond when he hopped, skipped and jumped with his grandfather to Philadelphia, then New York City and Old Greenwich, Connecticut, and finally on to Boston before returning home to Mississauga, Ontario, during the summer of 2004. It was an eight-day memorable trip. Here Chris enjoys a Philadelphia Phillies game at Citizens Bank Park.

Brad Shennette tagged along with his grandfather all the way to the Sunshine State in 2006. His Florida experience opened the door to a different world. At Homosassa Springs north of Clearwater he learned about manatees, alligators, and an hippopotamus named Lucifer after it had been fed!

Dad's Best Memories and Recollections

dered a fried catfish dinner. He thoroughly enjoyed the catfish with its eyes looking at him. Other than spending time in the large swimming pool at the condo's Hammock Pine site, we made daily excursions to such places as Tarpon Springs, the sponge capital of the world, and Clearwater Beach where we rode "the world's largest speed boat," the **Sea Screamer,** a thrilling outing in the Gulf of Mexico where fun-loving porpoises gracefully jumped out of water right next to our speeding boat. At Homosassa Springs Wildlife State Park, Brad had the opportunity to watch adorable and very large manatees feed. He was also fascinated to see various-sized alligators sunning on fenced-in sandy beaches. The highlight of the trip, at least for me, was watching Brad gawk at Lucifer, a huge hippopotamus eating lunch. After devouring, with his gaping mouth, half a dozen cabbages, lettuces, multiple carrots and apples, Lucifer began backing up in the water. The announcer, over microphone, warned sightseers to stand aloof from where Lucifer was heading, a cement wall at the back of the pool. Lucifer started wagging his tail like a windshield wiper, then let lose his inner entrails and flung here and there a rain of scatological muck causing Brad to become pop-eyed. I couldn't stop laughing. For sure, giggling people avoided Lucifer's flushing bowels. Brad's Florida trip was most unforgettable! His trip home aboard an Air Canada flight was his first airplane ride. He was now grown up! After Gay flew to Tampa a couple of days later to join me in Dunedin, I could hardly wait to tell her about Brad, highlighted, of course, by stories of Lucifer! Grandparenting can be so very memorable.

The youngest of three brothers to go wander-lusting with his grandfather was Mitchell Gary Shennette. Our trip, in 2007, was flying to California where son Charlie was living with his growing family in Burlingame, just south of San Francisco. Baby Gordon had just been born (07/07/07), and not only did Mitch get his first airplane trip, but he met his new cousin, Gordon, plus little Charlie, plus his grandmother, Gay, who was there to help out with the new arrival. Mitch was eleven years old at the time, a perfect age to get some life-lasting memories.

Other than visiting relatives, Mitch's timetable for the ten-days was unforgettable both for him and his grandfather. He took in a San Francisco Giants ballgame with his grandparents plus his uncle Charlie, but missed seeing Barry Bonds play due to the Home Run King's injury. We took the boat **Islander** to Alcatraz and spent a day visiting the most notorious of all jails, the former "home" of Al Capone and Whitey Bulger, the gangster who grew up down the street at the same time where I was raised in Dorchester. We walked across the Golden Gate Bridge on a very windy day (I thought Mitch was going to be blown right off the bridge into San Francisco Bay!), visited Muir Park with its massive Redwood trees, walked San Francisco's famous Embarcadero to Fisherman's Wharf where we ate at Alioto's famous fish house, visited San Francisco's world famous aquarium, saw multiple barking seals on Pier 39, travelled the world's most crooked road, Lombardo Street, took an overnight trip to Lake Tahoe and Squaw Valley, and visited my niece, Kerry Moulin, in Roseville. With son Charlie and little Charlie, we went to the Mavericks over by Pillar Point on the Pacific Ocean and, in awe, saw, what some claim, are the world's largest surf waves. This was a very memorable trip, that's for sure, both for me and Mitch. I think I will never forget the time we were driving up and down many of hills that so dominate San Francisco's landscape. As we approached a Lamborghini dealership at 999 Van Ness Avenue, Mitch asked if we could visit the dealer's showroom. I parked the car and suggested he get out, walk to the front door, pull it open and walk around the dealership room. Well, he went to the front door. I watched him from the car. He pulled and pulled to open up the double front door without budging it open. Finally, realizing the doors were locked, he came back to the car with a disgusting look announcing, quite seriously and categorically, that he would now never buy a Lamborghini. His favorite car had now shifted to a Maserati. Grandparenting is such great fun!

Over the last twenty-three or so years, six boys and two girls have entered this world and have made Gay and me very lucky grandparents. Because the three Shennette boys all grew up a mile or so from our

Chris and Brad's youngest brother, Mitchell, got his first airplane ride when he flew to San Francisco with his grandfather in 2007. Two of the many tourist sites he visited was Alcatraz across the Bay from Fisherman's Wharf where he tasted Dungeness Crab exclaiming that this seafood was "Oh, so good!"

house, grandparenting with them since their births has been a constant routine and a joy. My other five grandchildren, Charlie, Caroline, Gordon, Madelyn and Austin, the offspring of our two sons, because they reside in the Boston area, a full day's drive away from their grandparents, have made grandparenting a challenge. Nevertheless, Gay and I have been most fortunate to be in good health to see these five young New Englanders on a yearly basis. This is the result of our efforts to visit them at their various homes in the Boston area and the concerted effort on the part of their respective parents to bring their children and families to the home of their grandparents each year, especially to the family cottage in Muskoka. Needless to say, grandparenting New Englanders has been more difficult because of distance.

My son Charlie's two boys, Charles Henry, born, February 16, 2004, Greenwich, Connecticut, and Gordon Peter, born, July 7, 2007 (07/07/07), in Burlingame, California, despite the fact that they've moved around, have visited Canada every year of their lives. Young Charlie is proud of his first name. He now understands that his given first name makes him the sixth consecutive Charlie Humber to be born to Humber lineage since 1838, the year his great, great, great grandfather, Charles Austin Humber, was born on the Isle of Wight. Barely eleven years old as I write this vignette, Charlie VI, as his email address indicates, has learned to use electronic devices. He stores, literally, thousands of images on his iPad. He's a walking camera man and takes videos and photos everywhere he goes. For three consecutive summers he has gone to various camps in Parry Sound, just up the road from our cottage, and spends time at the family summer home, learning to enjoy campfire cooking, swimming with cousins and uncles, and pretending that "Orgoglio" lurks everywhere. Charlie VI especially enjoys sitting on grandpa's Morris Chair up in the cottage while watching television. Although Charlie VI is not overly fond of sports, his brother Gordon loves playing hockey, his team often coached by his father. I have really enjoyed watching the G-man play hockey and soccer games. I'm totally impressed by his goal-kicking left leg. But perhaps Gordon's top sport is squash, playing with his father at the University Club near Copley Square in Boston. Gordon is a good little athlete and with lots of encouragement is developing into quite a

Above: Gordon Humber, youngest son of Charles W. Humber, and fifth oldest of my eight grandchildren, says goodbye, 2014, to his grandparents' Golden Retriever puppy named Colt. Gordon was leaving his grandparents' cottage, **Pine Vista,** in Muskoka, heading back to Wellesley, Massachusetts, with his dad and his older brother, Charlie VI. It is always fun to tell Orgoglio stories to Gordon. It is one of papa's ways of "grandparenting".

Right: My grandson Charlie VI, says goodbye to Camp Kodiak in 2015 after spending three weeks at this wonderful camp near Parry Sound, just north of where his grandparents' cottage in Muskoka is located. It is wonderful to see my grandchildren trek north to Canada each summer where grandparenting becomes a priority....

Dad's Best Memories and Recollections

performer. My main hope for both boys is for them to continue to progress in their respective school work, to respect their parents and, as always, enjoy the grandparenting their grandparents have provided them since they were born…..

Since their marriage, June 6, 2003, Charlie's twin brother, Scott, and his loving wife, Molly, have become the proud parents of two girls and one boy: Caroline Emily, born, November 28, 2006; Madelyn Nicole, born, June 12, 2010; and Austin Nicholas who entered this world January 23, 2014. All born in Brookline, a Boston suburb, each of these three grandchildren have been raised in Hingham. Although Gay and I have visited together or independently Scott and his family each year at their two Hingham home, south of Boston, or their summer domicile in Chatham, Cape Cod, the family has additionally taken time out, each year, to drive to our Mississauga home for Christmas or to the family cottage, in Muskoka, during summer months making grandparenting such a pleasure. When Caroline was in Mississauga during one winter and was taken to a neighbourhood rink, she was so proud to show her grandparents how well she skated. With a smiling face she approached me. I promptly said, "Wow! You are a good skater! Do you know why you skate so well?" She replied that she was not sure. I then told her that she was a great skater because "You are my grand-daughter!" Well, the smile on her face was priceless. She knew I was kidding her but she loved it. Ever since, whenever she excels in something, I continue to ask her why she is so good at what she does and she always responds, "Grandpa, it's because I'm your grand-daughter!" Now that's grandparenting at its best!

Some three years younger than Caroline, Madelyn, a really determined young lady, spends a great deal of her time trying to out-perform her older sister whom she admires, and greatly and constantly imitates. I'm always kidding her that she's catching up to her sister. Her response is that she will catch up to Caroline sooner than later. She has all the ingredients to be a star performer in just about anything she chooses. This is where grandparenting comes in, though partially compromised by Madelyn's charm and her self-reliance. But the way she handles Colt, our Golden Retriever, suggests that she will be able to handle just about any situation she faces. As for Caroline and Madelyn's younger brother, Austin, this very young boy, at eighteen months, with his balance, his good looks, determination, his adorable smile and love of life is a joy to watch as he prepares to carry on with the Humber surname and his father's hockey prowess.

What a joy it has been to watch Caroline Emily Humber, my first grand-daughter and son Scott and Molly Humber's first of three children, grow up into a sparkling young lady. My oldest grand-daughter, born, November 28, 2006, loves her brother, Austin ("Buddy")Nicholas, born, January 23, 2014, and her sister, the vivacious Madelyn Nicole, born, June 12, 2010. Born in Brookline and raised in Hingham, Massachusetts, each is destined to pursue athletic dreams…

What has made my grandparenting evolve over the years has been Gay, my wife! She is the one who gets all the birthday cards, all the Christmas and holiday cards. She makes me write little notes on each card before they are mailed. She's the one who decides on the presents and special gifts we get for each grandchild. I love doing all of these jobs but without Gay, my grandparenting skills would be greatly diminished. Above all else, the key to grandparenting is giving love to grandchildren…. That's what grandparenting is all about, love making the world go round.

James C Potter

At age twenty, I enrolled at Brampton District High School(BDHS), northwest of Toronto. My desire was to graduate in the spring of 1957. My grade twelve English teacher, James C. Potter, surmised that I was potentially a drifter and possibly enjoyed the poolroom more than high school studies. His observation was intuitive because I had not attended school since 1954 and tended to be, in the eyes of some skeptics, somewhat rough around the edges.

Early in the first month of school, each student in Mr. Potter's English class was required to stand up at the front of the class and deliver an impromptu, three-minute speech. The topic I was assigned on a slip of paper was called "My Summer Job". I had three minutes to prepare it. When my time came, I spoke about my summer employment at the Toronto Western Hospital and what it was like to operate a maternity elevator in the same hospital where my grandfather, Gilbert Jarvis, had died fifteen years earlier. While delivering my speech, I well remember Mr. Potter at the back of the class roaring with laughter while I explained to my classmates in a rather awkward way that expecting mothers sometimes broke their water, right on the floor of my elevator, while I was taking them up several floors to the maternity ward. I explained how I had difficulty preventing husbands from following their laboring wives out of the elevator doors and down the hospital corridor to the delivery room. The rule was that only expectant mothers plus a waiting nurse were the only ones permitted to go beyond the elevator doors. At end of class, Mr. Potter pulled me aside and said something like, "Charlie, that was one of the best student speeches I've ever heard. You've got natural talent." He surely sparked in me an interest to work harder for his English class.

Following his retirement as a full-time high school teacher, Jim Potter taught at the old Britannia School House Museum, 1982-1985, on Highway 10 just south of Highway 401, Mississauga, Ontario.

During the course of my grade twelve year, I came to grasp what a superb teacher Jim was. He pumped into us grammar lessons. His brow would sweat as he passionately read Shakespeare to us. He tested us daily as we read chapters from **Great Expectations**. He had us memorize Hamlet's soliloquies. He made us go to the blackboard and write out answers to the questions he had given us for homework. We always had to write in complete sentence form and use correct grammar. He was most vigilant in monitoring our notebooks; he gave frequent assignments in creative writing; and he always cared how his students were doing. After my grade twelve year, I decided I wanted to be an English teacher. I wanted to be another Jim Potter. So, I took grade XIII English from Mr. Potter the next school year before I enrolled as a freshman at Temple University in Philadelphia.

Over the years, Mr. Potter became "Jim" as we became good friends. Sometimes I would visit him in one of his apartments in Brampton or at his summer home in Warkworth near where he originally began his teaching, at age nineteen, in a one-room school house, 1939. After our marriage in 1961, Gay and I had Jim over for dinner to our various homes multiple times. We were in constant contact with each other until just before he died, February 12, 2002, in Brampton. In fact, Jim came to our Sherwood Forrest home in Mississauga less than three months before he passed away. It was our "last supper". Joining our get-together was Wayne Getty who came down from Ottawa. Stan Barrett was unable to attend our reunion because of a life-threatening accident his son, Jason, experienced just the day before in

Dad's Best Memories and Recollections

Halifax. Jim would have immensely enjoyed our rendezvous as we were three of his favorite students from the 1950s. But then Jim would say this about all of his students no matter what decade he taught them.

Jim took several leaves of absence from BDHS to teach in places like England, Germany and Africa. I have saved the multiple letters he sent me written over a thirty-year period and all composed in wonderful penmanship. One of the first letters I received from Jim, dated February 10, 1959, happened when I was attending Temple University in Philadelphia. Jim writes to his former student, "Oh, yes, you must read **The Catcher in the Rye** by Salinger. It's your book. I associated you with the hero. Please read it! Please read it! Please read it!" In the same letter, he writes about seeing **West Side Story** and exclaimed "... Fabulous! See it if you ever get the chance!" Another of Jim's letters I received, dated January 12, 1961, was sent from Radcliffe-on-Trent, England. At the time I was living on Ladd Air Force Base, Fairbanks, while attending the University of Alaska. Jim mentioned how he used my Christmas letter as "a composition lesson in [his] grade twelve class," saying that his students "... think your writing is terrific." As usual, Jim was not just motivating his current students but also his former students. After he retired from teaching, my twin sons, Charlie and Scott, attended a one-day retreat at The Old Britannia School House, in Mississauga, where Jim taught students, 1982-85, as headmaster for students of all grades studying the pioneer era. Jim was all dressed up in period costume trusting that his "living history" classroom would inspire his students to experience what it was like to attend school during the reign of Queen Victoria. In a letter to Gay dated October 12, 1984 Jim wrote, "I just had to tell you how much pleasure I had last Friday in getting to know your two charming sons. What fine, fine sons you have.... They appeared to be extremely interested and asked questions and volunteered answers. How proud you must be of Charlie and Scott." This was Jim at his best --always interested in his students even if they were only part-time....

Overall, Jim taught school forty years -- in six different decades! Today, The City of Brampton has honored Jim by naming a public school after him and a major thoroughfare called James Potter Road. Those who were lucky enough to have Jim Potter as a teacher will remember him as a wonderful person who cared deeply for each of his students. He's a lifetime good memory.

Less than three months before he passed on, my favorite all-time high school teacher was entertained at our Sherwood Forrest home in Mississauga, February 12, 2002. Here Jim Potter and one of his former students pose for a photo-op.

Dad's Best Memories and Recollections

Group Captain A.J. Bauer

Group Captain Col. A. J Bauer commanded the Air Force base in Germany, Baden-Soellingen, 1971-1974.

The Canadian Armed Forces rank Group Captains above Wing Commanders and right below Air Commodores. Additionally, Group Captains are traditionally the Station Commanders of Royal Air Force Bases. Group Captain Col. A. J. Bauer commanded the Air Force Base in Germany, Baden-Soellingen, 1971-1974. I did not know Col. A. J. Bauer until some fifteen years after he retired from the Canadian Armed Forces. This was in the early-1990s when, as publisher of Heirloom Publishing Inc., I was looking for someone to write a biographical sketch of Air Marshall Billy Bishop, the famous Canadian World War I fighter pilot responsible for 72 aerial victories, the last five of this total coming, June 18, 1918, the very last day of his hunting sky Huns during World War I. No question about it, William Avery "Billy" Bishop, VC, CB, DCD, MC, DFC, ED, LL.D was the foremost British Empire pilot of World War I.

After I got to know A.J., he agreed to meet with me at the Royal Canadian Military Institute on University Avenue, Toronto. He accepted my proposal that he write a biographical sketch of Canada's first aerial Victoria Cross winner. In 1987, A.J. had founded Billy Bishop Heritage in Owen Sound, a Georgian Bay city two-hours north of Toronto. The main purpose for establishing Billy Bishop Heritage was to raise enough funds to buy the Billy Bishop boyhood home and establish the Billy Bishop Museum. All of this was established before I met Group Captain A.J. Bauer in 1992. In fact, Billy Bishop's boyhood home had become a major tourist attraction in Owen Sound before I had ever heard of Group Captain A.J. Bauer. When he finished writing the Billy Bishop story, it was published in **PATHFINDERS Canadian Achievers** (1994), Volume IV of CANADA Heirloom Series. At the same time A.J. was preparing his story, I had acquired some items that I wanted to donate to the Billy Bishop Museum. One of these gifts was a vintage airplane model of Manfred Von Richthofen's Fokker **Dr. I Dreidecker,** the scarlet red triplane the German ace pilot is best known to have flown during aerial combats in World War I. The Red Baron, as he was known, had 80 combat air victories, eight more than Billy Bishop recorded. The Red Baron remains the best known fighter pilot of all time. The three-winged plane was a large model, just big enough to fit into my Plymouth mini-van as I drove to Toronto from Providence, Rhode Island, where I had found the plane in an antique shop. I thought that this triplane would make a nice addition to the Museum. As well, I also acquired a first edition of Manfred von Richthofen's book called **The Red Battle Flyer,** 1918. It was a translated version of the German edition published in 1917 before the Red Baron died. Additionally, I had an aerial photograph of Owen Sound taken by the Bishop and Barker firm that went about in 1919 and 1920 taking aerial photos of all the various towns dotting the Ontario shores. These were the first aerial views ever taken professionally over Canadian landscape. Both Billy Bishop and Billy Barker were awarded the Victoria Cross for aerial combat and service during World War I. Because of poor management skills, their company went bankrupt after two years. Nevertheless, I thought that the Billy Bishop Museum should have this rare view of Billy Bishop's home town taken from the sky. I had it enlarged to 16"X 20". When I drove to Owen Sound to officially donate these gifts, A.J. met my wife and me at the front door, the gifts were accepted, and we went to Owen Sound's Billy Bishop Airport where he treated Gay and me to an airplane ride over Owen Sound.

Dad's Best Memories and Recollections

Later, A.J. and I rendezvoused in Toronto and drove to Montreal where A.J. had arranged for us to meet with Senator Hartland Molson, former President of the Montreal Canadiens, at the time the National Hockey League's most dynamic team. As well, Senator Molson was Chairman Emeritus of Molson Breweries. The purpose of our get-together was to solicit Molson Breweries to become a corporate sponsor of Heirloom's publication endeavors to generate heritage awareness about our country's rich culture and history. At the time, Senator Molson, an air pilot himself, was the Patron of the Billy Bishop Museum and A.J. thought that we should give Mr. Molson a chance to bring aboard Molson Breweries as a corporate sponsor of Heirloom Publishing. Needless to say, we succeeded in our endeavors and **PATHFINDERS**, volume IV of the CANADA Heirloom Series, profiles Molson Breweries in a major two-page spread.

When the next two volumes of the CANADA Heirloom Series were published, A.J. was also a contributor. In **WAYFARERS** (1996), he profiled Keith Greenaway, a pioneer arctic aerial surveyor; in **VISIONARIES** (1998), A.J. wrote about Robert Bradford, Canada's most acclaimed aviation artist. Certainly, Group Captain A.J. Bauer has been a memorable person in my life, one who has provided me with some very happy lifetime memories that I will cherish until the day I give up the ghost.

Owen Sound welcomed Billy Bishop following World War I. In this view, Billy Bishop "drives" his airplane down the Main Street, 1918.

Dad's Best Memories and Recollections

Double Trouble, October 17, 1973

By the time we finished our Thanksgiving dinner, 1973, we had completed four successive years of scrumptious turkey feasts up at the family cottage in MacTier. The October weather that year was perfect for spending a glorious Thanksgiving in Muskoka. The inflamed foliage was mesmerizing with orange, red and yellow leaves flickering and falling to the ground.... Wood smoke filled the air. The sigh of autumn was all around us. Uncle Bill Donaldson had joined us for our get-together at the cottage he had sold us in 1970. Bea Jenkins (BJ), Gay's mom, had come all the way from La Jolla, California, to be with us. Kristy was nine years. Karyn was not quite seven. Our first Golden Retriever, Canuck, was three years plus. I was thirty-seven; Gay was thirty-four years. And she was also very pregnant! She looked fantastic throughout the duration of her pregnancy, that is, until the last two weeks when she started looking as if she was going to give birth to a village, a phrase my mother used to describe herself before she gave birth to her set of twins in 1942. So, after feasting on Gay's traditional Thanksgiving dinner, we all prepared for the two-hour journey home.... The next week would be momentous....

Just about one week after closing up the cottage for the long winter, and while the family was enjoying dinner in our cozy Rexdale bungalow at 61 Westhumber Blvd., Gay knew something was happening as her water broke. It was October 16. Immediately, BJ took control of the girls while Gay and I, already packed up for the occasion, drove off to the Mississauga Hospital, just west of Highway 10 (Hurontario). This was the day we anticipated adding still another member to our family. The hospital, known today as the Trillium Health Centre, was called South Peel Memorial when Kristy and Karyn were born, 1964 and 1966 respectively. Since Gay had not yet gone into labour, she was admitted for observation. I then returned home to prepare multiple antique items I was consigning to a Max Storey auction sale in Brampton for the following day. In short time, the hospital called home indicating that Gay had gone into labour. I was there in a jiffy driving across the QEW in my 1969 Chevrolet Impala.

When I got to the hospital waiting room, I learned that all the babies born that day were male. I think some six or seven boys were born in a row. Because I was hoping for a son, I was somewhat disgruntled because the odds were for a girl to be born. Of course, all that mattered was that the baby, no matter the gender, was healthy. But I was still hoping for a boy! Well, I waited and waited.... It was getting close to midnight. I anxiously started wandering the hallways of the maternity ward, peeking through various windows, wondering how Gay was doing, wondering where she was, wondering if she was okay.... All along the wide hallway of the maternity ward were observation windows. At about one half hour after midnight, I watched two nurses at one maternity table swabbing two babies. It was interesting to observe them diligently taking care of such small individuals. Then one of the nurses noticed I was watching her handiwork with the two babies. I suppose she wondered who I was at such a late hour and mouthed through the glass window: "Are you Mr. Humber?" I nodded "Yes" and then she pointed two fingers at the two babies, exclaiming they were mine by re-pointing her fingers at me! And that's exactly how I found out I had become the father of twin sons.... Shortly thereafter I watched a different nurse deliver Gay on a gurney bed to a hospital room. She was still woozy. But, thank God, she was okay. I approached her bed. All she could do was smile. It was a smile that said multiple words. She was happy.... And God was good....

Anyone reading this vignette should be aware that parents in the early 1970s did not usually get to know the gender before their babies were born. Because ultrasound resources were not readily available in the early 1970s, Gay went into labour completely unaware of any forthcoming baby gender or, more surprisingly, that she was about to give birth to twins. We were told afterwards that because the babies were directly behind one another in the womb, their heart beats, detected in Dr. Jim Reid's office on multiple occasions, were detected as one. Even during the birth of the first born, Charlie, there was no evidence that Scott was about to follow his brother into this world. Once it was determined that a second baby was evident, an emergency force was put into play and Scott was born seven minutes after his brother at 12:16 a.m., October 17, 1973. Both boys were good sized, with Charlie weighing in at 7lbs 1oz, and Scott tipping the scales at 7lbs 4oz. Charlie was 19 inches long while Scott was 20 and one half inches long. But think of this: it was as if Gay was giving birth to a 14lb 5oz baby! One thing is for sure: she was carrying around some extra poundage! No wonder she looked as if she just might

Dad's Best Memories and Recollections

give birth to a village....

Gay remained in the hospital for ten days due to some unseemly complications. The babies stayed with her, of course, but she was unable to breast fed them. BJ stayed with us for an extra ten days making sure that the girls got off to school each day while I was teaching at Lawrence Park Collegiate Institute in Toronto. Nevertheless, we all found ways to visit with Gay every day. On the day she left the hospital, there was so much joy on everyone's face. It was like a miracle had happened. And now Kristy and Karyn got to understand what it meant to be the older sisters to twin brothers, boys who would grow up and complete a happy family....What a wonderful memory....

Top left: October 17, 1973, nurses hold twins, Scott, left, Charlie, right.

Top right: Hubby greets wife in hospital following birth of twin sons, October 17, 1973.

Middle left: Homecoming sign reads: "FEATURE FILM"; The Homecoming: Introducing the Humber Twins Produced by Gay Humber under the Direction of Chas Humber Co-starring Kristy, Karyn and BJ".

Middle right: Gay's Mom, BJ Jenkins, with twins, October 29, 1973.

Bottom left: Twins rubbing noses, getting to know each other, 1974.

Middle bottom: Kristy and Karyn hold brothers, summer, 1974, on the Morris Chair.

Bottom right: Charlie and Scott, moguls, nearing 30 years, 2003.

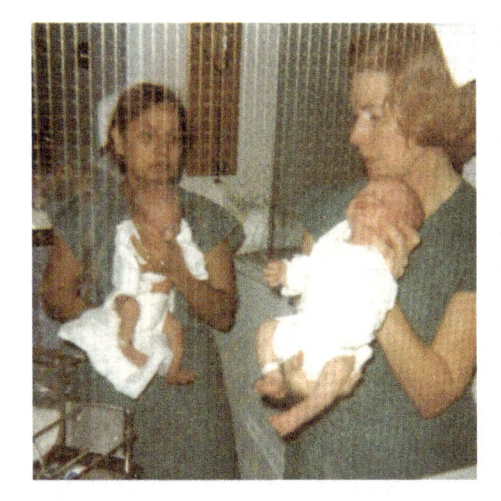

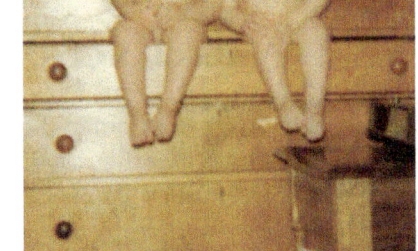

117 Dad's Best Memories and Recollections

Lord Mayor Wilbert Dick

Niagara-on-the-Lake is one of the most enchanting towns in Ontario as well as one of the most historic municipalities in the entire Dominion of Canada. Located on the western shores of Lake Ontario at the mouth of the Niagara River, this garden city originally was called Butlersburg when it was settled, 1781, by the famous Butler's Rangers, a much-feared Loyalist regiment during the American Revolution led by Col. John Butler. An early outpost, Butlersburg was renamed Newark in 1792 and was made the temporary capital of the newly formed province of Upper Canada when John Graves Simcoe arrived that same year as the first Lt. Governor. The town has had several name changes over the years but was officially named Niagara-on-the-Lake by the late 19th century.

When Niagara-on-the-Lake celebrated its 200-birthday in 1981, two very special personalities arrived to mark the occasion. One of these was Queen Elizabeth The Queen Mother who, in her eighty-first year, arrived to participate in the town's bicentennial festivities. Her Majesty was officially greeted and hosted by Lord Mayor Wilbert Dick whose title in Canada is very unique. In fact, one thing that each elected Lord Mayor of Niagara-on-the-Lake has in common with cities in the United Kingdom like London, Edinburgh, Manchester, Oxford and Glasgow is that they are all governed by Lord Mayors. Wilbert Dick was the only official Lord Mayor in Canada and all of North America when he served his community, 1978-1985.

Following the departure of The Queen Mother, Lord Mayor Wilbert Dick, on July 26, 1981, warmly greeted John Graves Simcoe, portrayed by none other than yours truly whose alter ego had been portraying Upper Canada's first Lt. Governor since 1977. A blaze of glorious musketry and an enthusiastic crowd, led by Lord Mayor Wilbert Dick, all dressed up in 18th century regalia, greeted the Governor at the naval docks. Here the Governor disembarked from the **Pathfinder,** similar to the longboat, **Onondaga**, that His Honour had taken in 1792 when he sailed from Kingston, Upper Canada, to Newark. Simcoe, in 1981, arrived with much pomp and circumstance at Navy Hall, the site of the first provincial Parliament, July 26, 1792. Before addressing the waiting crowd, the Governor reviewed the positioned troops. The Queen's Rangers, Simcoe's old regiment during the American Revolution, the 84th Highlanders, the Butler's Rangers, the King's Royal Regiment of New York (KRRNY), and Jessup's Corps were reviewed among others. The Governor's very first remarks, delivered in front of CBC television cameras, among others, extended salutary greetings from King George III. Simcoe, a.k.a. Charles J. Humber, stood in front of the twelve-foot Simcoe monument guarding the entrance to Navy Hall. It had been unveiled in 1953 to commemorate John Graves Simcoe's first Parliament. Each time John Graves Simcoe emphasized a sentiment, Lord Mayor Wilbert Dick applauded vigorously and the crowd responded accordingly. Upper Canada's first Governor reaffirmed that he had abolished slavery in Upper Canada in 1793; that he had promoted the publishing of Upper Canada's first newspaper; that he had founded the Town of York, now called Toronto; that he had undertaken to build North America's longest street, namely, Yonge Street; and that he had built strong military fortifications that successfully defended Upper Canada during the War of 1812.

The crowd loved the speech and applauded with gusto, encouraged by Lord Mayor Dick. After my speech, the Lord Mayor had the Governor sign the Town's guest book. On the opposite page to where Governor Simcoe was to sign was a page in beautiful penmanship where Her Majesty Queen Elizabeth The Queen Mother had signed just two weeks before. Since The Queen Mother took up a full page, I, as Simcoe, took liberty to fill up a full page. In my best penmanship that my grade six teacher would have applauded, I explained who I was, who I was impersonating, the importance of the occasion and that it was a privilege to sign the guest book opposite the page that the Queen Mum had signed. I drew to the Lord Mayor's attention that very fact as he closed the guest book, emphasizing that my page would be "kissing" the Queen Mum's page. He smiled knowing that I was a true Monarchist.

Some ten years later, when I was publishing **ALLEGIANCE: The Ontario Story** (1993), Volume III of the ongoing CANADA Heirloom Series, I solicited former Lord Mayor Wilbert Dick who had become Chairman, The Regional Municipality of Niagara. I suggested that his political jurisdiction consider subscribing to a one-page advertorial in the forthcoming book honoring Ontario's rich culture, history and heritage. He was pleased to oblige me, still convinced that I was none other than John Graves Simcoe. You can read this story on page 485 of **ALLEGIANCE: The Ontario Story**.

Lord Mayor Wilbert Dick greets John Graves Simcoe, (aka Charlie Humber), July 26, 1981.

Dad's Best Memories and Recollections

Grandmother Humber's 100th Birthday

    In 1975, my grandmother Lizzie (Biddle) Humber celebrated her 100th birthday, some thirty-two years after her husband, Charles Herbert Humber, died, 1943, in Goderich, Ontario. Nearly seventy-five years earlier, in 1901, my grandmother was in Buffalo, New York attending the famous 1901 Pan-American Exposition, when she, along with 50,000 spectators, witnessed the fatal shooting of President William McKinley, September 5, 1901. One particular person missing from my grandmother's centennial birthday party was my grandmother's youngest daughter, Edith Donaldson, who had passed away, at only sixty years, some five years earlier in 1970. Mind you, all of grandmother's six siblings had passed away except for one older sister, Lottie Holmes, my great aunt, who was happily present for this affair at age 101 years. The gathering, March 17, 1975, at Markarian's Steakhouse in St. Catharines, Ontario, would have totalled thirty-five family present had my sister, Priscilla, and her husband, Chuck Hurlbut, come with their two daughters, Beth and Jenny. But they lived in California at the time and it was just too far a distance to come for such an affair. The grand birthday party had been organized by my grandmother's oldest daughter, Fern Schweyer, age seventy-two years, and her daughter, my oldest cousin, June Van Fleet, from St. Catharines. Grandmother Humber was able to welcome and kiss six of her nine grandchildren (Priscilla, plus two other cousins who had died much earlier, Chuck and Phil Donaldson, were missing) and twelve of her fifteen great grandchildren (Peter Humber plus Beth and Jenny Hurlbut were not present) for her birthday party, in addition to her own two living offspring, Dr. the Rev. Charles M. Humber and his sister Fern Schweyer, aged 72 years at the time. Aunt Edie's husband, Bill Donaldson, from Hamilton, was there with grandmother's other in-law relative, my mother, Evelyn Humber, from Philadelphia.

    The years go by very quickly and grandmother's fifteen great grandchildren have raised, among themselves, an additional twenty-eight children, three of whom live in British Columbia, four in the Congo, in central Africa, five in Philadelphia, another five in Boston and the rest scattered around North America in various jurisdictions, mainly in Ontario. Grandmother Humber's 100th birthday party in 1975 was certainly one of the last times so many of our family relatives from the same bloodline assembled together as one big extended family. The modern age has taken its toll on such personal gatherings. Modern devices such as computers and iPhones and iPads have kept us all in contact, I suppose, but in a superficial way. The real personal connection, the hand shake, the hugs and kisses, the tactile gathering of the family for birthdays, anniversaries, Christmases, even funerals and weddings, are all getting harder and harder to attend despite modern technology such as faster and safer cars and buses, railroads and airplanes. Family gatherings are almost a thing of the past just as are rotary telephones, the telegram, home movies, walkie-talkies, tape decks and so much more. All this is so true no matter what one says about Skype and texting and Facebook and twittering and other modes of communication that are supposed to keep us connected in this escalating disconnected or unconnected world....

Grandmother Lizzie Humber's 100th birthday celebrations were held at Markarian's Steak House in St. Catherines, March 17, 1975. This view reveals Granmother Humber sitting in the middle of the family flanked by her older sister Lottie and her daughter, Fern.

119

Dad's Best Memories and Recollections

Stan Barrett

I first met Stan Barrett at Brampton District High School, 1956-1957. We were in the same grade XII home room class. Born, 1938, he was the third oldest of six sons born to Ray and Ida Barrett. Formerly from Shelburne, Ontario, at the time we met, Stan and his family were living in a first floor apartment in an Alfred Hitchcock-style home on Mississauga Rd., south of Huttonville. We became friends almost immediately and although our camaraderie did not fully develop until the following year when I was in grade thirteen and he was working and going to night school in Hamilton, Ontario, we double-dated a lot during our first two years of friendship. It was after my grade thirteen year, June, 1958, when Stan and I went to Barrie looking for summer work, that our life-long friendship solidified.

When we learned the **Toronto Telegram,** one of Canada's largest daily newspapers, was looking for a crew of door-to-door salesmen, we drove to Barrie in his Model A Ford and signed up as subscription salesmen with the **Tely**. Looking forward to our new jobs, the **Tely** booked us and several other crewmen at the Queen's Hotel, a prime watering hole, built in the 1850s and located on Dunlop Street East in downtown Barrie. The **Tely** paid our hotel rooms, Monday through Thursday; we were on our own Friday nights through to Monday mornings; the **Tely** paid for breakfast Mondays through Fridays; all salesmen were paid an automatic $6.00 per day salary; salesmen earned one dollar for each committed **Telegram** order as we went from door-to-door on a day-to-day basis. We offered ten-week subscriptions to prospective clients. Almost immediately we were making, literally, hundreds of dollars per week. Stan and I were exhilarated in making money, lots of it. We daily competed with each other to see who could make the most sales. It was always a close race. In the long run, Stan beat me in total sales that first summer. No other salesman came close to what we managed to earn either on a daily basis, a weekly basis or over the entire summer. We chuckled to ourselves as we approached our daily routes each morning and broke out with huge grins at day's end. Earning easy money was sheer joy. Stan and I, needless to say, were joyous all summer. On the weekends we often drove to Primrose Corners near Shelburne and fished the Boyne River for speckled trout. These were memorable, magical days walking the pristine Boyne, catching seven- or eight-inch trout in river pools shrouded with 100-year old cedar trees blocking our aggressive advances. We could always hear each other moaning after losing the big one – or – the biggest one ever! "Such, such were the joys…" of wild abandonment! Once in a while we ventured off to play tennis. We even took time to visit the Stephen Leacock Memorial Home, in Orillia, when it officially opened that July. We learned to appreciate Leacock's ironic sense of humor uncovered in Mr. Jim Potter's grade twelve English class, even transcribing Leacock's humor by sneaking dirty underwear between the bed sheets of Wayne Getty, still another friend and Brampton High School classmate working for the **Tely.**

Stan Barrett, **Toronto Telegram** salesman rehearses his sales pitch, summer, 1959, Empire Hotel, Huntsville, Ontario.

When that summer of 1958 working for the **Tely** ended, my hope was to return "home" to Philadelphia and begin my first year of undergraduate studies at Temple University. But immigration difficulties developed and I had to wait until the second term started, January, 1959, to initiate university studies. Since Stan lived near Huttonville and since I was bunking two miles away in Meadowvale, at Uncle Lester and Aunt Lefa Prosser's farm, the two of us continued to work together that fall, landing menial jobs at Eaton's department store in downtown Toronto. Because Stan owned a 1947 Pontiac, he usually picked me up each morning and off we'd go, day in and out, to Eaton's. Eventually, we finally did locate a rooming house in east Toronto where we boarded for a month or so.

Just before the Christmas break, 1958, I received the good news: my immigration papers had arrived! So, three days before Christmas, I took a Greyhound Bus to Philadelphia, joining up with my entire family for our first family reunion in several years. When I bid Stan farewell, I did so knowing that we would likely re-connect that next summer working for the **Tely.** My first term at Temple went well. When I returned with somewhat of a swagger that June to Canada, I re-connected with Stan, along with Wayne Getty, who had left Alberta to join us in Barrie. Since all three of us had re-secured our **Tely** jobs, we three Musketeers couldn't have been happier.

Dad's Best Memories and Recollections

Stan had come from a family that never had any member go to university. He had expressed interest in going to university the previous summer and I urged him to try Temple for a year. Lo and behold, he applied, got accepted and, still laughing at the world, we drove off to Philadelphia that September, 1959, in his 1932 Chevrolet two-door coup. It was an amazing adventure for both of us. Stan worked hard, got the good feeling of what it was like to confront the academic world and certainly proved to be a very fine student, studying from an apartment he rented on Montgomery Ave., bisecting Broad St. and running just south of the Temple University inner-city campus. After working for the **Toronto Telegram** during the summer of 1960, our third consecutive summer with the **Tely**, Stan decided to go his separate way and headed off to Acadia University in Wolfville, Nova Scotia, where his girlfriend, Kaye McCaugherty, from Streetsville, and his brother Bob were planning to attend. I went my own way and hitch-hiked to the University of Alaska in Fairbanks. As a consequence, Stan and I sort of drifted apart for several years, I marrying Gayle Jenkins, 1961, in Philadelphia, Stan marrying his high school sweetheart, Kaye, several years later, although just as I was about to graduate from Temple, June, 1962, Stan astounded both Gay and me with a knock on our door, in Lansdale, just north of Philadelphia. He had hitch-hiked from Wolfville, Nova Scotia, as a surprise. This "reunion" occurred as Gay and I were about to begin our teaching careers in Ontario.

Stan continued with his studies at Acadia, graduating, 1963. The same year, he won the top student/top scholar award. He was encouraged to apply for a Rhodes Scholarship but chose instead to join Canadian University Services Overseas (CUSO) and went to Nigeria, 1963-1965, where he taught school. Following his stint in Nigeria, Stan returned to Canada, eventually graduating with an M.A. in Social Anthropology from the University of Toronto, 1968. He pursued and earned his Ph.D. from the University of Sussex, England, 1971, at which time he returned to Canada and joined the University of Guelph faculty, 1971, retiring from there as Professor of Social Anthropology, 2006.

Now Professor Emeritus, Stan has written eight academic books. His most popular volume, **Anthropology: A Student's Guide to Theory and Method,** has been used in classrooms for more than two decades. Other books such as **Is God a Racist?: the Right Wing in Canada,** and **Culture Meets Power** have helped establish Stan, the former door-to-door salesman with the **Toronto Telegram**, plus a hockey player who was the backbone of Acadia's hockey teams back in the early 1960s, and a friend who has shared his Temagami cottage with his two high school buddies for decades, has left meaningful footprints on many trails. He has been an abiding friend for sixty years. Father of Jason and Mia, grandfather of a grand-daughter born in Montreal and grandson born in Thailand, and married to his better half, Kaye, for fifty years, Stan has been much more than just an unforgotten friend.... His friendship has been a series of fond memories, reflections and recollections....

As a student at Temple University, 1959-1960, Stan Barrett crosses Montgomery Ave. in North Philadelphia on his way to classes..

During the summer of 1958, while salesmen with **The Toronto Telegram,** "Three Musketeers" rented a home outside Barrie on the road to Shanty Bay, Ontario.

Dad's Best Memories and Recollections

John Kenneth Galbraith

If corporations actively sponsor opera, the Stratford and Shaw Festivals, sporting events, the National Ballet and local symphonies, I often wondered why corporations were not approached to sponsor specialty publications. Heirloom Publishing Inc. never went after government grants to prop up its all-Canadian publication house. This was because we felt that by taking government grants we were essentially welfare recipients munching on hard-earned taxpayer money. In fact we were adamant: Heirloom would never apply for government grants to prop up its publication house. Our mandate was to promote Canada's rich, culture and history on the world stage without drawing on the taxpayer for support. At the same time we also strongly felt that corporations should be approached and given the opportunity to subscribe to pages of space in our books. We believed we could induce them to tell their own stories in either a one-page or two-page spread and join with a gamut of other committed Canadian corporations who just might like the opportunity to sponsor Heirloom's mantra to celebrate Canada. The response we got, book after book, was wonderful. To attract the corporate state into sponsoring us was, we believed, a *tour de force*. In the process of recruiting such

John Kenneth Galbraithe (1908-2006) was very proud of his Ontario roots.

sponsorship, Heirloom also lobbied notable individuals identified with the business world, either locally or internationally, to accept our invitations to write special Introductions to the exclusive chapter profiling corporate sponsors agreeing to subscribe to advertorial space in our series of books. A few of those influential business personalities who accepted our invitation to salute our corporate sponsors in our Heirloom Series were Charles Bronfman, Co-Chairman of Seagrams Company Ltd., Dr. Peter George, President, McMaster University, Murray Koffler, Founding President of Shoppers Drug Mart, Frank Stronach, founder of Magna International, North America's largest automotive parts manufacturer, Maurice Strong, former President of Power Corporation, Petro Canada, and Hydro Ontario, as well as former United Nations Under Secretary General, and Diane Francis, former Editor of *The Financial Post* and Editor-at-Large, The National Post. Harvard University Professor, John Kenneth Galbraith, was still one other personality who accepted Heirloom's Invitation to write introductory remarks. His fabulous remarks introduced the business chapter called "Partners in Growth" for **ALLEGIANCE: The Ontario Story** (1994), Volume III of the CANADA Heirloom Series.

One reason Heirloom solicited Mr. Galbraith to write this special Introduction was because this most famous economist was born in Ontario. I thought it was a natural fit for him to salute the corporations making **ALLEGIANCE** possible. So, I called him at the Littauer Centre in Cambridge, spoke to his Harvard University secretary, and asked her if the former economic advisor to presidents Franklin D. Roosevelt, Harry S. Truman, John F. Kennedy and Lyndon B. Johnson would consider participating as a "contributor" to a forthcoming book celebrating his home province's bicentennial. He returned my call within a couple of days and we spoke about his birthplace, Iona Station, in southwestern Ontario, his association with the Ontario Agricultural College, now the University of Guelph, and about the concept for our forthcoming book which he greatly enjoyed hearing about, believing that our concept to attract corporate sponsors was most innovative. He was still active as professor emeritus at Harvard and because my sons, Charlie and Scott, at the time, were attending Brown University in Providence, Rhode Island, I made tentative arrangements to meet him at Harvard knowing that I would tie in his visit with a visit to my sons. But such was not to be as he had to return unexpectedly to his Vermont home at about the time I was going to venture to Boston. So, I missed my chance to meet the iconic John Kenneth Galbraith. Nevertheless, along with his

"Introduction," he mailed me a copy of his book, **The Scotch** (1964), a small volume revealing his life in southwestern Ontario. I have kept it plus several of his letters addressed to me in my archives. They are all brief. No wonder! As the man who spent fifty years as a professor at Harvard and wrote over 1000 papers and many academic books, including **The Affluent Society** (1958) and **The New Industrial State** (1967), he just did not have much spare time for anything. It was a pleasure to talk to him, to correspond with him and to have him participate in one of Heirloom's acclaimed publications. The introductory remarks that he penned for **ALLEGIANCE** are classic Galbraith. He certainly left me with fond memories.... The memorable Mr. Galbraith passed away in Cambridge, Massachusetts, in 2008. He was ninety-seven years old.

D16 • SATURDAY, JULY 17, 1999

He has friends in high places

John Kenneth Galbraith's memoir, Name-Dropping, is a gallery of highly polished, well-cut portraits of people the Canadian-born economist has known over a life almost as long as the century.

A16 THE TORONTO STAR Friday, January 10, 1997

Last liberal lion Galbraith still roaring at age 88

Famed economist decries 'war against poor'

BY JOHN IBBITSON
SPECIAL TO THE STAR

John Kenneth Galbraith, a

Galbraith awarded Medal of Freedom

By Alex Canizares
STATES NEWS SERVICE

WASHINGTON – Harvard economist John Kenneth Galbraith, 91, was honored yesterday with the Presidential Medal of Freedom, the nation's highest civilian award.

President Clinton awarded the medal to 15 people yesterday at a ceremony at the White House. The recipients "share in common a devotion to freedom and its expansion, to being good citizens, to serving their fellow human beings," Clinton said at the ceremony. "They have added distinction, richness, depth, and freedom to American life."

The Presidential Medal of Freedom was established in 1963 under President John F. Kennedy.

Clinton hailed Galbraith, who was US ambassador to India in the Kennedy administration, for promoting social justice through economic policy and working to create a "good society."

"It's ironic that he coined the phrase 'conventional wisdom' since he spent his life challenging

'It's ironic that he coined the phrase "conventional wisdom" since he spent his life challenging it.'
PRESIDENT CLINTON

it," Clinton said.

After the ceremony, Galbraith, a professor emeritus at Harvard University, said, "The thing I've invested most of my effort in is supporting a reasonably good way of life for all Americans, including those who live below the margin of pleasant sustenance." Galbraith also said he holds in high regard his work to curb the threat of nuclear war.

George McGovern, a former senator from South Dakota and Democratic presidential candidate in 1972, received a medal for sponsoring the Food for Peace program and expanding anti-hunger initiatives. McGovern is now representative to the UN Food

John Kenneth Galbraith, a Harvard professor emeritus of economics and former US ambassador to India, receiving his award from President Clinton yesterday during a Washington ceremony.

and Agriculture Organization.

Virginia Chafee accepted an award for her late husband, Senator John Chafee of Rhode Island.

Dr. Mathilde Krim, an AIDS researcher and educator, was awarded a medal for her work for nearly 20 years to search for a cure for the disease and spread awareness. Afterward, Krim said that the recognition of the presidential medal "says that we are doing something right."

Other recipients included the Rev. Jesse Jackson, retired General Wesley K. Clark, retired Admiral William Crowe, Children's Defense Fund president Marian Wright Edelman, women's labor activist Mildred McWilliams Jeffrey, worker advocate Monsignor George G. Higgins of Washington, and Johnson & Johnson CEO and antidrug activist Jim Burke.

Also receiving the award were immigrant rights activist Cruz Reynoso of California, the Rev. Gardner Calvin Taylor of New York, Senator Daniel Patrick Moynihan of New York, and Nazi hunter Simon Wiesenthal, who was unable to attend.

Economist Galbraith ponders the issues of century

Comes home to get us to buy his ideas in book

BY ART CHAMBERLAIN
BUSINESS REPORTER

The best-known economist Canada ever produced came to

123

Dad's Best Memories and Recollections

Dr. Wilfed G. Bigelow

Dr. Wifred Godon Bigelow, (1913-2005), co-inventor of the heart pacemaker, was inducted into the Canadian Medical Hall of Fame in 1997.

I believe it happened in 1956 when my maternal grandmother, Mabel Jarvis, was in her mid-seventies. Following her medical procedure, she became a pioneer, one of the world's very first patients to receive an implanted heart pacemaker. The cardiovascular surgeon who supervised this operation was Dr. Wilfred Gordon Bigelow. I met this wonderful man for the first time in 1993, nearly forty years after my grandmother's operation. The circumstances, however, were very different. At the time of our first get-together, I was the publisher and editor-in-chief of Heirloom Publishing Inc. whereas Dr. Bigelow was the retired head of the Cardiovascular Surgery Division at the Toronto General Hospital. I had taken liberty to fax Dr. Bigelow the story that Heirloom Publishing had prepared about the medical team, including Dr. Bigelow, who had developed the original heart pacemaker in 1951.

Heirloom Publishing's decision to tell the story of the pacemaker reflected our strong feelings that this medical achievement had saved millions of lives over the years and was a tremendous all-Canadian story to include among the 125 vignettes we were preparing to celebrate in our upcoming publication, **PATHFINDERS: Canadian Tributes.** As Heirloom's story revealed, Dr. Bigelow, along with two others, Dr. John Callaghan and Jack Hopps, created a small box-sized, electrical unit that could be used to restart a patient's heart after cooling. Following its original success, the pacemaker has undergone revolutionary changes. Whereas the original heart pacemaker was the size of a 1950s shelf radio, today's pacemaker is about the size of two toonies one on top of the other.

After reading the story that Heirloom had faxed him, Dr. Bigelow telephoned Heirloom's office in Mississauga, Ontario, and invited me to visit him at his Rosedale townhouse on Castle Frank Rd., Toronto. Born, 1913, in Brandon, Manitoba, Dr. Bigelow had received his medical degree from the University of Toronto, 1938. Following his service as a Captain in the Royal Canadian Army Medical Corps during World War II, where he performed battle surgery on the front lines, and after another year of post-graduate training at Johns Hopkins University under the tutelage of Dr. Alfred Blalock, "the father of cardiac surgery", Dr. Bigelow returned, in 1947, to the Surgery Unit of the Toronto General Hospital. At the same time, he was also appointed to the Surgery Department of the University of Toronto Medical School. As I prepared to meet Dr. Bigelow, I was aware of this biographical information including the fact that Dr. Bigelow headed the Surgery Department at the Toronto General Hospital from 1959-1977.

As I arrived, Bill greeted me at his front door while waving to Ken Thomson, his world-famous neighbor, who lived across the street. We sat around Bill's kitchen table and after some small talk he informed me how much he liked the story that Heirloom had faxed him. But rather than focussing on the story, he placed emphasis on what Heirloom had been accomplishing as a publication house, indirectly revealing to me that he was more interested in Heirloom's overall vision than he was in his personal story. In other words, he believed strongly in Heirloom's mandate to celebrate a variety of stories of Canadian achievement on the world stage, and it just didn't matter if the story saluted the heart pacemaker, the discovery of insulin or Mary Pickford.... Before I left Bill, as he wanted to be called, he presented me with his recent book, **Mysterious Heparin: The Key to Open Heart Surgery** (1990), signing it off with: "To Charles Humber — I hope this story will keep you in your all-important goal to make Canadians more aware of their great heritage."

Following the publication of **PATHFINDERS**, we both made an effort to stay in contact with each other. Occasionally I would drop in to his townhouse in Rosedale for a coffee at

Dad's Best Memories and Recollections

which time he was anxious to learn of our next project and who we might be celebrating as Canadian achievers. He encouraged me to consider other doctors in subsequent Heirloom books. These included a former classmate and Harvard University professor, Dr. C. Miller Fisher, the world's authority on carotid artery disease. Another was Dr. Wilbert Joseph Keon who established the world's first cardiac institute in Ottawa. He also encouraged me not to overlook Dr. William Edward Gallie, a titanic figure in Canadian surgery as well as Dr. Bigelow's mentor. Dr. Robert Salter, an orthopedic surgeon known as "the father of continuous motion" was still another doctor whose achievements became standard procedure in the world's operating rooms. I happily took his advice and Heirloom found a way to honor these outstanding medical doctors in our next two publications, namely, **WAYFARERS** and **VISIONARIES,** two volumes which, like the preceding **PATHFINDERS,** celebrated 125 stories of all-Canadian achievement impacting the world stage.

As the years drifted by, in early 1998, Dr. Bigelow invited my colleague, Angela Dea Cappelli Clark, and me to a luncheon at Massey College. The gathering was basically a swan song affair in which Bill took time out to thank Heirloom for all of its honest endeavors to recognize the tremendous contributions that Canadian doctors have made to advance medicine. He noted that in total we had celebrated, saluted and honoured over seventy stories of Canadian medical achievement in three consecutive volumes of the CANADA Heirloom Series. He encouraged us to publish a single volume exclusively about Canada's unsurpassed role on the medical world stage. My one main regret as publisher is that Heirloom never fulfilled those words of encouragement because our lease was about to expire and we were just not able to see ourselves sustaining the journey we had made since 1984 when several of us first launched **LOYAL SHE REMAINS.** Nevertheless, Bill sent me a precious letter which ends with "You, Charles, as editor have been publishing Canadian history with open-minded conviction for twenty years. Your books offer an easily read storehouse of important knowledge."

I was in New York City in 2005 when I happened to pick up a copy of **The New York Times** and discovered a photo of Dr. Wilfred Gordon Bigelow. It was embedded in a full-page obituary with the headline "Dr. Wilfred G. Bigelow, 91, A Pioneer in Heart Surgery". Needless to say, I was very dis*heart*ened to learn of the loss of such a friend....

Left: The original heart pacemaker with a more contemporary one the size of two silver dollars.
Right: Wonderful letter addressed to Charles Humber when Dr. Bigelow was 84 years.

May 4, 1998

Mr. Charles Humber
Publisher
Heirloom Publishing Inc.
6509B Mississauga Rd.
Mississauga, Ont.
L5N 1A6

Canada Heirloom Series

Dear Charles:

A wise nation fosters national pride and love of country by not only preserving records of its past great heritage but ensuring a public awareness of these achievements. This is the essence of "greatness".

The Canadian Heirloom Series of six books, performs this function by presenting stories of world class contributions and ventures with accuracy and interest. They are skillfully illustrated and each author is uniquely qualified to properly assess a contribution in terms of the global scene.

In the last three editions: Pathfinders, Wayfarers and Visionaries emphasized our well recognized and unique position in medicine during this century.

You Charles, as editor have been publishing Canadian History with open minded conviction for twenty years. Your books offer an easily read storehouse of important knowledge.

Yours Sincerely,

Bill.

W.G. Bigelow OC, MD.

Dad's Best Memories and Recollections

Bruce and Rick Humber

The Humber family of six lived in Lawrence Park, a North Toronto neighborhood in 1981. Near the end of June that year we got into our 1976 maroon-colored Buick station wagon and steered our way to California for the entire summer. The first leg of the trip took us directly to British Columbia and eventually Victoria where I was hoping to meet up with a distant relative by the name of Bruce Humber. I did not know much about this individual other than he was a former track and field star. This fact was rudimentary. What I was hoping to learn was how my side of the family was linked to Bruce Humber's side. When we finally reached Victoria, I was able to locate Rick Humber, the only son of the famous Bruce. He told me that when he first saw me he knew I was a Humber by my ear lobes. I was not able to determine exactly why we were unable to see Rick's father but I gathered that he was not well and was somewhat debilitated. Rick and I spent a brief spell connecting in a formal way and I came away with a better understanding of the connection between our families, a link that went back to the mid-19th century at a time when two brothers migrated to Canada from the Isle of Wight, that magical island off the southern coast of England. One of these two brothers was David Hess Humber (1818-1907), my great, great grandfather, while the second brother was Henry Humber (1812-1889). Henry and his wife, Sarah, immigrated to Canada West (Ontario) in 1851, some three years after his younger brother, David, had crossed the Atlantic, 1848, with his wife, Leah, and settled in the same community of Bowmanville in Canada West. Some twelve years later, 1863, Henry and Sarah's oldest son, Maurice, and his wife, Maria Matilda Behan, and their young family of two sons made the decision to migrate to British Columbia. Arriving in Victoria, via Cape Horn, the southern tip of South America, this family would yield another three sons. One became medical doctor Arthur A. Humber, father of Bruce Humber, former track star at the University of Washington and future Olympian.

Obituary for Bruce Humber who died at 74 years, August 17, 1988, as reported in the **Times-Colonist** of Victoria, British Columbia, where he spent his days except when he represented Canada at the Berlin Olympics, 1936.

Bruce Gordon Humber, far left, takes baton from team-mate in the 4X100 relay finals at the 1936 Berlin Olympics. Jesse Owens, second right, has just handed off baton to Ralph Metcalfe. The Canadian team was in position for the silver medal behind the record-breaking American relay team, but on the final exchange, the baton was dropped and Canada failed to reach the podium.

Dad's Best Memories and Recollections

After my 1981 get-together with Rick, I developed a clearer understanding of my Humber connection in British Columbia, realizing that my father, Charles Maitland Humber (1906-1988) and Bruce Humber (1913-1988) were third cousins and that Rick and I were fourth cousins.

Twenty-five years later, 2006, Rick and I re-connected when I made a cross-Canada trip by myself, in my brand new Honda Pilot, this time distributing my latest book, **Family Sleuthing,** to relatives and various friends in each province from Ontario to British Columbia. Victoria, British Columbia, was a key stop. Not only did I re-connect with Rick but I met his wife Dianne and was invited to stay overnight in their lovely home at 3270 Norfolk Rd., two blocks away from Humber Rd., named after Rick's father, Bruce. Rick kindly spent a full day with me, showing me the City of Victoria and the remnants of brick roads and brick buildings and houses, spread about old Victoria and built by Rick's great-grandfather, Maurice Humber (1834-1902), proprietor of Humber Bricks during the last quarter of the 19th century. For instance, in 1885 this brick-maker produced a total of three million bricks. The historic building he constructed at 505-511 Pandora Street in 1884 is, today, a heritage-protected two-story structure located in Old Town. Rick also told me that somewhere in his family archives is a photo of Bruce Humber with the world famous Jesse Owens. They had raced against each other more than twenty times during their careers. On the occasion when Bruce was inducted, 1969, into the British Columbia Sports Hall of Fame and Museum, Jesse Owens was in Victoria for the occasion. What is memorable about the photo is that both Bruce and Jesse, two friends, were smoking cigarettes. A well-known story Rick told me took place during the 1936 Olympics in Berlin. Bruce ran a strong second leg of the 4 X 100 final relay. For sure, the Canadian team was heading for the silver medal. Bruce had kept up with Ralph Metcalfe, perhaps the second fastest short distance runner in the world at the time. After Bruce handed off the baton to the third runner of his relay team, Howie McPhee, everything was fine until the last exchange when Lee Orr fatally dropped the baton. The team came in fifth behind the American team, powered by Jesse Owens' first leg. The race shattered the Olympic and world records, with both the Italian and German teams taking the silver and bronze medals respectively.

There is a letter in my own archives sent to me by John Turner, Prime Minister of Canada, 1984. As a young man he was a budding track star at the time Bruce Humber coached the Victoria YMCA Flying Y Club. This was the same time Bruce Humber coached the Helsinki-bound Canadian Track and Field Olympic Team in 1952. I had asked the former Prime Minister about my distant relative, Bruce Humber, and he told me, in a follow up letter, that Bruce Humber was one of the finest gentlemen he had ever met as well as an outstanding coach. On looking back, I fondly remember Rick when we met in 1981 and re-connected in 2006 when he took me about Victoria to show me historic places, including cemeteries associated with my distant Humber connections. Had I not met up with him in 1981, I probably would never have asked The Rt. Hon. John Turner about Bruce Humber back in the late 1980s in his Toronto law firm office. But then, had I not gone out of my way to re-connect with Rick in 2006, I would not have the information I've revealed in this memorable vignette.

Former high school teacher, Rick Humber, son of Bruce Humber, has lived in Victoria, British Columbia his entire life. In 2006, Rick showed Charles J. Humber many Victoria city landmarks associated with the pioneering Humber family who migrated to B.C in the mid-19th century.

Charles W. Dunn

Havard University Professor Charles W. Dunn (1915-2006).

During the 1992-1996 years, I travelled between Toronto and Providence, Rhode Island, during the hockey season, mainly to watch twin sons Charlie and Scott play Division I hockey for the Brown University Bruins. I usually took someone to keep me company for such hard-pressed, nine-hour trips. In 1994, towards the end of the hockey season, my companion on one of those trips was Hugh P. MacMillan. A retired field archivist for the Government of Ontario, "the honourable Hugh" helped make the 500-mile trip a great deal of fun sharing wondrous stories how he sleuthed historical documents from around the globe. On our way to Brown, the man from Glengarry expressed to me that he was hoping to introduce me to one of his good friends, a Harvard University professor whose specialty was Celtic Studies. Since we had extra time between the Friday and Saturday night games, and since travelling to Harvard from Brown constituted a one-hour drive, I actually looked forward to our drive to Cambridge and to the university from where my father received his Master's degree in 1947. To my recollection, I had never heard of Professor Charles W. Dunn. Needless to say, Hugh took liberty to inform me who this gentleman was, telling me stories about an erudite born in Scotland, 1916, the son and grandson of Presbyterian ministers, and a man who usually dressed in knee socks, wore a kilt and always was perked up in a tweed jacket. After graduating from McMaster University, in Hamilton, Ontario, and Harvard University, from where he earned both his M.A. and his Ph.D. degrees in Celtic Studies, Professor Dunn became legendary at Quincy House, where he was housemaster for over twenty years, as well as an internationally renowned scholar in Celtic folk-tales.

Sure enough, when we arrived at his beautiful home at 25 Longfellow Rd., Cambridge, he chipperly took us to his expansive reading room that was lined, wall to wall, with book shelving. And, yes, he was wearing traditional Scottish gear, and poured some good Scotch whiskey in sparkling Waterford glasses without asking whether we wanted ice. He was chippy to discover I had some Scottish blood through one of my United Empire Loyalist ancestors, Captain Alexander Clark. We continuously chortled and chuckled over stories galore associated with Hugh's latest discoveries in either Glengarry County, Ontario, or from Cape Breton, Nova Scotia, early jurisdictions where pioneer Scots settled in Canada....

During our enchanting visit, dominated by Professor Dunn's wit, charm and joviality, I could not stop scanning the Harvard University professor's book collection, which I estimated was between four and five thousand volumes. After noticing one particular text book, he encouraged me to browse through his library and before long one of the first books I pulled off the shelves was **A Chaucer Reader: Selections from the Canterbury Tales**, a volume he had actually edited and published through Harcourt in the early 1950s and, ironically, one I had used as a textbook in one of my Temple University classes. It was quite amazing when he asked me what my favorite Geoffery Chaucer tale was. When I told him it was either the "Miller's Tale" or the "Merchant's Tale", he laughed out loud, saying that all earthy people love those two particular tales. He started reciting Chaucer's "Merchant's Tale," especially the part where a young Damyan is waiting in a tree for his sweetheart, May, who found a way to escape her aging husband, Januarie, and climbed the tree to become engaged with her lover. When Professor Dunn recited the Chaucerian language it was thrilling to hear his voice. He'd have made a great actor in the Richard Burton style.

When Hugh and I departed to return for Saturday night's hockey game in Providence, after enjoying an early dinner, I took liberty to give the professor a present – a copy of **ALLEGIANCE: The Ontario Story,** Volume III of the CANADA Heirloom Series which I had edited and published just the year before. He seemed thrilled to accept it as he had spent a great deal of his life in Ontario. Professor Dunn died at age ninety years in 2006. The letter he sent me shortly after my visit is very memorable and reflects the genuine interest he had in meeting people and enjoying their company.... Upon his passing, the Harvard Dean of the Faculty of Arts and Sciences, Dr. Jeremy R. Knowles, eulogized that "Charles Dunn was one of Harvard's unforgettable figures -- a truly exceptional man."

Dad's Best Memories and Recollections

Prime Minister Jean Chrétien

Heirloom Publishing was most successful in soliciting a number of well-known personalities to write introductory remarks in the various volumes we published over a twenty-year period. Canadian Prime Minister Jean Chrétien was but one of these dignitaries. In 1993, Monsieur Chrétien became Canada's twentieth Prime Minister. In 1994, the Prime Minister kindly agreed to write the special introductory message to **PATHFINDERS: Canadian Tributes,** Volume IV of the ongoing CANADA Heirloom Series. Since Prime Minister Brian Mulroney had written, in 1988, the introductory message for **CANADA From Sea Unto Sea**, volume I of this same series, it was therefore not unprecedented for the current Prime Minister's Office to accept Heirloom's solicitation. In fact, it was not at all surprising when Heirloom's offer was accepted. Nevertheless it was very pleasing.... In fact, the PMO not only supplied Heirloom with Mr. Chrétien's "Introduction" but provided a special photograph of the Prime Minister taken by world-renowned photographer, Jean Marc Carisse, who had taken official photographs of every Prime Minister since the Rt. Hon. John George Diefenbaker, Canada's thirteenth Prime Minister, as well as each United States President since Gerald Ford.

PM Jean Chrétien welcomes Charles J. Humber to Parliament Hill, 1995.

In early 1995, following the publication of **PATHFINDERS** late in 1994, arrangements were made for me, as both the editor and the publisher, to make a special presentation of this publication to Prime Minister Chrétien in his Parliament Hill office. The date was arranged for a Monday in January, 1995. Because I was in Providence, Rhode Island where Charlie and Scott, my twin sons, were playing home-game hockey that weekend for Brown University, I planned to drive, with my daughter Kristy, from Rhode Island, on the Sunday night following their weekend hockey games. We hit the road rather late that Sunday evening and struggled through some heavy snow until we got to the other side of Albany, New York. We checked into a motel near midnight. Realizing that the snow was not going to stop, and realizing that the drive to Ottawa was going to be at least seven more hours, we had to get up early the next morning, 5:00 a.m. to be precise. The morning snow was everywhere. We finally reached Montreal about 10:30 a.m. but still had to make good time, in heavy snow, for my 2:00 p.m. appointment in Ottawa. Well, we managed to arrive just in time. We drove right to the front door of the Centre Block of the Parliament Buildings. We parked the car and I told Kristy to pick me up in one hour at the same spot. Entering the magnificent Peace Tower doorway, I wound my way up the steps to the Prime Minister's second floor office. I was just in time for my appointment and was ushered into the inner sanctum of the Prime Minister's Office. Mr. Chrétien was sitting at his desk and he rose as I entered, reaching out to me with his outstretched hand. I had a special encased leather-bound edition of **PATHFINDERS** under my arm and when he first saw it he appeared to be quite overcome. One of the first things he noticed about the book was the story of Dr. Norman Bethune. He wanted me to know that when he was in the Pierre Elliott Trudeau Cabinet he arranged for the funding of the Bethune Memorial House in Gravenhurst, Ontario. He made an effort to stress this point. He appeared to be much more animated about Bethune than he was about his own Introduction. I believe he was quite thrilled with the overall production, even though there was no French version. When he went on his trade mission to China later that year, **PATHFINDERS** was used as one of the official Canadian gifts, not so much because Canada's Prime Minister had written the Intoduction but because the Chinese greatly admire Norman Bethune to this day. With the story of this legendary doctor highlighted in **PATHFINDERS**, the Prime Minister was most happy to use this volume as a "cultural ambassador" in China. When Kristy and I departed Ottawa later that afternoon, I do not know if she realized just how much this trip meant to Heirloom. But the Canadian government, overall, was very supportive of **PATHFINDERS,** and I believe that a great part of that success was because the Prime Minister believed in what we were doing as a small, all-Canadian publication house with one mandate, namely, to generate heritage awareness and promote Canada's rich culture, history and heritage on the world stage. **PATHFINDERS: Canadian Tributes,** for sure, did just that....

Dad's Best Memories and Recollections

Bill McNeil

Over the years I've had the pleasure to know a number of popular radio and/or television personalities. The first coming to mind is Harry Boyle, who had been the Chairman of the Canadian Radio-Television and Communications Commission (CRTC), 1975-1977, before I met him in 1985. The Czar of Canadian Air Waves, the impish Harry wrote a chapter called "This History of Canadian Broadcasting" in **CANADA: From Sea Unto Sea,** a publication I edited and published in 1986 and which was revised in 1988 as Volume I of the CANADA Heirloom Series. A second personality who comes to mind is Robert Hurst, one of my former high school students back in the 1960s at Thomas L. Kennedy Secondary School, Cooksville, now part of the City of Mississauga. Bob rose up through the ranks of CTV, Canada's most listened to television station, to become its president, 2002-2010. **TV Guide,** in 2007, named Bob "the most powerful person in Canadian television news." The late John Fisher, perhaps better known as "Mr. Canada", the third personality in this category, was a significant mentor and a wonderful friend who encouraged me to follow in his footsteps before he died. But it was Bill McNeil, one of John Fisher's best friends, who proved to be one of the most likeable, charming and most sincere men I ever met in the ever-changing world of communications. Born, 1924, in Glace Bay, Cape Breton, Bill was gracious, sincerely charming, even when smoking cigarettes, and his warm baritone voice was mellifluous whenever he spoke. My memories of Bill McNeil are fond, reflective and indelible....

Bill worked the coal pits in Sydney, Nova Scotia, for eight years before getting his first job facing a CBC microphone in Sydney. Eventually he was made moderator of **Assignment**, 1956-1971, one of the most listened to coast-to-coast radio programs throughout the 1950s and 1960s. This was followed by hosting or co-hosting CBC's weekend radio broadcasts called **Fresh Air** or **Voice of the Pioneer**. Over the years he interviewed more than 600 pioneers, people who homesteaded the Canadian prairies, or went to the various gold rushes in the Yukon and northern Ontario, or were veterans of the two World Wars, or survived the Great Depression of the 1930s. When he retired from the CBC in 1992, after serving the Canadian government-sponsored CBC empire for forty years, his last two broadcasts were held live in a packed Roy Thomson Hall, downtown Toronto, where people from across Canada came to salute one of the most beloved voices in Canadian radio programming ....

When his good friend, John Fisher, died, 1981, both Bill McNeil and I became directors of the John Fisher Society, a non-profit organization formed to perpetuate and promote John's legacy. This is when I first met Bill. We became fast friends and frequently met for lunches to discuss how to sustain John's love affair with Canada, especially after I became President of the Society. He also wrote chapters for the CANADA Heirloom Series. In the meantime Bill interviewed me multiple times on his coast-to-coast radio programs, discussing the John Fisher Society and how listeners could participate in keeping Canada's 1967 Centennial Commissioner's legacy alive. When **CANADA From Sea Unto Sea** was published, I took liberty to dedicate this volume to John Fisher while Bill McNeil published his own book entitled **John Fisher.** I treasure the signed copy he gave to me.

Over many coffees, Bill educated me how radio programming had changed since the 1930s. He reminded me that people used to sit in their living rooms and listen to the radio while knitting or crocheting or reading the evening newspaper. Radios, he reminded me, were pieces of polished furniture. People enjoyed watching their radio as if it were a live person. They listened hour after hour to radio programs, especially the news. I told him how my own mother and father used to listen to their bee-hive shaped radio in their dimly lit living room in Hagersville, all the while keeping

Dad's Best Memories and Recollections

their eyes on the lighted dial. Bill reminded me that during World War II, reports coming from the "front" were riveting. Listening to the CBC during the Second World War was often a harrowing experience as uneasy listeners heard the guttural voice of Adolf Hitler. These radio broadcasts generated much fear in North Americans and paved the way for millions of people to buy War Bonds. Bill reminded me that the old days of radio programming were the golden years. This was a time when broadcasters saw themselves as humble guests in people's homes. That has all changed today because broadcasters, for the most part, at least according to Bill, only see themselves as hosting listeners. They are not averse to swearing over the airwaves because they have somehow earned their right to express themselves as they see fit. They thrive on being offensive, choosing controversial topics, not because they generate ratings but because they feel entitled to discuss whatever they want. Bill felt that radio broadcasting had degenerated. He longed for the good old days when dignity and reverence ruled the day and when there was conversation between radio hosts and their listening audience.

Bill passed away in 2003 of kidney failure. When he died, a small part of Canada also passed away....

February. 27, 1986: Bill McNeil, Elward Burnside, Len Woolsely, George Fisher, Lou Cahill, Charlie Humber, President, John Fisher Society, John White, John Fisher Jr. The John Fisher Society donated $10,000.00 to the Ontario Heritage Centre back in the 1990s to perpetuate the name of "Mr. Canada" in the newly refurbished building at 10 Adelaide Street East, Toronto. The Hon. John White, Chairman, accepted the donation from the President.

Wayne Getty

A close friend for nearly sixty years, Wayne Getty enjoys a moment of reflection at the Humber cottage in MacTier.

I was twenty when I returned to high school in 1956. One of the first students I befriended was Wayne Getty, born in India, 1940. In the same class was Stan Barrett. As "Musketeers," the three of us have persevered as close friends for nearly sixty years. As the rebellious sons of Baptist ministers, Wayne and I often met up after school at Burrow's Billiards in downtown Brampton, Ontario. One day while playing snooker, Wayne casually asked if my father was known for punning and further inquired if my father's name was "Charlie" implying that both fathers were likely classmates at McMaster University during the Great Depression. Our friendship quickly bonded, especially after Wayne invited me to his house for a family rendezvous. Over dinner, Wayne's father, Orville, fondly recalled my father as a student as did Wayne's mother, Bertha. Wayne's four younger siblings, Norville, Ronald and Ian, plus their sister, Margaret, were each born as the children of missionaries in Coonoor located in south-central India where Wayne was enrolled in the Breeks Memorial School, the Christian school where Lord Thomas Macaulay coined the syllabi for India's educational system. Macaulay's 1835 mandate abolished Sanskrit and the Persian language, enacting English as the instructive language for all colonial-ruled schools in India.

Wayne did not complete his grade twelve year at Brampton District High School, partially as the result of adjusting to a worldly environment. Instead, he entered a work force which, ironically, seduced him further into his ever-expanding secular world. During this time, the two of us spent many hours in Toronto's various downtown theatres watching such iconic movies as **Bridge on the River Kwai** and **Bus Stop**. We also snuck into Maple Leaf Gardens, April, 2, 1957, to catch Elvis Presley perform such Billboard hits as "Heartbreak Hotel" and "Hound Dog." When Wayne's parents moved to Alberta, 1958, Wayne had been discovering an ever-expanding, free-thinking world for eighteen months by working as a bankteller in downtown Toronto and as an orderly at the Brampton Memorial Hospital. That same summer, he joined his two Musketeer friends, all three of us signing up as salesmen with the **Toronto Telegram**. All the while, Wayne's parents beseeched their oldest to complete high school. When the 1958 summer ended, Wayne reluctantly migrated to Alberta and enrolled at Three Hills Bible School, north of Lethbridge. Here Wayne endured difficulties adjusting to a system that implored students to heed the call of Christian service. Such missionary-minded fundamentalism with authoritative commitment to devotional service was just too formidable for Wayne to accept, all of which activated him, once again, to stray from school. After more struggles and rebellion, the uncompliant Wayne finally graduated from high school in Picture Butte near Lethbridge. By 1964, Wayne had decisively completed his B.A. degree in Sociology from University of Calgary.

Ever since I first met Wayne, his most endearing quality has been his compassion, a homage he likely reaped from his missionary parents. Such consideration for others moulded him into a controversial mouthpiece for Canada's First Nation peoples. Upon completing his undergraduate degree, Wayne was first employed by the Alberta Government to work with the Indian Bands of Rocky Mountain House. From 1967-1970, his intense and strident work with First Nation peoples aggravated the local judge, the RCMP, the local police and local citizens for his relentless and passionate work, leading to Wayne's termination by the Government. After completing his M.A., 1971, Wayne was, 1971-1975, employed by the Indian Band at Morley, a Reserve in the Alberta foothills.

During the three years Wayne worked for the Alberta Government, he was fired three times for insubordination. Ironically, after each termination, a different Department of the same government rehired him. Admittedly, Wayne rebelliously refused to implement certain government policies. He did so because he adamantly knew he was right and the government wrong. In every case, the policy was changed after Wayne's dismissal because the agency realized Wayne had been right. To this day, Wayne believes his crowning achievement while working for this Government was assisting aboriginal women to retain or regain their Indian Status after marrying non-Indians.

In 1975, after completing his M.S.W., Wayne accepted a teaching position at Olds College north of Calgary. He found still another position in Yorkton, Saskatchewan, 1987, as Director of Indian Services. Before moving on to the Ottawa suburb of Orleans, 1989, he had accepted employment with the Dept. of Fisheries and Oceans, becoming the Federal Government's Claims Negotiator on all aspects of Federal Fisheries for the new Comprehensive Claims under negotiation with Indian Bands across Canada who had never signed "Treaties." After being professionally diagnosed as disabled, 1997, a weary Wayne retired. Today, upon reflection, Wayne claims his greatest achievement in Ottawa was ensuring that aboriginal groups got a just and rightful share of coastal fisheries. He also made certain that the Nunavut peoples had the right to kill one whale per year for food, social or ceremonial purposes. Wayne claims that such controversial legislation was "just and necessary."

Dad's Best Memories and Recollections

Over the years, several women have shared their lives with Wayne. These include Myrna, who married Wayne in 1963. Their three children are Wayne Jr., born, 1964, Michael, born, 1967, and Leah, born, 1968. Wayne Jr. and Leah live today in Calgary while Michael lives in Utah as an internationally noted paleontologist. Following his divorce from Myrna in 1980, Wayne's relationship with Elaine Rollinmud on the Stoney Indian reservation led to the birth of Fawn in 1982. Had they married, Elaine would have lost her Indian Status by marrying a non-Indian. After Fawn's aboriginal mother passed away, Wayne met Roognapha (Roong) Jaroensok in Thailand, and soon thereafter brought her to Canada. After their marriage, 1983, Fawn became an integral part of Wayne's expanding family. Christopher was born, 1984, and Sabrina, 1988. As well, there are two step-siblings: Lily, Roong's daughter from her first marriage, and Nuning, Roong's niece. Both were born in Thailand, immigrated to Canada and were legally adopted by Wayne whose compassion easily embraced his growing family.

Today, Wayne's eight children have each been educated and have become productive citizens. His children are good friends with each other, forming a close-knit extended family. Wayne visits each of his children at least once a year, including Nuning, a professional engineer living in Arizona. Several children, including Wayne's estranged wife, Roong, are involved in the proprietorship of three wonderful Thai restaurants in the Ottawa area. One of these restaurants, located in Hull, Quebec, opposite The Museum of Civilization, called **Papaye Verte**, is owned by Lily and her husband, Vince Bobyan, and managed by Wayne's youngest daughter, the delightful Sabrina. It offers the finest Thai food in the Ottawa area and has become a mecca for tourists and federal bureaucrats.

Though Wayne has lived, over the years, in faraway places (he currently lives with partner, Mai, six months each year in Rayong Province, Thailand), the two of us have remained very close, and not just via the internet. For instance, Gay and I with our two daughters, Kristy and Karyn, visited Wayne and Myrna in 1964 in Calgary.

In 1981 when we travelled across Canada to California we came as a family of six and visited Wayne in Calgary. Wayne and Myrna also visited us in Madison, Wisconsin, 1967, when I was a graduate student at the University of Wisconsin. At the time I hitch-hiked to Alaska, 1960, I stopped for a couple of days in Lethbridge visiting the entire Getty family. Wayne and Roong also came to daughter Kristy and Erik's wedding in Mississauga, 1989. Wayne, with various family members, has visited many times our family cottage in Muskoka. Over the years Wayne was enticed by me to write chapters and provide illustrations in the seven-volume Canada Heirloom Series that Heirloom published from 1986-2000. One chapter in **Canada's Native Peoples** (1989) was named "Indians of the N.W.T., the Yukon the British Columbia Interior." Several times, Wayne, with his head shaved or with a massive beard and a head of hair to stuff a pillow, has trekked with me to Lake Temagami in northern Ontario to visit Stan and Kaye's cottage on Rabbit Lake. One time Wayne even met me in Kingston, Ontario. We drove through snow, 1995, to upper New York State to watch my twin sons, Charlie and Scott, students at Brown University, play varsity hockey against both Clarkson and St. Lawrence universities. Staying in contact with each other over all these years, in spite of vast distances, suggest that much more than friendship, loyalty, compatibility and compliance have bonded us. Even though our political leanings are quite opposite, we are kindred spirits with effortless passion. We have generated happy memories of each other that we will take like torches to our graves.

Below: Wayne Getty admires his close friend's first paycheck as a salesman with the **Toronto Telegram,** July, 1958.

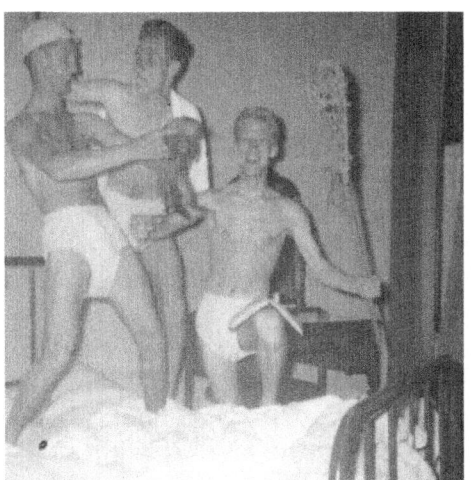

"Three Musketeers" act up in their bedroom suite at the Orillia Hotel, summer, 1958, after cashing in their paychecks. Left to right: Stan Barrett, Wayne Getty, Charlie Humber.

Below: Wayne Getty from Alberta, on his cross-Canada trip, from Calgary, visits friend Charlie Humber in Etobicoke, 1970.

Dad's Best Memories and Recollections

Fields Corner Reunions in MacTier, 2009 and 2010

After more than sixty years, three buddies from my teenage years, all in their seventies, drove, in 2009, from Boston to the historic railway town of MacTier, two hours north of Toronto, where my family cottage overlooks 500 feet of Stewart Lake frontage. Donnie Gillis, Earl Boyd and Salvatore Sansone came in Donnie's new GMC Savanna Conversion Van and would stay at the post-and-beam summer home for five days. Reminiscing about the old days, my three hellhound friends enjoyed themselves so much that they returned the next year for another five days. Those two gatherings provided a reflective time for us, giving each of us a collective opportunity to recall our post-World War II years together, to remember old girlfriends, to feast on foods and recall former coffee shops and restaurants like the Quality, to remember Ma John's Pool Hall or the Lucky Strike Bowling Alley, or Mallows Café, to watch gangster movies like we used to at the old Fields Corner or Dorchester Theatres, and to tell stories about crime figures we knew and mobsters we didn't care to know like Whitey Bulger, Joe Barboza, Trigger Burke, Steve Flemmi, the Bennett brothers and Specs O'Keefe. Each of their ominous shadows stretched precariously across our Dorchester neighborhood.

Donnie was born, June 15, 1936, at Boston City Hospital. Growing up in Dorchester, he had three brothers and two sisters raised by parents who themselves were born in Cape Breton, Nova Scotia, an area in Canada mainly settled by Scottish Highlanders in the late 18th and early 19th centuries. Donnie's father, Angus Leo, was born in Judique, Inverness County, and Christine MacNeil, his mother, was born in St. Rose, Inverness County. Both could trace their family roots to Scotland which was emotionally abandoned by their ancestors in 1801. Ever since I can remember, Donnie always talked about his family's roots in Cape Breton. Donnie's parents met during the Great Depression and were married, 1933, in Boston, where they raised their six children, mainly in Savin Hill and Fields Corner. Donnie went as far as grade eight at the Grover Cleveland School on Charles Street, Fields Corner, where he got to know "Tootsie" Wahlberg and his brother, Don, the latter becoming the father of both Donnie and Mark Wahlberg of Hollywood fame. Donnie Gillis was one of my close friends during the late-1940s to the mid-1950s before he joined the Army and served with the 82nd Airborne Division. Married fifty-five years in 2015, Donnie and Loraine raised five children in Hull who are all university educated. Donnie and Loraine visited **Pine Vista** in 2006.

Left to right: Donnie Gillis, Earl Boyd, local MacTier plumber, Paul Ignani, and Salvy Sansone, at **Pine Vista**, MacTier, 2010. Three old buddies introduce a new buddy to the ways of post-World War II Boston.

Earl Boyd, born, November 14, 1935, was one of the biggest babies ever born in Dorchester, weighing close to 14 pounds. Born in Boston, like Donnie, Earl traced his ancestry to Scotland. But unlike Donnie, Earl's ancestors were Scottish Lowlanders. They came from Kilmarnock, birth-place of Johnnie Walker Whiskey. It is also where the famous Kilmarnock Castle was established in 1316 A.D. by Robert Boyd, an Earl Boyd ancestor, whose land was given to the established Boyd family by Robert of Bruce. This oral history came down through Earl's grandfather, Charles Boyd, who migrated from North Ireland to Maine in the 19th century. For the most part, Earl passed this information on to me while up at the cottage. He was examining a **National Geographic World Atlas** found on one of the coffee tables. While using a magnifying glass to study a detailed map of Scotland, he told me his fascinating family history. Throughout all those tumultuous years when Earl and I branded our friendships with guys like Billy Gallant, Jackie Flaherty and Paul McDonnell, I had the

Dad's Best Memories and Recollections

misconception that Earl was Irish, not Scottish!

    Salvy, born 1937, was the son of Giovanni Sansone who passed through Ellis Island, New York City, from Bari, Italy, in 1919. Bari is located on the Adriatic Sea near the southern tip of Italy. This is where Pope Benedict XIII was born. Ten years older than his wife, after Giovanni married Josephine DiPalma, also from Bari, they raised eight children (she had seventeen pregnancies) of which Salvy was the second youngest of this family. Raised mainly on Gibson Street in Fields Corner, Salvy became a licenced plumber and a Massachusetts Plumbing Investigator, 1994-2008. He also taught night school classes in Plumbing for thirty years. Good-natured and likeable, Salvy was the Rocky Marciano of our gang. One never got mad at him because of his infectious smile. But if he decided that you should be taught a lesson, you might wake up the next day wondering what hit you.

    Today it is rare for anyone to stay in close contact with old friends following their teenage years. We grow up, get married, become parents, move away, get new friends and interests, and fade into old age. For some reason, the guys I grew up with have remained in close contact with each other. Perhaps it is because we are survivors.... And the guys I'm referring to are not just Donnie, Earl and Salvy, but so many others such as Ralphy Minichiello, Billy Barry in Tampa Bay, Pinky Peacock in Phoenix, Arizona, Allan Gillis, Donnie's younger brother, Ronnie Barron, Red Malone, Paul Labbe and twins Franny and Joe Fitzgerald, Jackie and Tommy Flaherty, and Patty O'Brien.

    Recalling the heavy footprints we left behind, we now realize that someday we will depart this life to re-group in the next life bearing torches for each other.... The two summers of 2009 and 2010 have made those torches burn brighter ....

Below: Getting ready to return to Boston, Salvy Sansone, Earl Boyd, Donnie Gillis, waving goodbye to MacTier, 2009. All guns were packed away.

Top right: Left to right: Earl Boyd, Salvy Sansone, Donnie Gillis and Charlie Humber ready to order lunch at Severn Falls Riverside Restaurant, located on the Trent-Severn Waterway, 2009, just south of MacTier.

Bottom right: Following the two reunions in MacTier, Ontario, the old Fields Corner Gang reunited, October, 2010, Twcksbury, Massachusetts: left to right are Billy Barry (from Tampa, Florida), Al Gillis, Paul Labbe, Ralphie Minichiello, Salvy Sansone, Earl Boyd (all from Massachusetts) and Charlie Humber (from Canada). Missing is Donnie Gillis, who took the picture. Note the Ontario licence plate!

Dad's Best Memories and Recollections

BATTLE OF ORISKANY AUGUST 6, 1777

Unless one served in the United States Navy aboard the U.S.S. **Oriskany** or comes from Upper New York State, the name Oriskany probably means very little. But historians easily argue that a key turning point of the American Revolution took place, August 6, 1777, at the Battle of Oriskany. Advocates for both sides of the famous battle have claimed victory over the years. And there is no question the outcome would have been far more precise had the Loyalist militia, instead of retreating after decimating General Nicholas Herkimer's revolutionary infantry, had forged onwards and taken Fort Stanwix and assumed unquestionable control of the Mohawk Valley. But circumstances were such that the King's Royal Regiment of New York, in addition to Col. John Butler's forces and the Mohawk Indians, led by Chief Joseph Brant, all retreated even though Gen. Herkimer had been mortally wounded and his brigade of 800 revolutionary soldiers decimated by half. This paved the way for the Continental militia to gain an upper hand on the front lines and paved the way for British General John Burgoyne and his Loyalist militia, which included Jessup's Rangers, to surrender two months later at Saratoga, October 17, 1777. The defeat of General Burgoyne and his Loyalist forces at Saratoga ensured that New England was secured by the revolutionaries and foreshadowed the eventual defeat of Great Britain and Loyalist forces at Yorktown, Virginia, October 19, 1781.

Over the years, the small town of Oriskany, just outside Utica, New York, has either held celebrations or has been commemorated. The Oriskany Battle Field Monument, at 85 feet, was dedicated in 1884. More than 6000 people gathered to glorify this shrine, a monument saluting the "bloodiest battle of the American Revolution." They came by wagons, canal steamboats and carriages. The United States Postal Service has also recognized the Battle of Oriskany with stamps in both 1927 and 1977. Moreover, Oriskany is the principal setting of the 1939 movie **Drums along the Mohawk,** a movie that suggests "America was born at Oriskany."

In the second year of my term as National President of the United Empire Loyalists' Association of Canada, I was invited by the Central New York State Parks, Recreation and Historic Preservation Committee to participate in the 100th anniversary of the erection of the Oriskany Monument. I indicated it would be my pleasure to drive from Toronto to attend such a ceremony and wondered if my twin sons, Charlie and Scott, could participate in the forthcoming ceremonies August 6, 1983. Since my nine-year old sons' great-grandfather, many times over, Nicholas Amey, had fought with the Jessup's Rangers under Gen. Burgoyne, I felt it would be an educational experience for them, dressed up in period costume, to participate in such a celebration. In that they were the living descendants of those U.E. Loyalists from the Mohawk Valley who resettled in Canada after the Treaty of Paris, September 3, 1783, I felt their participation was appropriate. My suggestion was applauded. We consequently drove from Toronto, arriving at Oriskany on August 6, 1983. The three of us participated in a very enthusiastic memorial service. While my twin sons raised the British flag on the grounds of the Oriskany monument, I knew they were participating in the experience of a lifetime. It is certainly one of my all-time fondest memories.

Twins, Scott and Charlie Humber dressed in reproduction Loyalist outfits, prepare to hoist the Loyalist flag at Oriskany, New York, August 6, 1983. Invited to participate in the ceremonies honouring the one hundreth anniversary of the building of the 85-foot high monument at Oriskany, the not-quite ten year-old twin sons of Dominion President Charles J. Humber are standing on the very battleground where two of their loyalist forefathers fought more than 200 years ago.

Dad's Best Memories and Recollections

Above: United States postage stamp commemorates General Nicholas Herkimer who died at Battle of Oriskany, Auust 16, 1777.

Right: Letter sent to Charles J. Humber, President, United Empire Loyalist Association of Canada, following August 6, 1983 ceremonies at Oriskany, New York.

Below: Left to right standing in front of the 85-foot tall Oriskany monument, August 6, 1983: Col. Joseph Reynolds, Scott Humber, Charles J. Humber, President UELAC, Major Walter Cookenham, Chairman of the Celebration Events and Charles Humber, Jr.

OFFICE OF PARKS AND RECREATION · CENTRAL REGION Jamesville, New York 13078 315-492-1756

Orin Lehman — Commissioner
Charles T. Mitchell — Regional Manager
Laurence D. Martel — Regional Chairman

President Charles Humber
Master Scott Nicholas Humber
Master Charles William Humber
United Empire Loyalists
Dominion Headquarters
23 Prince Arthur Avenue
Toronto, Canada M5R-1D2

On behalf of the Central New York State Parks, Recreation and Historic Preservation Commission, I want to personally thank you for attending our Centennial Celebrations and adding so much to the day's activities. The raising and lowering of the flag, the friendly remarks, and the colorful presentations added so much and was enjoyed by all who were here.

I am enclosing copies of the photos that were in the newspapers. The addresses you requested are as follows: Mr. Walter Cookenham, College Hill Road, Clinton, New York 13323 and Mr. (Colonel) Joseph D. Reynolds, Commandant, 9 Third Street, Medford, MA 02155.

Sincerely,

Roger Myers
Historic Site Assistant
Oriskany Battlefield/
Steuben Memorial

Above: Flintlock mechanism belonging to the gun of Nicholas Amey who fought at the battle of Saratoga, October 17, 1777. The flintlock has remained in the family for at least 235 years.

Dad's Best Memories and Recollections

Calvin Katz

I've known Calvin Katz ever since I joined The Toronto Postcard Club back in the early 1980s. I was not an original member of this club which in 2015, after thirty-four years, is one of North America's largest postcard clubs catering to the collecting whims of deltiologists. These vintage postcard collectors pursue everything from Santa Claus cards, to early photo cards of main streets in villages and various towns, from map cards, to cards illustrating trains, trans-Atlantic boats, cats, post offices, fire stations, even patriotic cards or specialty cards celebrating July 4, Easter, Thanksgiving or, in general, everything and just about anything. I've even met people who collect cards illustrating marbles, rabbis, airplanes, mountain scenery in addition to motels, Route 66 cards, and the San Francisco earthquake. Calvin was a charter member of the Toronto Postcard Club. His specialty has been collecting photographic postcards depicting vintage Toronto scenes (1900-1920). I noticed immediately in my early association with Calvin that he was very knowledgeable, that he possessed a discriminating eye and keenly understood the merits of bargaining. He was as good as anyone I had ever met in making transactions in the antique trade at all levels. Within months of knowing him, Calvin was coming to my North Toronto home in Lawrence Park where we would trade cards and share our collections into the wee hours of the night. We developed a unique friendship with a common denominator of respect, camaraderie, and the appreciation that we both had a good eye for quality.... Today, we are very good friends sharing visitations up in Muskoka where we both have owned cottages.

After graduating from high school, Calvin gained admittance to the University of Toronto but higher education did not suit him. Neither did Teacher's College which he also tried out. After marrying his teenage sweetheart, Pam Cherner, 1969, Calvin obtained a taxi licence and has owned his taxi business now some forty-five years even though he no longer drives his cab but leases it out. Born in 1948, he was originally going to be called Kalman but somehow Calvin became his name, a very interesting given name for a young boy whose prevalent connections were with synagogues, not churches. In order to support his growing family of

Postcard members get together. **Best in Show** was awarded to Charles Humber, middle, February 23, 1992. Calvin Katz, far right and Brent Timmins, far left, are congratulating the two-time winner.

Dad's Best Memories and Recollections

four children, Calvin has dabbled in antiques, especially ephemeral material, more particularly, postcards. He also plays poker once a week and tells me that I should never play against him, principally, because I'd lose – every time! I think I believe him. Today, Calvin is an eBay entrepreneur and has acquired a high rating in the trade. After some fifteen years of transactions, Calvin has had over 32,000 sales.

One evening, about 1985, Calvin and Pam were visiting Gay and me at our home. I had a particular card he had come to purchase and after the transaction, Calvin and Pam left to return home. What happened following their departure was reported in the club's publication that the Toronto Postcard Club produces four times a year. I've reproduced it as is:

MY MOST INTERESTING EXPERIENCE

I'm sure that every one of you has had an interesting, out-of-the-ordinary-experience because of collecting postcards. This one happens to be mine.

First, permit me to share a bit of background. About ten years ago, I was just starting to get really involved in researching my postcards. One of my favorite pastimes was to verify the location of unidentified postcards.

This was an unsettling time in Toronto. It was a sultry summer. A few young girls had been murdered, and a 22-year old nanny was missing.

After working hard all day (I'm a full-time taxi driver), I found it hard to relax or sleep, so I decided to indulge in something useful: trading post cards. My wife, Pam, decided to accompany me, and off to my friend, Charlie Humber's we went.

Charlie had a photo card which he professed to be of a store on Geary Avenue, a street in central west Toronto. The only trouble was that there was no caption on the postcard signifying the exact location of the setting.

After a little, good-natured haggling, the trade was made. It was time to go home. It was still fairly early and Pam and I didn't really feel like trying to sleep in the sweltering heat. Then the idea occurred to me. Why not drive down to Geary Avenue and see if we could verify the location on the card.

Geary is a small street running into a dead end on a service station parking lot. We started at the beginning and drove right along the whole street, with no sign of the store. Determined as I was, we pulled right into the service station lot.

Remember, I said some girls had been murdered and one was missing. Well, sitting on this lot were five police cars. By this time it was one o'clock in the morning. As we turned to leave, they pulled out in hot pursuit, with their lights flashing and sirens blaring. They must have thought that my wife was the missing girl, and that I had pulled into the lot with some evil thought in mind. They cut me off, and with guns drawn, demanded that I leave my car. They then asked me what I was doing there at that time of the night. Imagine my embarrassment when I told them I was researching postcards.

When I was finally able to convince them I was telling them the truth, they laughed, and one of the officers, who had been servicing that area for over twenty years, was even able to show me where the store had been.

We left for home thinking that postcard collecting almost had me arrested for kidnapping and murder. And some people say that postcard collecting is a dull hobby.

I've always maintained that post card collecting is an enthralling hobby. As I understand, this tickling inclination to collect has replaced both stamp and coin collecting as a passion with researching one's family tree the only hobby challenging postcard collecting as the *numero uno* hobby. Today, Calvin still collects postcards. In addition to helping his son Jason run a Domino's Pizza franchise in Dundas, near Hamilton, he also posts "stuff" on eBay for clients, including me. Together we enjoy watching people from around the world purchase our stuff that we once treasured.

Two War Memorial Dedications

The toll of American servicemen who sacrificed their lives during World War II exceeds 400,000. Shortly after this global conflict, war memorials commemorated the fallen across the United States. They honored those who had sacrificed their lives to protect our freedoms. Plaques were affixed to buildings, landmarks were named after heroes, books were dedicated to the brave, films honored the courageous, and awards were given out commemorating so many who gave their lives. American Legions all across the United States erected statues. Not to be forgotten, city and town squares were named after servicemen who did not return home. Two particular Boston squares were given recognition in my Dorchester/Roxbury neighborhood when I was growing up in post-World War II America. I did not attend these dedication services although I used to walk in their shadows almost on a daily basis. But it was only recently that I discovered the relevance of their existence in one of my father's scrapbooks. They were revealed in newspaper clippings and acknowledged the participation of a Baptist minister, who was my father, the Rev. Charles M. Humber, at these memorial services.

The first of these squares is located at the corner of Dudley Street and Howard Avenue, two blocks from where my father's church, Bethany Baptist Church, was located on West Cottage Street. It is called the **William M. Atkinson Square** and memorializes a young man who lost his life during World War II while serving aboard the **U.S.S. Franklin**. His aircraft carrier was crippled eighty miles off the coast of Japan, March 19, 1945, by a Japanese air attack that caused the death of over 800 American sailors.

The **U.S.S. Franklin** was the most heavily damaged U.S. carrier to survive World War II. It had served at such places as Iwo Jima, Guam and Manila Bay and survived numerous kamikaze attacks. Actual footage from the devastating attack that killed William Atkinson is included in the film **Task Force** (1949) starring Gary Cooper. My father gave the prayer dedicating the square to this American hero, Sunday, May 20, 1951.

Rev. Charles M. Humber, at the microphone, gave the prayer at the Dedication Service for the William M. Atkinson Square located at the corner of Dudley Street and Howard Avenue, Dorchester, Massachusetts, May 20, 1951.

Dad's Best Memories and Recollections

Roxbury Citizen

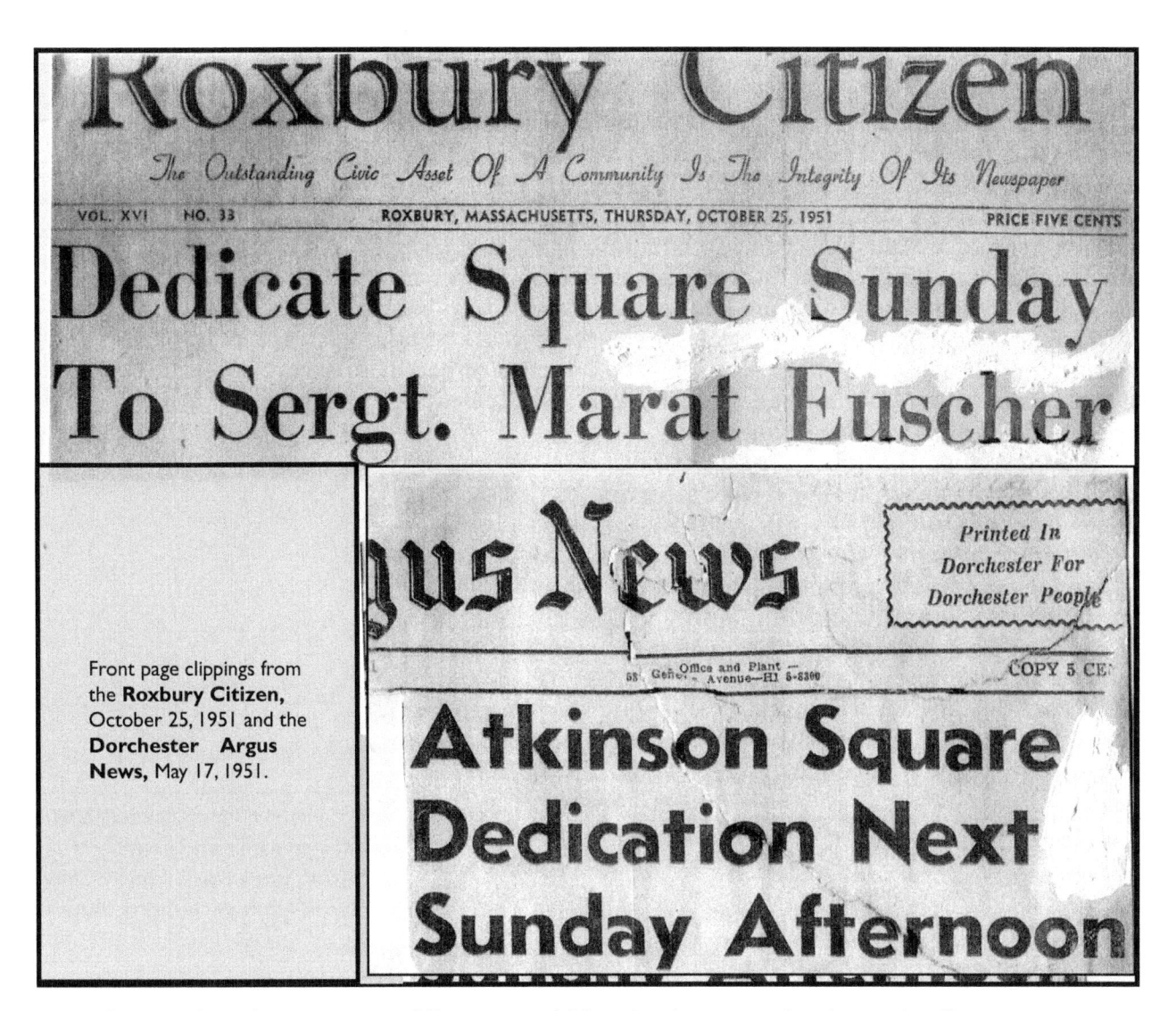

The Outstanding Civic Asset Of A Community Is The Integrity Of Its Newspaper

VOL. XVI   NO. 33   ROXBURY, MASSACHUSETTS, THURSDAY, OCTOBER 25, 1951   PRICE FIVE CENTS

Dedicate Square Sunday To Sergt. Marat Euscher

...gus News

Printed In Dorchester For Dorchester People

Office and Plant — 55 Gene... Avenue—HI 5-8300   COPY 5 CE...

Atkinson Square Dedication Next Sunday Afternoon

Front page clippings from the **Roxbury Citizen**, October 25, 1951 and the **Dorchester Argus News**, May 17, 1951.

Located at the junction of Dennis and Moreland streets, Roxbury, the **Sergeant Marat Euscher Square** is dedicated to a fallen veteran whose family attended Bethany Baptist Church. The dedication ceremony, Sunday, October 28, 1951, attracted a gamut of Boston politicians and local American Legion officials. My father was the principal speaker at this service honoring a fallen hero. Dad, according to reports, recalled that Sergeant Euscher, a former Boy Scout leader, was killed in action on January 9, 1945, at Rimmling, France. One politician participating in the memorial service was City Council President William F. Hurley, closely affiliated with former Boston Mayor, James Michael Curley. He presented my father with a book written by Joseph Dinneen called **The Purple Shamrock** (1949), a biography of the former Mayor Curley who at various times throughout his political career served two prison terms for corruption.

These two Squares are similar other ones throughout America. They number in the thousands. But my discovery of my father's participation in these two memorial services has prompted me to reflect not so much about his participation in these services but to ponder on the servicemen who sacrificed so much to preserve our freedoms. On my last trip to Boston in November, 2014, I located these two squares and had goosebumps that sixty-plus years earlier, 1951, my father had participated in the deication of these two squares. These are fond recollections.

John W. Holmes

First published in 1986 under the corporate name of Loyalist Press, **CANADA From Sea Unto Sea (CSS)** was not marketed through book stores but via the Canadian postal service and directly to various Canadian government ministries and numerous corporations. The company was created in 1985 to capitalize on the huge success of **LOYAL SHE REMAINS** which had sold 50,000 copies in 1984 to commemorate Ontario's bicentennial celebrations. This 650-page tome (CSS) was then re-published in 1988 under a new corporate name, Heirloom Publishing Inc. The Board of Directors of Heirloom Publishing Inc. appointed me as both publisher and editor-in-chief. Re-introduced as Volume I of the CANADA Heirloom Series in 1988, this illustrious edition clearly promoted Canada's rich culture, history and heritage and sold some 35,000 copies while Heirloom was preparing Volume II of this same series, namely, **CANADA's Native Peoples.**

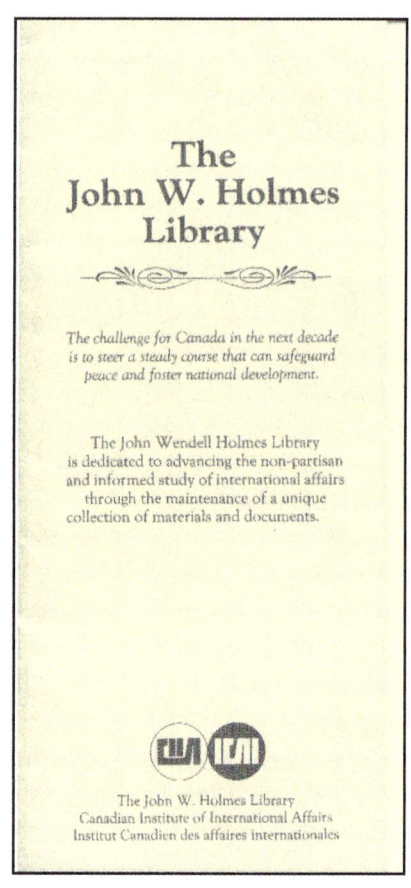

One of my responsibilities as editor-in-chief was assembling a gamut of thirty individuals, professional historians, who had a Boswellian touch. Each was commissioned to write designated chapters for this upcoming "cultural ambassador." We needed big names to make an impact. No longer were we targeting just Ontario book lovers but Canada at large. It took much wheeling and dealing – and arm-twisting – to bring aboard a group of distinguished historiographers who already had an established name. One proposed chapter in the mix was called "Canada under the Dove." My mission was to locate someone who was either a Professor of International Affairs at some university or somebody who had served Canada as a diplomat. I was guided to John Wendell Holmes....

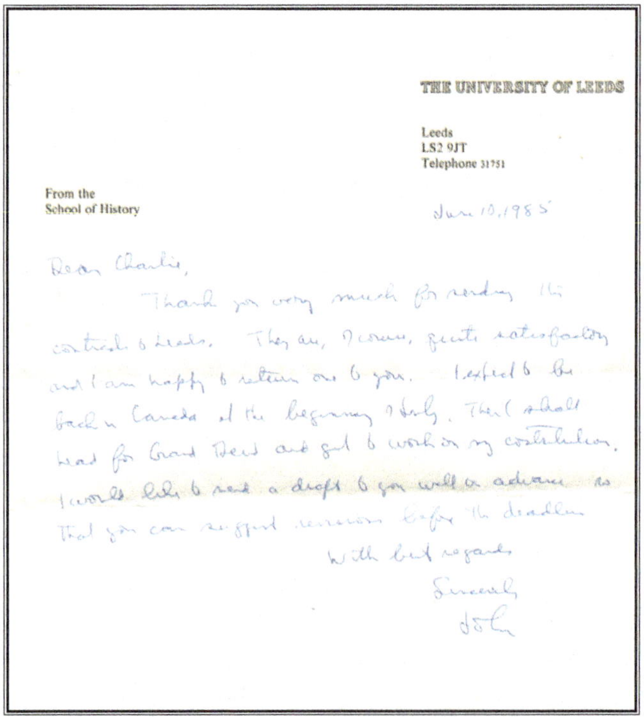

This very distinguished Canadian had served with Canada's Department of External Affairs during World War II. Following this conflict, he was made Canadian Charge d' Affairs (Ambassador) to the Soviet Union, 1947-1949. In 1950 he became Canada's Acting Permanent Delegate to the United Nations. Thereafter, he became the Director-General of the Canadian Institute of International Relations (CIIR) where eventually The John W. Holmes Library was opened in 1985 on the grounds of the University of Toronto to coincide with John's seventy-fifth birthday. Dedicated to advancing the study of international affairs, the library has been housed, since 2007, at the Centre for International Governance Innovation, under the guidance of the Basillie School of International Affairs, on the campus of the University of Waterloo. The John W. Holmes Library honors a very special man who, in his time, became legendary as a professor at various universities while exhibiting grace, wisdom and skill in his classrooms.

Not only did John Holmes agree to write the

The John W. Holmes Library, in 2007, was moved from the University of Toronto to the Basille School of International Affairs, University of Waterloo.

Before the advent of the internet, people wrote personal letters. This one was sent from the University of Leeds in England, 1985, and it reveals John's polished demeanour with his editor in Mississauga, Ontario.

Dad's Best Memories and Recollections

142

proposed chapter in **Canada From Sea Unto Sea,** he also knew my limited background in the subject matter and made sure that he was in no way offended when I would appear at his office at the University of Toronto and share with him my editorial comments. In fact, he was always so cordial suggesting in a diplomatic way that "perhaps we should not use this word or phrase but rather substitute them for still another word or phrase." Of the forty-five illustrations I had researched to enhance his chapter, he thoroughly enjoyed reviewing my selection and generously complimented me for my research and "aplomb"(to use his word) in writing the extended captions for each illustration. Once the full chapter was printed and illustrated and I had the chance to share it with him before publication, he was most pleased with Heirloom's overall endeavours to publish his very special chapter in such a prestigious publication. He certainly knew how to make one feel proud.

Mourning John Holmes: An architect of peace

By Thomas S. Axworthy

Yesterday afternoon, at the University of Toronto, the separate worlds of academe, diplomacy and politics came together, if ever so briefly, to mourn the death of John Wendell Holmes.

Ever since his first organizing drive for the Canadian Institute of International Affairs (CIIA) in 1938, as a teacher, writer, public servant and animator, John Holmes represented for over 50 years all that was civilized, elegant and creative in Canadian diplomacy.

Joining the Department of External Affairs in 1943, just as that ministry was fashioning the Golden Age of Pearsonian internationalism, Holmes was a member of the foreign policy generation that, in his own words, "shaped the peace."

These originators of Canadian internationalism believed, first of all, in the role of diplomacy. Diplomacy is the art of communication and negotiation between the powers; as a Dutch diplomat of the 17th century wrote "on the one hand, the Ambassador is a messenger of peace, on the other hand, he is an honorable spy."

Above all, wrote Holmes, a diplomat must appreciate the paradoxes of life in order to "negotiate the adjustment and ease the pain" of change. Diplomacy, therefore, involves more than foreign trade. There is a requirement for a state to sell goods, but even more important is the requirement to sell good ideas.

The Holmes generation was equally dedicated to a Canadian approach to international problems that emphasized the oneness of our Earth. To the stern-faced representatives of the superpowers, how idealistic Canadian diplomats of the Holmes era must have appeared with their constant advocacy of international control of nuclear weapons, a strengthened United Nations, and ideas for expanding the frontiers of international law.

To the end of his days, Holmes was a tireless advocate of international organization: He saw it, not only as an urgent necessity, but as a way in which a middle power could maximize its influence. Today, with planetary interdependence daily dramatized by disasters like Chernobyl, the AIDS epidemic, the greenhouse effect, or the problems of Third World debt, this country must return to a global agenda, rather than the continental cocoon of a Fortress North America.

Typical of his generation in so many ways, yet Holmes was distinct in another. Whatever the many virtues of the postwar Department of External Affairs, a belief in participatory democracy was not among them. Holmes was different.

He began his involvement with foreign policy as an organizer for the CIIA, a non-partisan organization dedicated to the rational discussion of public issues, and he left External Affairs in 1960 to return to this first love: "There is an essential place in the making of foreign policy," he wrote, "for loud advocacy, loud praise, and loud invective, and there is a place for quiet diplomacy. The public has a right to know and the government has an obligation to keep international confidences."

More than any other single individual, John Holmes was responsible for involving his fellow citizens in the arcane world of foreign policy. Tireless in his devotion to public discourse, Holmes repeatedly travelled across the breadth of Canada.

John Holmes was an idealist; but an idealist who lived his ideals, rather than simply mouthing them. As Lord David Cecil reminds us, what one lives for may be uncertain, how one lives is not. It was very certain how John Holmes lived.

Friendship, in Francis Bacon's phrase, "redoubleth joys and cutteth griefs in halfs." John Holmes' whole life was dedicated to doubling the joys and cutting the griefs of his friends.

Whether helping students with curriculums, colleagues with their concepts, or international agencies with their calamities, Holmes was ever ready with a quip or a kindness. In my travels abroad, from Bonn to Boston, from London to Lagos, the first question of almost all my foreign acquaintances was "But of course, you know Holmes?"

At the mention of his name, eyes twinkled and frowns disappeared, as everyone recalled a favorite anecdote. What better epitaph could one wish for than at the mention of one's name, the world breaks into a smile?

☐ Thomas S. Axworthy is vice-president of a Canadian foundation and former principal secretary to ex-prime minister Pierre Trudeau.

JOHN WENDELL HOLMES: As the noted teacher, writer, public servant and advocate of participatory democracy looked in 1981.

The **Toronto Star** reported the passing of John W. Holmes, September 29, 1988.

Each year, since 1989, Glendon College, York University, hosts the annual John W. Holmes Memorial Lecture sponsored by the Academic Council of the United Nations Systems (ACUNS). A man of charm and wit and a phrase-maker of great skill, John W. Holmes told me personally that he deplored the television age where ten-second judgments were made or where calamitous events were judged in moral terms. The hand-written letters he mailed me when he was visiting professor at Leeds University, Great Britain, 1985, are keepsakes and provide happy memories. They came from a man skillful as a diplomat and a diplomat who was a man of skill.

John W. Holmes passed away just before the second printing of **CANADA From Sea Unto Sea** was released, in 1988, as Volume I of the CANADA Heirloom Series.

New Year's Eve, 1951

I do not remember exactly when I first became a Boy Scout. I belonged to Troop 4 in Roxbury which I probably joined in 1948. The Troop's home base was Bethany Baptist Church located on East Cottage Street where my father, Rev. Charles M. Humber, was minister, 1948-1952. Shortly after I became a Star Scout, I was discharged from Troop 4 during the summer of 1952 when I was at a Boy Scout Jamboree located at Loon Pond near Middleboro, Massachusetts. One day I and another scout disobeyed regulations and took a canoe out into the middle of the pond where the canoe flipped over. The result was that the both of us lost our Troop membership. But, I did have many good times with Troop 4 over a four-year period. One of the most memorable took place on a camping trip that began on December 29, 1951 and ended on New Year's Day, 1952. Below is the report I wrote, completely unedited, that re-captures that memorable experience I had with my Troop. The report was written at the encouragement of my mother and father. Mom typed it for me so she could share my story with relatives in Canada. I just discovered this report after some sixty years. It came to me sometime after my mother's passing in 2005. It was stuffed in a big brown envelope my brother gave me when I was visiting him in Philadelphia. The report came with a gamut of other memorabilia that mother had diligently saved over the years. Recently, while examining my family archives in my Mississauga, Ontario, home, this report came to light once again. Because it is so interesting, these reflections are being shared with you. The report is filled with a fifteen-year old boy's happy recollections, a boy who often was recalcitrant, often rebellious, but one who loved adventure. This one certainly has generated fond memories.

Top: Camp Hemenway, on Great Hill, six miles from Tamworth, New Hampshire, is still standing 60 years after our 1952 Boy Scout New Year's Eve campout. **Below:** Boy Scout registration, 1951-1952, for Charles Humber.

It was Saturday the 29th of December, 1951. The time was 10 o'clock in the morning. The place was Scoutmaster Al Chamillard's home, Roxbury, Boston. We were all ready (9 of us) to leave for a Boy Scout camp in New Hampshire, a total distance of about 130 miles.

As we got about nine-tenths of the way there, Mr. Chamillard's car had a flat. It was snowing like fury and we were all freezing. The last town we went through was Tamworth, 6 miles from our campsite. We finally fixed the flat, and we found our way to the bottom of a mountain called Great Hill. It was very late in the afternoon. The camp, named Hemenway, was about three-quarters of a mile up Great Hill, and we had to walk in three or more feet of snow up the Hill! We took our clothing and other stuff, leaving behind the food. Up, up, up we went, our feet getting heavier every moment. It was still light, and when we reached one-quarter of the way there, some of us collapsed. We thought we would never make it. It was getting dark now and some were dropping back. As we reached two-thirds of the way we were freezing, and some of us were leaving bundles and clothing behind in order to reach the camp. After about an hour we reached the cabin. It was dark and the snow shone as the moon beamed on it. We surely were glad to get inside. We waited to get warmed up, and then a few of us went back to help the others who were lagging behind. At last all of us -- Al Chamillard, Scoutmaster, Gordon MacKenzie, Assistant Scoutmaster, yours truly, Charlie Humber, Ducky Adams, Herbert Gately, George Chamillard, Albert Chamillard (Junior), Freddy (?), and Arny VanderWoude -- finally reached the cabin. We found our bundles wet.

The stove was getting hot. We knew we had to go back to the car and get some more stuff, mainly the food which would otherwise have frozen. Off we went. It was about 7:30 and it was so quiet! We reached there safely, and coming back it was a very tough job, even though we now had a pathway for us to walk on.

Dad's Best Memories and Recollections

After reaching the cabin, there were still two things to do: get water and choose beds. Six would sleep downstairs and three upstairs.

We had to get water and three of us went down to a pump-- I'd say about sixty yards from the cabin. When they came back, we were starving. So… for food we had bacon and eggs. After we had eaten we went to bed, hoping for a better day to come.

We all slept in the next morning, and getting up at about nine (Sunday) we saw quite a nice cabin. It was foggy out. We had planned to go to church, but it was too hard to carry out, so we dropped the plan. We found outside the cabin two big piles of wood. That was good for us, because it saved us going hunting in the snow for it. The next thing we did was to go back to the cars and get some more equipment, such as a saw, extra food, rope, etc. When we came back (about 2:30) we found a nice hot dinner waiting for us.

After eating, Mr. Chamillard went into town to fix his tire and get some more food. While he was gone, we had a snowball fight, and sort of straightened the cabin up. We wanted to explore the grounds around us, but it was much too foggy. The next thing was to get more water. We found the shack where the pump was, more attractive than the night before. It was getting late now, and we wanted a campfire, and then a little snack before going to bed. The campfire was not a long one, and so to bed. It was a "good night, sleep tight" after a hard-working day.

The next morn was the day before New Year's. Wood was sawn, water was got, and our food vanished quickly (an excellent breakfast!). We could see very nicely, for it was a fine clear day. The sun was shining brightly. Snow balls were easily made. We could see such mountains as White Face, Passaconway, Paugus, our own hill -- Great Hill, and, of course, the most beautiful, Mt. Chocorua, which could be seen clearly from our cabin window.

In the afternoon we decided to take a ride around in our cars. Gordon took his group. Mr. Chamillard took his. We went through Tamworth, stopping at the stores for some treats. A question was asked by one of the boys if many wild animals were hunted around there. The reply was, "Oh yes, many such as deer, porcupines, fox, wolf and the odd bear." Soon we continued the car ride. What a beautiful site it was -- on top of these high mountains! We saw such things as Chocorua Lake, Big Lodges, and much beautiful scenery. We got stuck several times on the ice. In fact once both cars were stuck and we could not turn around so we had to back-trail a mile.

The most interesting feature of this trip was the time we saw The Huskies (Eskimo Dogs) in Husky Town. There must have been about fifty huskies, and all were howling for all they were worth. When we came back we were ready to eat anything. So for a reward, we had two beautiful chickens, a la king style, with peas and potatoes. After we ate, we sat around looking forward to New Year's Eve. We all were happy, waggish and jocular, all except Gordon who was getting a bad attack of asthma. Soon it was twelve o'clock. A good shout "Happy New Year!" was given, and a Dagwood midnight snack was had, and off to bed we went….

In the morning we were awakened by Mr. Chamillard. It was time to pack and clean up the cabin. We ate our last meal, cleaned ourselves up, and were talking of the New Year ahead of us. At 10 o'clock, we took all our equipment to the cars, and left it with Gordon who was not feeling too well. It was very cold on the way back to the cabin but we were also able to enjoy the beautiful scenery before us.

We were not looking forward except being a housewife although Mr. Chamillard was the main housewife. As Mr. Chamillard was washing the dishes, he suggested that we take a trip to the tower just beyond our cabin. What beautiful scenery it was!

When we reached the cabin from the tower for the last time, we had to clean up, and make a lunch for ourselves. What a time!

Finally we were ready. Off we went. The trip to Boston was short and sweet. We all arrived home safely and I trust that we all thanked God for looking after us.

Surely the memory of this adventurous weekend shall stay in our hearts for the rest of our lives…..

February 14, 1952

Charles J. Humber

Christmas Letter, 2008

I was seventy-two years when I wrote the following letter. Charlie and Scott were living in the United States; Kristy and Karyn lived in Mississauga where Gay and I have also lived since 1987. Reproduced below is my special 2008 Christmas letter to my wonderful four children.

December 16, 2008

To my four children with love at Christmas:

Your grandfather Humber loved playing Santa Claus. He enjoyed seeing his own four children, moreover, put our home-made stockings up over a false fireplace during our dark early days in Boston when we were as poor as church mice. This was particularly true between 1945 and 1948. And your grandfather Humber loved being Santa Clause especially after we all went to bed. If you take time out to interiorize yourself into your grandfather's mind, you will better understand what he was attempting to do under the dire conditions that he was trapped in at 1145 Dorchester Avenue in Boston. I remember after one particular winter evening, about 1946 or 1947 when I was either ten or eleven years old, all six of us, as a family, bundled up and went from our mid-19th century, rented tenement building, two flats, second and third floors, down to Savin Hill Station at the foot of Bay Street, and took the subway to the Washington St. Station in down town Boston. "Rudolph the Red-Nosed Reindeer" had just been recorded by Gene Autry and was fast becoming a very popular Christmas hit just as it still is today. The song was being played over big, awkward-looking loud speakers all along Washington Street where Jordan Marsh and Filene's Department Stores were prominently located. These were Boston's Sears or Hudson Bay Stores of the time. At the same time that we as a family were marvelling at the Christmas season that Boston was so famous for promoting, Dad couldn't help but notice this colossal reproduced image of himself dressed up as Santa Claus. I think he was totally surprised by the tapestry-looking image although he must have known about the prospects of such a banner being used for Christmas promotion in downtown Boston. Anyway, the image was some four or five stories high, just huge and very colorful, and was draped from the top of Filene's Department Store building facing Washington Street. It drooped down to just above the first floor big windows facing the busy sidewalk filled with bustling Christmas shoppers. He was pleased as Punch to see himself hanging four or five stories high (remember that funny grin he used to get?). Feathery snow was falling all about us and the sidewalks were fast-covered with the thick, clean white flakes blowing everywhere; music was emanating thrillingly from various store fronts, each blaring out joyous Christmas music. Salvation Army personnel were singing Christmas carols and all the store windows were alive and aglow with Christmassy scenes. Even Boston's famous hotdog stand, Joe and Nemo's, was blaring out Christmas songs as people were lining up to buy 10 cent hotdogs. It was all so magical for young eyes. All six of us were wintery cozy in second-hand clothing likely purchased at the Morgan Memorial. Our cheeks were blustery red. There was no sign of hunger on our perky, wine-red faces. Just happiness and wonder…. You guys were not even a twinkle in my eyes during those precious formative years. Mom and Dad, and Paul and Priscilla, and Anna and I were all one big happy family that wintery and frosty day. We truly loved each other as a family…. Mom was so serene and happy and so proud to be with her family on such a provident occasion. I remember so well her puffy, fur-collared winter coat…. It was maroon-coloured. And Dad was so pleased to see his face – some five-stories high – a

Dad's Best Memories and Recollections

big colorful flag-like tapestry affixed to the side of Filene's. He had his traditional rimmed hat on. The wide brim of his old-fashioned hat was covered with snow. The scene is still so clear in my mind's eye to this day. His white silk scarf is still so vividly etched in my memory. It was a special, Dickensonian time that has stood still for me over all these years. .... I cherish this image of our family standing together on Washington Street some sixty years ago. I remind you that your grandfather's effort to bring joy to others when portraying Santa to us, his four children, or to countless others, was legendary. His photo was in the newspapers most every day. You may not know it, but my Dad played Santa for seven or eight years in Bean Town and, later, in the City of Brotherly Love.... The money he was paid by Filene's, I'm sure, put a turkey on our kitchen table each Christmas.

Still another Christmas is soon upon us. I just thought I'd share this happy memory of more than sixty years ago. I trust you will have similar memories of your own youth and will find a way to share your memories of this time of the year with precious loved ones. Your mom and I certainly tried to make Christmas meaningful to you guys over many years.

**Love you guys,
Pops**

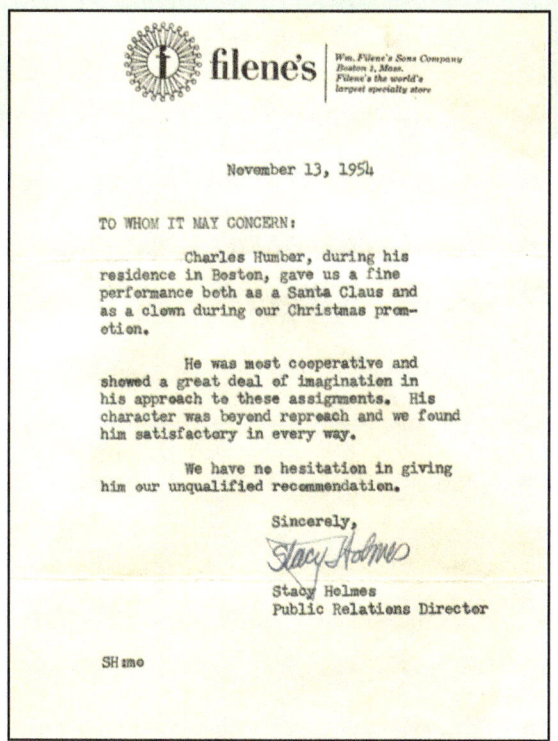

Above: For nearly 100 years, the leading department store in Boston was Filene's. Rev. Charles M. Humber played Santa Claus in this downtown Boston store in the 1940-50s.

Top right: One of many thousands of promotional photographs taken each year to promote Santa in his workshop at Filene's. Here is Santa, aka Rev. Charles M. Humber, bringing Christmas Cheer and celebration for Christ's birthday to well-wishers.
Bottom right: The iconic Filene's clock that protruded over Washington Street from Filene's, a Boston landmark for years.

Dad's Best Memories and Recollections

C. A. Humber's Tool Chest

Filed away in my family archives is a letter written by Henry Howarth Humber (1875-1933), one of many great uncles I never met. In 1901 or 1902 he had moved from the shores of Lake Huron to the town of Leduc in Canada's North West Territories. My great uncle Henry mailed his letter, February 27, 1904, to his father, Charles Austin Humber, my great-grandfather, who had been living in Goderich, Ontario, since 1872. The letter reveals how much Henry misses his father's iron-handled wooden chest jammed full of tools. He writes to his father 2000 miles away, "I wish I had your box of tools. I am continually borrowing saws and one thing or another." Procuring tools in those days was no easy task, especially if you lived in a pioneering community like Leduc, 160 miles or so north of Calgary, Alberta. C.A. Humber's tool chest back in Goderich was totally loaded with carpentry tools that would have fulfilled Henry's building dreams.

In 2007, Charles J. Humber, left, donated his great-grandfather's tool chest to Lang Pioneer Village. Joe Corrigan, right, manager of the historic village, accepts the gift that is signed and dated on the inside "Allandale, 1868, Charles A. Humber".

Other than my great uncle's letter, I never knew anything about this tool chest, that is, until 1984 when I was visiting a cousin living in Stratford, Ontario. She wondered if I might be interested in my great-grandfather's tool chest. Helen (Humber) Sinclair, Mait and Linnie Humber's only child, was born, 1910, some three years after her grandfather, C.A. Humber, had died in a tragic home accident. Thus by deduction one assumes that my great uncle Mait, Henry's younger brother, inherited the tool chest following the death of their father. Because Henry's brother, Mait, lived in Stratford, just down the road from Goderich, the tool chest he inherited remained with him throughout his adult life. And when Mait died in 1950, my second cousin, Helen, inherited the tool chest. Some thirty-five years after her father's passing, Helen and her husband, Ray Sinclair, gave this treasured family heirloom to me in 1984.

I cherished the tool chest as a family keepsake, but I really did not know what to do with it. It had no functionality in our house. One day when cleaning it up, I noticed my great-grandfather's signature, "C.A. Humber", inscribed on the inside lid of the box. I also noticed in very clear script, on the same inside lid, some significant information indicating that this tool chest was made in the town of Allandale, 1868, one year after Canada became a nation. Because of my family research that led to the publication of **Family Sleuthing,** 2006, the name Allandale resonated with me. I knew that such a town no longer existed because Allandale, as a village, was renamed Lang in 1872. This name change occurred at the same time my great-grandfather, Charles A. Humber, moved to Goderich. Among the chattels he had shipped to Goderich was the documented tool chest, the same chest great uncle Henry in Leduc sorely pined over.

Today, the village of Lang has essentially become an historic site known as Lang Pioneer Village, a 1967 Centennial project located south of Peterborough, north of the town of Keene and on the Indian River that wanders through Otonabee Township to Rice Lake. Today this site has twenty-five restored buildings. The village itself is a living museum and is a mecca for those chasing local history. Back in early 2007, I approached Joe Corrigan, Manager of Lang Pioneer Village, and inquired about the possibility of my donating my great-grandfather's tool chest to the museum. He was most receptive to the idea and in the spring of 2007, I drove to the village and met with Mr. Corrigan. He was very pleased to accept the Charles Austin Humber tool chest as a gift. The museum also bought a copy of **Family Sleuthing** for their library! Even though history suggests that my great-grandfather left an indelible mark in Goderich, it was most satisfying for me to know that my great-grandfather, who taught in Keene, and was a carpenter in Keene along with his brother Orenzo and their father David Humber, should have his tool box on permanent display at Lang Pioneer Village. This is a nostalgic reminder that he was once a part of this community where a living museum continues "…building the future from the fabric of the past."

Dad's Best Memories and Recollections

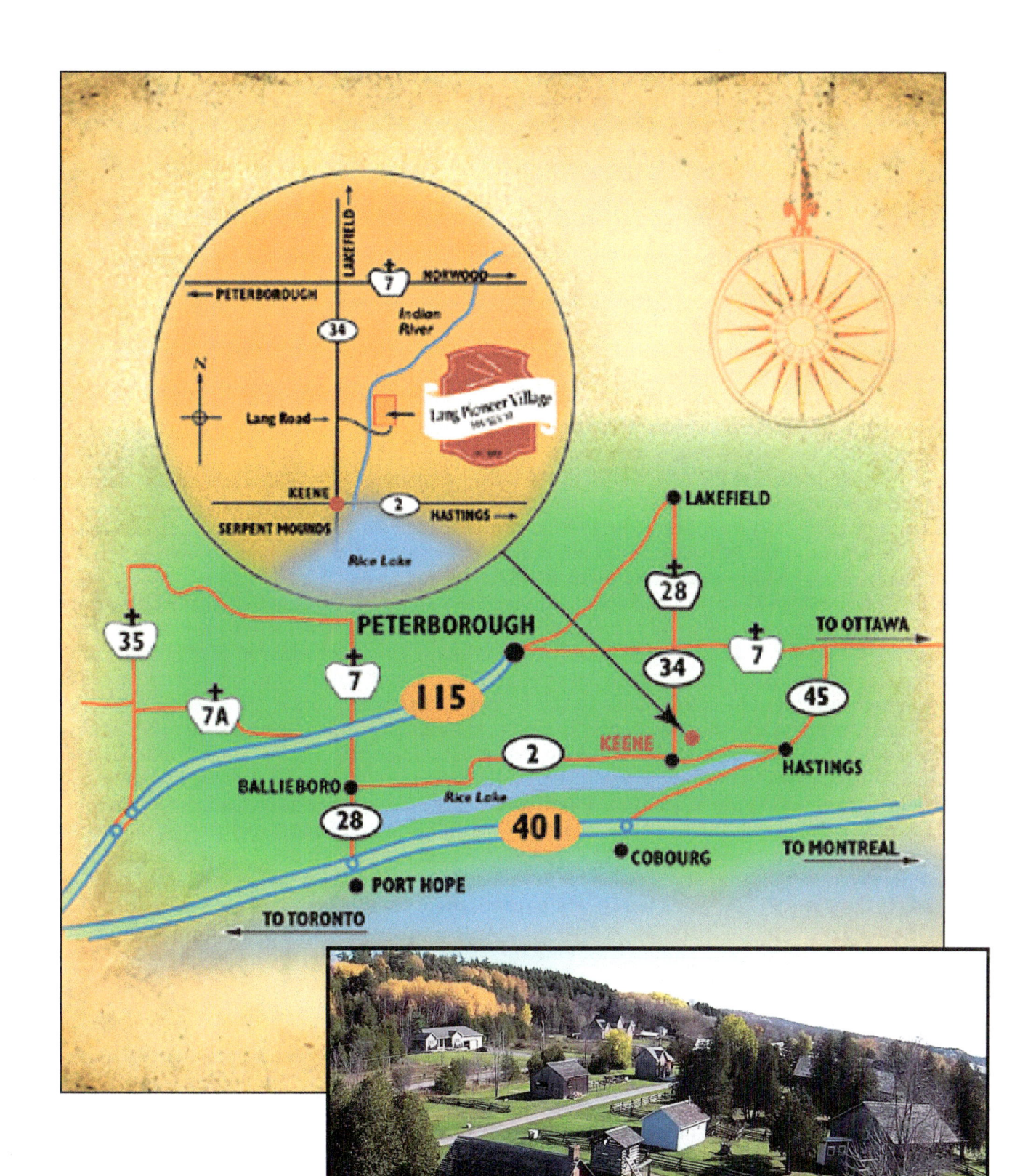

Above: Map giving directions to Lang Pioneer Village founded as a Centennial project in 1967. **Right:** Aerial view of the village today with its 25 restored buildings.

Dad's Best Memories and Recollections

G. Blair Laing

The two years, 1982-1984, that it took to publish **LOYAL SHE REMAINS**, the top-selling publication in 1984, were the same two years I served as National President, The United Empire Loyalists' Association of Canada. The administration offices for both of these missions were side by side at 21 and 23 Prince Arthur Ave., respectively, just one block north of Bloor Street and to the west of Avenue Rd. There was much hustle and bustle in those days as the Province of Ontario celebrated its Bicentennial, 1984, and the City of Toronto celebrated its Sesquicentennial, the same year. During this period, David M. Stewart of The MacDonald Stewart Foundation, in Montreal, seconded me. This development sprung me lose from teaching so that I could better concentrate on editing **LOYAL SHE REMAINS**, assist the provincial government in promoting its upcoming bicentennial celebrations, and prepare for the onslaught of presidential duties beckoning my attention during those two very busy years.

While preparing **LOYAL SHE REMAINS**, I developed a friendship with, perhaps, Canada's most-respected art dealer, G. Blair Laing. His gallery was located at 194 Bloor Street right behind the offices of the UEL Association on Prince Arthur Ave. One proposed major chapter in **LOYAL SHE REMAINS** was to examine "The Arts" in Ontario. I had commissioned Don Webster, Curator, Canadiana Department, Royal Ontario Museum, to write this chapter. To embellish Webster's chapter, I needed appropriate illustrations. So, at the beckoning of Lord Ken Thomson, a long-time admirer of Mr. Laing, I took advantage of my proximity to the Laing Galleries and introduced myself to this connoisseur art dealer. We immediately became good friends to the extent we had tea together after hours in his second floor apartment located directly above his gallery. He basically took a liking to me partly because I was the National President of the UEL Association but additionally, I believe, because I was a collector of Canadiana whose furniture was prominently illustrated in Howard Pain's well-known tome, **The Heritage of Upper Canadian Furniture** (1978). Being a Presbyterian from Westmount, Montreal, G. Blair Laing also liked the idea that I was the son of a Baptist minister. At the outset of our friendship, he told me the story of a man who was driving his Model A Ford through the countryside. While looking out his car window, he exclaimed to the passenger next to him, "Look – in the sky! Over there! See that cloud?" He paused, then he exclaimed: "That's a Baptist cloud!" The passenger replied, "How do you know that it's a Baptist cloud?" Well, can't you tell? It's the only cloud in the sky and he's looking for an argument!" He then gave me a smile, an indication that he liked conversing with me....

And converse we did. But more than anything, he educated me. He told me fabulous stories of his "hunting" trips across Europe and England looking for Canadian art. It was his duty, he felt, to repatriate great works of art. His main love affair was with post-impressionist James William Morrice, "Canada's greatest artist." And because he believed that Morrice was, indeed, Canada's best, he would show me Morrice after Morrice paintings in his private collection, gesticulating with his hands as he pointed to the Modernist features of Canada's most prominent painter. G. Blair Laing told me during these sessions that art dealers have a significant, dignified role in influencing public taste and promoting certain artists. He reinforced this position by pointing out that, because of him, the exotic sculptures of Henry Moore were recognized and accepted in Canada. Moore's semi-abstracts, often a reclining human body, more often than not, female, stand prominently as bronze sculptures outside such places as the Art Gallery of Ontario and Toronto's City Hall. Blair's friendship with Henry Moore had a lot to do with these acquisitions....

By 1987, my term as UEL president had come and gone. Because of the success of **LOYAL SHE REMAINS**, a number of us associated with the publication of this 700-page best-seller were

The gallery of pre-eminent art dealer and collector, G. Blair Laing was a Bloor Street landmark for decades.

motivated to establish a publishing company. We were inspired to leave the premises of Prince Arthur Ave. and move to Mississauga near the junction of Mississauga Rd. and Highway 401. In the process the first printing of **CANADA From Sea Unto Sea** (1986) was published and our vision to become an imposing publication house was vaulted high. In the meantime, my friendship continued with Blair Laing. The superb books he published, **Memoirs of an Art Dealer,** Volumes I and II, plus his stunning **MORRICE a Great Canadian Artist Rediscovered,** reinforced G. Blair Laing's reputation as a person whose contribution to Canada's art world was second to none. After donating, 1990, his entire collection of 83 James Wilson Morrice paintings to the National Art Gallery of Canada, in Ottawa, he truly became Canada's patron of the arts. Dying in 1992, G. Blair Laing never saw his Morrice Collection exhibited at the National Art Gallery. My fond remembrance of Blair is truly a great memory. It's my enjoyment to share his story with you.

April 20-22, 1991 • $1.25 a copy

Art dealer Blair Laing: 'I had nothing to do with the valuations'

Art donation system isn't picture-perfect

By Philip Mathias
Financial Post

A MAJOR collection of James W. Morrice paintings donated to the National Gallery of Canada in 1989 is raising questions about whether art donations can be used to gain huge unfair tax advantages at the expense of Canadian taxpayers.

The donation of 84 Morrice paintings was appraised at $15 million for tax purposes, even though its market value may have been only about $8 million. A donor of such nationally important fine art is permitted to reduce his taxable income by the full appraised value of the donation.

Donated by Blair Laing, the 80-year-old dean of Canadian art dealers, the Morrice collection exposes:
• weaknesses in the National Gallery's appraisal rules.
• flaws in the functioning of the watchdog body, the Canadian Cultural Property Export Review Board, which has the responsibility for preventing fine-art donations from being used as a tax dodge.
• ambiguities in guidelines established by Revenue Canada to ensure that appraisals come in at fair market value.

David Mitchell, a Toronto-based fine art consultant and appraiser, says "the whopping value of this 'gift' in relation to the works donated is being discussed quietly but with concern in ... [many] art circles."

There are also questions about the quality of some of the paintings taken in by the gallery, Mitchell says. (See accompanying story.) The gallery announced the donation on Dec. 6, 1989.

"I had nothing to do with the valuations ..." Laing says. But Laing chose the appraisers, in keeping with National Gallery policy, a gallery official told The Post.

The appraisers were paid by the gallery. Some institutions consider this a conflict. But National Gallery policy permits a non-arm's-length relationship between donor and appraiser.

Recognized expert

According to research conducted by The Post, the collection's value at the time it was donated was about $8 million. The official $15-million value is an average of evaluations done by two appraisers.

One was Walter Klinkhoff, a leading Canadian art dealer, in his 70s, based in Montreal. Klinkhoff is a recognized expert in Canadian paintings but also a self-professed friend of Laing's.

"We have known one another for probably 40 years and done business with one another," Klinkhoff said, "... so, yes we've always been friendly."

The acceptance of Klinkhoff by the National Gallery as an appraiser has been called into question for two reasons: his closeness to Laing, and the fact that he sells Morrice paintings from time

See DONATION, page 4

MORRICE
A GREAT CANADIAN ARTIST REDISCOVERED

G. BLAIR LAING *March 1985*

To my friend Charles J. Humber with best wishes
G. Blair Laing

WITH AN INTRODUCTION BY JEAN SUTHERLAND BOGGS

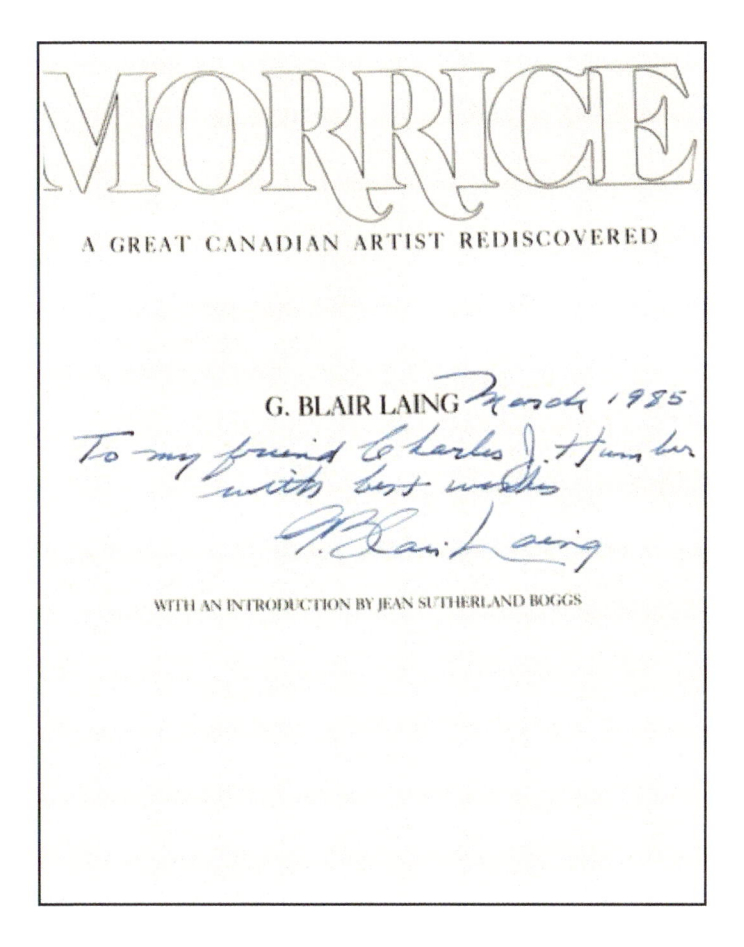

Left: Within a year of this article appearing in **The Financial Post**, G. Blair Laing passed away.
Above: G. Blair Laing's last book celebrated Canada's greatest artist. He happily signed my copy.

151 | Dad's Best Memories and Recollections

Sir William Campbell House

In 1969, following my graduate studies at the University of Wisconsin, one of the biggest chores Gay and I had was furbishing our newly acquired three-bedroom house at 63 Westhumber Blvd., in Rexdale, Ontario. Rather than buying new or second hand furniture, we decided to fill our home with antiques. So off we went to the many farm auctions taking place each weekend outside Toronto. Before long, our residence was bulging with furniture, not so much because I was a compulsive buyer but because the cost of antiques was so reasonable especially at a time when inflation was rampant. Antique furniture was escalating in price so fast that antique dealers were looking to restock their stores almost on a daily basis. In fact, it was not unusual to buy several items at a farm auction and on the way home drop into antique shops and turn a quick profit. Wheeling and dealing became a constant part of my life during the 1970s. Gay and I upgraded our antique collection almost on a monthly basis. Before long we had assembled what became known as the **Humber Collection**. Many of our pieces were loaned to exhibitions or were illustrated and referenced in various books and magazines about antiques. By the mid-1970s, I was even teaching an evening course in Antiques for the Etobicoke Board of Education.

Early in 1973, antique dealer Les Donaldson, a pioneer in the antique business, whose store was in Galt (now Cambridge), about an hour west of Toronto, had just acquired a cupboard that was nearly 200 years old. It was perfect for storing clothes and accessories for the anticipated birth of our third child (instead, Gay gave birth to twin boys later that October!). I negotiated a price of $1700.00, a considerable sum in those days. Beautifully painted to simulate burl walnut, it was entirely crafted in pine. In reality it was a linen press, made in Scotland, imported to Canada and purchased by Les, who was known throughout his life as a much respected dealer. An antiquarian, Les really knew his stuff. In fact, he took much time to educate me about what constituted quality antique furniture, originality, provenance, age and so much more. The linen press cupboard he sold me in the spring of 1973 was crafted in 1787. The entire piece was completely original, clean and ready for use. Gay was happy although she wondered if I had perhaps paid too much....

Four Humber siblings, left to right, Kristy, Charlie, Karyn and Scott, stand in front of the Les Donaldson cupboard before it was sold to the Campbell House, 1978.

While this transaction was taking place, two additional matters surfaced that directly impacted our family. The first of these was a letter from antique dealer Carl Hutchinson whose shop was located in Queenston, near St. Catharines. In his eighties, Carl had hustled for antiques since before the Depression. His wife, Nancy, mailed us the letter in June, 1973, exclaiming that Carl finally had bought the best cupboard he had ever owned or ever seen. Later identified as the Grobb cupboard (see elsewhere in this volume), I was totally flabbergasted after driving to the Niagara Peninsula to see it. To be blunt, as the elderly couple unveiled it in their small barn, I was completely overwhelmed. Carl gave me to the end of the month to pay for it. My next door neighbour in Rexdale, Bert Trew, who was a bank manager in downtown Toronto, loaned me the money, a whopping $2500.00. Clinching the deal for the Grobb cupboard left me no choice but to sell the Donaldson linen press cupboard to help pay off the bank loan. This development led to a second matter that potentially could have upset our plans. In other words, while these two transactions were being processed during the spring of 1973, there was, at the same time, an ongoing story in the media about how Toronto's last surviving Georgian home, the Sir William Campbell House, had been moved through downtown Toronto to the northwest corner of Queen Street and University Avenue and was slowly being restored. The high-profile move was orchestrated by the Advocates' Society, barristers, who had come together in 1963 to form a Society as a forum for discussion, education and fellowship. After raising the money to move the historic house a mile across mid-town Toronto, in 1972, the Society began restoring this grand Georgian house masterpiece and initiated filling it with period furniture. This generated in me an idea.... Perhaps those in charge of refurbishing the Campbell House, built in 1824 by a man born in Scotland in 1758, just might be interested in the Les Donaldson cupboard. William Campbell had come to Toronto in 1811. He became Ontario's Chief Justice of the Ontario Supreme Court, 1825-1829. Sir William Campbell was, indeed, an important historic figure! One could not possibly blame me for thinking that those in charge of refurbishing the stately Georgian home just might show interest in my cupboard, especially since it was crafted, 1787, in Scotland, William Campbell's birth place. A high school classmate, Alan Emerson, an Advocates' Society member himself, made a presentation, on my behalf, to the powers in charge of restoring and refurbishing the Campbell House to its former glory. He met with such personalities as Barry Pepper, and Hyliard G. Chappell among others, and the deal was consummated for even more than what I had originally paid for it. This deal was finalized in 1978. I was, needless to say, absolutely thrilled with the transaction. No question about it, both parties benefited from the transaction, but I, at least, was getting our household out of debt.

Today the William Campbell House is much more than a meeting place for advocates or barristers. It has a unique dining room named after one of its founders, John Josiah Robinette, the first president of the Advocates' Society when it was founded in 1963. An offshoot of the Robinette Dining Room is a separate enclave where my former cupboard proudly stands. Nearly thirty years after selling the cupboard to the Advocates' Society, the grand overseers of the Sir William Campbell House, I had the desire to pay the landmark property a visit and see my old cupboard one more time. So I touched basis with James ("Jamie") Clark, youngest son of one of my former Heirloom partners, Angela Dea Cappelli Clark. James, a partner with the law firm Stern Landesman Clark, was able to arrange for a luncheon get-together at the Campbell House. This was back in 2003. During our luncheon sojourn at the Campbell House, Jamie, always thoughtful, took several photos. It was a meaningful reunion to meet up, once again, with the cupboard that caused me potential bankrupties back in the 1970s but in 2003 brought back fond memories as I touched it and admired it. This happenstance, for me, is a really nice memory....

Top right:: Date 1787 painted on the two doors of the Campbell House cupboard, some 35 years older than the Sir William Campbell House. **Above left:** Charles J. Humber stands in front of the cupboard he sold to the Advocates' Society
Right: Moving the Sir William Campbell House, built 1822-24, through downtown Toronto, from Adelaide and Frederick Streets to the NW corner of University Avenue and Queen Street West, a distance of one mile.

Bert Case Diltz

Bert Case Diltz (1894-1992)

After completing a full year of studies at the University of Alaska (Fairbanks), 1960-1961, my *inamorata* and future wife, Gayle Jenkins, from La Jolla, California, and I, at the time from Philadelphia, along with Jim Walker from Altoona, Pennsylvania, drove down the Alaska Highway from Fairbanks all the way to Philadelphia, Pennsylvania. The City of Brotherly Love was our destination for the next school year, Gayle teaching primary school in Lansdale, just north of Philly, and I was finishing up my undergraduate studies at Temple University from where I hoped to complete my degree in English Literature, June, 1962.

On our way through Toronto, I decided that it would be a good idea to stop in at the Ontario College of Education (OCE) up on Bloor Street near Spadina Ave. I wanted to learn what had to be done to meet qualifications to teach high school in the Province of Ontario. I entered the main door of the institution after just fixing a flat tire. So I was not particularly dressed up to make a formal inquiry. Nevertheless, I went to the office, wearing jeans and feeling grubby. A lovely lady out of the Victorian age came over to meet me. I told her my situation and that I was making general inquiry what particulars were needed to qualify as a prospective secondary school teacher. She looked into the adjacent room, went in, came back out almost immediately and said that Dean Diltz would be pleased to meet me. Scruffy as I was, I entered the inner sanctum of the Dean's office. There he was, the legendary Bert Case Diltz.

When I was in grade twelve at Brampton District High School, it was Mr. Diltz's text book we used to study poetry in Mr. Potter's English class. I was not at all intimidated by the fact that the Dean had his polished black shoes up on his desk. I was neither intimidated by the huge cigar he was puffing! In fact I felt quite at home with this man who seemed to be so down to earth. I asked him what qualifications I had to meet for enrollment in the Ontario College of Education. He asked me curt questions about where I was currently attending school, what were my aspirations in life, why I wanted to be a teacher.... I answered his questions honestly, after sitting down at his request. He sized me up and said something like, "I like your style. You're dropping in to inquire about a teaching position after attending the University of Alaska. Now you're going back to Temple. And you want to come to Toronto and start your career in the classroom. Well, let me give you some words of encouragement. We need people like you to teach our young people. Go and finish your degree. Come up during the Easter break when there will be jobs awaiting you. Various boards of education from across the province will be booked at all the big hotels. Get signed up with a school board and you will automatically be qualified to enroll during the summer for a temporary teaching certificate." He got up from his swivel chair, cigar in his mouth....As he tightened his belt, he said, "Don't forget to look me up when you enroll for the summer course. I'd like to see you again ...." We shook hands and I left the premises of OCE. I could hardly wait to tell Gay about our future. It felt secure.

Later I would find out that Bert Case Diltz was a World War I veteran who had fought at Ypres, Somme, Vimy Ridge, Paschendaele, Amiens and Mons. This Dean was a man's man. He was no sissy. I certainly clicked with him and can say that he certainly impressed me and left me with a great memory. He encouraged me to be a teacher as much as Jim Potter did years earlier... Great memory....

Ted Williams

Growing up in Boston meant that you probably followed professional sports. Each day I went to high school, I would cross Dorchester Avenue at Bay Street, walk into Serino's Variety Store at the corner, and glance at the Sports Section of the **Boston Globe** to follow Ted Williams before the local bus turned the corner to take me up Bay St. to the Savin Hill subway station and on to Boston Latin School. When television became popular in the late 1940s, before I went to high school, I used to deliver **The Boston Daily Record,** an evening newspaper. All extras had to be sold, usually totaling ten issues. So I would trot into the several taverns or bars in my neighborhood locally-known as "Dot Ave." I was twelve or thirteen at the time. With newspapers bundled under my arm, I sold them to those finishing their ales and beers and watching the Red Sox on the tube. Most taverns in those days had their TVs hanging over their bars running vertically to their front doors. I always stayed there in the corner between the front door and the bar until Ted Williams came to bat. Then it was off to deliver my **Daily Record** to the 100 newspaper customers I had in various tenement blocks in my neighborhood. Broadcaster Curt Gowdy would support his team by sipping on a bottle or two of Narragansett Lager Beer that he was promoting through advertisements. By the seventh inning, Curt often got into the first stages of inebriation and began slurring his words. His eyes got droopy.... All the rummies in the bars loved Curt as he had become one of them – as he did just about every baseball night – drinking lager beer. Selling newspapers to these guys was no big deal. They'd always give me a "jit" (five-cents) and always told me to keep the change (newspapers sold for three cents in those days).

I was a huge Ted Williams fan while growing up in Boston. In 1952, Ted Williams was recruited by the U. S. Marines to serve his country – for a second time! This time his service took him to Korea. On Wednesday, April 30, 1952, the Red Sox held a special Ted Williams Day at Fenway Park. It was a Wednesday afternoon and I was in school. There was no way I was going to miss this game. So I skipped school, walked through the Fens to Fenway Park, and bought a ticket out in center field. I went by myself to watch my hero play. The score going to the bottom of the seventh inning was 3-3. Detroit's Dizzy Trout, no slouch of a pitcher (he would win 170 games for the Detroit Tigers) was on the mound. Ted got up to bat with one player on first base and unbelievably, my hero slammed a homerun into the right field stands to win the game 5-3. In what a lot of people thought was his last game, the "splendid splinter" did return to the Red Sox two seasons later and actually played six more seasons, hitting a career total of 521 homeruns. Had he not served three years with the Marines during World War II and two more years during the Korean War, it is very probable he would have broken Babe Ruth's record of 714 homeruns. It certainly was a thrill to attend Ted Williams Day! And when the game was over, I hustled over to where the players departed Fenway Park. I just wanted to see my hero one more time. Sure enough, I watched him go to his parked car. He gave out no autographs, but he did look my way when I wished him well and that was all I needed. The great one had actually noticed me! What a memory. I was not quite sixteen years....

Dad's Best Memories and Recollections

Max Storey, Auctioneer

I started going to auction sales in 1969 shortly after Gay and I purchased our first home in Etobicoke, one of Toronto's five boroughs. We decided, at the outset, to furnish our house with antiques. The first antique I bought was a Tiffany-style lamp at a Max Storey auction sale in Brampton (we still own this lamp in 2015). This took place at the Junior Farmer's Building on Elliott Street. Touted as "best in the business," Max Storey mesmerized everyone with his mellifluous voice that needed no microphone. His witty jargon, risqué jokes, teasing remarks endeared him to a faithful following, all of whom enjoyed listening to a World War II veteran who honed his voice bellowing in a submarine. Before his auctions started he threw men cigars and women chocolate bars. He would hold up a pair of silver-plated Burdizzo pinchers used to castrate bulls and announce that these were necessary for women who needed to rule their husbands. He would hold up a bed-pan and call it a guzunda. Why? Because it guzunda the bed! He would lift a blanket beater high above him, informing the audience that its purpose was multiple, including controlling children. He really was a one-man vaudeville show and could hypnotize his eager following with his trilling: "gimmee, gimmee, gimmee – I have seven-fifty, gimmee eight, gimmee me eight…." He would point his cane, shift his hat, pull up his pants, sip from a glass that did not smell like water….. His drink was called the Rockwood Special (half rye, half water). He would harmonize "Two, two tood-a-loo, give me two, give me two, who'll gimmee two…." His banter was comical. He was front and centre on the stage, a gifted entertainer, a midway barker.

During the winter months, he sold indoors. These were consigned auctions. The front of the hall of the Junior Farmer's Building was filled with everything from colored glass to stoneware jugs and crocks, from silver pickle cruets to flow blue dinner plates, from chopping blocks to treen and toleware, from furnishings and candle sticks to quilted bed coverings and rugs….The crowds were huge. Concession stands were busy. People came together as if the auction was a family reunion. This is where I first met Gordon Ball and Brian Reid and so many others in the antique trade. After several years, I was also consigning things to Max Storey. It was fun to buy something for fifteen dollars and have Max sell it the next year for thirty dollars! People who bought and sold in those days were mini entrepreneurs, thanks to Max. Every

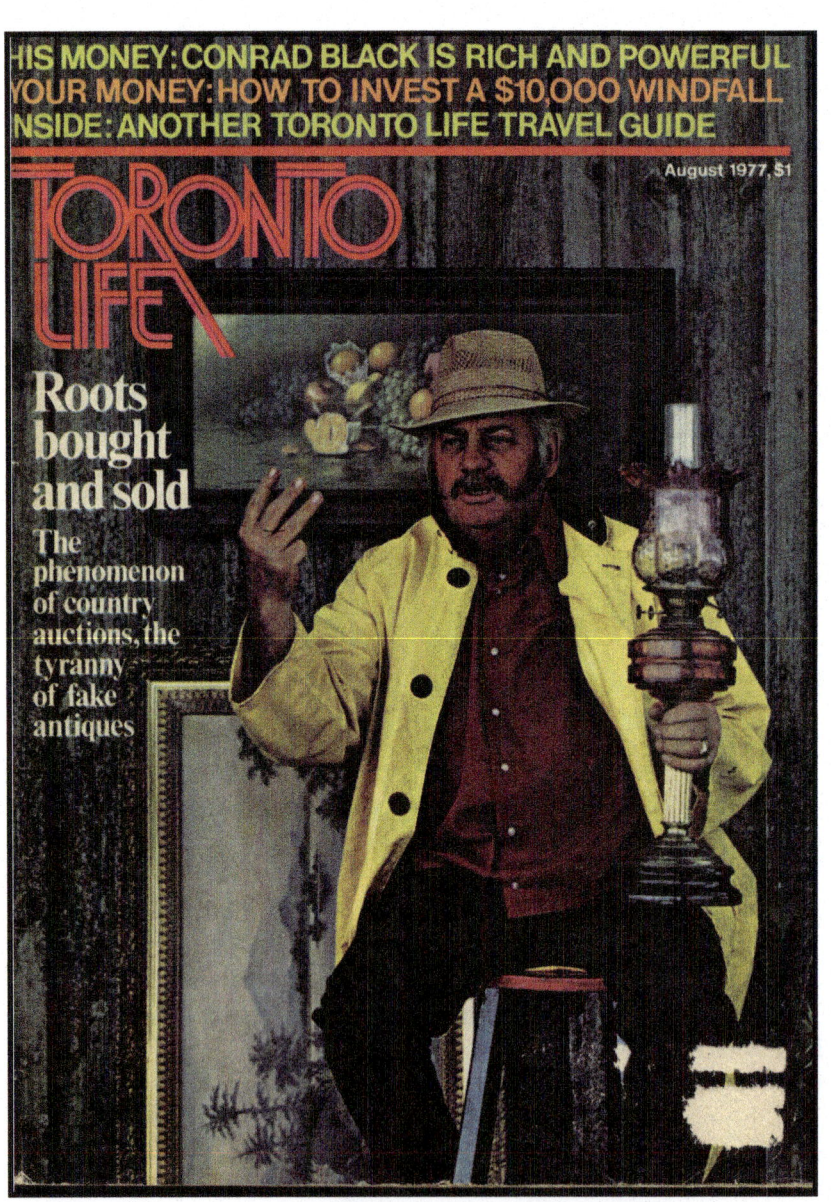

Auctioneer Max Storey should have been a baritone opera singer. His voice did not need a microphone. Here he is on the cover of **Toronto Life,** August, 1977, trilling for thirty dollars.

year I consigned to Max at least 100 or so items. He put money into my pockets and indirectly paid for a lot of family things like skates, scarves and mitts for winter months, and water noodles, sand shovels and sandals for the summer months up at our cottage.

When my Aunt Lucille and Uncle Stewart Longfield sold their home in the old town of Meadowale, 1980, I was able to get Max Storey to auction off their chattels from their spacious backyard lawn. At one of the last auctions he ever conducted, April, 1990, I bought a lovely little Puslinch Township bench from an Alastair McLean farm sale out in Wellington County east of Waterloo. To this day, I still use it as a little table reposing next to my leather-covered wing back chair in the family room of our Mississauga home. I often think of Max as I use it. Gay would never let me sell it.

Over the years, I probably attended 75 Max Storey auction sales. In that one usually spends somewhere around three hours per sale waiting for items to be auctioned off, I imagine that I have spent, over the years, the equivalent of at least one full month of my entire life going to, listening to and bidding on items at Max Storey sales. Passing away at age 79 years in 2001, Max is a highlight memory…. Sometimes when I go to sleep at night I can still hear that resonating voice chirping away and getting the final bid for a future family heirloom….

Right: Last Max Storey auction sale I attended, April 21, 1990. I purchased a little bench that I still use daily 25 years after the sale.

Below: When my Uncle Stewart and Aunt Lucille Longfield were giving up their Meadowville home in 1980, I enlisted Max Storey to auction off their chattels.

THE WOODBRIDGE ADVERTISER

AUCTION SALE
for
STEWART LONGFIELD
to be held at his home in Meadowvale—4th house South of Church (on 2nd. Line West)
on
SATURDAY, SEPT. 6
at 11 A.M.

FURNITURE: Large pine table with side drawers, Maple desk and chair, round Oak dining table with 3 leaves, set of 6 dining chairs, Windsor armchair, 3 pce. bedroom suite-bed, dresser and washstand, 3 pce. bedroom suite with burled inlay, Oak buffet - Jacobean, high back stool (Brunt etching), enamel top table, set of 5 old kitchen chairs, large mahogany desk, old pine cupboard, drop leaf kitchen table (pine), drop front secretary, wicker fernery, 2 slat back rockers, sev. good small tables, Colonial gramphone, 2 occasional chairs, small pine table, double bed (walnut), Pineapple, old chest of drawers, 2 old trunks, pine tool box, small pressed-back chair, J.H. chair, rocking chair, horse collar armchair, pr. of twin beds with mattresses, kitchenette table and four chairs, modern love seat, wooden table and 4 chairs, chesterfield and chair, few picture

---

This Small Bench was bought at this Sale!

AUCTION SALE

FOR

ALASTAIR & IAN McLEAN

to be held at the farm Lot 30, Conc. rear of 9 of PUSLINCH TWP. From Morriston go East on Wellington Road 36 over 401 to 2nd farm on left

ON SAT. 21 APRIL AT 11 A.M. 1990

APPLIANCES -
Frigidaire Frig.
Enterprise elec. Stove 24"
Maytag auto. Washer
Maytag Dryer
Filter Queen Vacuum
Viking chest Freezer
Coldspot upright Freezer
Zenith coloured TV 25"

FURNITURE -
Walnut Sideboard
Walnut Bedroom Suite - Bed, Dresser & Washstand
Elm table w. spooled legs 3' x 3'
Walnut Settee w. Cameo back
Oak ex. table
Set of 4 Pine Kitchen chairs
Set of 6 side chairs w. pierced seats
Wingham Clipper Cook Stove
Nest of 3 tables
Oak Rocker - excel.
Wingback chair
Walnut oval coffee table
Oak 2 drawer nite stand - very unusual
2 Walnut Library tables
Bowmanville Rocker
Slipper chair
Oak armchair
Oak Sideboard
Lamp table
Pine cupboard - 3 drawers, 2 doors C.1850
2 Pine Blanket Boxes
Pine top for Flat Back
Dresser & Washstand
Spooled crib
Folding Bookcase
Pine Chest of Drawers - excel.
2 small Pine Kitchen tables
Piano Stool
Spinning Wheel - small
Hoosier cupboard

GLASS & CHINA -
R.S. Prussia cake plate - Floral
Large patterned Compote - excel.
Cake Stand; 4 Goblets
Limoges covered vegetable
Copper Lustre bowl & 2 creamers
Few Flo Blue pieces
Pressed Pitcher w. Cherries etc.
Green sugar shaker
H.P. Nippon tray
End of Day Vase
Blue Willow platter
Amber Pickle Cruet Liner
9 Oil Lamps - all different
Selection of good old plates
Carnival Glass
Few pieces of Irish Sprig
Several Toilet Set pieces
Collection of China Roosters
Noritake cup & saucer
Cheese Dish
Soup Tureen; Large Ladle - British Silver
Covered Vegetable - Wheat pattern
Shade for a Hanging Lamp - Painted
Square etched shade for Hall Lamp
2 Beaver Sealers - qt. & pt.

MISC. -
Gingerbread Clock
Mantel Clock
3 Swing mirrors
Pr. Brass candlesticks
Copper Boiler; Exercise Bike
About 25 Pictures & Frames
Selection of Silverware - mostly Rogers Bros.
Large selection of old Books
Several old Quilts
Goffering Iron - excel.
Dolls Iron & Trivet; Sev. Irons & Trivets
Dietz Union Driving Lamp
3 sleigh Bells, cutter Bells & cow Bell
Very unusual square Teakettle
Ink Wells; Brass Pail; Crocks & Jugs

Century Farm since early 1800's - First Sale ever
An excellent offering of Antiques - all original
TERMS: Cash or cheque with I.D.
For Info. call Ian weekends or evenings 1-519-821-6075 - Lunch available
Not responsible for accidents

Max Storey,
Rockwood, Auctioneer.

Dad's Best Memories and Recollections

The Sunshine State Beckons

My trip to Florida in the mid-1980s was anything but a vacation. It was an attempt to control a struggling health issue. I needed getaway time to recuperate. My sister Anna and her husband Jim Rolen's home in Palmetto, south of Miami, seemed to be the best destination to meet my recovery needs. Unfortunately, it would take another twenty years for Florida to beckon Gay and me to vacation there and enjoy its sunshine and sandy beaches following my recovery trip to Palmetto. And although we flew to Florida in 2004 for a ten-day respite, still another purpose for our travelling there was to finalize research for a family book project called **Family Sleuthing.** Thus our 2004 trip to the land of alligators was multi-purposed.

At the time we flew to Florida in 2004, I was not quite sixty-eight years. Our flight there would be the first of eight trips to the Sunshine State over the next twelve years. Visiting Florida that year was really special because it afforded me opportunities to obtain valuable information for my research that focused on a great uncle, Dr. Albert Milton Humber (1866-1960). I had previously found out through various clippings in Detroit newspapers that my great uncle had been Henry Ford's doctor. I also learned that this oldest brother of my grandfather had a son named Austin, one of sixteen first cousins that my father had on his father's side of the family. However, such information was not sufficient to write a key chapter about one of my father's favorite uncles. Albeit, when I found out that Austin's former wife, Elynor, was living in Clearwater, Florida, I had the good fortune to contact her. In short time, Gay and I made hasty plans to visit Florida, to meet Ellie and to learn about her former father-in-law, a man I had never met. Our trip was timed to coincide with a hockey tournament in Tampa, one in which our sons, Charlie and Scott, were playing. This was April, 2004. Our trip proved to be very memorable....

When Gay and I flew to St. Petersburg, rented a car, and checked into Dunedin's Best Western Hotel fronting the Gulf of Mexico, Ellie was a very spry eighty-four years and living in Hammock Pine, a gated community located near our hotel. Shortly after booking into our hotel room, we heard a door knock. It was Ellie. She surprised us with gifts welcoming us to Florida. She was more like sixty years of age. For the next week we dined and travelled to various sites she thought we should see in Florida. We became good friends. We toured historic Ybor City, travelled the Clearwater Beach area, walked the famous St. Petersburg Pier and travelled as far north as Tarpon Springs and Homosassa. Throughout this duration, we also had to find time to travel to Brandon, east of Tampa, to watch our twin sons play in a hockey tournament. In short time, our first Florida trip together was over far too soon. But, thanks to Ellie, I got all the info I needed to complete my great uncle's story. Our 2004 trip is now an entrenched happy memory.

Below: Cousin Dr. Gilbert Punches, my aunt Grayce's elder of two sons, has lived in Vero Beach, Florida, most of his adult life where he had been an anesthesiologist. Retired today, he likes to play the stock market.... **Right:** When Gay and I first visited Florida, we met Ellie Humber in Clearwater, 2004. Ellie provided me with enough information about her former father-in-law, Dr. Albert Milton Humber, for me to write a full chapter about him in the 2006 publication, **Family Sleuthing.** Gay and Ellie flank Charlie Humber.

Dad's Best Memories and Recollections

The next year, 2005, Ellie found a place for us to rent in Hammock Pine, the same complex where she lived. We travelled there in our Honda Odyssey via Clemmons, North Carolina, where we stopped for an overnight visit with cousins Don and Cynthia Ruble. In Florida, we stayed for a month, from middle of April to middle of May. In addition to making various excursions to Vero Beach to visit cousin Dr. Gilbert Punches, we also toured Sarasota and its environs including the Ringling Bros. Museum complex, the Dali Museum in St. Petersburg, a Blue Jays ballgame at Tropicana Field in Tampa, and multiple antique shops, malls and shows. The very next year, 2006, I drove with grandson Brad Shennette to Florida (see the story "Grandparenting" elsewhere in this volume). Gay flew to Tampa two weeks later as she did not wish to stay a full month away from our year-old Golden Retriever puppy named Zebby. Since our relationship with Ellie had blossomed we invited her to fly to Mississauga. She arrived in late August, summer, 2006. She loved Toronto, the CN Tower, Muskoka and, of course, our year-old puppy. Because Hammock Pine was not available in 2007, we skipped going to Florida that year. The next year, 2008, when Hammock Pine became available, Gay unfortunately developed pneumonia. Because she was unable to go, I decided to wing it on my own and travel in my Honda Pilot to Florida. Once again I stopped in North Carolina to visit with Don and Cynthia Ruble. The vacation in Florida went by so fast. I had several great times re-connecting with an old buddy, Billy Barry, whom I had not seen for over fifty years. Originally from Dorchester, I grew up with him in the 1950s. We played some good old-fashioned Fields Corner eight ball then found one pool hall in Clearwater that had a snooker table. As well, I did a lot of antiquing looking for vintage postcards during that 2008 sojourn in Florida. While returning to Canada late that spring, I drove to Alexandria, Virginia, for a three-day stay with my sister Anna. It is always a pleasure to visit with my "sastroid".

Top: The largest collection of Salvador Dali's art work, outside of Europe, is displayed in this prominent St. Petersburg Museum. Gay and I were enthralled with his impressive work in 2005 when we visited the museum. **Bottom:** The domed stadium called Tropicana Field has been the home of American Baseball League's Tampa Bay Rays since 1998. Gay and I have enjoyed multiple visits there, including one game with son Scott.

I had thought that our vacationing days in Florida were probably over in 2008, as the lady who rented her place to us in Hammock Pine permanently moved there from New Jersey. Some two years slipped by before there was any additional motivation to go to Florida. But in 2010 our good neighbours on Stewart Lake in Muskoka, Calvin Riva and Helen Healey, had just purchased a place down in Florida and were wondering if we might like to rent their abode when they were not there. Because they knew us as neighbours and friends (I've known Calvin since he was a boy), their offer was fair and we asked when the place would be available. The time was perfect so we opted to rent their "home away from home," in a place called Rotonda West. For each of 2012 and 2014, we rented from mid-April to mid-May. We found their winter home very comfortable, especially the lavish screened porch covering their attractive swimming pool, their barbecue and all the TV sports channels one could hope for in

When Floridian Ellie Humber visited Toronto in 2006, our sign greeted her as she approached our car at Toronto's International Airport.

Top: We have stayed at 202 Caddy Rd., Rotonda West Florida, on two different occasions, enjoying the winter home of our Stewart Lake neighbors, Calvin Riva and Helen Healey. In this view, Gay is enjoying Florida's sunshine by their luxurious pool. **Lower Left:** Billy Barry and I re-connected after nearly fifty years of going our own ways. We grew up in Fields Corner, an area of Dorchester, Massachusetts, in the late 1940s and early 1950s. We rendezvous now regularly when Gay and I visit Florida.... **Lower right:** Warren Mendham, grandson of Dr. Albert Milton Humber, flew to Toronto prior to his 90th birthday to meet Gay and me for the very first time in 2008. We also stayed with my cousin in his Fort Lauderdale home on two separate occasions. He shared wonderful memories with us and introduced us to his lovely daughter, Jeanette Quiton, and her family as well as his son, Jeff. Warren passed away in January, 2015.

sunny Florida. Their hacienda is located in Florida's southwest coast, south of Venice. Actually, Rotonda West is an area of land that is, broadly, a circular-shaped community with a population of nearly 10,000 people. Its landscape can actually be seen with the naked eye from satellites. Because of its geographical location, Rotonda West afforded us opportunities to visit cousin Judy (Daso) Herb in Naples and cousin Warren Mendham and his family in Fort Lauderdale. In fact, 2014 was the last time we actually saw Warren as he passed away in January, 2015, after we visited and stayed overnight at his residence. We also took a boat-ride tour from Fort Myers to Key West and back. Driving flat lands from Naples over Alligator Alley to Miami was a real different experience. I enjoyed visiting the house in Palmetto where my sister Anna Rolen used to live. And we certainly enjoyed visiting the Thomas Alva Edison and Henry Ford winter estates in Fort Myers. A wonderful pleasure was driving over the four-mile long Sunshine Skyway Bridge linking Manatee and Pinellas Counties. It was a thrill to see Tampa in the distance and boats gliding the waters of the Bay.

In 2014, son Charlie flew from Boston with his two boys, Charlie Jr. and Gordon (the G-Man), down to Rotonda West for four days. It was so good to see them. I think the highlight of their trip was going to Myakka State Park and skimming across the lake in a flat bottom boat. My grandchildren really enjoyed seeing all the alligators (as did their father, and grandparents!).

Obviously, we would not have continued to travel to the Sunshine State if we did not enjoy the climate, the variety of trees and plants, the various sites and friendly people. They have all generated many happy memories and there is no question: these Florida memories are lasting. We also are looking forward to future excursions to Florida. If we go in 2016, I will not yet be 80 years....

Top: This impressive 25-foot tall statue in Sarasota, Florida, recreates the famous photo taken in Times Square following Japan's 1945 surrender. It is a sure eye-catcher. Gay and I first saw it in 2014 after son Charlie and his two boys flew down from Boston.

Centre: Myakka State Park was probably the first place my two grandsons, Charlie Jr. and Gordon, saw alligators. Their grandparents enjoyed sharing with them the lore that alligators are friendly with Orgoglio.

Bottom: Florida's Skyway Bridge linking St. Petersburg with Bradenton to the south is some four miles long with a breath-taking view of Tampa Bay and the Gulf of Mexico. It is a lingering memory to cross it which we do at least a half-dozen or so times with each Florida visit.

Farr's Mills, 1815-1828

Some two hundred years ago, when Toronto was first known as Town of York, 1793, a much smaller settlement emerged along the banks of the Humber River. Its location would be near today's intersection of St. Phillips and Weston Roads in Etobicoke, one of the five municipalities making up today's Greater Toronto Area. This settlement was known as Farr's Mills, 1815-1828. A hamlet at best, it consisted of two mills and several roadhouses struggling to survive as a community just south of what is today's Highway 401. James Farr, the leading man of business at Farr's Mills, re-named his community "Weston" after his ancestral home in England. Before he moved from the newly named Weston, 1828, my great, great, great grandfather, James Farr, fathered son Thomas Farr, born, January 22, 1822. Where he was born is the now long-forgotten Farr's Mills....

When I set out to publish **FAMILY SLEUTHING** (2006), I did not know much about the defunct Farr's Mills. I doubt if my mother knew much about her great-great-grandfather James Farr or that there was a community formerly named after him. Back in 2004 and 2005, when I was researching the Farr family, I met up with Martin Proctor of the Weston Historical Society. He spent many hours researching the Farr family in the Weston Historical Society facilities. His knowledge about the Farr family, especially J. T. Farr, founder of J. T. Farr & Sons, one of Canada's largest General Motors Dealers back in the 1930s, was insightful. I did learn over the years from relatives that Farr was a prominent Weston surname, intermarrying with such other Weston families as Bull, Pink, Coulter, Cruikshank, Barker, Ellerby, Fairchild, Steadman, Wardlaw, Rutherford, Snider, and Cowieson. J. T. "Toat" Farr, as mentioned above, not only operated a prominent car dealership, but his famous lacrosse playing son, Ellerby Farr (EG), won, in 1926, the prestigious Mann cup, the Stanley cup of lacrosse. I also learned that Thomas Farr, my mother's great-grandfather, married Hannah Ellerby, in 1843. My mother's great grand-parents lived out their last years in still another mainly forgotten community named Thistletown, where Kipling Avenue and Albion Road intersect in north Etobicoke.

A distant relative, Lambert Farr, a grandson of the original James Farr, willed to me back in the 1970s a family photograph, taken, circa 1880, depicting Thomas and Hannah Farr, with their eleven children, including my great-grandmother Mary Ann (Farr) Scott. It hangs prominently on the walls of the Humber cottage in MacTier to this day. It is illustrated on page 194 of **FAMILY SLEUTHING**.

In the process of digging into Farr family history, I also discovered an historic plaque, affixed to an old millstone erected in 1957 by Toronto and Region Conservation Authority. Located in a parkette on Weston Road where St. Phillips Road runs into Weston Road, in part the plaque reads, "James Farr, who owned the mill, 1815-1828, operated five run-of-stones in his mill. The lower and older part of Weston was known as Farr's Mills." Such historic sites generate thoughtful memories and recollections....

These two illustrations depict the memorial in today's Etobicke erected, 1957, by the Toronto Region Conservation Authority, honouring Farr's Mills, formerly a community long gone, along the banks of the Humber River.

Dad's Best Memories and Recollections

Mr. Speaker Steve Peters

I'm not sure when Don Cosens first brought Steve Peters to my Mississauga home, but it was sometime during the mid-1990s when Steve was the Mayor of St. Thomas, in southwestern Ontario, 1991-1997. Over the years, I've seen Steve, now a retired politician, at various functions, including auction sales, in his hometown of St. Thomas, or at various antique shows or historical society meetings. He certainly was one of the most popular Assembly House Speakers in the history of the Ontario Legislative when he controlled the inner sanctum of Queen's Park, 2007-2011. A graduate in History from the University of Western Ontario, Steve has had an ongoing love affair with Canadiana throughout his life, mainly mentored over the years by two friends, George Thorman, a former high school teacher of history in St. Thomas, and former auctioneer, Don Cosens, "Mr. Everything," especially when it comes to the history of Elgin County, a political jurisdiction in southwestern Ontario dominated by the memories of Mitch Hepburn, Guy Lombardo, Mahlon Burwell and Col. Thomas Talbot.

The citation written across the bottom of this photograph reads: "Charlie, great to welcome you to Queen's Park, St. Pt, 2011". Standing left to right on the staircase of the Legislative Assembly Queen's Park are Don Cosens, Charles Humber, Speaker Steve Peters and Ed Ralph.

One day in the spring of 2011, Don called me to say that Steve Peters, before he retired as the Speaker of the Legislative Assembly, would like to recognize several of his friends in the Speaker's Gallery. These three friends were Don, Ed Ralph and me. The special date was to be the final day of the Second Session of the 39th Parliament of the Ontario Legislative Assembly, the same date Steve would retire as a member of Ontario's Provincial Parliament, twelve years as an M.P.P. representing Elgin-Middlesex-London. The invitation took me by total surprise as it was such a genial gesture on his part to recognize personal friends in such fashion. Naturally, I would do anything and everything to show up.

When the day came, Monday, May 30, 2011, the three of us met in the Ontario Parliament Building and were ushered to the Speaker's Gallery. Before the Session began, it was really quite an experience to sit in a special designated place in the Gallery opposite Speaker Steve Peters sitting in the Speaker's Chair. He called the Session to order and while wearing his robes and white collar, professionally rose and announced that he would like to recognize three friends. He said, "Seated in the Speaker's Gallery this morning I'd like to take this opportunity to welcome a good friend of mine, Don Cosens, along with friends Charles Humber and Ed Ralph. Welcome to Queen's Park today." We then rose, stood by our seats and were recognized.

Following the session, we all gathered in the Speaker's Suite located in the Legislative building. Here Steve had his own kitchen, bedroom and facilities, plus a dining room to entertain his special guests with lunch. Steve's essential role on this special day is most memorable.

H. C. Burleigh, M.D.

Dr. H. C. Burleigh, former soldier, family doctor, beloved historian, passionate genealogist, writer and friend, stands out as the key individual who unlocked the many mysteries about my great, great, great grandfather, Nicholas Amey, who settled as a United Empire Loyalist in Millhaven, Ernestown Township, Lennox and Addington County, 1784. I discovered Dr. Burleigh in 1972. A lover of antiques, I was impressed with him at the outset when I knocked on his door in Bath, Ontario. His house was a mid-19th century dwelling with interior atmosphere generated by antique furniture, books, filing cabinets, paintings, rugs, crocks, and much more. He was in his early seventies when he answered my door knock. At first, he was a little reluctant to give away family information to a stranger on a mission. After conveying my sincerity and that I was willing to pay for service, he understood my frustration as a novice researcher and invited me inside while he looked for a booklet he had written about the Amey family. It was 12 pages long and filled with valuable info. One paragraph resonating with me was reading about Nicholas Amey and his brother, Jonas, ethnic farmers from the Saratoga District of Upper New York State, who had sided against the 1776 colonial uprising. Banished to Canada after the American Revolution, all they really wanted, prior to the 1776 outbreak, was to live off their land and live freely from government infringement. So when the two Amey brothers tried to return to Upper New York State, May, 1801, to be with their dying father, a notice was posted in the Saratoga District where they, for decades, had formerly resided on farmlands that were invidiously confiscated after the rebellion. The statement overwhelmed me....

> Whereas in the course of the late glorious contest for liberty and independence, many persons residing in this, and other of the United States, regardless of their duty, having basely deserted the cause of their country, and voluntarily joined the Enemy.... Resolved therefore that, if any person who hath voluntarily joined the late enemy and who shall hereafter return to this District [Saratoga], such person will be treated with severity due to his crimes and infamous defection.

I often returned to Dr. Burleigh's Bath residence throughout the 1980s. It was a joy to share with him new ancestral findings. The more we sojourned, the more he supplied me with answers. He put me in contact with Amey descendants. They were just as gracious as Dr. Burleigh. They included Ibra Conners of Ottawa and Ada Johnston of Bath. They supplied me with photos of the 1740 Amey (Emigh) house in New York State (see Emigh House story in this volume). After all my research, I finally came to learn the family background of Alice A. Amey, my great-grandfather Charles Austin Humber's bride whom he married in Millhaven, just west of Kingston, way back in 1864.

When Dr. H.C. Burleigh died in 1980, this wonderful man's research of over 800 families from the region was donated to Queen's University. His research is now a goldmine for genealogists.

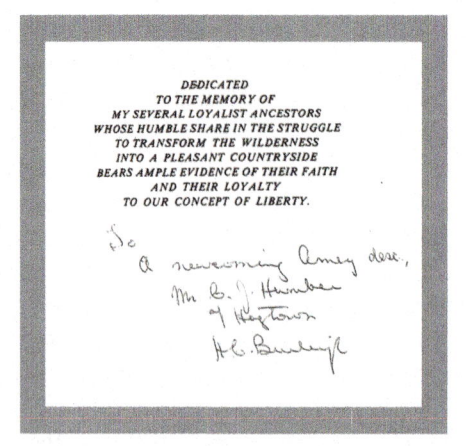

Left: Article in **Napanee Beaver**, November 21, 1973. **Above:** Inside **Forgotten Leaves of Local History** (1973) inscribed by Dr. H.C. Burleigh to C.J. Humber. **Right:** One of many pamphlets written by Dr. Burleigh in 1977.

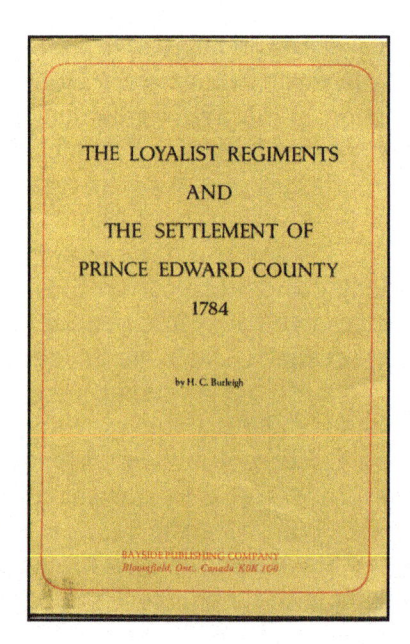

Dad's Best Memories and Recollections

100th Anniversary Dinner UELAC

Back in 1970, there was an article in the **Toronto Star Weekly** listing various organizations, service clubs, historical societies, benevolent societies etc. that one could join. Among the fifty organizations profiled was The United Empire Loyalists' Association of Canada (UELAC). Because I had been told over the years that the paternal side of my family was descended from United Empire Loyalists, I became intrigued with my family's history. Dad provided some particulars, including family letters revealing information that was often in the spirit of truth but almost always led to dead ends. I contacted the UEL Association and after serious family research became a certified member of the Governor Simcoe Branch, one of twenty branches, at the time, of the Association. By 1976, I was voted the Simcoe Branch President. At the same time I was added to the executive branch of the national UELAC, 1976, and became its nationally elected President, 1982, a position I held until 1984 while various provincial bicentennial celebrations in both the Maritimes as well as in Ontario took place. This time of my life was very hectic. I was a Board member of the John Graves Simcoe Association; I had been seconded to the MacDonald Stewart Foundation in Montreal; I was Vice President of the Toronto Post Card Club as well as a member of the Executive Committee, Monarchist League of Canada. In addition to these responsibilities, I was also the President of the John W. Fisher Society. On top of all this I was a father of four active children and an over-worked husband. When my UEL presidency ended, 1984, I retired from the Association to become publisher of Heirloom Publishing.

Thirty years later, when the UEL Association of Canada celebrated its 100th anniversary on June 7, 2014, I joined a full-house gathering of dignitaries at Toronto's Eaton Chelsea Hotel, including ten past presidents. It was a very memorable occasion honouring one hundred years of the UEL Association, founded 1914, as well as those thousands of UELs who came to Canada after the American Revolution.

The Past Dominion Presidents of the United Empire Loyalists' Association of Canada. The photo was taken Saturday, June 7, 2014, at the Eaton Chelsea Hotel, Toronto, prior to the Centennial Celebration Gala dinner. Front row, left to right: Myrna Fox, 2002-2004; J. Okill Stuart, 1994-1996; Bernice Wood Flett, 1996-1998; Back row, left to right: Frederick H. Hayward, 2008-2011; Charles J. Humber, 1982-1984; Arnold N. Nethercott, 1990-1992; Douglas W. Grant, 2004-2006; Peter W. Johnson, 2006-2008; C. William Terry, 2000-2002; Robert C. McBride, 2011-2013
Absent: Evelyn Drew, 1974-1976; Gwendolyn Smith, 1984-1986; Lt. Col. Frank Cooper, 1988-1990

Maurice F. Strong

Maurice Strong, "international civil servant"

Probably the most influential and best-known international figure I've ever met was Maurice Strong. This super salesman, who never finished high school, rather early in life, aspired to global recognition not only in the business world but in the world of diplomacy as well as the world of environmental concerns. Today he is a household name at the United Nations. Some call him an "international civil servant" while others label him "godfather of the environmental movement." He is also one of the world's most controversial figures in that he represented Secretary General of the United Nations, Kofi Annan, in Japan, 1997, when the Kyoto Protocol was formulated and claimed that global warming is "man made."

I became aware of Mr. Strong following the publication of **CANADA From Sea Unto Sea** in 1988. In a personal letter to me dated, September 14, 1989, Mr. Strong placed an order for volumes I and II of the CANADA Heirloom Series. Most interesting was a reference in his letter he made to the late John W. Holmes, a contributor to the Canada book, stating that this former Canadian diplomat was a fine man that "…we will all miss…." As this letter passed my desk, I reflected how thoughtful it was for Mr. Strong to write such a personal letter.

Mr. Strong, born 1928, originally started working for the United Nations when only eighteen and then, the next year, 1949, he was back in Canada working for James Richardson & Sons as an oil and mineral resources consultant in Calgary. By age twenty-five, he was Vice-President of Finance, Dome Petroleum, at the time one of the largest oil companies in Canada. He became President of Power Corporation, based in Montreal, 1963-1966. Before he was named President, Petro Canada, 1975, he was appointed to head up the Canadian International Development Agency (CIDA), 1970. He was anointed Secretary General for the United Nations Conference of Human Environment when it held its first Earth Summit, in Stockholm, Sweden, 1972. He subsequently was appointed Chairman of the second Earth Summit held in Rio de Janeiro, 1992. He was, to say the least, a very busy man focussing more and more on environmental issues….

My personal encounter with Mr. Strong took place when he was Chairman, 1992-1995, of Ontario Hydro, Canada's largest utility firm. I thought it would be a smart move on Heirloom's part to invite Ontario Hydro to support Heirloom's next book, **PATHFINDERS: Canadian Tributes**, Volume IV of the CANADA Heirloom Series. When I called his office to make an appointment, his efficient secretary took my call, indicating she would pass on my message to Mr. Strong. Shortly thereafter he personally returned my call and suggested a time for a meeting. At our get-together, he was quick to agree to my proposal that Ontario Hydro should become a corporate sponsor of Heirloom's next book project. At the same time, he made a pre-publication order for 50 books. It was then I suggested to him that he might give consideration to writing the introductory remarks to the very special chapter in the forthcoming **PATHFINDERS** profiling, advertorially, Heirloom's corporate sponsors. I proposed that Heirloom would write the "Introduction" for him, if he so wished, and that he could approve, revise it or even re-write it. He agreed to my proposal. After drafting the special Introduction and sending it off to him for his response, low and behold, Heirloom received a letter from him approving the Introduction as written, saying, "I don't think I can improve on your draft and am pleased to have you use it just as is." Needless to say Heirloom's staff was delighted with this satisfactory development. We all agreed, at Heirloom, that it was an honour to have his name, in such a way, associated with our forthcoming publication.

Whether Maurice Strong, who has some sixty honorary degrees and whose papers have gone to Harvard University, is the fox who has been given the assignment, and all the tools necessary, to repair the global henhouse to his liking, this controversial figure has certainly demonstrated with me on a personal level that he was a man with gracious deportment and cordial demeanour generating nothing but a pleasant memory after our brief association. Without question, he is the best connected and most controversial environmentalist in the world enabling individuals like former United States Vice President Al Gore (1993-2001), an environmental activist without peer, to cash in on the lucrative cottage industry of "man-made" global warming.

Right: Letter sent to Charles J. Humber, September 14, 1989, indicating Mr. Strong's feelings about diplomat John W. Holmes, who, before he passed on in 1988, wrote a chapter for **CANADA: From Sea Unto Sea.**

Lower right: Letter sent to publisher of Heirloom Publishing indicating that the proposed Introduction written by Heirloom's President was totally acceptable as is. The Introduction is found on page 337 of **PATHFINDERS**, Volume IV of the CANADA Heirloom Series.

M. F. Strong
72 Chamberlain Avenue
Suite 100
Ottawa, Ontario
K1S 1V9

September 14, 1989

Mr. Charles J. Humber
Publisher
CANADA Heirloom Series
Heirloom Publishing Inc.
2233 Argentia Road
Suite 304
Mississauga, Ontario
L5N 2X7

Dear Mr. Humber:

Thank you very much for your letter of July 5, 1989 which unfortunately has only recently caught up with me as I now make my principal residence and office in Ottawa.

I also want to thank you particularly for your kind comments in regards to John Holmes. He was a fine man, and we will all miss him.

I am enclosing an order form for one set of the Canada Heirloom Series which I very much look forward to reading.

Best regards.

Yours sincerely,

Maurice Strong

KS/ds
Encl.

THE FINANCIAL POST

The man with survival plan for the world

Maurice Strong works for Earth Inc.

By Eric Reguly
Financial Post

[newspaper article text]

Strong lives like a travelling salesman. Two years of circling the globe preparing for the Earth Summit drained him.

Above: Typical media coverage Maurice Strong has received for decades as a crusader for saving the planet.

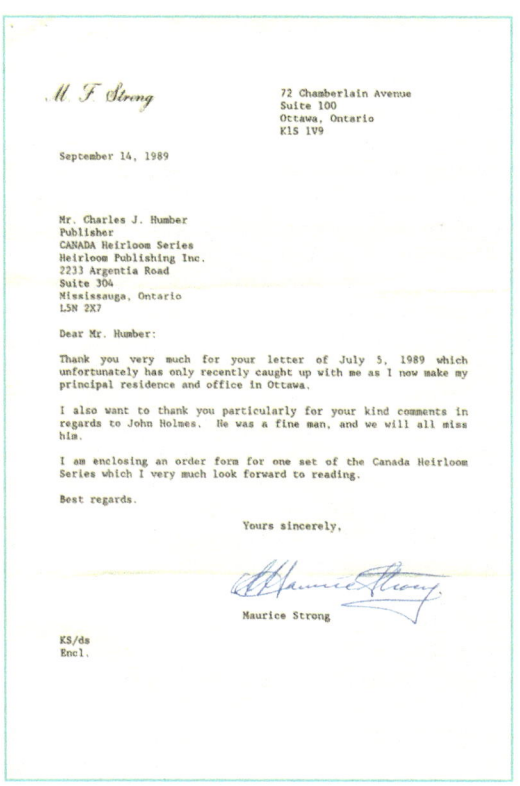

M. F. Strong

November 3, 1992

Mr. Charles J. Humber
Publisher
Heirloom Publishing Inc.
2233 Argentia Road
Suite 304
Mississauga, Ontario
L5N 2X7

Dear Mr. Humber:

My son, Ken, has sent me with the copy of your letter addressed to him of September 21, 1992 the information on your proposed new publication 'Pathfinders: Canadian Tributes'. This promises to be a fine publication in keeping with the high standards I have come to admire in you and I would be pleased to provide an introduction to the chapter profiling "Canadian Corporate Achievers". While it is seldom that I adopt a suggestion exactly as drafted, I don't think I can improve on your draft and am pleased to have you use it just as is. If you need me to sign it directly, please let me know, although I assume you could use the signature from this letter.

I do hope this important new initiative will be successful.

Yours sincerely,

Maurice F. Strong

MFS:mb

167 Dad's Best Memories and Recollections

Louis Mayzel

Louis Mayzel was an original Board member of the John W. Fisher Society following the death, in 1981, of Canada's 1967 Centennial Commissioner. When I joined the Board the following year, Louie was quick to befriend me, taking liberty, as well, to introduce me to one of his very close friends, Rabbi Jacob M. Kirchenblatt, a co-founder of Beth Shalom Synagogue on Eglington Avenue, Toronto. In another vignette in this volume, one story tells how Louie Mayzel, Rabbi Kirshenblatt and I went together on a trip to Israel in 1984. Before our memorable trip, both Louie and "Kirshy" thought it best to take me to see Gideon Saguy, Israeli Consul General in Toronto. I had shown both of them the ceremonial armband that once belonged to Field Marshall Hermann Goering, indicating that I would like to donate the "artefact" to the Yad Vashem Holocaust Museum during my upcoming trip to the Holy Land. Believing my gesture was a good idea, Louie expressed opinion that I should definitely share my plans and thoughts with the Israeli Envoy in Toronto. After sharing my proposal with Consul Gideon Saguy, the Envoy thought my plan was a most intriguing idea. Shortly thereafter he contacted relevant dignitaries in Israel. Thanks to Mr. Saguy and Louie Mayzel, my trip to Israel would include a special presentation ceremony of the armband to officials at the Holocaust Museum.

In getting to know Louie, I found out that he was a man with an extraordinary amount of love in his heart. Not only did he generously pay for my trip to Israel, but I saw how the mind of a philanthropist worked in Toronto, his adopted city. While he supported Israel in so many ways, he also was most generous in supporting the children of police officers killed in action in Toronto going back to 1952 when Constable Edmund Tong's life was taken. This act of love continued in 1962 when police officer Frederick Nash was tragically killed leaving behind four children. When police officer Michael Sweet was murdered, 1980, Louie reached out to the constable's family and helped them overcome their tragic ordeal by establishing education funds.

Louis Mayzel in the Terry Fox Book Store on York Street, Toronto, greets twin bothers, Charlie and Scott Humber, introducing them to the story of Canada's famous marathoner.

A Toronto land developer, Louis Mayzel took it upon himself to save one of Toronto's most historic dwellings from the wrecker's ball. After he bought the derelict structure in 1962, he oversaw the transference of the property to the Etobicoke Historical Society. The iconic Montgomery's Inn, built, circa 1832, is located at 4709 Dundas Street West in Etobicoke. As a result of Louie's generosity, the fieldstone structure is a cherished remnant from Upper Canada's colonial days and is recognized as one of the best preserved historic sites in Toronto.

In 1980, my family of six were all up at the family cottage in MacTier when Terry Fox initiated his Marathon of Hope, a cross-Canada run to draw attention to the plight people have coping with cancer. Terry, of course, was a prime example of one fighting cancer as he took to the road with one leg. Unfortunately, his race came to an abrupt halt in Thunder Bay, Ontario as he approached the halfway mark of his historic run from St. John's, Newfoundland to Vancouver. The media coverage was massive as it reported Terry's heroic efforts to run across Canada with one leg. Unfortunately, Terry died within a year, June 28, 1981, with the timely result that The Marathon of Hope was formulated as an annual run initiated by Terry Fox's family. At the same time a prominent historian claimed that in a couple of years Terry Fox would be forgotten, a statement that irritated Louis Mayzel who went out in 1982 and bought up all the books that had been published about Terry Fox, including Leslie Scrivener's best seller, **Terry Fox: His Story.** Louie opened the Terry Fox Book

Store on the first floor of a building on York Street, Toronto, selling the books at cost to the public and donating the books to schools and libraries everywhere. He was determined that the Terry Fox legacy would be perpetuated. Today, 2015, The Marathon of Hope has raised well over 600 million dollars for cancer research. The annual Terry Fox marathon, which takes place each September since 1981, is considered to be the largest one-day fundraising event for cancer worldwide. Louie kept the Terry Fox legacy alive, that's for sure, going so far as to create the Terry Fox Rose Garden in Jerusalem's Liberty Rose Garden in 1984.

Louie Mayzel, born in Poland, 1900, migrated to Canada in 1930. He couldn't speak English and only had five cents to his name. But he worked hard and happily became a Canadian citizen in 1935. He told me many times that his love affair with his adopted country was powerful. Such love motivated him to present one of his rose gardens outside Israel's Parliament, the Knesset, to Margaret Birch, Ontario's Deputy Premier, in December, 1984. He called it The Ontario Bicentennial Rose Garden. Louie Mayzel left this world for a better world, May 27, 1985, six months after taking me on my most memorable trip to Israel in 1984.

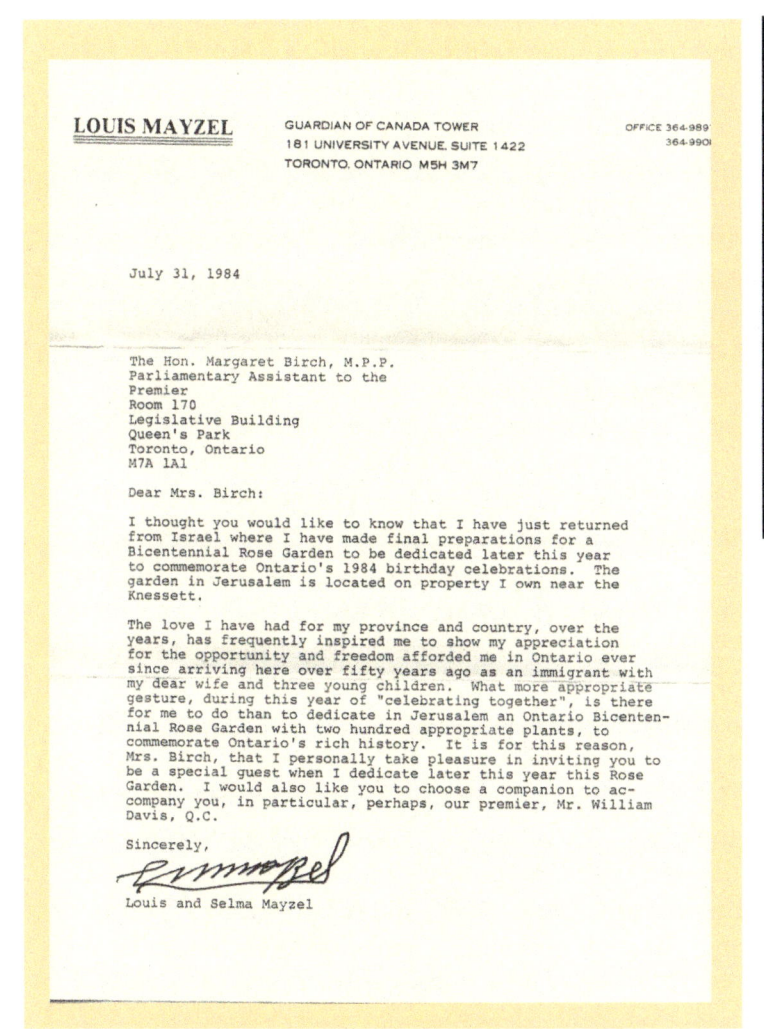

Above: Three months before Louis Mayzel took Deputy Premier Margaret Birch and her assistant, Naomi Goldie, along with Rabbi Kirchenblatt and Charles J. Humber to Israel, Louie Mayzel wrote a letter to Mrs. Birch expressing his unabiding love for his adopted homeland.

Above: on December 7, 1984, the Ontario Bicentennial Rose Garden was dedicated outside the grounds of Israel's Knesset. Jerusalem Mayor Teddy Kollek, recognized Louis Mayzel for his commitment to Israel and extended an appreciation to Ontario Deputy Premier Margaret Birch, for representing her government at the dedication ceremonies. In this view, Mrs. Birch stands ready to present a copy of **LOYAL SHE REMAINS** to Mr. Kollek. Louis Mayzel, who sponsered this ceremony, is seen standing, centre left, in front of Charles J. Humber, co-editor of the bicentennial publication.

Dad's Best Memories and Recollections

C. Miller Fisher, M.D.

Heirloom Publishing was preparing to publish **WAYFARERS: Canadian Achievers**, Volume V of the CANADA Heirloom Series, in 1995. This forthcoming publication would celebrate 125 Canadians whose achievements on the world stage impacted with lasting positive consequences. After profiling Bill Bigelow in Volume IV of this series, Dr. Bigelow, the co-inventor of the heart pacemaker in the 1950s, suggested that one doctor Heirloom might consider profiling in any upcoming volume of the Heirloom Series should be Canadian-born Dr. C. Miller Fisher, one of Dr. Bigelow's 1938 graduating classmates at the University of Toronto School of Medicine.

Upon my inquiring more about this doctor, Dr. Bigelow suggested I make another visit to his Rosedale townhouse for lunch at which time he would gladly tell me about Dr. Fisher, a world-famous neurologist. I learned that Dr. Miller Fisher was the first to provide detailed descriptions of lacunar strokes, the first to identify transient ischemic attacks as stroke precursors, and identified the link between carotid atherosclerosis and stroke. These were medical terms I was unfamiliar with at the time but, because they were important in understanding stroke causes, I felt Dr. Fisher's story must be included in Heirloom's forthcoming book. Before contacting Dr. Fisher, however, I hoped to re-familiarize myself with the Montreal Neurological Institute where Dr. Fisher had been a Wilder Penfield protégé. It turns out that Dr. Fisher's research was so profound under Penfield's guidance that Harvard University enticed Dr. Fisher to leave Canada in the early 1950s and come to Boston where he would be provided with the most up-to-date facilities to fulfil his research needs. Dr. Fisher accepted their offer and remained fifty years at Harvard where he became the world's authority on carotid artery disease.

Dr. C. Miller Fisher (1913-2012) identified the link between carotid atherosclerosis and stroke.

I did not realize I would be in for a treat when I directly called Dr. Miller at his Massachusetts General Hospital office. Upon contact, he was intrigued with the idea that I would actually drive all the way from Toronto to Boston just to interview him. But Boston was my "home" town, so to speak, so it was no big deal to return there. As well, since my sons, Charlie and Scott, were attending Brown University, any visit to Boston could be tied in with seeing them. Moreover, I always wanted to walk through the front doors of the Mass General where my father, Rev. Charles M. Humber, took lectures from world-famous cardiac specialist, Dr. Paul Dudley White, that is, before Dad earned his Pastoral Care Certificate in 1947. So, it really was a thrill for me to make this special trip.

I arrived in Boston during the spring of 1995. Dr. Fisher greeted me at his office door. He was dressed in a white lab coat. He excused the glass slides that were stacked everywhere engulfing a huge microscope. The slides, he said, contained specimen dissections from the cadavers of post-mortem stroke patients…. He claimed there were some 10,000 slides in his office. I took plenty of notes. The doctor was polite and soft-spoken. It was simply astonishing to meet the very man who established that the plugging of the carotid artery was the essential cause of strokes. I was in the presence of a very special human being, whose research would save countless lives in our lifetimes! When we bade each other farewell, a saint shook my hands….

Dr. Fisher, at ninety-eight, passed away in 2012….. He was an advanced soul generating joy and making happy memories for me. Today the Harvard Neurology Residency program at Massachucettes General Hospital is named after this internationally respected Canadian doctor.

Dad's Best Memories and Recollections

Col. Strome Galloway

I've always felt that people of my generation were very fortunate. We were born just several years before the outbreak of World War II (1939-1945) resulting in our not serving in military warfare. We were also not old enough to serve in the Korean War (1950-1953). When the Vietnam War surfaced its ugly head in the mid-1960s, we were now too old to enlist or be drafted for military service in that my generation was now in its thirties. Thus, it has always been a privilege and honor to meet up with military personal who served their country, particularly veterans from the Second World War. One such veteran I was lucky to connect with and develop a friendship with was Col. Andrew Strome Ayers Carmichael Galloway, better known as Col. Strome. Shortly after the Monarchist League of Canada was founded, 1970, I joined as a member, not knowing that Col. Strome Galloway from Ottawa was a co-founder. When Prime Minister Pierre Trudeau, whose closeted anti-Monarchist agenda led to the creation of the League, Col. Strome Galloway was at the forefront pushing an anti-Trudeau agenda and a pro-Monarchist platform. Once in a while I would meet up with the Col. at meetings. We struck a cordial relationship. Then when I became National President of the United Empire Loyalists' Association of Canada, 1982-1984, I used my position to approach Col. Strome Galloway to write at least one chapter in the forthcoming publication called **LOYAL SHE REMAINS**, a book being prepared to commemorate Ontario's bicentennial, 1784-1984. More than accommodating, he agreed to write two chapters for this publication venture, the first one called "The First War to End All Wars" and a second chapter called "The Second War to End All Wars". In editing his work I realized that I was reading chapters written by a very special person who loved his country dearly and had profound knowledge about the two wars he was commissioned to write about. Little did I realize when he was commissioned to write the World War II chapter that he had been a commanding officer during the eight-day Battle of Ortona. Ortona was a city port half way up Italy's eastern seaboard. From December 20-28, 1943, an all-Canadian force brigade ferociously fought and defeated the Mussolini-Hitler forces at seaport. In the process, this unit lost 1375 men in the action. Some might claim that it was the biggest and most important battle of the Italian campaign. What amazed me is that Col. Galloway barely mentioned this battle in his World War II chapter. Following the publication of **LOYAL SHE REMAINS**, we became good friends. Thus, when I travelled to Ottawa for research at the National Archives, I would connect with this fine gentleman who would take me to the Army Officer's Mess and encourage me vociferously to continue publishing volumes about Canada, stressing he would be a willing contributor for any of my books. While at the Army Officers' Mess, he pointed out to me a colorful portrait of General Sir Percy Girouard. It was hanging above the table where we were sitting. The Col. claimed that this remarkable Canadian hero was likely unknown to 99% of all Canadians. I had not heard of this French-Canadian myself. Then the Col. said, "Charles, you must include him in your next book. Make him one of the next 125 portraits of unknown or forgotten Canadians whose achievements have impacted worldwide with positive consequences". Then he went on to tell me of the achievements of this Canadian military leader in 19th century Africa, in particular, how he built strategic railroads in the Sudan for Lord Horatio Kitchener's campaign, in South Africa, as a force in the Boer War as well as in Nigeria where he eventually became governor. His overseeing of building strategic railways in Africa averaged better than one mile a day of construction. I looked at the very impressive portrait of Gen. Percy Girouard hanging in the Army Officers' Mess. The painting reveals the General wearing a typical red Fez hat. Strome told me he discovered this historic Canadian while he was teaching at Kingston's Royal Military College, noting that there was no known image of this heroic figure who had attended this college so Strome posed as General Percy Girouard for the artist who had been commissioned to paint the portrait, mustache and all. I thought this was amazing and when Col. Strome wrote the story of Girouard, the only image I used was the one hanging in the Army Officer's Mess in Ottawa. Take your pick whether the portrait is of Gen. Girouard or Col. Galloway.

The Grobb Cupboard

The more I chased antiques in the 1970s, the more frustrating it was to be a collector because there were virtually no Canadian antique reference books to guide people like me. Nevertheless, I probably did have some advantage over many collectors in the late 1960s and the 1970s. While they were charging off to auction sales to buy up the estates of farmers who were giving up generations of family ownership to land developers, these same collectors were, for the most part, uninformed or ill-informed about what they were chasing. On the other hand, because I had spent my formative years as well as my university days in the United States, through osmosis of some kind, I developed an awareness of antiques that many in Ontario had not yet aquired. It was also a very vexatious time, for we, as a society, were witnessing the end of an era in Ontario. Hundreds and hundreds of farms and country estates were being vacated, so to speak, to land developers and speculators. This boom was happening all across the province. Auction sales were everywhere, sometimes twenty or thirty a week in just the greater Toronto area. There was somewhat of a frenzy to buy up antiques as most seemed to understand that this estate market would soon dry up. During the process of chasing antiques, mostly furniture, I discovered many wonderful antique dealers, one in particular in the St. Catharines area. He was in his late seventies and for the most part retired. Knowing that he had been an antique dealer for over fifty years, I surmised that there were antiques he must have seen in the 1920s, 1930s and throughout the WW II years that he was unable to buy because he did not have enough money. I went to his house in the historic Niagara Peninsula area and rolled out five $100.00 bills, peeled them off on his kitchen table, and said to Carl Hutchinson something like, "Go and find me the very best cupboard you've ever seen but could not acquire because you did not have enough money." Both Carl and his wife were shocked that someone would or could be so plucky, venturesome or temerarious. At the time I do not believe any antique cupboard made in Ontario ever sold for five hundred dollars or more! But Carl knew I meant business. I explained to him exactly what I was hoping to find, namely, the best Germanic cupboard in the Philadelphia-Chippendale style. One such cupboard just had to be in the surrounding area that had been settled in the 1790s by Germans from Pennsylvania. We shook hands on the proposal. Almost a year went by before I received a letter from Mrs. Hutchinson stating that they had found "my cupboard". I anxiously drove to their place. They asked me to follow them to their barn where the cupboard was awaiting me all draped in burlap. When they unveiled it I was absolutely amazed. It was the very best case-made example of Upper Canadian craftsmanship I had ever seen. I asked, gingerly, what the price was and they quoted me five times my deposit, stating they had been told that it was crafted by an early German artisan by the name of Grobb, either Abraham or his son, John. I was in shock! But I said "sold!" asking only that they hold the cupboard until that weekend when I would return with the rest of the money. I had to seek out my next-door neighbour, a bank manager, and borrow $2,000.00 dollars. I definitely was going to be broke! In the meantime, I knew, just absolutely knew, as I clicked my heals, that my cupboard, made, circa 1810, by John Grobb of the Vineland area, was the definitive purchase one could ever make. This cupboard, without question, was *numero uno* in the trade.... How could I go wrong!

I purchased my cupboard before Phil Shackleton's **The Furniture of Old Ontario** (1973), Henry and Barbara Dobson's break-through publication, **The Early Furniture of Ontario and the Atlantic Provinces** (1974), Donald Blake Webster's **English-Canadian Furniture of the Georgian Period** (1979), and last but not least, Howard Pain's massive best seller, **The Heritage of Upper Canadian Furniture** (1978) were published. Although the Grobb cupboard was eventually illustrated in these publications, sometimes very prominently, this outstanding example of Upper Canadian craftsmanship gave our family a great sense of pride when we lived in North Toronto. In addition to these previous publications, the Grobb cupboard, over the years, has been featured in various newspaper articles like the **Toronto Star** (November 22, 1980, p. F10), and **The Canadian Collector** (May/June 1982, pp 37-39); it was also showcased at the Country Heritage Loan Exhibition in Etobicoke, October 4-7, 1974, handled by Henry and Barbara Dobson. It was a landmark exhibition that is often compared to the famous Girl Scout Loan Exhibition of 1929, held in the

Dad's Best Memories and Recollections

American Art Galleries, New York City, the forerunner of Parke-Bernet which eventually became Sothebys in 1967.

When we decided to expand our summer home in Muskoka and build a post and beam retreat for our expanding family, we had to raise money. Thus when a well-known antique dealer in Grey County approached me and Gay up in our cottage, on behalf of a prominent antique collector in Western Canada, he suggested he could broker a deal between the two of us clearly indicating that such an attractive deal was not only possible but probable. After several months of dedicated negotiations, a satisfactory deal was consummated making all parties concerned pleased. The cupboard had been a part of our family for nearly thirty-five years. But Gay and I let it go. The price we asked and got is irrelevant. What is relevant is that this walnut-crafted cupboard substantially paid for most of the upgrades we made to our wonderful "castle in the wilderness" in beautiful Muskoka. You might say that we gave up the best of the very best to get the very best for our sunset years....

The Grobb cupboard has always been surrounded by quality Canadiana such as the box-stretcher table rendered in virgin-growth walnut made circa 1790s either in Pennsylvania or Upper Canada.

Dad's Best Memories and Recollections

Deltiology

Charlie Humber was winner of The Toronto Postcard Club Annual "Best of Show" award in both 1982 and 1992.

It's a toss-up as to what the world's most popular hobby is today: coin or stamp collecting? But other hobbies are gaining popularity. One of them is sleuthing ancestry. With the rise of the internet, collecting ancestry data soon could be the number one hobby. Close behind is deltiology, the hobby of collecting postcards. "Deltiology" is coined from the Greek deltos meaning "writing tablet."

Postcards (or writing tablets) with images on them were illegal until 1898. This rule was enforced because all postcards delivered by post offices were meant for business or strictly for communication, not for pleasure. Thus the picture postcard did not really come into vogue until 1898 following the relaxation of international postal guidelines.

The golden era of postcard collecting is associated with the years 1898-1916, a time that slowly gave way to mass production. The period is often referred to as the Edwardian Period. With every subject matter imaginable, postcard collecting proliferated. They were printed and posted during this golden era by the millions. People sent postcards to pen pals everywhere. Enthusiasts filled up postcard albums, sharing their collections with others involved in the same hobby. The postal carrier was kept busy. Postage was cheap: one cent per card until World War I when postage soared to two cents per card – an act that terminated post card collecting.

All this activity was going on before the movie industry took off and before people had their own Brownie cameras. The itinerant photographer was active knocking on doors. He was as much a travelling salesman as the Fuller Brush man was in his day. By the hundreds, these salesmen did not miss a single town or village, taking bravado black and white photos of backyard activities such as Mrs. Eloise Murphy milking cows or Ben Schwartz scrubbing potatoes on his back stoop or proud little Grant displaying his fish catch from the local river. Church functions, St. Patrick's Day parades, the wearing of derby hats or the smoking of cigars, horses pulling milk wagons, railway engines chugging smoke, and steam boats churning the waters of the St. Lawrence or Lake Muskoka were all subject matter for the photographer who took amazing photos and printed them in lots of six or twelve for a sum. People did not fully realize that their postcards were actually recording social history. And all too often, after their deaths, their albums were unfortunately discarded. Albums that survived, unwittingly, have preserved much of our visible past with the consequence that postcards are being re-collected today by discriminating deltiologists worldwide although they tend to limit their specialized topics to railway stations, Christmas cards, famous people, and main street scenes....

After World War II, postcard collecting had run its course. But a phenomenon was lurking. Collectors began realizing that postcards, especially from the golden era, actually preserved the visible past. More than ever, deltiologists began comprehending that collecting ephemeral items like postcards was almost a duty. The phenomenon was similar to the revolution that the iPhone or the iPad advent has created today. Before long, emerging deltiology societies, like the Toronto Post Card Club, realized that they were part of a movement whose aim was to preserve our visible past. These clubs discovered that they were much more than social historians or archivists. They were preserving history. They held conventions and staged postcard contests. Today many millions of these precious images are now archived in thousands of collections.

For me, it has been a great experience to collect postcards. When I started collecting in the early 1970s, postcards from the golden era were selling for peanuts. Flea markets might offer an entire album of postcards, circa 1910, for twenty dollars. Today, the same album might fetch hundreds. Over nearly half a century, I have traded and sold many wonderful cards, at least 50,000. A real plus in this fascinating hobby is meeting so many wonderful people who passionately travel across North America looking for visible history to preserve. Postcards depicting Muskoka, where our cottage is located, plus map postcards, and scenes of Boston where I grew up, are areas that fulfil my current collecting passion. More particularly, postcards sent or received by various relatives over the last 100 or so years have become my main interest. Scenes depicting where former relatives have lived, worked or served are not just collectable for me, but are treasured family memorabilia. They generate a sense of identity. I have now collected over 400 of these "family cards" all of which establish a platform of best memories and recollections. Illustrated in this vignette are examples of three of my postcards that depict my family heritage: (1) my great uncle Henry H. Humber standing in front of the Humber Block and next to his car, in 1912, outside his jewellery store in Red Deer, Alberta; (2) the 1913 winning Western Ontario Baseball League Champions, the Stratford Classics, managed by league co-founder, my great uncle, Mait Humber, seen, in this view, second row, second from left; and (3) photo of my father, Charles M. Humber, a University of Toronto chemical engineering undergraduate, sitting, age twenty-three, at Egerton Ryerson's desk, Queen's Park, Toronto, where he worked during the summer of 1929 for the Ontario Ministry of Education. No question about it – collecting postcards is most memorable and also quite thrilling.

My Belfast Connection

As a family of four in May, 1969, we were living in Madison, Wisconsin. I had just completed my second year of graduate studies at the University of Wisconsin. Our money supply was not very flush. So, when I was offered an opportune position at Lawrence Park Collegiate Institute (LPCI), in North Toronto, it was hard to refuse. The school's principal, Bill Noble, was a top notch administrator. He had checked up on my credentials through his network and without ever meeting with me offered me a position at perhaps the most respected public high school in Metropolitan Toronto. This was all done over the telephone. When I accepted his offer, I was leaving behind my goal of graduating from the University of Wisconsin with a Ph.D. in English Literature. But I was thirty-three years of age. Gay and I had two pre-school daughters, the oldest of whom, Kristy, was about to start kindergarten in September. We also felt that we would like to add at least one more addition to the family. So, my dreams of completing a doctoral degree came persuasively to an end. Upon returning to Canada, we bought a home in North Etobicoke and I took up teaching high school as the new Assistant Head of the English Department with Belfast-born Kenneth Egerton Weir as the school's English Department Head.

Kenneth Egerton Weir was Chairman of the English Department, 1969-1994, Lawrence Park Collegiate Institute, where I was Assistant Head 1969-1977.

We met for the first time after Ken, later that summer, cordially invited me to his house at 60 Castlefield Ave. His home was about one half mile south of the school where we would both teach in rooms next to each other up on the school's third floor. This was also going to be Ken's first year teaching at LPCI. When I met Karin, Ken's wife, she was most friendly, very charming and assured me that Ken and I would work well together. She was absolutely right.

We also discovered we had much in common. I was very impressed with Ken's spoken English which was articulated Johnsonially. And although he was not raised a Baptist as was I, his background in the early 1950s included four years of study at Three Hills Bible School, Alberta, suggesting he had evangelical leanings similar to those of Billy Graham. In fact, I would later find out that when Billy Graham visited Belfast in April, 1946, Ken, at seventeen years, was there at Templemore Hall to hear a young man who would become the greatest preacher over the next half century. Ken proudly told me that he was born in Belfast where he had graduated from Queens' University, mentioning, also, that his father had worked on the RMS **Titanic** in Belfast before it went on its tragic maiden voyage, April, 1912. He also informed me that he was looking forward to establishing a debating club at LPCI and suggested that between the two of us we should be able to recruit some fine students for both the Debating Society and the Public Speaking program. He also mentioned that he was a gold-medal winner in debating at his *alma mater*. This comment was somewhat daunting to me as I had virtually no knowledge of parliamentary debating procedures. Upon reflection, Ken's university debating success was ironic in that my father, as well, was also a debater in the 1930s. As a McMaster University student, my father, C.M. Humber led his team to the Canadian Intercollegiate Finals, at Bishop's University, Lennoxville, Quebec. Of course, with Ken's strong background in English literature we fast became compeers and confreres. We both taught English literature at the senior level and often shared lesson plans and compared notes. Eating lunch together in the English office was routine. Our debating teams accelerated and won awards and we took pride in our students who excelled in literary comprehension. In other words, we made a great tandem and the entire school knew we were a team who demanded excellence from our students.

Dad's Best Memories and Recollections

When I left LPCI, 1978, to teach at Oakwood Collegiate Institute, I remember how my students at Oakwood competed with Ken's students at LPCI in both public speaking and debating championships. The last of the prestigious gold medal contests in public speaking, funded over a twenty-year period by late Toronto businessman, Harry Jackman, was held at the University of Toronto Schools (UTS) in the late 1970s. Two of the finalists were, ironically, from both Oakwood and Lawrence Park. The $3000.00 first place gold medal award went to Micah Barnes, my top student that year. Ken, always the gentleman, graciously congratulated me for being the coach of the winning speaker, the recipient of the last gold medal prize in Toronto Public Declamation contests. But the climax came shortly thereafter when my Oakwood debating team also won the City Championship that same year. And the school we debated for the championship was, once again, Lawrence Park. Ken just shook his head as his debating team was absolutely awesome, but Oakwood's team was up to par and won the trophy.

Over the years, our two families have stayed in contact. Ken and Karin, with Shannon and Tommy, journeyed to our cottage in the early 1970s. They have continued to visit us since we built our post and beam addition to the old cottage. As I approach my eightieth birthday, I have kept my family dentist in North Toronto. After my session with him, I usually drive over to visit with Ken and Karin who always prepares a scrumptious lunch for me. Ken, my all-time favorite teaching colleague, as he gets older, still has that sparkle in his eyes even though, in his eighty-eighth year, his eyes are telling him that he should wear his glasses more often. He surely has given me muscular memories and constantly has afforded me recollections of our great times together.

Upper right: Prior to leaving high school teaching in 1983, I had served as Ken Weir's Assistant Head of the English Department, LPCI, 1969-1977, and as Gil Baker's Assistant Head at Oakwood Collegiate Insitute, 1977-1983. In this view, Ken and Gil visit me in my Heirloom Publishing Inc. office in Mississauga, Ontario, circa 1999.

Below right: Ken Weir and I drove down to Providence, Rhode Island, to watch my twin sons play hockey for Brown University, 1995. Charlie, left, and Scott, right, flank Ken who loved the intellectual atmosphere of the Brown University campus.

Dad's Best Memories and Recollections

Isle of Wight, 2002

Since my earliest days, the name Isle of Wight has haunted me. It was from this historic island, located in the English Channel, four miles from Portsmouth, that my Humber ancestors migrated to Canada in 1848. I've always desired to visit the Wight. This fancy was especially kindled after the largest folk festival of all time took place there, August, 1969 when Bob Dylan, the Band, The Who, Tom Paxton, and Joe Cocker were highlight performers along with guests John Lennon, George Harrison, Ringo Starr, Keith Richards, Eric Clapton and Elton John….

At the age of sixty-five, I finally arrived on the Wight. I landed, June 16, 2002, at London's Gatwick Airport. This was five days before Gay would arrive. I took the two-hour train ride to Portsmouth where I stayed overnight at the Westfield Hall Hotel. I preceded Gay for a chance to familiarize myself with the Isle of Wight's geography. It also availed me to interact with Harold Humber, a distant cousin, who pre-arranged to meet me, in Portsmouth, at the famous Wightlink boat launch. He lived with his wife, Edith, in Carisbrooke, a Medieval town smack in the middle of the Wight, twenty-three miles wide and thirteen miles deep. After we crossed the Solent, we drove from Ryde in his three-wheeled Reliant Robin to his home at 14 Gunville Rd.

When Gay Humber arrived on the Isle of Wight, June 2002, she was met by this 3-wheeled Reliant Robin MK2 SL owned by Harold Humber.

Over the next five days, Harold took me all over the Wight in his Royal Blue three-wheeler. It was a fun car to whiz about. Harold's interest in our common family heritage was most evident as he truly enjoyed showing me Humber gravestones in various churchyards all over the Island. A highlight was venturing to the old Parish of Kingston where we located the remarkably restored dwelling where my great-grandfather, C. A. Humber, was born, 1838. Dr. Michael Howard, the owner, invited us to tour his property located on Emmethill, near Beckfield Cross. It was a thrill to visit this ancestral home and to hear stories about it before it was restored. After leaving my great-grandfather's birthplace, we passed Billingham Manor where David Hess Humber, Charles Austin's father, was born. It really was bewitching to travel over the same roads that so many of my Humber ancestors had trudged for generations. The Medieval Parish Church down the road in Shorwell, St. Peter's, is where David Hess Humber was baptised, April 2, 1818, and where he married my great, great-grandmother, Leah Draper, November 17, 1837. To walk in and about this 1000 year-old church and its environs was a very tingling experience.

On Gay's arrival date, Saturday, June 22, Harold and I drove to Ryde to meet her. On the way back to Harold's place, Gay agreed to take time out to visit Carisbrooke Castle, a 1000-year old landmark where Charles I was imprisoned before he was executed in 1649, by Oliver Cromwell's government. On the next day, June 23, before we bid Harold and Edith farewell, we went to the Arreton Methodist Church for Sunday Service. Harold, as the preacher, invited me to read the Scripture, Isaiah 51, verses 6-8. Following the service, three of us drove to Shanklin to meet his daughter who had also found for us, in Shanklin, two bed and breakfast accommodations, respectively, named the Lincoln and Glen Hotels, over the next six days.

For nearly a week, Gay and I travelled by bus all over the Wight. One day we visited Osborne House, Queen Victoria's summer residence in East Cowes, built in the 1840s. One of the tour guides, upon noticing my name tag, said to me, "Why not consider moving back to the Wight. We need more Humbers here!" Another day Gay and I ventured to Needles Park, in Alum Bay, located at the extreme western end of the island. It is a dramatic landscape of chalk erosion protruding from the English Channel, perhaps the Wight's most famous landmark. From high above a chalk cliff, Gay took a chairlift to the beach below while I walked two miles along Tennyson Downs to the lofty

Dad's Best Memories and Recollections

Tennyson Memorial. The Downs, some five hundred feet above sea level, are very spectacular and the walk to the Memorial Monument is so breathtaking. From the ground I picked up two pieces of chalk, wrapping them in paper on which I scrolled Alfred Tennyson's famous line: "I'm a part of all that I have met." I placed it under the impressive Tennyson Monument to commemorate my friendship with former classmate Stan Barrett and the chuckles we've had over the interpretation of that famous line. Among the places Gay and I visited over the next week included Sandown Pier, Shanklin Chine, Ventnor's Zig Zag Road where we also visited the famous Spyglass Inn, noted for its past smugglers and pirates. In Shanklin, we dined at such places as The Steamer Inn, The Plough and the Barleycorn, as well as the Crab Inn where Henry Wadsworth Longfellow wrote some of his best poetry. We visited the most famous thatched-roof village in England, Godshill, where the local church has been standing since before the Norman Conquest. We also visited the oldest place of continuous worship on the Isle, Bonchurch, mentioned in the **Doomsday Book**. One day, while researching the Humber surname at Newport's Registry Office, Gay shopped the Isle of Wight's capital.

A peak highlight for both of us was a day trip across the Solent to Portsmouth, visiting the restored HMS **Victory,** the warship that my great-grandfather, Cornelius Biddle, trained on before he left for the Crimean War. We also visited **The Mary Rose**, Henry VIII's famous vessel that sunk in the Solent and was raised from the deep after 437 years. The Royal Navy Museum was an ideal museum to visit before returning to Shanklin for one last night, leaving the Wight the next morning, June 30, for Gatwick. Upon departure, we took with us ultimate memories.

Top right: While visiting the Royal Navy Museum in Portsmouth, June 2002, we came across a wonderful collection of ship figureheads, all carved mythologically.
Middle right: Dr. Michael Howard shakes hands with C.J. Humber, great-grandson of C.A. Humber, born in this house on Emmethill, 1838.
Bottom right: From this point in Portsmouth Harbour, just across from the Isle of Wight, The Royal Navy plied the seven seas and ruled the oceans. Here Gay Humber reflects on the time that Admiral Lord Nelson sailed past this world-famous Spice Island Inn to confront the enemy at the Battle of Trafalgar, October 21, 1805.
Bottom left: One of the highlights of our trip to the Isle of Wight was visiting the Tennyson Monument overlooking The Tennyson Downs some 500 feet above the English Channel and Alum Bay.

Dad's Best Memories and Recollections

The Big Chute

Above: Governor Simcoe, aka Charles J. Humber, cuts the ribbon with Douglas G. Lewis, M.P., officially opening the Big Chute, August 5, 1979.

Below, left and right: Official Opening Big Chute Marine Railway brochure, August 5, 1979.

Other stories in this publication call attention to multiple occasions when I "impersonated" John Graves Simcoe (1752-1806). A most significant figure in the history of Ontario, Simcoe is sometimes referred to as "Lord Simcoe," a title he never had. Previous to his tenure as Upper Canada's first Lieutenant Governor (1791-1796), J. G. Simcoe had been commander of the Queen's Rangers, a British regiment that recruited mainly Loyalists. Some historians claim that the Queen's Rangers did not lose one conflict during the American Revolution.

Following the war, at age thirty, and after arriving in Upper Canada, 1792, Simcoe built the Town of York on the shores of Lake Ontario between the Don and Humber Rivers. It became Upper Canada's capital. Called "Muddy York," it was renamed Toronto in 1834, today North America's fifth largest metropolis. Simcoe also initiated the building of two major roads, Dundas Street and Yonge Street, the latter, today, the longest street in North America. His Honour also introduced a system of courts, trial by jury, freehold land tenure and English Common Law. He built Fort York. He abolished slavery forty-one years before Wilberforce in Great Britain accomplished a similar law and sixty-five years before Abraham Lincoln dismantled slavery. The "underground railroad" that so many runaway slaves followed to Canada prior to the Civil War could thank Simcoe's 1793 Abolition Act for guiding them as a beacon of hope.

During the 1970s and 1980s, as a Director of the John Graves Simcoe Association, at the time an agency of the Government of Ontario, I took advantage of the opportunity afforded me to dress up in a Queen's Ranger's replica uniform and impersonate John Graves Simcoe. Giving speeches promoting Simcoe's legacy became routine for me. Various societies and associations invited "Simcoe" to such places as Montreal's Le Chateau Champlain Hotel, Toronto's Royal York Hotel and the Royal Connaught Hotel in Hamilton to give talks about Simcoe's historical importance. In fact, some people were convinced that I was John Graves Simcoe reincarnated.

One of the "best memories" I've recorded elsewhere in this volume occurred when I, as John Graves Simcoe, threw out the first pitch at a Toronto Blue Jays game. The August 3, 1980 event got national coverage. Nevertheless, I believe the "best memory" I have impersonating John

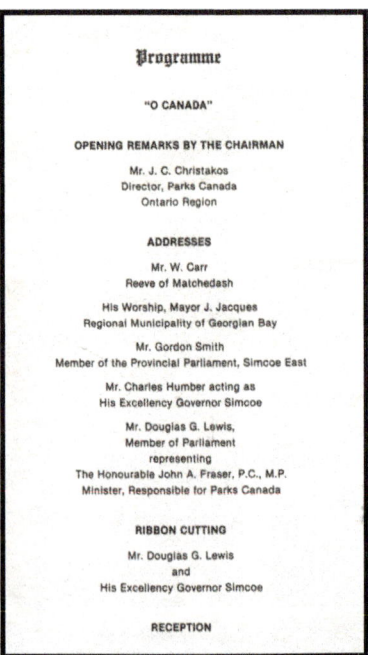

Dad's Best Memories and Recollections

Graves Simcoe occurred when "Simcoe" was invited to open the Big Chute, a Trent-Severn Waterway National Historic Site located just off the TransCanada Highway near Port Severn, some twenty-five minutes south of the Humber cottage in MacTier.

On August 3, 1979, three freight canoes, ranging from twenty to thirty-five feet long, and carrying, all-together, some forty voyageurs, including Hugh P. MacMillan, "brigade commander," were launched at Swift Rapids on the Trent-Severn Waterway. They paddled down the river bringing John Graves Simcoe, in his regal splendour, to our destination, the Big Chute, an Indian word for "fall of water." Upon our arrival, we noted the drop of gushing rapids hydrologically re-engineered so that cruise boats, up to 100 feet long, might be accommodated by slipping onto a metal cradle, on railway tracks, that could go up or down rapids tumbling some sixty feet. It is North America's only marine railway.

One newspaper (**The Beacon,** August 9, 1979) reported a crowd of some 5000 people. Many were waiting in a flotilla of boats for our paddling canoe brigade making its way to the official opening of the Big Chute. It was awesome to see a multitude of boats waiting for the dignitaries and the ribbon cutting ceremonies. Gay's mother, Bea Jenkins, and Gay herself, plus Kristy, Karyn, Charlie and Scott, our four children, were present. The downside of the event was son, Scott, age six, who, monkeying with his twin brother, was rushed to a hospital. Thank God he was okay after a falling accident on the cement steps that ran downhill parallel to the marine railway. Other than that incident, it was an event I shall always cherish — cutting a ribbon in the midst of the Canadian wilderness with people patiently waiting in their cruise boats to move on to Georgian Bay, down the marine railway, and from there onwards to, perhaps, Chicago, the Mississippi River, or even the Gulf of Mexico. But the entire affair at the Big Chute has generated for me over the last thirty-seven years a once-in-a-lifetime very good memory….

Above right: Voyageur Governor Simcoe arrives aboard a freight canoe with an entourage of voyageurs at Big Chute with a flotilla of boats awaiting for the official opening of the Marine Railway, August 5, 1979.

Right: Getting ready to "slide" down the world's most formidable Marine Railway after it was officially opened. Simcoe stands on the flatbed top layer with his followers who guided him from Holland Landing to the Big Chute.

Dad's Best Memories and Recollections

Aloha Hawaii

During my early years, I never dreamed of going to Hawaii. I had no reason to think about those eight volcanic islands in the mid-Pacific. I do remember watching Arthur Godfrey on his popular CBS TV show in the early 1950s plucking away on his ukulele with Haleloke, the popular Hawaiian hula dancer, swaying her hips and singing Hawaiian songs. But her performances never persuaded me to be Hawaiian-bound. In my thinking, pre-Cambrian Shield Muskoka was all the beauty I ever desired to see except, possibly, New England. But when my son Charlie moved to the San Francisco area and additionally bought a condo on Hawaii's Big Island, 2005, my thoughts of going to Hawaii heated up. This was reinforced when Gay's brother, John Jenkins, and his wife, Alice, moved from San Louis Obispo, California, to Waimea, a town at the base of the Kohala Mountains on the Big Island. Ironically, their home was very close to where Charlie had bought his condo with its hypnotic view of the Alenuihaha Channel separating Hawaii's Big Island from Maui and its often visible Mount Haleakala twenty-nine miles away.

Gay and I made two trips to Hawaii before Charlie sold his condo in 2009. His *dulce domum* was located at Hali'i Kai at Waikoloa, a very beautiful resort complex offering outdoor grills and a mixture of Hawaiian drinks, especially Mai Tais, right next to an ocean-front swimming pool with a sunset view. The first of these trips took place in December, 2007; a second trip ensued, February, 2009, when an old buddy, Skip McConkey, from Victoria, British Columbia, joined Gay and me for a week's retreat at Charlie's condo.

On December 26, 2007, following Christmas at Charlie's residence in Burlingame, just south of San Francisco, Gay and I flew to Hawaii. Our trip preceded Charlie and Elizabeth's flight along with their two sons, Charlie Jr. and baby Gordon, in addition to Charlie's twin brother, Scott, and his wife, Molly, plus Caroline, their daughter. They had flown from Boston for a Christmas get-together in Burlingame before the twin brothers and their families flew to Hawaii, joining up with their parents on the Big Island. The younger generation, seven strong, stayed at Charlie's condo while Gay and I, after meeting John at Kona's International Airport, stayed at John and Alice's lovely home. Over the next week, tour trips provided insight into the Big Island's attractions. John, an excellent tour-guide, took Gay and me to all sorts of places while driving around the 266-mile rim of the Big Island of Hawaii. He also took us across the interior of the Big Island along Saddle Road that separates two massive volcano mountains, Mauna Loa and Mauna Kea, the latter being 13,796 feet high, one of the world's most active volcano mountains.

Business card view of swimming pool at Charlie's condo at Hal'i K'ai, near Kona, on the Big Island of Hawaii.

Left: Waipi'o Valley on the Big Island of Hawaii. The drive to the valley's floor is a 2000 foot drop. **Right:** Before entering Volcano House Restaurant in Hawaii Volcanoes National Park, two Charlie Humbers, son and father, stand in front of the impressive outdoor wall painting of the very active Kilawea Crater.

Dad's Best Memories and Recollections

There are so many Big Island ventures to recall. All are memorable. Two lookouts where John and Alice took us were spectacular. After showing us the incredible Poloulu Valley from a special prospect, they next drove us to the Waipi'o Valley Lookout, driving down a zig-zag road, at less than five miles an hour, a drop of some 2000 feet that eventually led to a beach strewn with lava-black sand and crashing waves. Behind us cascaded waterfalls tumbling some 1300 feet to a propagating green valley. Both valleys were breathtaking but Waipi'o's Valley was special.

Various members of the family, on a daily basis, explored the Big Island. One morning on our way to Hilo for brunch at the world-famous Ken's Pancake House, we stopped at Laupahoehoe State Park on the breathtaking Hamakua Coast. At this site, a tsunami, on April Fool's Day, 1946, with waves at fifty feet high, wiped out an entire community, including a school with its four teachers and twenty students. Down the road at Hilo another 150 lost their lives in the same tsunami. Following our brunch, a natural instinct was to visit the Pacific Tsunami Museum in Hilo before venturing off thirty miles to Crater Rim Drive, an eleven-mile circular road that loops the world's most active crater, Kilauea Caldera. Seen from the rim of this world-famous landmark are steam vents puffing and bellowing from earth fissures on the floor of the crater that is known to thrust red hot lava hundreds of feet into the sky. Before leaving the site, we took time to visit the Thomas A. Jaggar Museum plus the Hawaii Volcanoes National Park Visitor Center. We then called it a day and took refuge for the night in two cabins reserved for Charlie and little Charlie, Gay and me, plus John and Alice. The overnight site was near the famous Volcano Café.

Other daily trips were made to Pu'uhonua o Honaunau National Park, where we visited a restored ancient village, a place of refuge for natives fleeing certain death long before there was contact with western civilization. On another day trip, while some visited the surf and beaches of the Kona Coastline, others paddled across Kealakekua Bay to visit the historic site where British explorer, Captain James Cook, was killed by natives, February 14, 1779. A prominent obelisk monument was erected on the site in 1874 and is visible across the Bay. A highlight gathering on our first trip to Hawaii took place one evening when our sons and their wives took Gay and me out for a gala evening of dinner and wine, served outside in candle light, at Brown's Beach House, at the Fairmont Orchid Hotel on the Kohala Coast. John and Alice agreed to babysit Charlie Jr., Gordon and Caroline at Charlie's condo.

When I learned that Charlie was selling his condo, he made it possible for us to take advantage of his respite one more time. Thus Gay and I returned for one last fling in February, 2009, with Skip McConkey joining us flying in from Victoria. Although we visited with John and Alice on several occasions, Gay and I independently rented a car for the duration of our stay and travelled the Big Island with Skip. We did not just visit historic sites but coffee plantations, car shows, flea markets, antique stores, various cigar and book stores as well as historical settings such as the statue in Kapaau that commemorates King Kamehameha I. This national figure is the historic hero of Hawaii who conquered the Hawaiian Islands by 1810 and established the Kingdom of Hawaii embodying the eight islands of Hawaii under one flag. One highlight with Skip was watching him haggle for a ukulele in Kona on the very day he returned to British Columbia. And on the day before Gay and I returned to Canada, we took John and Alice out to a splendid restaurant called the Bamboo Restaurant and Gallery in Hawi. It was a lovely way to sip on a Mai Tai one last time while saying goodbye to two wonderful individuals who went out of their way to make our two Hawaii trips so very memorable…. We have yet to return for a third time…. Until that time our memories guide us.

Top right: Skip McConkey with Gay enjoys the Hamakua Coast near Laupahoehoe State Park where a devastating tsunami hit in 1946.
Bottom right: Our final get-together with Gay's brother and his wife, John and Alice, took place at the Bamboo Restaurant and Gallery in Hawi on Big Island of Hawaii, February 2009.

Dad and Kik's Trip to New England, 2014

In November, 2014, my eldest daughter and I drove to Exeter, New Hampshire. The main purpose of our trip was to watch Kristy's (Kik's) youngest son, Mitchell, my third oldest grandchild, play varsity hockey for Phillips Exeter Academy, a top-rated preparatory school, founded, 1781. Since I grew up in Boston, 1945-1956, our trip also afforded me an opportunity to share with Kik my boyhood schools, my Savin Hill and Fields Corner stomping grounds, in Dorchester, and perhaps meet several of my old buddies or visit key places in and around Boston to quench her curiosity about her father and his so-called squandered youth.

I picked up Kik in my Honda Pilot at her house at 5:00 a.m., Wednesday, November 12. We headed for Buffalo's Peace Bridge, crossing the U. S. border after getting our coffee fix at Tim Horton's at the Duty Free Shop in Fort Erie. It took eight hours to drive to Exeter. We checked into the Hampton Inn before heading off to the Exeter hockey arena to watch the Big Red play a pre-season game. Afterwards, we took Mitch out for dinner before dropping him off at his dormitory. Mitch exuded praise for Exeter and seemed most happy as a student as well as his overall development as a hockey player. The arena was a very lively setting, packed with Exeter teenagers cheering on their classmate heroes, the Big Red…. It was most interesting to compare noisy teenage hockey fans cheering on their classmates to the so-called sophisticated fans in Toronto watching their relatives shoot pucks, shaking their fists at opposition players or yelling at referees while looking only for wins, not the development of their offspring's playing skills….

Located in Exeter, New Hampshire, Phillips Exeter Academy, is where my grandson, Mitchell Shennette, attended, 2014-15. A highly selective, co-educational independent school, founded, 1781, Exeter prepares its graduates for higher education while maximizing their athletic endeavours. It's hockey program is tops and for these reasons Mitch chose Exeter as his last step before going to university.

After eating breakfast and checking out from our hotel, we drove to the Exeter campus where Kik had a pre-arranged meeting with Exeter's college counselor. At the same time, I went over to the hockey arena where I had an appointment with hockey coach Dana Barbin. His enthusiasm for Mitchell Shennette as a human being and a developing hockey player at the Academy was encouraging. Feeling upbeat, I left coach Barbin on a good note. Kik and I next drove to Freeport, Maine, 80 minutes northeast of Exeter, where one of my all-time favorite stores, L.L. Bean, is home-based. After a two-hour shopping spree, we drove south to Essex, Massachusetts where Kik and I experienced one of New England's best known seafood "palaces" called Woodman's. And feast we did before driving to son Charlie's home in Wellesley, just west of Boston, in time to see grandsons Charlie Jr. and Gordon go to bed. Son Charlie's house is such a treat to visit. I love to admire some of our former antiques in his house, especially General Nathanael Greene's desk which I gave him, after driving to San Francisco, 2006, before he returned to the Boston area.

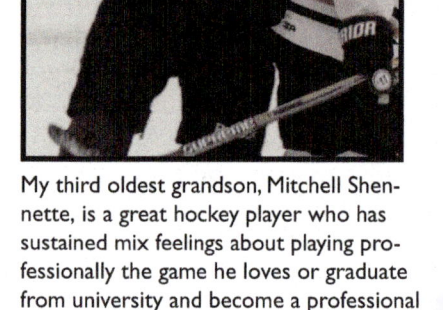

Celebrating its 100th anniversary in 2014, Woodman's of Essex is one of the best seafood stops in all of New England. It specializes in fried clams and clambake.

My third oldest grandson, Mitchell Shennette, is a great hockey player who has sustained mix feelings about playing professionally the game he loves or graduate from university and become a professional businessman.

After breakfast the next day at the Maugus Restaurnant, 300 Washington St., Wellesley, we did a bit of shopping in Needham at Trader Joe's before driving to Dorchester. While touring my old eighbourhood, we stopped in to see Paul Labbe who was still living at the corner of Ellsworth St. and Dorchester Ave., just north of Fields Corner, in the same house where he grew up in since the 1930s. After saturating Kik with Fields Corner hangouts etc. and showing her where Elmer "Trigger" Burke, back in the 1950s, used his machine gun in an attempt to silence Speck's O'Keefe from squealing on his famous Brinks Robbery (1950) partners, we returned to Wellesley, met up with Charlie who took us to dinner at the Brae Burn Golf Club where he is a member. The 18th hole of this course is called the "Jones Tee," named after the famous Bobby Jones Jr. who won the United

Dad's Best Memories and Recollections

States Amateur Golf Championship at Brae Burn in 1920. After our lovely dinner, we returned to Wellesley, had a libation, chewed the fat and went to bed.

On Saturday, November 15, we got up and travelled to Marlboro, west of Wellesley to watch Caroline, my granddaughter, Kik's niece, play in a hockey tournament at the Marlboro arena. It was so much fun to tie her skates before she went on the ice. She's a good little player and should go very far in her hockey endeavours. Next we drove back to Wellesley where Charlie picked us up and we drove back up to Exeter to watch Mitch's first official game of the season. Exeter won the game, 5-1, over Brewster Academy. Following the game, Charlie and I went to a post-game party on Elm St. in town where the coaches were celebrating their first league win of the season. Meanwhile, Kristy took Mitch out to dinner. In short time we said goodbye to Mitch and the three of us, Charlie, his sister Kristy, and I returned to Wellesley....

On Sunday, November 16, Kristy and I left Wellesley to watch grandson Gordon play hockey in Newton with his father being the coach. After the game, we bid goodbye and left for Hull on Boston's south shore. Here one of my best boyhood friends, Donnie Gillis, lives. Donnie and Loraine's son is a graduate of Wesleyan University in Connecticut and I thought it might be a good idea for Kik to discuss Mitchell's aspirations to play hockey at this institution with Donnie Jr. Our visit was somewhat short in that we had to get to son Scott's new residence in Hingham at 4 Sayles Rd. And what a lovely place it was for Kristy and me to spend the evening. The next day, while Scott took Kristy to the airport, I took granddaughter Madelyn to school after which I travelled into Abington to have lunch with an old buddy, Ronnie Barron. After our luncheon, I drove to Quincy and visited with Salvy Sansone who recently had lost a leg to diabetes. I wanted to cheer him up and he probably was the one who cheered me up. Later I visited with Earl Boyd who lives behind the Dorchester House on Dot Ave. I just love to see my old buddies, street warriors from sixty years ago. No question about it, we are survivors. How much longer do we have to cherish old memories together?

After staying overnight at Donnie's in Hull, I got up, on Wednesday, November 19, and drove to Exeter, once again, to watch Mitch and the Big Red Hockey team defeat New Hampton from New Hampshire, 8-1. After the game I saw Mitch briefly then drove to Wellesley, hooked up with son Charlie at the University Club, just off Copley Square. We had one of the best dinners ever sitting at the bar. It was such a delightful time to watch how my son interacted with so many people who kept coming up to him to acknowledge his squash game and how it keeps improving. The dinner was fabulous and along with the fond memories I have driving to New England with Kristy and sharing my youth hangouts with my oldest daughter, it was absolutely great fun to touch bases with Mitch, watch three of his hockey games, then spend some quality time with both my sons and my five wonderful grandchildren, including baby Austin who is just precious. The entire trip sure has afforded me so many great, great memories, so many happy reflections and numerous recollections. This was particularly true as I motored back to Canada, missing the biggest storm of the century in Buffalo by-passing it and driving home to a worried wife in Mississauga via Watertown in upper New York state and Ganonoque on the other side of the St. Lawrence River. What gargantuan memories!

Centre below: While attending a hockey game, my daughter Kristy introduced me to selfies. Here she takes a selfie of us, at a hockey game in Exeter, New Hampshire. **Below left:** Fields Corner was the area of Dorchester where I was most comfortable as a teenager growing up in post-World War II America. **Below left centre:** Paul Labbe has been an ongoing friend for over sixty years. He was a fierce street warrior who understood, as well as anyone, the underbelly of Boston. **Below right centre:** Ronnie Barron is one of some sixty or so friends I grew up with in Dorchester, either Fields Corner or Savin Hill. **Below right:** In order to get home from New England, I had to bypass the biggest storm of the century in Buffalo by travelling to Ganonoque, Ontario, via Waterford in Upper New York State.

Dad's Best Memories and Recollections

Visiting Britannia, 2001

When one of our two sons took a job with the Blackstone Group, 2001, his company re-located him to London, England. His residence was 61 Eaton Square in Belgravia. Such notables as Sean Connery, Rex Harrison, Neville Chamberlain and Stanley Baldwin were former residents of that plush area. In fact, the apartment where son Charlie lived was the immediate past address of Donald Sutherland of **M.A.S.H.** fame. In early, 2001, one half year before New York City's World Trade Centre was attacked, 9/11, Charlie invited his parents to visit him. That April Gay and I landed at Heathrow Airport and headed directly to Charlie's Eaton Square residence.

Gay and I were not typical tourists. On the go every day, a.m. to p.m., we rarely took time to eat in fancy restaurants or shop in exalted places like Harrods or attend theatre productions. We usually took London's Tube to places.... In doing so, we always had to "Mind the Gap." Sometimes we ventured outside Londinium (London's original Roman name). We went to Cambridge, spending a full day there visiting Cambridge University, visiting colleges like Corpus Christi where Christopher Marlowe attended (I wrote a term paper on Marlowe while attending the University of Wisconsin!), Jesus College, where poet Samuel Taylor Coleridge attended, and Christ College, where my favorite Renaissance poet, John Milton, attended. When Charlie, Gay and I made our trip to this famous university, founded, 1209 A.D., we greatly enjoyed King's College Chapel. Authorities claim the Chapel's medieval stained glass windows are unmatched.

This iconic sign is a warning to passengers boarding any of the stations in London's famous Tube. If you are careless you might get trapped inconveniently in the gap between the subway train's door and the platform. In your best interest, "Mind the Gap."

Other places beyond central London we ambled to were Greenwich and Southwark. A favorite place we visited in Greenwich, the home of Time and Prime Meridian, was the National Maritime Museum. After admiring J.M.W. Turner's huge (12' X 12') painting, "The Battle of Trafalgar," one better understands why Britannia ruled the seas for so long. It was intriguing to visit the dry-docked **Cutty Sark**, some say the fastest clipper ever! The following year, 2002, we had an awseome experience in Portsmouth touring HMS **Victory**, the warship my great-grandfather, Cornelius Biddle, trained aboard before going to the Crimean War. Upon crossing London Bridge, the borough of Southwark greets you. Here looms London's oldest Gothic Cathedral. Southwark Cathedral is where William Kemp, Shakespeare's original Falstaff, lies buried. John Harvard, a member of this Cathedral, crossed the Atlantic and founded Harvard College, 1636. We also visited The George, rebuilt, 1677. It is London's last surviving galleried coaching inn.

It was fun venturing to London landmarks like Trafalgar Square, Buckingham Palace, Piccadilly Circus, and St Paul's Cathedral, where a favorite poet, John Donne, was Dean. We also toured Westminster Abbey, the British Parliament Buildings, the restored Globe Theatre, and the residences of Charles Dickens and John Wesley. The Winston Churchill War Rooms were so intriguing to visit. Apsley House, the home of Artur Wellesley, the Duke of Wellington, was a winning experience. We loved Covent Garden and its Royal Opera House. We took an "in the gloaming" Jack the Ripper Tour and visited such places as Madame Tussauds, Sir Arthur Conan Doyle's fictional Baker Street home for Sherlock Holmes, and the Sir John Soane Museum, famous for William Hogarth's original paintings ,"A Rake's Progress." A boat ride down the Thames River, passing under bridges and by iconic landmarks like the Tate Museum of Modern Art, the Millennium Ferris Wheel (London's Eye) as well as the Tower of London (which we later visited for a full day) was all bewitching. We visited Canary Wharf, the visionary project of Albert Reichmann of Toronto's Olympia and York fame. We had lunch at the Wig and Pen Restaurant, the only building on the Strand that did not

Above: Built in the 1830s, the 170-foot tall Nelson's Column stands in Trafalgar Square in Central London. **Left:** There is a marker designating the exact spot where Admiral Horatio Nelson was slain, aboard the HMS **Victory** at the Battle of Trafalgar, 1805.

Dad's Best Memories and Recollections

burn to the ground during the Great Fire of London, 1666. While visiting the Monument, built, 1671-1677, that commemorates the Great Fire, we learned it was designed by Sir Christopher Wren who also designed St. Paul's Cathedral. The 202-foot Monument is the tallest isolated stone column in the world. Going to Speakers Corner at the northeast corner of London's Hyde Park was great fun. Here mainly crackpots stand on homemade platforms and spill out their trilling passions to an ongoing hoard of hecklers. Nearby, a plaque in the middle of crossroads, reveals where the notorious Tyburn Gallows once stood. Here, for six hundred years, Newgate prisoners were cart-drawn to a hand-made "tree" for public hangings.

The highlight of our trip probably occurred when Charlie took his parents to the Connaught Hotel for a farewell dinner. Charlie brought with him a vintage Chateau Lafite-Rothschild. The *maitre d'hotel* approached us at our table about de-corking our bottle to give the wine a chance to breathe. The cost for that was sixty pounds! Then he said, "You know, it's an expensive wine!" I asked him "How much?" Smiling, he went and got a book. He then pointed to the price. The going rate was nearly 5000 pounds! Needless to say, we enjoyed our wine that night. You could actually bite the taste! Like our soiree dinner, our ten-day trip to Britannia was so memorable!

Top left: One tourist site most visitors make sure to see in London is Buckingham Place. At the time we visited, the "Changing of the Guard" was taking place. It is an awesome and most memorable ceremonial occasion. **Top right:** At son Charlie's invitation, 2001, Gay and I visited our son in London. Charlie joined his parents on many of our tour trips. Here Charlie poses on the Tower Bridge, probably the most famous bridge in London crossing the Thames River. **Bottom left:** The Tower of London is probably the #1 tourist attraction in London. Gay and I spent a full day here, the home of the Crown Jewels, Chastity belts and the Bloody Tower where two princes were murdered by King Richard III. It was fascinating to see where such famous individuals were executed, including Anne Boylen, wife of Henry VIII, beheaded in 1536, Sir Thomas More, beheaded in 1535, Lady Jane Grey, beheaded in 1554, Earl of Kilmarnock (William Boyd), beheaded, 1746, ancestor to one of my very good teenage buddies, Earl Boyd. It was also interesting to learn of the beheading of Thomas Cromwell, in 1540, as he was the Governor of the Isle of Wight where many of my Humber ancestors originated before migrating to Canada in 1848. In this image Gay intermingles with two Beefeaters, ceremonial guardians of the Tower of London. **Bottom right:** London's Madam Tussauds, the world's most famous wax museum, is a major tourist attraction. One of "dad's best memories" was planting a kiss on Queen Victoria even though Her Majesty had been dead 100 years!

50th Wedding Anniversary

My parents, Charles Maitland Humber (1906-1988) and Evelyn Audrey Jarvis (1907-2005), were married in the Knox College Chapel, University of Toronto, on August 22, 1934. The groom's Best Man was Percy Howard Schweyer (1904-1962), Dad's brother-in-law. The bride's Maid of Honour, Lefa Scott Jarvis (1916-1997), was Mother's youngest sister at eighteen years. The 6:00 p.m. wedding was performed by Dad's influential uncle, Rev. Fred Charles Elliott, from Ingersoll. The reception was held at the home of the bride's parents, Gilbert and Mabel Jarvis, who lived at 444 Markham Street in Toronto. For their honeymoon, Mother and Father were driven to the outskirts of Toronto from where they hitch-hiked to Ottawa. For the next week they went from Ottawa to Montreal and back to Toronto. They each had one suitcase. I remember Dad telling me that when he and Mom arrived in Ottawa their wedding was reported with a photo on the front page of one of Ottawa's newspapers.

Over the next forty-seven years, Dad and Mom lived in many places. They began their lives together in Hamilton, Ontario, before moving to St. Lambert, just south of Montreal, Quebec, in September, 1935. After returning, 1937, to Hamilton, living at 165 Bold St., they moved to Hagersville, 1938, then Toronto, 1942, and then Rouge Hills (Pickering), east of Toronto. From there, their journey through life took the family to Boston, 1945. Their next big move was to Philadelphia, 1955, then to Conshohocken, Nesquehoning and Clarion, all successive jurisdictions in Pennsylvania. By 1981 Dad and Mom, in full retirement, were invited to live with son, Paul Humber, and his family, at 327 Green Lane, in Roxborough, West Philadelphia. These splendid sunset years were savoury times in which both parents were cared for by Paul and his loving wife, Prudence, and nourished by three grandchildren, twins, Paul David and Ruth, and their younger brother, Peter. Together, they brought much joy into the lives of my parents. In three years, 1984, Mom and Dad would celebrate their fiftieth wedding anniversary in MacTier, Ontario.

Certificate of Marriage for Charles M. Humber and Evelyn A. Jarvis signed and dated by Rev. F.C. Elliott of Ingersoll, Ontario. Lefa Jarvis was Maid of Honour and Percy Schweyer was Best Man.

Gay and I opted to host my parents' fiftieth wedding anniversary in MacTier, some two hours north of Toronto, a place where, since 1970, our family cottage has been home to many relatives. Mom and Dad's reception, August 22, 1984, at the Foote's Bay Community Centre, was organized by several women from the Foote's Bay United Church, headed by Hazel Lusk. The whole affair was staged about one mile from our Stewart Lake cottage. Approximately fifty relatives and friends joined for the festive occasion, including my father's sister, Fern Schweyer, from St. Catharines, and my uncle Bill Donaldson, husband of Dad's youngest sister, my aunt Edie, who had passed away fourteen years earlier. Bringing them was cousin, Dave Donaldson, from Hamilton. Joining in the party were my youngest sister, Priscilla, and her husband, Chuck Hurlbut, from Ohio, plus their two daughters, Beth and her husband, Craig Shoemaker, plus Jennifer. Sister Anna and Jim Rolen plus their daughter, Linda, came from Miami, Florida. Additionally, brother, Paul and his wife, Prudence, and their twins, Paul David and Ruth, drove from Philadelphia to participate in our parents' Golden Wedding celebrations. My mother's only brother, Gordon Jarvis, came with his wife, Marie, along with two sisters, Lefa Prosser, plus Lucille Longfield and her husband, Stewart, from Brampton. Several cousins came. Ted Donaldson, the son of Uncle Bill's brother, Sid Donaldson also came. Ted actually built the Foote's Bay Community Centre in addition to our cottage which he built in 1956 for Uncle Bill. Gay and I bought Bill's cottage in 1970. After several years the cottage was dubbed **Pine Vista**.

To prepare for the Golden Wedding reception, Gay and I were able to rent the Leckie cottage right next to our cottage. Essentially the immediate family split up with Mother and Father staying at **Pine Vista.** The two sets of twins, Charlie and Scott, and Paul Jr. and Ruth, all aged eleven years, slept in a three-room tent. It was a very busy time with just one septic tank and shower to meet the needs of some twenty people over several days of celebrations.

Gay organized the church ladies to prepare for the early afternoon buffet dinner. Mom and Dad were the exception in that they were ceremoniously waited upon. Flowers were delivered with Mom and Dad both wearing corsages. There was a head table where Mother and Father sat with their four children. As she did in 1934 when Mom and Dad were married, my Aunt Lucille sang the wedding song, "I Love You Truly." There was hardly a dry eye in the Community Centre. After the banquet, Mom and Dad's eldest presented a slide show depicting fifty years of happy memories. Daughter Anna proposed the toast to her parents while youngest daughter, Priscilla, read a poem written for the festive occasion. Son Paul gave the invocation prayer and as well as the dinner grace. Mom and Dad were humbly overwhelmed by all the adulation and love extended their way. They thoroughly enjoyed all the hugs and kisses. It was a glorious time, a memorable time, a time for joy, remembrance and fond recollection. After several days of family togetherness, partings became sweet sorrows. Mother and Father were the last to depart. I trailed after them on Highway 400. It was tough to finally wave goodbye to them as they veered off to Pennsylvania along Highway 401 while I carried on to our home in North Toronto.

But the whole affair was very memorable, an event of a lifetime I have held close to my heart ever since....

Above: Golden Wedding Annniversary cake served to some fifty guests who attended the celebration, August 22, 1984.
Top left: Mom and Dad, ready to cut the cake, are flanked, by their four children, left to right, Charles Humber, Priscilla Hurlbut, Anna Rolen and Paul Humber. Sitting off to the right are twins Charlie and Scott Humber and their cousin Ruth Humber.
Top right: Charles and Evelyn flank Fern Schweyer, Dad's oldest sister who was 81 years when this photo was taken at the anniversary dinner at Foote's Bay.
Bottom left: Following their memorable Golden Wedding Anniversary celebration at the Foote's Bay Community Centre, my parents spent the next several days enjoying the company of their four children and nine grandchildren at their eldest son's Muskoka cottage. In this view, Dad, in his seventy-eighth year, and Mom, at seventy-six years, relax under a white pine tree that is today very mature and majestic.

Dad's Best Memories and Recollections

Brian and Betty, the Very Best of the Very Best

THE SPECTATOR Saturday, May 18, 1996 Page H10

A Georgian Masterpiece

Dochstader Hotel, built in 1845, is now a spacious one-family home

Left: On May 18, 1996, **The Hamilton Spectator** showcased Brian and Betty's home, the former Dochstader Hotel, on River Road West between Caledonia and Cayuga, Ontario.

Below: Betty and Brian share an intense moment at either Charlie or Scott Humber's wedding, 2001 or 2003.

Many people have walked with me on my journey through life. As wayfarers, some have walked with me for lengthy distances but veered off our path to pursue other interests. Some have left indelible impressions on me, but took different turns and all but disappeared from my life. Others, over many years, have travelled in tandem with me. Brian and Betty are two of those unforgettable individuals. They have not only shared their journey but have brought a great deal of joy over the years both to me and to my family.

Betty Mitchell is originally from the Burin Peninsula, a finger-looking jut of land, some eighty miles long, that penetrates the Atlantic Ocean from the southern coast of Newfoundland. Newfoundland is one of those rare places where people, like Betty, when they leave their homeland to discover their passion elsewhere, tend to leave a portion of their hearts behind them....

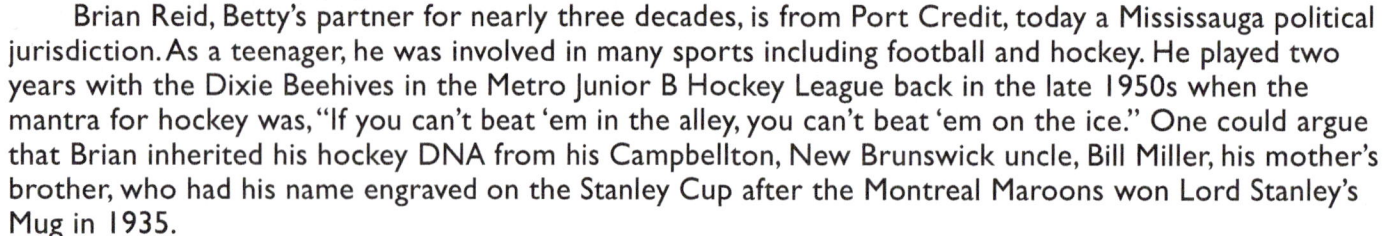

Brian Reid, Betty's partner for nearly three decades, is from Port Credit, today a Mississauga political jurisdiction. As a teenager, he was involved in many sports including football and hockey. He played two years with the Dixie Beehives in the Metro Junior B Hockey League back in the late 1950s when the mantra for hockey was, "If you can't beat 'em in the alley, you can't beat 'em on the ice." One could argue that Brian inherited his hockey DNA from his Campbellton, New Brunswick uncle, Bill Miller, his mother's brother, who had his name engraved on the Stanley Cup after the Montreal Maroons won Lord Stanley's Mug in 1935.

Brian and Betty's home is the historic 1845 Dochstader Hotel, the only building still left from the days when Mount Healy was a busy 19th century village on the west bank of the Grand River between Caledonia and Cayuga. They bought the 9000 square-foot "hotel" with its nineteen rooms in 1990. The Georgian dwelling includes nine bedrooms, a ballroom, a former tavern and a coach house which Brian and Betty have conveniently converted into a recreation room. Here multiple guests have assembled and enjoyed Havana cigars from Brian's extensive tobacco collection. Here they have sipped the best ever Manhattans prepared by Betty. Here multiple TV Sports are watched by hockey and baseball aficionados. Over many years, the Dochstader has rocked!

The "Best of the Best"?
Brian

Dad's Best Memories and Recollections

190

Since purchasing the Dochstader Hotel, Brian and Betty's home has become a mecca for dinner parties enriched by joviality, laughter and exquisite hospitality. One of the most memorable affairs took place on New Year's Eve, 1999, when everyone from the rural neighbourhood came to say goodbye to the 20th century and cheered the birth of the 21st century. Brian and Betty over the years have also found unique ways to party. They've hired stretch limousines to take their guests on joy rides through the countryside before surprising the entire party with a lavish dinner served by a coterie of food providers. On one occasion, they hired a team of actors to perform a "Murder Mystery" in their upstairs ballroom and invited the neighborhood of some sixty guests to guess "Who done it?" The fun-loving proprietors of the Dochstader have also hosted hayrides pulled by teams of horses in the midst of one very dark and cold winter night. On another occasion they convened a Halloween Party where guests masqueraded as historical figures. Two people showed up as King Henry VIII! One Christmas, 2002, Brian and Betty hosted the entire Humber family with a seven-course Christmas turkey dinner. There must have been a hundred candles saluting the gala affair. On the occasion of Betty's 60th birthday, Brian hired a river boat to take a group of some sixty people on a dinner cruise along the Grand River. Their gracious hospitality has been rewarded because just about everyone along West River Road, in Haldimand County, has joined in lasting friendship.

Over the years, Brian and Betty have joined Gay and me on memorable excursions. One of the first ones we took was to Dorset, Vermont, back in the late-1990s where a prominent antique show, "on the village green," is staged every other year. To celebrate our trip, we opened a bottle of wine and lunched at a picnic table in Upper New York State in Canandaigua and watched the sunlight dance on the impressive Finger Lake with the same name. Betty and Brian shared with us our parental joy when our twin sons, Charlie and Scott, were married respectively, 2001, in Old Lyme, Connecticut, and in Middleton, Rhode Island, 2003. It was sheer joy to have them attend and meet so many relatives on those two wondrous occasions, including my ninety-seven year old mother.

Brian and Betty have journeyed many times to our cottage, bringing with them their friendship and ultimate desire to share in good times. On my 70th and 75th birthdays they've made the trip north to MacTier, in Muskoka, where they charmingly interacted with all members of the family almost as if they were long-lost family relatives. The greatest memories I have of them is that they've just simply fit in and become one of us. Indeed they are family, especially when it comes to antiques, Manhattans, a love for good-living, good food and robust laughter. President of Park Thermal International, a leading North American supplier of Thermal Process Technology co-founded by Brian's father, 1938, Brian exudes with professional aplomb and a delicate balance of aloofness and interaction that make him not just a very fine salesman but a very good friend complemented by Betty who has the distinct ability to make anyone believe that they have known her since her childhood days in Newfoundland.

Top: Brian Reid gets ready for New Year's Eve 2000; Manhattans and Martinis were flowing. **Second from top:** Brian, Charlie Humber Sr., Scott Humber, Charlie Humber Jr. and Erik Shennette digest Christmas dinner, 2002, with Cuban cigars at the Dochstader Hotel. **Second from Bottom:** Brian and Betty take a moment to reflect with Gay on the tranquility of the Sir John Johnson estate in New York's Mohawk Valley, circa 1998. **Bottom:** Betty celebrated her happy 60th birthday in 2008, on a dinner "cruise" down the Grand River.

Dad's Best Memories and Recollections

Goderich, a Last Hurrah

I'm not sure how many trips I made to Goderich before 1985, the year Dad and I made our historic jaunt there. It was the only time the two of us went exclusively together to his hometown. Our timely excursion occurred some three years before he passed away, July 9, 1988. I can now look back and fondly remember that, in 1942, at age six years, I celebrated Christmas in Goderich where my grandparents lived. They lived in the middle house of three former Humber homes, side by side, along Victoria St. S. It was truly a family affair as the Bill Donaldsons from Hamilton and Percy Schweyers from Nelles Corners also came for that memorable Christmas. And when my grandfather died, 1943, I remember the trek Dad and Mom made with their four children from Toronto in the family's 1930 Model A Ford. To make such a trip in March to attend the funeral was a bleak occasion. One thing I vividly remember about this particular trip was taking note of the trees on Victoria Street that were being tapped for maple sugar. Glistening silver-looking buckets hanging on thick tree trunks five feet above the sidewalks caught the slow drip, drip of the sap. Twenty years later I also recall driving my aunt Edie Donaldson to Goderich to attend the funeral of a school chum by the name of Delight Munch. My grandmother, Lizzie Humber, accompanied her youngest daughter for the over-night trip. The next time Goderich came on the scene occurred when my grandmother, on March 15, 1978, passed on in St. Catharines, one week shy of her 103rd birthday. Her internment service was conducted by my father in the Maitland Cemetery chapel. Grandmother Humber rests in the same plot with her husband, my grandfather, in addition to C.A. Humber and his wife, Alice A. (Amey) Humber, my great-grandparents. All who attended the ceremony will remember, following the service, how Dad tapped a corner of the closed casket, a timely earthly farewell to his Mother.

Standing on the front walk of his Goderich home on Victoria Street, bearing his family's surname, is Charles Maitland Humber, aged 2 years, 1908.

I really had no reason to visit the beautiful town of Goderich following my grandmother Lizzie Humber's passing in 1978. The three houses, once Humber-owned on Victoria St. between St. David and East Streets, all had been sold off years before she passed. So there was no immediate connection to Goderich for me other than to visit a town where my great-grandfather, Charles Austin Humber, along with his family, had moved to in 1872, or to visit the town where both my grandfather, Charles Herbert, or my father, Charles Maitland, were born, respectively, 1873 and 1906. But when Dad and Mom decided to trek from Philadelphia to Ontario in 1985, Dad indicated that he'd like to have one last excursion to Goderich. Arrangements were made for Dad and me to leave Mom behind with younger sisters, Lucille Longfield and Lefa Prosser, in Brampton, while a father and his namesake son journeyed together to his birth place for an overnight "Last Hurrah." It would be a memorable trip, for sure….

As we approached Maitland Cemetery on the east side of Highway 8, just a couple of miles south of Goderich, Dad indicated that he'd like to drive through and see the prominent gravestone memorial honoring both his parents and his grandparents. After taking a tour of the Cemetery and finding the impressive gravestone, and taking photographs, we returned to Highway 8 which leads directly to Victoria St. We slowly drove right past the three "Humber houses." Full of sentiment, Dad enjoyed seeing the three residences and while driving past them he indicated that he'd like to stop and take a walkabout. After stopping, we got out and moseyed about the three properties that seamlessly stretched a full block. No question about it, Dad really enjoyed this opportunity and touched the porch railing of the middle house, recalling two wedding receptions that had taken place on the veranda and all the relatives that had come to the two weddings of his sisters, Fern Schweyer, in 1925, and Edith Donaldson, in 1929.

In addition to being a devout Christian, Dad was also a deep-feeling human being. An example of his warm-hearted personality was reinforced after recognizing his effusive attraction to Goderich sunsets. Thus, while we were standing on the sandy beach below the famous Goderich bluffs, we watched the setting sun slip below the Lake Huron horizon, a frozen-in-time moment. Then, almost on cue, we quickly got into our car and drove to the top of the 60-foot bluff overlooking Lake Huron and watched the sun sink below the horizon a second time. This was something Dad wanted to do, namely, observe the Goderich sunset twice in one evening something he hadn't done since he was a boy! It was such a lovely evening. The sky was so clear. Seeing the two sunsets almost simultaneously was a marvellous treat for Dad! Prior to undertaking this achievement, while we were on the sandy Lake Huron beach below the bluffs, Dad doffed his shoes and socks and walked ankle deep into Lake Huron. He just wanted to feel the cold water of Lake

Dad's Best Memories and Recollections

Huron one more time. I am convinced he felt he was re-capturing his Goderich youth in the very same water he pranced around in when he was a pre-teenager during World War I. It was a thrill for him and a marvellous experience for me to watch my endearing Father recapture such joy….

We then journeyed to the town Square. A unique landscape design, the Square is really a circular road-grid encompassing green space. It is like a wheel with eight streets poking out in all directions from its centre. Here we sat down on a bench facing the very spot where the C.A. Humber & Son jewellery store operated from 1890 to 1928. It was twilight. The evening was lovely. On the park bench next to us were two elderly gentlemen. I decided to strike up a conversation and asked if they were "Goderich old boys". They replied "All their lives." The conversation evolved to the extent they wondered who we were. So, I indicated that my Dad, sitting next to me, was born in Goderich and that his father formerly operated a jewellery store across from where we were sitting. I also informed them that "People claim I am the spitting image of my grandfather." I also told them that my father, my grandfather and I all had the same first name. They then said that my name must be "Charlie Humber!" It turns out that they did not directly remember Dad but they did remember my grandfather because of his well-known store and the fact that my grandfather was so involved in the Goderich community. Dad and I eventually checked into the historic Bedford Hotel for our one night stay. Before checking out the next morning, we went to the Bedford restaurant where dad desired to eat breakfast mainly because it was a place where he and his father had eaten in earlier years. Dad tried to find the same spot he used to sit at when he was just a high school student. Before breakfast, Dad asked the waiter for "Two on a raft looking at you." The waiter was caught off guard. Then Dad responded, "I've changed my mind. Make that order a shipwreck." We all chuckled at what Dad had said. It was an expression he would have used seventy years earlier. It simply meant that he wanted scrambled eggs for breakfast, not two eggs on toast! This was vintage Dad as he explained his prank joke to the waiter.

As we parted Goderich, Dad opened the window of the car, peered out and yelled in a jingle, "So long, it's been good to know you…." It was as if he expected that somebody was listening. It was certainly a memorable trip….

Top far right: When visiting Goderich, August, 1985, Dad wanted to visit the gravesite of both his parents and grandparents memorialized by this impressive marker in the Maitland cemetery.

Bottom far right: The Bedford Hotel on Goderich Square is where my grandfather used to take his son for breakfast or a treat. Dad and I recaptured this event by staying overnight and ordering breakfast the next morning before leaving Dad's hometown for the last time and returning to Brampton. Dad viewed bottom left under canopy.

Top Left: This is the home that Charles Herbert Humber and Lizzie Humber moved back to in the late 1920s. It was originally their matrimonial home in 1901. Here two wedding receptions were held for the two Humber daughters and it was from this porch that my grandfather's coffin was taken down the front steps, in 1943, and driven to Maitland Cemetery where he was buried.

Bottom left: Stars and stripes flew for many years aloft the Humber house on East and Victoria Streets as successive United States consuls took over the house in the 1890s. Shortly after Dad's birth, 1906, the Humber family repossessed this house until father left Goderich in 1925, to attend University of Toronto.

Dad's Best Memories and Recollections

Les Donaldson, Dean of Antiques

Canadian antique dealer for 50 years, Les Donaldson (1907-1989) was unquestionably the "Dean of Antique Dealers". A prince among his peers, Les, though born in Scotland, he died, some might say, more Canadian than the red maple leaf.

After wandering into his antique shop at 13 Salisbury Ave., Galt, Ontario, during the 1970s or '80s, one would eventually be greeted by Les Donaldson sitting at his "untouched surface" harvest table in the kitchen of his circa 1890 gabled house. The "Dean of Ontario Antique Dealers" is what Les Donaldson's contemporaries called him after Canada's 1967 Centennial.

Les was a pioneer in the Canadian antique trade going back to the outbreak of World War II. He was Canada's Roger Bacon, the iconic American dealer from just outside Exeter, New Hampshire, who, more than anyone else during his era, educated a new generation of Americans and beckoned them to preserve their country's past by collecting it…. This is exactly what Les Donaldson did for nearly fifty years. As a much-respected Canadian antique dealer, he caused the generation following him to preserve their visible past by not just collecting it but by cherishing it. Les used to quote George Santayana: "Those who forget the past don't deserve the future."

I first met Les Donaldson in 1970. As I cautiously entered the antique world, Les became my oracle, my fountain of knowledge…. He was much more than an antique dealer. He was also a gifted instructor, teaching those who followed and listened to him that they should either be a dealer or a collector, but not both! He also stressed that the true collector must embrace history and become an antiquarian. When I visited his home on the Blenheim Rd. where he and his wonderful wife Nell lived for most of their married lives, he would deliberately quiz me like a professor and banter back and forth with me about the "mechanics" of furniture, often over a drink. I remember how he used to tell me that most collectors can be trained to have a reasonably good "eye" much like athletes learn their skills through training, conditioning and hard work. He stressed that, yes, there are those very special sporting figures, rare individuals, who are naturally gifted. And that, yes, they do train and train, but their natural talent cannot be taught because it is a gift. He felt the same principle applied to antique collectors. He was convinced that the budding collector either has it or doesn't have a discriminating eye, one that instinctively understands taste, form, and quality. He certainly believed that the antique collector can and does learn to develop a keen eye for taste and quality but the one that has the gifted "eye" also has a distinct advantage over the come by chance collector. Les also tended to pooh-pooh the so-called phrase that "beauty is in the eye of the beholder" emphasizing that most anyone can distinguish between a graceful woman and one who is haggard and scraggy. It was so fascinating to hear Les expatiate his thoughts in such a way. They generate great memories….

Back some forty years ago, I often chose to attend auction sales out near Les so that I could visit him on my way home and share with him what I had just purchased. On one such day in the very early 1970s, he gently pulled the rug out from under my feet reminding me that I had forgotten his mantra: judge all furniture by the following four principles: form, condition, name of maker and provenance. He pointed out to me the weaknesses of my purchase, showing me flagrant deficiencies in the object I thought had great appeal. These included the fact that the drawer in the one drawer table had been replaced. Les also pointed out that one inch or so was missing from the height of table and that the entire surface was scraped to the bone! He was so right. His observations, moreover, were instantaneous. His eye was so accurate. That was a lesson I never forgot.

What people liked the most about Les was that he never tried to show anyone that he knew more than they did. Also, he never tried to sell anyone anything if he thought the prospective buyer was not ready to own it. This is why he attracted the young and the old, female as well as male, and the informed as well as the uninformed. His affable demeanour, plus his immense knowledge, gravitated people to his shop, to browse and to chew the fat with him. It was a happy event to meet with him in his shop. Besides, he had a great twinkle in his eye....

After five years of friendship and purchase of a fantastic cupboard from Les Donaldson that I had to sell in order to purchase still another cupboard (see the story elsewhere in this volume about the Sir William Campbell House), not only did Les and I strike up a lasting friendship, but I began to buy paintings from Nell his adorable wife whom he had married back in 1937. In fact, after our twin sons were born in October, 1973, I asked Nell if she would consider painting an idyllic scene of both Charlie and Scott as living on a romantic landscape estate somewhere out in the country. Not only did she agree to paint a rendering of my twin sons but wondered if she and Les could drive to Rexdale from Galt and see the twins. They were not quite two years old at the time but she wanted to see them before she painted them as five year olds. They also wanted to see the Grobb cupboard (see the story of the Grobb cupboard elsewhere in this volume) which had replaced the cupboard I had purchased from Les. When Nell entered our home in 1975, she perfectly understood from photographs I had given her the physical differences between the identical twins. Gay and I were amazed at her trained eye! And when Les saw the Grobb cupboard, he had to admit that I was now a top of the class student and had truly learned the importance of form, quality, style, condition and provenance. He was so pleased that his "student" had graduated from his antique shop, *summa cum laude*!

Born, 1907, Salcoats, Scotland, Les came to Canada at age two years. Raised in Galt, he married his sweetheart, Nell Anderson, and the two of them raised one son, Bill, and daughters Agnes and Barb. Les was an antique dealer for almost fifty years. Les always wanted to "die at a good country auction right at the height of the bidding." He didn't quite get that wish, but when he gave up the ghost, October 3, 1989, two years after Nell's passing, Canada not only lost the Dean of Canadian Antiques but a prince among his peers.... What a memory he has left me....

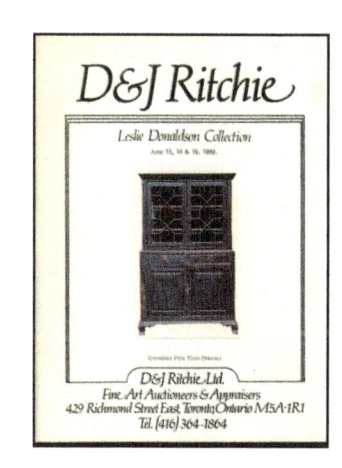

Above: The Les Donaldson collection was sold, June, 1982, by D. & J Ritchie, Toronto, Ontario.

Left: After Les Donaldson became your friend, you would meet his wife Nell. Soon after I met Nell, 1974, I bought a couple of her oil paintings. I then commissioned her to paint a scene with twins Charlie and Scott Humber, playing with their rocking horse and with their "family estate" in the background. This oil painting is destined to become a family heirloom. Notice the Golden Retreiver, a breed Humbers have raised for nearly one-half century.

Dad's Best Memories and Recollections

The William Morris Chair

Exactly when my parents, Charles and Evelyn Humber, acquired the "Morris chair" is not known. They likely got it following their move from Hamilton in 1935 to 176 L'Esperance St., St. Lambert, Quebec, where I and my sister, Anna, were born, 1936 and 1937 respectively. One thing is for sure – the Morris chair not only stayed with Mom and Dad over the next four decades but travelled with them to many jurisdictions. It journeyed from Montreal to both Hagersville and Toronto, in Ontario. From Ontario it went to Boston. When the Humbers moved to Pennsylvania in 1955, the Morris chair went with them. And from Philadelphia it went to Nesquehoning, in northeastern Pennsylvania, before Dad gave it to me in either 1972 or 1973. When I returned to Canada with the Morris chair, it immediately travelled to the family cottage in MacTier, two hours north of Toronto, the place where our summer home our haven has been since 1970. I have now owned the chair longer than my parents. And when they got it, the chair was already some forty years old. By definition, the Morris chair is now a legitimate antique and very collectible.

Even though my immediate family has learned to call the chair by its proper name, no one has ever inquired why it is called the "Morris Chair." There is an explanation. William Morris (1834-1896) was closely associated with the *avant-garde* British Arts and Crafts Movement, a spirit of restlessness during the last quarter of the 19th century. It reacted to the traditional skills of craftsman being lost to the Industrial Revolution. This movement emphasized craft and the decorative arts over machinery and assembly lines. Industrialization was considered evil. William Morris, at the forefront of this movement, rebelled against the dehumanizing the machinery age caused and combined his dislike of the degrading movement with his love of Romance and the poetry of Keats, Coleridge, Shelley and Wordsworth. In 1861 he founded Morris & Company and five years later began making his famed Morris chair with its reclining back and more often than nought its Gorgon carved heads at the end of arm-rests. The defining characteristics of the Morris chair, in addition to its declining feature, are serpentine and gargoyle shaped carvings. These chairs were made in dark oak by the thousands and were copied innovatively by Gustav Stickley and his own vibrant movement at the same time in the United States. Eventually, these innovative movements gave way to Modernism, still another movement that continues to impact the current century.

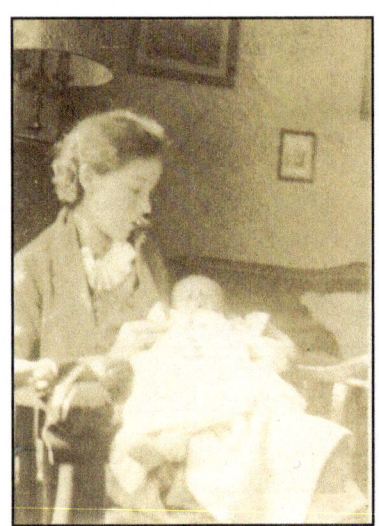

The Morris chair phenomenon has no comparison. It is unique in furniture design and arguably has never

Above left: Evelyn Humber sitting in the Morris chair, with her first-born, Charlie, in St. Lambert, Quebec, 1936.

Above right: Siblings, Anna and Charlie, in Morris chair, Hagersville, Ontario, 1938.
Left: Rev. Charles M. Humber sitting in Morris chair with his four children, Anna and Charlie, standing, and twins, Paul and Priscilla, on their father's lap, Christmas, 1942, in Toronto.

Dad's Best Memories and Recollections

been superseded. Part of its success can be traced to the stunning fact that it was referenced in the social media of its day, including various songs, movies and books. For instance, at least two Irving Berlin songs refer to the famed Morris chair. In **You'd be Surprised** (1919), the lyrics proclaim: "At a party/ Or at a ball/ I've got to admit/ He's nothing at all/ But in a Morris chair/ You'd be surprised." Berlin also makes reference to the Morris chair in the song "**All by Myself.**" Such personalities as Bing Crosby and Al Jolson made the song popular but it was Aileen Stanley, in 1921, that had the English world following her in the roaring twenties when she sang, "I sit alone in my Morris Chair/ So unhappy there/ Playing solitaire."(I suggest you Google her rendition of this song. Fabulous!). Additionally, Eddie Cantor makes reference to the Morris chair on the opening night of the 1919 Ziegfeld Follies. He exclaimed in his song **You Don't Need Wine to have a Wonderful Time** "Why should we care if the wine isn't there/ We still have the sofa and the Morris chair." In the World War I patriotic song, **If He Can Fight Like He Can Love, Good Night Germany,** the lyrics go "…I know he'll be a hero over there, 'cause he's a bear in any Morris chair." As well, the movie **Three Stooges Rockin' Through the Rockies** (1940), Curly says, "I once shot a Morris Chair from underneath Sitting Bull." And although these references are rather old, stodgy and comical, they drew attention in its day, somewhat unwittingly, to the Morris chair and helped make it the popular icon it is today, that is, if you can find one. And references to the famous Morris chair still appear in the contemporary works of Dan Brown as well in the earlier works of Pearl S. Buck, John Steinbeck and Kurt Vonnegut.

There is no question that the Morris chair up at the cottage brings me many happy memories. If I want, I can visualize every one of my family, past and present, sitting in it, enjoying life, laughing, telling jokes, watching movies, or napping. It is an iconic chair and, hopefully, it will remain with the family for the next 100 years. It is the anchor that helps bind our family together, year after year. I just love Gay telling me when I've been away that one or another of my grandchildren has asked her, "Can I sit in Papa's chair?" It brings a smile worth millions….

Above Right: Living room at 1145 Dorchester Avenue, Boston, Christmas, 1951, with Charlie in Morris chair, and dog Rusty being petted by twins with sister Anna looking on.

Lower left: Up at the cottage, 1974, sitting in the Morris chair is the proud papa of twin brothers, Charlie and Scott, not quite one year.

Lower right: Charlie VI, 2015, sits in Papa's Morris chair at the Humber cottage, in Muskoka, Ontario.

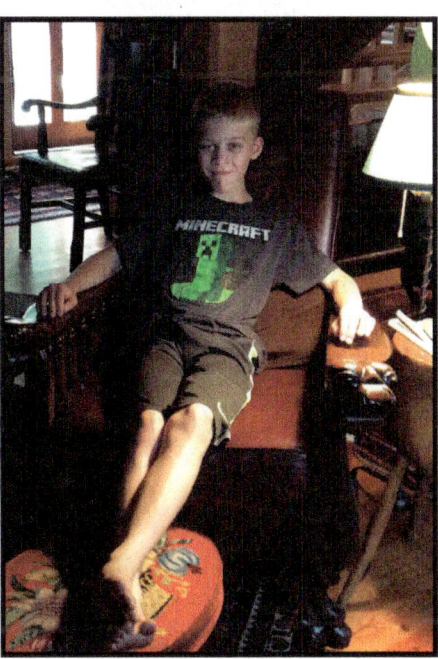

Dad's Best Memories and Recollections

Dunn Court, Dorchester

Dunn Court doesn't exist anymore. In the late 1940s, when I was growing up in Dorchester, Boston's largest neighbourhood, Dunn Court was, at best, considered a dirt road, maybe 300 feet long. It went west from Dot (Dorchester) Ave. to Deer Street. Across Dot Ave. from Dunn Court, was Bay Street, a bus line route that ran east some four blocks to the MTA's Savin Hill Subway Station. (Google The Kingston Trio's 1959 hit song called "Charlie on the MTA"?)

The wooden-clapboard tenement building where the Humber family of six lived, 1945-1955, like most housing units in Dorchester, was three stories high. The century old, flat-roofed apartment complex had three doorways, each leading to three floors made up of four-roomed apartments. We lived at 1145 Dorchester Ave, three doorways up from Dunn Court. Nine different families, in a perfect situation, would live in these flats. It was from here on school days, while attending Mather School on Meeting House Hill, that four Humber siblings left their doorway fronting Dorchester Ave, turned right and after twenty-five paces or so, would turn right again at Dunn Court.

Dorchester Ave. circa 1946. Tenement complex on right is where the Humber family lived. The doorway next to the white store on extreme right was our doorway. Dunn Court is between the two tenement buildings.

As we walked along Dunn Court, we would pass another three-story apartment complex to our right. There were two entrances in this circa 1840 tenement building, one at each end with each doorway leading to three flats one above each other. A second building that typically housed three floors stood aloof at the end of Dunn Court. Two of my best friends, WeeWee O'Neil and Jimmie Dodds lived in this unit.

Dunn Court came to an abrupt end at Deer Street. To our left, as we walked toward Deer Street, was an open field, big enough to play either baseball or touch football. I clearly remember, after we moved to Dorchester from Toronto, October, 1945, watching an actual lamplighter, wearing an old Tam o' Shanter, climbing up a ladder on Dunn Court and leaning against the extended metal prongs of the street lamp and lighting up the only gas lamp standing on Dunn Court. This field was my backyard, so to speak. Not only did Jimmie Dodds and both Wee Wee and Jackie O'Neil live on Dunn Court, but others lived in flats overlooking Dunn Court. They were Jackie Gill, Mikey Flaherty, Frankie Parks, Johnny Rogers, Donald (Do Do) Goode, Charlie Turner, Jackie Joyce, Jackie McIlaney, the Noonan brothers as well as Bobby Willard and Jimmy (Pucker) Mahoney. We were "brothers." None of us had any TV until 1949. Families had party-line telephones. Clothes were hung out across from our back windows on very long clotheslines connected to the Dunn Court tenement buildings across our backyards. After turning on our radios, we waited for the tubes to light up in order to hear "The Amos and Andy Show" or the "Bob Hope/Bing Crosby Show".

The scrubby playing field on Dunn Court was our "field of dreams." Here we would flip coins or toss baseball bat handles to choose team players. We played baseball until dusk. We were nine, ten or eleven years, in grades four, five or six, while playing baseball and pretending we were Joe DiMaggio or Ted Williams, Bobby Doer or Johnny Pesky. It was a thrill to play touch football believing we were Johnny Lujack or Doc Blanchard, Glenn Davis or Sid Luckman. Hitting a baseball over the house in dead centre field was the ultimate challenge. Only Wee Wee O'Neil could do that. He became our mythological hero. He could have played for the Boston Red Sox but the roads of our lives diverged. I guess I'll never know what happened to him. I've been told he died from alcoholism. After Christmas, after everyone bought real Christmas trees, the Dunn Court field became the perfect place to assemble 100 or so discarded Christmas trees and burn them late some January evening. The sky would light up, that's for sure! It's a wonder that the ashes from the bonfire did not fall on tenement building roofs and burn them down.

Dad's Best Memories and Recollections

Every community has a known busy body. For the boys of Dunn Court, it was an old woman by the name of Katie Callaghan. She didn't like boys and used to, with a broomstick, drive us away from "her sidewalk" on Dot Ave. abutting Dunn Court. When playing in the Dunn Court fields, she would sit on a stone in her grubby backyard and watch us play. If our ball went near her backyard area, she would try to get it before us. She was always dressed up like some Halloween witch with black shoes and stockings. Her long black skirt, a black shawl, looked more like a blanket. She enhanced her dress code with a peaked witch's hat. Her nose sloped down her face and at the end of it was an unhealthy-looking mole. She was terrifying to be near and she cackled when she chased us. Although we were somewhat scared of her, when she chased us we almost died laughing as we always were able to outrun her.

Today, there is not a mention of Dunn Court on any Boston map. Most of the tenement buildings surrounding the roadway are long gone. Our tenement building burned down in the early 1970s. A parking lot plaza catering to Vietnamese is now a memorial to my boyhood home and dreams. In the 1940s, just as we turned onto Dunn Court, straight ahead and about one story above me, was a blue sign, some eighteen inches long, with a white strip around its edges clearly stating, "Dunn Court." It was nailed to the side of the building. I'd give anything to have that sign hanging today inside our cottage. Not that I need something to remind me of the fields where I learned to play baseball and football, but Dunn Court for me is a precious memory offering haunting history. As a family of four, we Humber kids often traipsed across that playing field to and from school. To most individuals it means nothing. But to me that playing field that no longer exists represents my lost youth. It makes all the difference in the world to me.

Left top: This was Dunn Court's "Field of Dreams". The tenement block to the left faces Dorchester Ave. The street lamp, lower left, was a gas lamp and it was lit manually each night.
Left bottom: The Dunn Court playing field went up to the building with no windows. To hit the ball over this tenement block was to hit a home run! Deer Street is to the right running into Roach Street in the far background.
Right Brother Paul with Rusty on our third-floor fire escape overlooking our backyard and Dunn Court as well as the Dunn Court playing field. Katie Callaghan can be seen sitting against her backyard fence just waiting for a ball. Mather School is looming in far background in this circa 1950 view.

Dad's Best Memories and Recollections

UNIVERSITY OF ALASKA FAIRBANKS 1960 - 1961

As a sophomore at Temple University, 1959-1960, I worked part-time in the university's library. At the time, Billboard Country and Western's #1 song was "North to Alaska" sung by Johnny Horton. As well, a top movie that year, starring John Wayne, had the same title. One of my jobs at the university library was clearing up all the university and college catalogues in the reference room and re-stacking them, in alphabetical order, on book shelves. One particular bulletin caught my eye. This was the University of Alaska catalogue that had intriguing photos of its far north campus isolated beneath the breathtaking *aurora borealis*, as captured in photo at left. The campus itself was located on a hilly plateau on the outskirts of Fairbanks. As I perused the names of the professors and the various programs at the university, I said to myself, "What a neat place to attend!" Romantic inclinations reminded me that the Territory of Alaska had just been made the 49th State. I decided, on the spot, that the U. of A. had a swagger and was a place I'd like to attend. In short time I started an application process to leave Temple University for one year in order to attend the University of Alaska the upcoming year, 1960-1961. My application was accepted before I left Philadelphia and returned to Canada for my summer job. To confirm in their minds that I had decided to go "North to Alaska," my parents journeyed from Philadelphia to Canada at the end of August to give me their blessings and farewells. High school girl-friend, Doreen Wiggins, drove me to the junction of Highways 400 and 7, just north of Toronto. There we bade each other goodbye. The story of my 3000-mile hitch-hiking experience to my sub-arctic destination can be read elsewhere in this production. Nevertheless, my trek north to Alaska took nine days. I was ecstatic to arrive there safely as a student. And what a year it was!

I arrived on the campus one day before classes started. When checking in, I was dismayed to learn that all dormitory accommodation was taken. Because the university had admitted more students than it could accommodate, officials were coerced into arranging with Ladd Air Force Base to place fifty of its incoming students, all over twenty-one years, in one of the Civilian Bachelor Quarters (CBQ) on the base. In some respect this was good luck for me as it meant that I, as a student, had access to the base Civilian Club where all non-military people gathered to eat at significant discount prices compared to food costs on campus or elsewhere. As well, starting at 6:00 a.m. and continuing to midnight, bus service took students from Ladd AFB directly to the campus and back. The drive was less than fifteen minutes either way. For students not housed in dormitories, it turned out just hunky-dory for the displaced students, especially for me, as the Civilian Club is where I eventually met one special person working on the base as a teacher. Her name was Gayle Jenkins. In thirteen months we were married. She was from California; I was from Ontario; Alaska is where we met; Philadelphia is where we were married!

The university was a very active campus. One of the first things I noticed was a sign posted in the Student Union advertising work for students needed to assist in harvesting cash crops at the university's sub-arctic experimental farm. I signed up. When the campus bus took us to the fields, I was flabbergasted looking at cabbages weighing nearly fifty pounds. Carrots were a foot long and fatter than cucumbers. Lettuce heads were larger than basketballs and radishes were as big as baseballs. I couldn't believe their weight and size but learned that during the summer, because there was sun beaming nearly twenty-four hours per day on the fields, vegetables got to be humongous! The university paid money-hungry students very well to harvest vegetables.

Students came from all over the United States to attend the University of Alaska, enrolling in arctic engineer-

View of the Civilian Club, in the far background, centre, on Ladd Air force Base, Fairbanks, Alaska, 1960. Photo was taken from the CBQ (Civilian Bachelor's Quarters) where fifty over-aged students from the University of Alaska bunked during the academic school year, 1960-1961. The Civilian Club was their dining hall where students interacted with other civilians on the base such as school teachers.

Dad's Best Memories and Recollections

200

ing, geophysics, mining, arctic research and much more. When I arrived, the student body was 2000 strong. My affable room-mate, Fritz Blayney, from Oshkosh, Wisconsin, ended up working for Continental Airlines before becoming Senior Vice-President of Oasis Hong Kong Airlines, 2006. Across the hall from me was, Dick Mitchell, my best friend on the campus. Originally from Fresno, his career took him to Nepal as a research scientist. After completing his Ph.D., he moved to Toronto to work at the Royal Ontario Museum before taking a job at the Smithsonian Institute in Washington. We remained in contact while he lived in Montana and since his move to Muskegon, Michigan, 2015, we plan on exchanging visits.

Leaving Mount McKinley (Denali), the northern lights, and minus -50⁰F temperatures behind, Gay and I drove the Alaska Highway that spring of 1961 to Philadelphia in her 1958 Ford Fairlane. Upon introducing her to the family and choosing a wedding date, Gay flew home while I took four summer courses at Temple. When Gay returned to teach in Lansdale that September, I began my final year at Temple. On November 22, 1961, my father, a Baptist minister, married us at Mantua Baptist Church in Upper Darby. Over that Thanksgiving weekend, we honeymooned in New York City. And upon my graduation, 1962, the two of us happily bid goodbye to Philadelphia and moved to Ontario, our home base, on and off, ever since. Upon reflection, I now know that had Johnny Horton not recorded "North to Alaska", I might never have gone to Alaska and met Gay. What memories!

Upper left: Photo taken in the CBQ Barrack on Ladd Air Force Base, Fairbanks, Alaska, 1960. Room-mates Fritz Blaney, far right, and Charlie Humber, wearing sweater. Seen in same view is Pete Mazzaglia from Boston and Larry Adcock from Alabama. **Upper right:** Longtime friend, Richard Mitchell from California and Charles "Judge" Green III from Missouri eyeing their bounty: dahl sheep horns and two racks of moose antlers along with other game including parka squirrels and arctic rabbit. **Lower left:** Championship trophy won by "Chuck" Humber, Billiard Champion, 1960, University of Alaska. **Lower right:** Dr. Charles M. Humber, father of the groom, married Charles J. Humber and Gayle Jenkins, in an evening wedding, November 22, 1961, at Mantua Baptist Church, Upper Darby, a suburb of Philadelphia. Chuck Hurlbut, future brother-in-law, stands far left, beside best man and brother, Paul Humber. Sisters Anna, Maid of Honor, and Priscilla, bridesmaid, make up the rest of the wedding party.

1967-1970

Bascom Hall, built 1857, rests atop the hill that dominates the University of Wisconsin campus in Madison. The oldest and most famous building on campus, Bascom Hall houses most of the administrative offices of the university. It's as well known as the Wisconsin State Capitol just down the road.

While teaching at T.L. Kennedy Secondary School in Cooksville, Ontario (1962-1966), my ongoing passion was to pursue graduate studies in the U.S.A. Though the universities I targeted were far away, my belief was that piggybacking adventure with studies maximized life experiences, a formula that prompted my leaving Temple University, in Philadelphia, back in 1960-61, to enroll for just one school year at the University of Alaska, in Fairbanks. I narrowed my Graduate School selections to the Universities of Texas, Washington, and Wisconsin. Each had reputed Graduate School programs in Renaissance Studies, my major area of interest. When my school board granted me a "leave of absence," Gay and I prepared our big move to Wisconsin, January, 1967.

As a family of four, we lived at 2340 Park Towers located on Hurontario Street, just north of the Queensway, in Mississauga, formerly Cooksville. Kristy was not yet three years and Karyn was but six weeks old. Following Christmas at L. & L. Farms, in Meadowvale, and a New Year's Eve stop in Hamilton with Uncle Bill and Aunt Edie Donaldson, we "migrated" in our 1964 Ford Galaxy pulling a U-Haul Trailer to Wisconsin. While attaching the U-Haul to my car I was asked by some Cooksville local where I was going. When I responded "to the States," he replied: "It's a regular three-ring circus down there, eh!" This was forty years before the Barack Obama years! And, yes, the USA was socially dysfunctional at the time with the Vietnam War and LSD generating massive anxiety problems. Upon reaching Chicago, the snow was a foot deep and even deeper in Madison. We drove directly to the International Student Centre on campus where we were guided to a professor who agreed to house us until we found appropriate apartment accommodation. Luckily, this happened the very next day.

Our two-bedroom apartment at 1711 Camus Lane was near the campus and legendary Rennebaum's Drugstore where Gay worked part-time. When she worked at Rennie's, I babysat; when I went to classes or to the library, Gay was in charge at home. We lived at Camus Lane until mid-August. During our eight-month stay, Alan and Chris Emerson, from Toronto, came and stayed with us in our crowded conditions. In between the spring semester and summer school classes, we bought a tent and camped out at Wayalusing State Park on the Mississippi River, just across from Iowa. We also visited Wisconsin Dells. But, regretfully, after completing the equivalent of one year's graduate courses, we returned to Canada. Re-hired by our former Board of Education, we needed to raise additional monies to continue with any future Ph.D. program. So we had no choice but to return to Canada. While living at 1759 Bloor Street, east of Dixie Rd., Mississauga, and while we both taught that year (1967-1968), I also enrolled as a graduate student at the University of Toronto enrolling in Northrop Frye's world-famous course, "The Bible and Classical Mythology."

Returning to Madison that summer, of 1968, and for the next school year, 1968-1969, we left behind Pierre Elliott Trudeau, Canada's new Prime Minister. My plans were to skip the Master's degree program and proceed directly towards a Ph.D. Our home was 204K Eagle Heights, the university's residence for graduate students with families. My closest friend became Emanuel Seko, from South Africa. He lived two doors down from our unit and was pursuing, like me, a Ph.D. in Renaissance Studies. Taking courses from such luminary professors as Ricardo Quintana, Mark Eccles, Harry Hayden Clark, A.B. Chambers and John Shawcross helped make this the most memorable time of my

Above: Emanuel Seko was my closest friend on campus. Originally from South Africa, he escaped apartheid and trekked to Nigeria where he and his family got caught up in the 1968 Biafran Conflict. Escaping with his family of five, once again, including two sons and daughter, Jane, and his wonderful wife, Mildred, Immanuel journeyed to the University of Wisconsin where our two families integrated. A students majoring in Renaissance studies, Immanuel, upon completing his Ph.D., moved to Spartanburg, South Carolina, where he taught Shakespeare and Milton for more than thirty years at the University of South Carolina. We exchanged numerous visits over the years, he coming to Canada no less than four times. The last time we visited was 2014, in Spartanburg, South Carolina, when Gay and I linked up with Emanuel, now a widower, living alone in his house surrounded with books and various awards. Recalling our friendship over the years and what might have been had I stayed on and completed my doctoral degree, we laughed at what a tandem we would have been together at any university.

Dad's Best Memories and Recollections

graduate studies. We also bought a new 1969 Chevrolet Impala. Sister Anna and Bill Lubliner, on their way back from California, stopped for a visit that summer. Brother Paul and his wife, Prudence, also stopped on their cross-country trip. Mom and Dad also visited. Close friend, Wayne Getty, from Calgary, with his pregnant wife, Myrna, came for a brief stay, bringing with them their two young sons plus a camper trailer.

We were very lucky to find a middle-aged Pilipino couple to babysit Kristy and Karyn while Gay taught grade one and I went to classes. Student demonstrations during this 1968-1969 timeframe escalated across the U.S.A. and Madison was no exception. In

Taking time out from graduate studies at the University of Wisconsin was always difficult. The ongoing demands of graduate work, Gay's work schedule, and the two girls kept both Gay and me pre-occupied twenty-four hours a day. But we did find time to criss-cross the huge campus and its various landmarks including the famous Der Rathskeller or Picnic Point where we often would go during warm months to enjoy yummy sandwiches on the shores of Lake Mendota at the end of a hot summer's day. We were a very close family operating with precision to accommodate the needs of each family member. Take note of the handlebar mustache that one particular cerebral student fashioned during his Madison days.

fact, the National Guard was called in to quell student rioting on campus on several occasions. Tear gas permeated everywhere! A chaotic economy and the Vietnam War had taken their toll. Now in my thirties, I had yet to settle down. We could also see ominous dark clouds on the economic horizon. Teaching jobs were forecast to be limited. Considering that I had two grinding years to go to complete a doctoral degree, we were getting a little nervous about our future security. As the spring of 1969 loomed, we thought pragmatically. We concluded that the road to a Ph.D. was not necessarily beneficial to our family that we hoped soon to expand. So, when I got an unsolicited call from Mr. Bill Noble, the principal at Lawrence Park Collegiate Institute, in North Toronto, offering me the Assistant Headship of the English Department at his school, I accepted his offer knowing that I would no longer be pursuing a personal dream at the expense of my family. Leaving Gay and the girls behind at Eagle Heights for the summer of 1969, I drove to Toronto, staying in Weston with Alan Emerson to complete a summer school program at the Ontario College of Education to upgrade my teaching certificate. Additionally, while Neil Armstrong landed on the moon, I purchased a raised bungalow at 61 Westhumber Blvd., in Rexdale. At the end of August, I then drove back to Wisconsin, picked up Gay and our two daughters, a loving family, and, together, we happily returned as a family of four to Toronto where we kick-started our normal lives all over again. Though the path to my M.A. degree was cumbersome, our venture to and our recollections of the mid-west are all very memorable. The girls, moreover, will never forget the Red Owl store or the Octopus Car Wash, two Madison business landmarks that caused Kristy and Karyn to hide in the back seat of car every time we passed these monuments that "lurk for the innocent."

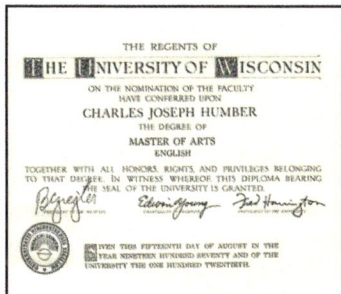

While living in Madison, Wisconsin, 1967-1969, we travelled in our car visiting the university arboretum, the city zoo, parks, the overwhelming Capitol, and, more often than naught, picnic tables overlooking Lake Mendota. Two visible Madison landmarks were the Red Owl grocery store sign and the extra large Octopus Car Wash sign. The Red Owl sign looked very threatening suggesting the owl wanted to peck you with its beak. The Octopus sign with its multiple arms looked as if the creature was reaching out to grab you. Every time we drove by these ominous signs, I forewarned Kristy and Karyn to hide in the back seat of the car. And every time we drove past these signs, they always asked if it was okay to re-appear. Of course, we said the threat was gone, but they looked back to make sure the owl was not trying to catch us or to see if the arms of the Octopus were able to catch them. It was a lot of fun raising the two girls! The M.A. certificate, far right, was the culmination of hard work, dedication and family sacrifice.

Dad's Best Memories and Recollections

Newfoundland, "Whadda ya'at b'y"

When attending school in Boston or Fairbanks, Alaska, or playing snooker in Brampton, Ontario, Newfie jokes were common. Wherever I've lived, such jokes have been prevalent and silly. Fortunately, belittling Newfies as low IQ or unworldly is passé today. Furthermore, wherever I've gone I've come across people from "the Rock" and, without exception, they've not only spoken with an endearing accent but demonstrated friendship and charm. Such traits highlighted the main reasons why Gay and I committed to a Newfoundland visit in May, 2002. The ten days of discovery there and the history lessons learned about Canada's tenth province are most memorable....

In 1949, when Newfoundland became a province, it had been Great Britain's first possession in North America with Sir Humphrey Gilbert claiming Newfoundland for Queen Elizabeth in 1583. A gargantuan rock off Canada's east coast, Newfoundland, essentially an island, constitutes some 110,000 square miles. This does not include Newfoundland's bigger half, Labrador. Some historians claim that, St. John's, the capital, is the oldest incorporated city in North America. In fact, during the Feast of Saint John, 1497, when Italian explorer John Cabot, representing King Henry VII of England, sailed into natural harbours along Newfoundland's eastern coast, one of the safe anchorages he entered was dubbed St. John's. The historic city, today, is Canada's 20th largest municipality.

Gay and I flew to St. John's, May 30, 2002. For our first three days, we stayed at the Bluestone Inn on Queens Rd. Being tourists in St. John's and criss-crossing downtown streets such as Duckworth and Water was great fun. Before we left for other regions, it was fascinating to experience various restaurants that have made St. John's so notable. For sure we wanted to experience a libation called Newfoundland Screech, a rum-drink made in St. John's that is 40% alcohol. One of the twenty-six pubs on George Street, a three-block midway of ambience, is the perfect place to test the drink. Seafood is the menu in St. John's! We feasted on lobster or snow crab at the Peppermill on Water St., Chucky's Fish and Chips on Kings Road, the Murray Premises Hotel, and Rumpelstiltskin's on Hill O' Chips.

Upon leaving the Bluestone Inn, we rented a car for the next week, a 2002 Pontiac Grand AM. Cape Spear, a chunk of rock that juts out into the Atlantic Ocean further than any other point in North America, was our first stop, just south of St. John's. Here the oldest lighthouse in Newfoundland, built, 1836, still operates. Standing high on elevated cliffs overlooking the cold Atlantic creates an opportunity to watch humpback whales and 12,000 year-old icebergs.

From Cape Spear we journeyed southwards, stopping at Bay Bulls where O'Brien's Whale and Bird Tours took us out to the largest Puffin bird colony in North America. We also saw a fabulous iceberg that was grounded in Witless Bay. Newfoundlanders are unhappy about icebergs "parking" in their harbour because it means their summer is going to be shorter and colder. We did so much on this excursion into the Avalon Peninsula. We visited Ferryland where Lord Baltimore settled in 1621 before he founded Baltimore, Maryland. At the tip of the Avalon we visited Cape Race where the **Titanic** sent distress signals, in 1912, enabling the world to learn of the loss of 1500 people when the famous liner struck an iceberg. One of the most exciting attractions we saw on our drive south was visiting St. Mary's Ecological Reserve, where a prominent bird rock is home to one of the largest sea bird colonies in Newfoundland, mainly gannets and kittiwakes. The nesting ground was just a stone's throw from the precipice cliff from where we stood. Fog made the place eerie and haunting with all the birds mating and calling to each other in the creepy mist and shrouding vapor. The noise is deafening. After staying overnight at Rita Hagan's bed and breakfast in Aquaforte, the next day we learned that nearly twenty-five years earlier, on Christmas Day, Rita's husband was axed to death by a schizophrenic next door neighbour. This fact haunted us the next

Left: Grounded iceberg in Witless Bay near Bay Bulls
Right: Bird Rock at Cape St. Mary's Ecological Reserve, Avalon Peninsula, Newfoundland.

Dad's Best Memories and Recollections

day. Rita Hagan was such a wonderful host. She would have loved for us to return each year. She passed away in 2012.

After reaching the southern terminus of the Avalon Peninsula, we looped backwards, driving through Placentia and Argentia, bypassing the Mae West mountain chain as we scurried to the Bonavista Peninsula. At its tip is the setting where John Cabot anchored his ship, the **Matthew,** now rebuilt as a classy tourist attraction. A great experience was visiting Ryan Premises, the restored complex of a fish merchant's operation in the 19th century. The Bonavista Peninsula is jammed with attractions. The abandoned film setting of a 19th century fishing village facing Conception Bay made for the TV series, **Random Passage**, was an exceptional stop. We also visited the setting of one of our favorite movies, **Shipping News** (2001), near Trinity. Here we also stayed at our favorite Bed and Breakfast of our trip called the Campbell House. At Bay de Verde we saw many foreign fishing boats and small "icebergs" grounded in the harbour. The closer we got to the icebergs the more we felt we were freezing. At Clarke's Beach we stayed at Sleepy Hollow B.& B. The owner, Lewis Roberts, took us to his own museum in the next town, Bareneed, where he displayed hundreds of his creations made from discarded electronic parts showcasing his bizarre techno folk art. One of our surprise stops was at Brigus where famed arctic explorer and navigator Bob Bartlett's home, **The Hawthorne** (1830), had been turned into a museum. We really enjoyed visiting this former home of

Left: Campbell's Bed and Breakfast cottage, near Trinity, Bonavista Peninsula. Gay waving from back of sleeping quarters
Centre: C.J. Humber examines St. John's Harbour with **Holland America** cruise ship docked and the Basilica, silhouetted on the horizon overlooking the harbour. **Right:** The Cabot Tower on Signal Hill overlooking both St. John's Harbour and the Atlantic Ocean.

one who accompanied Robert Peary on his 1909 North Pole trip. On returning to St. John's, we loved visiting windy Signal Hill overlooking the Atlantic. Here Guglielmo Marconi became the first person ever to receive Trans-Atlantic signals. The Cabot Tower on this historic site overlooking St. John's Harbour was built to coincide with Queen Victoria's Diamond Jubilee as well as to commemorate John Cabot's 400th anniversary of landing in St. John's. On our return to the Bluestone Inn, we also visited Quidi Vidi, an old Portuguese fishing village beyond Signal Hill. Here we visited Mallard Cottage touted as the oldest wooden structure in North America. We also saw Quidi Vidi Brewery that makes its Iceberg Beer brand from icebergs. The last visit of our ten-day trip was The Basilica Cathedral of St. John the Baptist. When completed, 1855, the Basilica was one of the largest churches in North America. It is a major tourist stop in St. John's. Dinner that night at Chucky's was, of course, lobster. Exhausted, I went to sleep counting places we saw: Come by Chance, Dildo, Heart's Desire, Heart's Delight, Conception Bay. Since flying out, June 9, we've been planning to re-visit the Rock and recapture memories. Whadda ya' at b'y?

Percé on the Rocks

It's so true: North America's declared natural landmarks are stunning. The easterly portion of Quebec's jutting landscape, the Gaspé Peninsula, where Percé Rock looms, serves to reinforce this assertion. When I read about the Rock or saw it promoted in television ads, I said, "Someday, I'm going to Percé Rock!" That time came in 1994.

Above: Percé Rock is one of Canada's stunning natural landmarks, a gigantic stone sitting in the water at the tip of the Gaspe Peninsula in eastern Quebec. The massive block of reddish-gold limestone brings into view one of the world's largest natural arches. Samuel de Champlain after seeing the "pierced hole" in the world-famous monolithic rock called it *Rocher Percé*. **Right:** Located 2 miles off the coast of Quebec's Gaspé Peninsula, Bonaventure Island is roughly circular in shape and has an area of just over one and one-half square miles. With more than 280,000 birds nesting, the island is a tourist's delight and home to one of the world's largest bird sanctuaries.

Gay agreed that a Quebec getaway was a good idea. So, when the school year ended, we journeyed to *la belle province,* staying in *ville du Québec* for two days. The ramparts surrounding *vieux-Québec* are fascinating and not because they are the only fortified city walls remaining in North America but because their stone arches suggest a medieval presence. We so enjoyed old Quebec. Founded in 1608 by Samuel de Champlain, this section of the city was designated a UNESCO world heritage site in 1985. Before leaving Quebec City, we also toured the Plains of Abraham, walked the Dufferin Terrace, and took the Quebec Funicular to *vieux-Québec* below Cap Diamond. The Château Frontenac towers over the old city. The most notable structure along the St. Lawrence River, it is probably the most photographed hotel in the world. It is where my Uncle Charles A. Elliot worked as an accountant after serving in World War I.

Driving along the south shore of the St. Lawrence River is enrapturing. We stopped at Saint-Jean-Port-Joli, Canada's wood-carving capital. Here I located old friend, Benoi Deschênes, whose carvings are internationally celebrated. He gave me a photograph of his award-winning wood sculpture, *Les Voyageurs,* granting me permission to reproduce it on page 19 of **Pathfinders: Canadian Tributes**, volume IV, the CANADA Heirloom Series.

From that town on the south shore of the widening St. Lawrence River, we trekked to the Gaspésie where the famous *Rocher Percé* stands. Seeing it from a distance is breathtaking, even mystical. Multiple times I stopped the car to take perspective photos of Percé Rock. From a distance, it emerges on the horizon like a massive ship under sail or perhaps a beached super tanker. One can detect, miles away, one of the world's largest natural arches giving the reddish-gold rock a luminous appearance. Standing 300 feet high and nearing 300 feet wide, its length is 1400 feet. The limestone monolith is not only mythical but a geological wonder. At low tide, Percé is linked to the mainland by a sandbar. To follow the sandbar and touch Percé Rock as Gay and I did was allegorical and a thrill.

The town of Percé is an old French fishing village. We were able to locate a motel on an elevated section of the

Left: The 112-foot Cap-des-Rosiers Lighthouse is the tallest in Canada. It is situated on the south shore of the St. Lawrence River as it empties into the Gulf of St. Lawrence. Gay, pictured, and I enjoyed a French Canadian lunch with red wine, crackers and cheese at the base of this historic lighthouse. **Right:** Called the "Cross of Gaspe," it was first erected as a wooden cross when Jacques Cartier landed on the shores of Quebec in 1534. A 32-ton single-piece of granite in the shape of a cross, it was erected in Gaspe in 1934 to commemorate Cartier's 400th anniversary of his landing in the new world claiming *Nouveau France* for Christianity and the King of France.

Dad's Best Memories and Recollections

town so that we could scan the bay and watch the setting sun light up Percé Rock. The island further out, Bonaventure Island, beckoned us to travel there the next day. The next morning, aboard the **Felix Leclerc** boat cruise, we navigated past Percé Rock to the easterly side of Bonaventure Island where a sheer cliff rising 225 feet is home to the largest gannet colony in the world. Hovering and flying above seals and whales, more than 200,000 birds in flight are one of the wonders of the world to watch. But be careful of the wind as their residue is malodorous.

Visiting the Gaspé Peninsula had several minor stops. One was at the Cap-des-Rosiers Lighthouse, a National Historic Site. Here we picnicked beneath the tallest lighthouse in Canada. The Cap-des-Rosiers lighthouse stands at 112 feet and was built in 1854. We also spent time in the town of Gaspé where Jacques Cartier landed on July 24, 1534. This was nearly 100 years before Boston was founded by Pilgrims. In 1934, 400 years later, a 32-foot solid, granite cross, weighing 32 tons, was erected near the site where the famous French explorer claimed *Nouveau France* for Christianity and the King of France. It's one of the most empyrean crosses in the entire western world.

Passing along Baie-des-Chaleurs is much like enjoying an impressionistic painting unfolding beside you while driving the length of the magnificent Baies-des-Chaleur highway. It's a most serene road. We stayed overnight in Daniel-Gascons, the town where Hazel McCallion, Mississauga's former mayor for thirty-six years, was born. After crossing into New Brunswick, we soon passed through Rexton, stopping to visit the birthplace of Bonar Law (1858-1923), the only British Prime Minister to have been born outside the British Isles. As we drove through Bouctouche, I reflected that this was the small town where one of Canada's greatest entrepreneurial families, the Irvings, were born and raised. His family today is recognized as Canada's second wealthiest. On our way to Prince Edward Island, we also passed through Shediac acclaimed as the lobster capital of the world.

After taking the ferry from New Brunswick to Prince Edward Island (Confederation Bridge, linking PEI and New Brunswick, was completed three years later, 1997), we drove directly to Charlottetown, the provincial capital, where we stayed overnight. Inquiring about available tickets to the Charlottetown Festival Theatre, we were lucky enough to purchase a pair for the fabulous show **Puttin' on the Ritz,** the Irving Berlin musical that hit Broadway in 1927 and has been an ongoing hit ever since. The Charlottetown Festival has staged, since it opened in 1965, the musical based on Lucy Maud Montgomery's novel, **Anne of Green Gables.** We toured Charlottetown in a double decker bus before venturing off for Lucy Maud Montgomery's home in Cavendish and where **Anne of Green Gables** was written, 1908. A whimsical home, we were so impressed with the gardening and the number of Japanese tourists who, by the busload, were paying tribute to one of Canada's best known literary names. After visiting the estate, we travelled to Saint Anne's Church in New Glasgow and feasted on lobster. This is a must destination for anyone visiting PEI and wanting to enjoy the best basement church supper anywhere! One thing is for sure: it was about the only time we enjoyed something without discussing Percé Rock.

Top: Saint Anne's Church in New Glasgow, Prince Edward Island, offers the best lobster food feast in PEI. The basement dinners provided by the church are a must for tourists wanting to whet their lobster appetite. **Bottom:** Lucy Maud Montgomery's home in Cavendish, Prince Edward Island, is an iconic Canadian destination. Here **Anne of Green Gables** was written. This all-Canadian story has sold over fifty million copies since 1908. The novel is compulsory reading for Japanese students who often come to Canada to get married on the grounds of the estate. **Below left**: While driving home to Ontario from the Gaspe, we passed through Maine stopping at L.L. Bean in Freeport. The hat I bought has travelled everywhere with me for the last twenty-two years. I might even be buried with it!

Gay and I were not sure how to head back to Mississauga following our week's trip through Quebec, New Brunswick and PEI. We decided not to return the same way we came. Rather, we journeyed through northern Maine, hustling our way to Freeport, where the famous L.L. Bean store is located. Anyone interested in where I bought my famous green hat that I wear every year up at the cottage, well, you got it right -- it was at L.L. Bean's!

There is no question that our trip's highlight was Percé Rock. French writer Andre Breton says that the Percé Rock is an "iceberg of moonstone". I say it's one of those places that could be more memorable than a lobster dinner....

Launching **LOYAL SHE REMAINS**, 1984

When I was elected President, The United Empire Loyalists' Association of Canada (UELAC), in Waterloo, Ontario, May, 1982, I was teaching high school for The Toronto Board of Education. My UELAC portfolio was a two-year term. This meant my term would coincide with the Government of Ontario's official plans to commemorate the province's 1984 Bicentennial with alluring celebrations. And since more than 800 communities across Ontario had already committed to celebrating the province's bicentennial, for sure, 1984 was destined to be a big year!

Fortunately, through the auspices of the late David Macdonald Stewart, the Macdonald Stewart Foundation of Montreal seconded me to its non-profit organization. This freed me from teaching responsibilities for at least the next two years and enabled me to determine the best way for the UELAC to participate in this upcoming celebration. Indeed, I was most anxious for the UELAC to find an appropriate way to celebrate not only the province's bicentennial but to honour our UE Loyalist ancestors who came to Canada as defeated refugees from the American Revolution and substantially participated in the creation of a new society in a new land.

Around the time I was seconded, an individual by the name of William Koene approached me and inquired about the possibilities of the UELAC producing, in conjunction with him, an illustrious book celebrating Ontario's history with emphasis on the United Empire Loyalists. I quickly arranged for Mr. Koene to make a proposal to the UEL Council. In short time the Association agreed to his proposal with the understanding that all liabilities and responsibilities for the entire publication venture would remain with Bill Koene and his own company and providing there was some sharing in any profits. In short time he assembled his staff which included a promotion and sales staff and an editorial department. Roles such as publication co-ordinator, production and design co-ordinator, direct-mail co-ordinator and general office staff were also integral to the project.

There is much content to be included in any book acknowledging Ontario's rich history. I was soon made the co-editor for the entire project along with Mary Beacock Fryer. An ambitious two-year program was set into motion with multiple authors commissioned to write a gamut of some thirty chapters. The publication was named **LOYAL SHE REMAINS**, a title taken from the provincial motto: "As She Began Loyal, Loyal She Remains," a motto, of course, referring to the fact that the first wave of immigration to the province were UE Loyalists who brought with them unquenched loyalty to the British Crown. These same sentiments are as true today as they were in 1784. This is clearly evident as multiple new citizens of the province swear their loyalty to the Monarchy almost daily.

A 600-page book celebrating Ontario's elaborate history included not only the coming of the UE Loyalists, but chapters on the War of 1812, the Great Depression, World Wars I and II, the History of Education, Religious Faith in the Province, Pioneering Achievements, the Arts, the Simcoe Years, Sporting Heroes and so much more....

Far left: In early 1984, the Royal Ontario Museum was the venue to announce the forthcoming publication **LOYAL SHE REMAINS**. Former Governor General Roland Michener has the pleasure of cracking a joke at the expense of Charles J. Humber, co-editor and President of UELAC. **Left**: Beginning July 7, 1984, the **Toronto Star** serialized **LOYAL SHE REMAINS** for 10 consecutive weeks. This resulted in blockbuster sales from across the province during the 1984 Ontario Bicentennial. This installment was the first excerpt.

Dad's Best Memories and Recollections

While the writers were commissioned and producing their respective chapters for the book, still another group, headed up by Reg Dawe and Angela Dea Cappelli Clark, was raising funds. This was done through corporate sponsorship. We felt if corporations were willing to sponsor Ballet, Opera, Theatre, Sports, Marathon Runs, Symphony, the Stratford Festival and others, why not induce corporations to sponsor a project that the government of Ontario was behind! Besides, it was a way for corporations to show that they supported a book project that was generating much-needed heritage awareness and promoted our rich culture. They were given the opportunity to subscribe to one- or two-page editorials recording their proud history. It was a massive undertaking. Thus, while the editorial work was going on, the sales team was travelling the province, soliciting corporate sponsorship and raising funds. When it was all over we enticed subscriptions to more than 100 pages of space from corporations wanting to tell their respective histories in concise vignettes. This sponsorship funded the entire publication. Without their support, **LOYAL SHE REMAINS** would never have got off the ground. It really was a brilliant strategy. Of course, once the book was published, all corporate sponsors had a supply of wonderful gifts for clients and customers. Indirectly helping market the publication were special individuals agreeing to write various introductory messages. These included Ontario Premier Bill Davis, former Canadian Governor General Roland Michener, and distinguished Canadian Senator Eugene Forsey. As President of the UEL Association, as well as co-editor, I was privileged to write the Prologue.

LOYAL SHE REMAINS sold just over 50,000 books, ten times a Canadian best seller! We officially announced its forthcoming publication at a Royal Ontario Museum gala in much reported fanfare. At the Annual Convention of the UELAC at Queen's University, Kingston, Ontario, May, 1984, **LOYAL SHE REMAINS** was officially launched. I was dressed up as John Graves Simcoe and officially made a presentation to the Right Honorable Roland Michener in front of the largest ever gathering of Loyalists ever to attend a Loyalist convention. As well, on July 3, 1984, in consort with Canada Post that issued a Loyalist commemorative stamp at Toronto's Black Creek Pioneer Village, **LOYAL SHE REMAINS** was re-launched generating constant sales over the summer.

Essentially, **LOYAL SHE REMAINS** was not sold in book stores. Rather it was marketed directly to the public at Fall Fairs, Parades, Sporting Events, through various mailing lists and wherever people gathered. **The Toronto Star** reviewed sections of the book in full-page spreads for ten consecutive weeks. This in itself generated massive sales both directly and indirectly. The book was also selected as the official gift to a number of well-known personalities. When Premier the Hon. Bill Davis presented a special edition to Pope John Paul II, who visited Toronto in 1984, the publicity generated a multitude of sales. And when Her Majesty The Queen visited Ontario, I was privileged to present Her Majesty with a special edition on behalf of the UEL Association as well as the people of Ontario. The publicity these events generated was monstrous. There is no question that the publication of **LOYAL SHE REMAINS** is one of my life's highlights, sustaining me with fine memories that I will take to my grave with much satisfaction.

Above: First day issue, July 3, 1984, of Canada Post's Loyalist stamp.
Right: LOYAL SHE REMAINS was launched a second time at Black Creek Pioneer Village, when Canada Post issued its United Empire Loyalist stamp, Toronto, July 3, 1984. Dignitaries participating in the launch, left to right are: Russ Cooper, Manager of Black Creek; Dea Cappelli Clark; Charles Humber; Bill Koene; The Hon. Bob Nixon, Leader of Ontario Liberal Party; Reg Dawe, at podium; The Hon. Margaret Birch, Ontario Deputy Premier; Mayor Dennis Flynn, Etobicoke; Mary Fryer; Geof Fryer; Joan Aggis, Adminstrator.

Family Sleuthing Revisited, 2006

Other than my wife Gay, I doubt if anyone understands what an effort it took to publish **Family Sleuthing**, a publication endeavour that surely ranks as one of my life's most cherished accomplishments. Although full-time research on the project didn't really start until 2001, the overall platform for this endeavour probably originated in my early years in that I have always shown curiosity about my family's roots on both sides of the family. Perhaps this is one reason why so many of my relatives, before they passed on, left me boxes and various sized manila envelopes of ephemera and photographs that they couldn't or wouldn't throw out but wanted someone like me to save their memorabilia for posterity. This in itself is a best memory....

Although my father never really talked much about his family roots, he did enjoy recalling and telling stories about various uncles and aunts he had visited over the years. This instilled in me a curiosity about the Humber line especially when I started reading letters Dad had inherited from his aunt Aggie Cassels, his father's only sister, who had married an athletic legend from Stratford by the name of Roderick Cassels. I also discovered through sleuthing that a great many of my father's relatives were champion athletes winning a variety of tournaments or individual and team awards for such sports as track, lacrosse, curling, hockey, lawn bowling, cycling and baseball. I discovered that many were Masons who were pinnacle achievers in this organization and in other fraternal societies such as the Shriners. When I found out that I had a distant relative, Bruce Humber, from Victoria, who was an integral part of the Canadian Track and Field team that went to the Berlin 1936 Olympics, I was impressed if not fascinated. In doing just rudimentary research, I found that many of my relatives were pioneers in various communities across Canada, including Fort Qu'Appelle, and Mortlach in Saskatchewan, and Portage la Prairie in Manitoba, Leduc and Red Deer in Alberta, and Victoria, the capitol of British Columbia. As well, such Ontario communities as Bowmanville, Keene, Peterborough, Stratford, Port Rowan, Essex, Goderich, and the general Kingston area of eastern Ontario were all settled by past relatives. On my mother's side of the family tree, I learned that the Scott, Jarvis, Blair, Ellerby and Farr "clans" were from Prince Edward County or, subsequently, from the greater Toronto area. Many were farmers, apple growers, auctioneers, preachers, merchants, boat builders, fishermen, and general nineteenth century entrepreneurs, even artists, who were never dependent on government handouts. Other than several descendants from the first generation of UE Loyalists who came to Canada as destitute refugees from the American Revolution, 1783-84, no relative on either side of the family has come to Canada over the years and relied on any government assistance of any sort.

Before **Family Sleuthing** was published in the fall of 2006, I had travelled as far as the Isle of Wight, in England, to learn more about my Humber roots there. I met up with a distant cousin, Harold Humber, a lay preacher, who took me and Gay to various ancient places where my Humber lineage had worked, including Carisbrooke Castle and Osbourne House, and various medieval churches such as St. Peter's in the Parish of Shorwell. This type of discovery was very impressive and consequently has generated for me many unforgettable memories. My travels have also taken me to Winnipeg and Portage la Prairie, in Manitoba, to Calgary and the foothills of the Rocky Mountains, in Alberta, to Vancouver, to Everett, Washington, and to Roseburg, Oregon, to Prescott, Arizona, as well as to closer destinations like Detroit and Flint, Michigan, in addition to Newfoundland and Quebec. Of course, anywhere in Ontario where past relatives have lived at one time or another I became a self-appointed family archaeologist, digging and excavating family stories, especially way down in the far reaches of Essex County, southwestern Ontario, where one of my great-grandfather's sisters, Keturah Keane, moved in the mid-19th century.

In the process of all this family research generating "best memories," I was happy to learn that many of my ancestors really made outstanding contributions to society, all of whom I've referenced, one place or another, in **Family Sleuthing.** The cement poured, for instance, for the world-famous Peterborough Lift Lock north of Rice Lake, was poured by Orenzo Humber, one of my great-grandfather Humber's brothers. The same family built churches including one that still stands on the Hiawatha Indian Reservation on Rice Lake. One of my ancestors, maternal great-grandfather Cornelius Biddle, who fought in the Crimean War, trained aboard HMS **Victory**, Nelson's famous flagship at the Battle of Trafalgar. It really was amazing to learn these facts and to learn that Phineas and Charlie Reeves of Port Dover and Port Rowan are known as two of the most sought after decoy carvers in North America. Still another relative, maternal great-grandfather W. B. Scott was co-founder of the Emporia Business

Dad's Best Memories and Recollections

College, forerunner of Emporia State University in Kansas. This gingery knowledge tends to instill pride in family and generate much ponderous satisfaction. One of the largest General Motors dealerships in Canada was founded in Weston, Ontario, by World War I veteran, J.T. "Toat" Farr, one of grandmother Jarvis's uncles. His son, Ellerby, won the Mann Cup in 1926, the Stanley Cup of lacrosse. Such discoveries have been precious to me and have perpetuated lasting memories. One of my great uncles, moreover, on my mother's side, Farr Llewellyn Scott, was a North American checker player champion. An uncle of mine, Percy Schweyer, was a golf champion of Norfolk County in southwestern Ontario while still another relative, Mike Weir, won the Master's golf championship back in 2003. My mother's brother, Gordon Jarvis, played the trombone for Tommy Dorsey in the U.S.A. and in Toronto for Toronto's top bands in the 1930s led by the Romanelli brothers. My father, Charles M. Humber, a student at McMaster University, reached the finals in 1934 for the Inter-University Debating League Cup, emblematic of Canadian championship. Many of my relatives have won grand prizes in quilting contests, particularly my grandmother Mabel Jarvis when she lived in Brampton. Two of my cousins represented Canada in various rifle contests, including David Donaldson who was sent to England in 1955 where his team won the Alexander Graham Bell Championship at Bisley. Another cousin, Grant Schweyer is registered as a Canadian Sniper. He has won many blue ribbons and gold medals in musketry in the American South re-enacting Civil War combat. Not to be outdone, my father competed in the King George Challenge Shield Championship Rifle Match, in London, Ontario, while attending Goderich Collegiate, 1924.

Many prominent personalities from the past and linked to the family include Hollywood's Tom Mix, the notorious Billy the Kid, and Henry Ford whose medical doctor for a time was my great uncle, Dr. Albert Milton Humber. Howie Morenz, voted the greatest hockey player of the first half of the twentieth century, was coached by another great uncle, Mait Humber, my grandfather's brother. He also founded the first professional baseball league in Canada. Another great uncle co-invented the punch clock so that the coming and going of employees at the Ford plants in Michigan could be tracked. Red Fife Wheat, the strain that turned the Canadian prairies into a global bread basket, was developed by the Fife family who inter-married with the Humber family in Peterborough County.... The apprenticeship system created for the Grand Trunk Railway, later Canadian National Railway, and which generated tens of thousands of jobs over several decades, was created by my great uncle Mait Humber of Stratford.

When I think about all of these achievements, I find great satisfaction to have recorded most of them for posterity in **Family Sleuthing**. I feel I have lived a magical life filled with happy memories. I'm proud that my immediate family of today have all been educated. My father led the way. He not only graduated from two Ivy League schools, Columbia and Harvard, but three other universities, University of Toronto and both McMaster and Boston Universities where latterly he attended Divinity School with Martin Luther King Jr. His four children followed in their father's footsteps, all graduating from universities. My own twin sons, Charlie and Scott, have certainly generated fond memories for Gay and me when they both went on scholarships to Ivy League Brown University. My two daughters, Kristy and Karyn, have also graduated from university, the former from University of Toronto, the latter from both York University and Central Michigan University. Today, both are professionals, one a nurse while the other is a professor at both Humber College and Guelph/Humber University. And now Gay and I have eight grandchildren to watch grow up and mature. Four were born before the publication of **Family Sleuthing**. During our sunset years, we trust that each of them, plus the four grandchildren born after the publication of this family treasure book, will proceed through life, generating as many happy memories for themselves as they have given their grandparents. If they can fill their memory baskets as full as their grandparent's storehouse of memories, they will be awesomely wealthy, especially if they raise Golden Retrievers like their grandparents have done over a forty-year period.

The Canadian Statesman.

Family Sleuthing – a celebration of family

Author traces his roots back through Bowmanville in book

By Julie Cashin-Oster
Special to The Statesman

Elizabeth Traskos, far left, Elizabeth Brandon, Bonnie Snyder and Charlie Humber stand at the gravestone in Grand Lawn Cemetery in Detroit where the remains of Frank Humber and his wife Elizabeth Passmore Fulford lie buried. This trip was just part of Mr. Humber's journey as he compiled his family tree before penning his book Family Sleuthing. Many of his relatives originally hailed from the Bowmanville area, a fact also highlighted in his book.

'A publication that started out as a brief tribute to my family more than five years ago, slowly developed into a hardcover family tome celebrating, saluting and honouring the lives and legacy of both sides of my family tree back into the early 18th century and beyond.'
– Charles Humber

BOWMANVILLE -- The fascination with our past begins in grade school when we are given the task to create a family tree. For most that is as detailed as it gets, but for Charles Humber researching his roots took five years and turned into a 400-page hardcover book complete with illustrations.

The Canadian Statesman in 1894 saluted David Hess Humber (Charles's great-great-grandfather) as one of the town's early pioneers. This occurred during Bowmanville's centennial year. The first section of the book pays tribute to David Hess Humber and his wife, Leah Draper, Bible Christians who were inspired to come to Bowmanville in the mid-19th century from the Isle of Wight, England. The most prominent and affluent Bible Christian Church in Canada at that time was in Bowmanville.

"These Bible Christians came to Canada with four children, one of whom was my 10-year-old great-grandfather, Charles Austin Humber, who went on to become a prominent Goderich citizen. One of his six children, born in Keene, Ont., became Henry Ford's doctor in Detroit. Still another of his children, also born in Keene, invented Henry Ford's punch clock," said Mr. Humber, author of *Family Sleuthing*.

"Four more children were born to this family, likely all in Bowmanville between the years 1850 and 1860. These were Keturah, Herschell, Francis German and Oliver Wellington."

One gets a good view of who Bible Christians were in mid-19th century Canada. Long gone as a religious sect, they eventually merged with the Canadian Methodist Church in the later 19th century. There is an illustration of the old Bible Christian Church in Bowmanville being demolished in 1961.

There is a rare illustration (originally printed in The Canadian Statesman) of an auction sale that took place outside of Bowmanville in 1871. The sale was conducted for a nephew of David Hess Humber, John Henry Humber, who came to Bowmanville in the early 1850s with his parents, Henry and Sarah Humber, also from the Isle of Wight and some 20 years after David and Leah. The story of Henry and Sarah and their Bible Christian family is detailed in the first section.

"A publication that started out as a brief tribute to my family more than five years ago, slowly developed into a hardcover family tome celebrating, saluting and honouring the lives and legacy of both sides of my family tree back into the early 18th century and beyond," he said.

The book includes more than 650 illustrations and is divided into nine sections with 65 biographical stories.

Although there is reference in *Family Sleuthing* to each member of the Humber family of 10 living in Bowmanville, only Parysatis (b. 1850), Herschell (b. 1853), Francis German (b. 1854), and Oliver Wellington (b. 1860) were born in this town. None of this family died there.

However, David lived in a retired home in Bowmanville, operated by a Mr. Brimacombe, up to the last six months of his life, dying in Warkworth at the home of Bowmanville-born daughter, Parysatis, in 1907, at age 88.

His second wife, Lydia Patten, died in a House of Refuge in Cobourg in 1905. She and David were living in Bowmanville from 1891 to 1901 according to the Canadian Census.

"Being the oldest of my generation, everyone kept passing things off to me on death -- I had boxes and boxes," Mr. Humber said. "Humber is the oldest surname in the English language. Both sides (father and mother's) have deep roots in family, with strong ties to the Empire Loyalists. I researched both and was surprised it came out even. The book is equally divided between mother and father."

Mr. Humber, a retired high school teacher, left a 50-60 hour week job in publishing and five years ago started crisscrossing North America researching his ancestral roots. From British Columbia to Arizona, he just got on a plane and visited people. Some he knew from his parents, others he just looked up.

"I would just call people out of the blue, everyone was always fascinated."

Publishing only slightly more than 300 volumes with the idea of satisfying relatives in the twilight of their years, the book sold out. Mr. Humber sold books to 30 families in 30 states, seven provinces and four continents. Half the people not related love to use it a source material to write a family book. Genealogy is the number one hobby in the world -- surpassing the top two -- stamp and coin collecting.

"You have to have passion, tremendous passion to do a book like this, 'stick-to-wardness,'" he said.

If you are interested in taking a look at *Family Sleuthing* it can be found at the Clarington Public Library.

You can reach Charles Humber at gchumber@sympatico.ca.

The Goderich Signal-Star

Humber honours humble Goderich beginnings through *Family Sleuthing*

Carolyn Parks
special to the signal-star

Charles Joseph ("Charlie") Humber enjoys history – and has a keen interest in that of his family.

His book "Family Sleuthing—Chasing Sunsets & Falling Leaves" traces many generations of his large family from the early 1800s to today and in the process, provides an interesting look at community and social life during that period.

Interestingly, the Humber family has a Goderich connection. At age 35, Humber's great grandfather, Charles Austin Humber (1838-1907), moved to Goderich with his wife and children in 1872.

During the next 35 years, he was an active businessman and citizen. Although a millwright by trade, he founded C.A. Humber & Son jewelers on The Square.

Charles Austin also served many terms on town council, and was at various times involved with the Goderich Board of Trade, The Goderich Mechanics' Institute, lawn bowling, curling and a member of North Street Methodist Church.

The youngest son of Charles Austin was named Maitland Alexander Humber (1877-1950) after Goderich's large river and affectionately was called 'Mait' by family and friends.

In 1873, the author's grandfather, Charles Herbert Humber (1873-1943) was born at Goderich where he lived throughout his life, eventually taking up his father's jewellery business.

As a jeweller, he acted as an agent for numerous railways, charged with inspection and monitoring of the watches of many hundreds of railway engineers.

A seriously important job—if watches were not scrupulously synchronized, rail tragedy could result. Charles Herbert served on Goderich Town Council more than 25 years.

The author's father, Charles Maitland Humber (1906-1988) was also born at Goderich.

With a Bachelor of Science degree from the University of Toronto, Charles Maitland enrolled as a divinity student at McMaster University graduating in 1935. He taught Chemical Engineering at the University of Toronto and undertook pastoral charges at various churches in Canada and the United States.

Author Charlie—a long-time teacher of English literature and eventual publisher—spent five years compiling and writing "Family Sleuthing."

"Through this book, I learned who I am as a person," he reports, "and developed a more thorough understanding of my ancestors. It was interesting to learn how history evolved and involved them.

"I wanted to honour and celebrate the relatives who went before me and leave something tangible about our family's heritage for my children and grandchildren."

Humber's meticulous research has done just that.

In addition to a wealth of information "Family Sleuthing" contains a vast collection of photographs and illustrations, gleaned from 10,000 documents.

Charlie Humber will address the Goderich Genealogical Society on Oct. 3 at the Huron County Museum in Goderich beginning at 7:30 p.m.

Enquiries about "Family Sleuthing" can be made to (905) 823-6154.

Above left: Bowmanville's **The Canadian Statesman**, one of Canada's oldest newspapers, reviewed **Family Sleuthing,** June 13, 2007, page A7. **Above right: The Signal-Star** of Goderich where three generations of Humbers lived, reviewed **Family Sleuthing**, September 26, 2007. **Bottom left: The Stratford Beacon Herald** reviewed **Family Sleuthing**, January 13, 2007, page 3. **Bottom Right: The Haldimand Press** reviewed **Family Sleuthing,** March 14, 2007, page 1.

The Beacon Herald

Family book highlights Maitland Humber's role in Stratford's history

Father of the CNR apprentice system

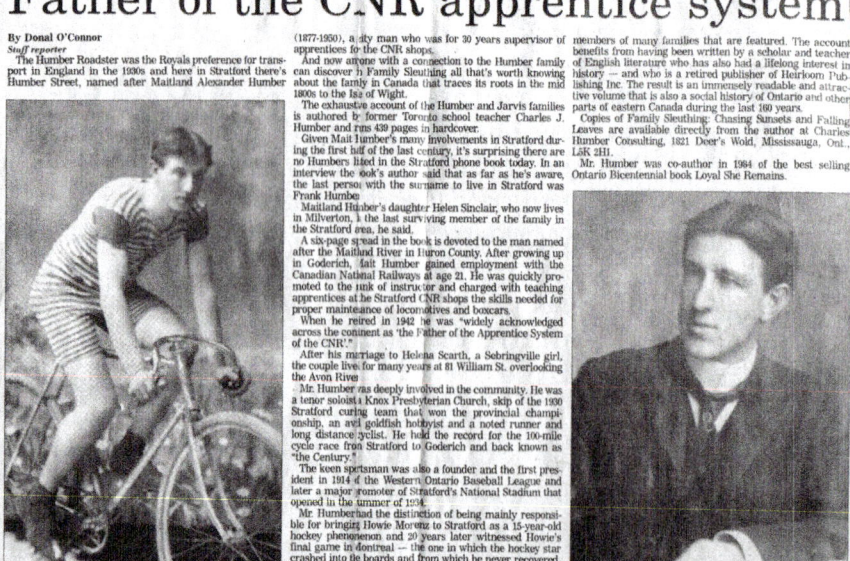

By Donal O'Connor
Staff reporter

The Humber Roadster was the Royals preference for transport in England in the 1930s and here in Stratford there's Humber Street, named after Maitland Alexander Humber (1877-1950), a city man who was for 30 years supervisor of apprentices for the CNR shops.

And now anyone with a connection to the Humber family can discover in Family Sleuthing all that's worth knowing about the family in Canada that traces its roots in the mid 1800s to the Isle of Wight.

The exhaustive account of the Humber and Jarvis families is authored by former Toronto school teacher Charles J. Humber and runs 439 pages in hardcover.

Given Mait Humber's many involvements in Stratford during the first half of the last century, it's surprising there are no Humbers listed in the Stratford phone book today. In an interview the book's author said that as far as he's aware, the last person with the surname to live in Stratford was Frank Humber.

Maitland Humber's daughter Helen Sinclair, who now lives in Milverton, is the last surviving member of the family in the Stratford area, he said.

A six-page spread in the book is devoted to the man named after the Maitland River in Huron County. After growing up in Goderich, Mait Humber gained employment with the Canadian National Railways at age 21. He was quickly promoted to the rank of instructor and charged with teaching apprentices at the Stratford CNR shops the skills needed for proper maintenance of locomotives and boxcars.

When he retired in 1942 he was "widely acknowledged across the continent as 'the Father of the Apprentice System of the CNR'."

After his marriage to Helena Scarth, a Sebringville girl, the couple lived for many years at 81 William St. overlooking the Avon River.

Mr. Humber was deeply involved in the community. He was a tenor soloist at Knox Presbyterian Church, skip of the 1930 Stratford curling team that won the provincial championship, an avid goldfish hobbyist and a noted runner and long distance cyclist. He held the record for the 100-mile cycle race from Stratford to Goderich and back known as "the Century."

The keen sportsman was also a founder and the first president in 1914 of the Western Ontario Baseball League and later a major promoter of Stratford's National Stadium that opened in the summer of 1934.

Mr. Humber had the distinction of being mainly responsible for bringing Howie Morenz to Stratford as a 15-year-old hockey phenomenon and 20 years later witnessed Howie's final game in Montreal — the one in which the hockey star crashed into the boards and from which he never recovered.

Mait's only daughter Helen Sinclair is credited by the members of many families that are featured. The account benefits from having been written by a scholar and teacher of English literature who has also had a lifelong interest in history — and who is a retired publisher of Heirloom Publishing Inc. The result is an immensely readable and attractive volume that is also a social history of Ontario and other parts of eastern Canada during the last 160 years.

Copies of Family Sleuthing: Chasing Sunsets and Falling Leaves are available directly from the author at Charles Humber Consulting, 1821 Deer's Wold, Mississauga, Ont., L5K 2H1.

Mr. Humber was co-author in 1984 of the best selling Ontario Bicentennial book Loyal She Remains.

THE HALDIMAND PRESS

Humber's History

Family Sleuthing Traces Generations

Detailed family histories are usually of interest only to members of the clan which is focused upon. Yet, a 439-page hardcover book bearing the title *"Family Sleuthing, Chasing Sunsets and Falling Leaves,"* as 'sleuthed' and written by Mississauga, ON resident Charles J. Humber, will surely serve to revive a goodly number of memories for certain Haldimand County seniors who knew the author and his family circa the 1940's and those of the Schweyer family to whom his father was connected through marriage.

Mr. Humber has kindly donated sufficient copies of this book to the Haldimand County Public Library to provide one for each of the five Branches: Caledonia, Cayuga, Dunnville, Hagersville, Jarvis and Selkirk.

The connection between the author and Haldimand County began in 1925 when his father's sister, Fern Humber, married Percy Schweyer the youngest child of Jacob and Alice (Nauman) Schweyer who was born and raised at Cottonwood Mansion. Mr. Humber himself became directly connected to Haldimand when, in 1938, he and his sister, Anna, moved to Hagersville with their parents after his father was named Pastor of the Hagersville Baptist Church.

Family Sleuthing author, Charles J. Humber, was born at St. Lambert, Quebec, July 14, 1936 first of the four children of Charles M. and Evelyn (Jarvis) Humber. His father was ordained at Hagersville some months after moving to Haldimand and pastored in Hagersville for four and one-half years before the family left to reside in Toronto in 1942. Rev. Humber had accepted a teaching position at the University of Toronto and at the same time, became Pastor of Victoria Park Avenue Baptist Church.

As illustrated in a birth notice reproduced in the book from a July, 1942 issue of The Hagersville Press, the Humbers' two younger children, twins Paul and Priscilla, were born at Mrs. Moulding's Nursing Home in Hagersville just weeks prior to the family's move to Toronto.

By 1948 Rev. Humber was enrolled at Harvard University in Massachusetts and his family were enjoying Summer vacations at *"Hiawatha,"* a cottage located near Selkirk at Woodlawn Park on the Lake Erie North Shore that was owned by the Hagersville Baptist Church. Ineligible to return to the U.S. in the Autumn of 1948 because of expired immigration documents, the four Humber children attended S.S. No. 2, Walpole for some months. Then known as "McGaw's School," our Press readers now know the former one-roomed *Little Red Schoolhouse* as "The Wilson MacDonald Memorial School Museum" which presides over the intersection of Rainham and Cheapside Roads, just west of Selkirk.

In the section of the book devoted to his sister, Priscilla, Mr. Humber reflects on the Humber kids time at McGaw's School and some of the local pupils they mingled with for that brief period of time and other recollections of that era of his parental family's life.

While your editor was not able to meet with "Charlie" Humber on the two separate occasions when he visited the office of The Haldimand Press with a copy of his book, we have since shared a number of enjoyable telephone conversations. On those occasions he recounted some interesting anecdotes and indicated on which pages of the book one might discover his references to this County. As well we also learned of a 'common thread' he and your editor share in that we both trace to ancestors who resided in Huron County.

Charles Humber

As noted at the outset of this account, many Press readers will not find much of the material included in this personal tome to be of personal interest to them. Yet, for those enchanted with local history and/or genealogy there are enough references to local places and people—as well as plenty of period photographs and reproductions of general interest vintage documents—that it should prove well worth a trip to your Haldimand County Public Library Branch to peruse its pages.

For those who might like to contact Charlie Humber personally, his e-mail address is:

gchumber@sympatico.ca

The Heritage Gazette of the Trent Valley

ISSN 1206-4394 Volume 12, number 2, August 2007

Charles J. Humber, *Family Sleuthing: Chasing Sunsets and Falling Leaves*, (Mississauga, Charles Humber Consulting, 2006) Pp ii, 439; hc $100. ISBN 0-9694247-9-5

The production quality of this volume is overwhelming. It was printed and bound in India, and the quality and clarity of the pictures and the many documents is exceptional. The book is a pleasure to read. The project was begun in 2001, and a query appeared in the *Heritage Gazette of the Trent Valley* in 2002. Charles J. Humber is well-known for his extraordinary helmsmanship in the production of *Loyal She Remains*, a book that honoured the 200th anniversary of Loyalist settlement in Ontario.

This book is ambitious in different ways. It focuses on a string of the family that begins with David Hess Humber and Leah Draper. The book is threaded around the families of successive generations: Cornelius Biddle and Elizabeth Fry; Samuel Jarvis and Valletta Blair; William B. Scott and Marry Ann Farr; Charles H. Humber and Lizzie M. Biddle; John G. Jarvis and Mable A. Scott; Charles M. Humber & Gayle Jenkins.

I have travelled across the great Humber bridge that joins Lincolnshire and Yorkshire and naturally thought this family would come from that region. However, the seed of this line is the Isle of Wight. Charles Humber takes us in his footprints as he searches for his family in the archives of the Isle of Wight. He includes a nice picture of an incredibly neat Newport Records Office. He reconstructs the life of the agricultural laborers of this area, and notes the bind of the family to the Bible Christians, a tie that was particularly important when they emigrated to the Bowmanville area in 1848; later near Harwood. Some members of the family stand out. The terrible death of C. A. Humber who died of an accident while pulling a bathtub down stairs; when a stair collapsed he fell and suffered a concussion on a radiator. The book includes excellent copies of the oil paintings of him and his wife painted by George F. Hargitt (1838-1926). His wife was an Amey, a Loyalist and Huguenot familiy.

Angelina Humber married into the Fife family of Peterborough county. Several members of the family that emigrated to Bowmanville area settled in the area around Rice Lake.

The story moves quickly to other parts of the province: Goderich, Stratford, Stony Creek. We also get visits to China and to the Canadian west. Subsequent sections of the book take us to many other areas. The branches of the family seem to converge on the counties of Norfolk and Haldimand and then branch out from there.

Humber is a storyteller and the book is very readable, if somewhat daunting given the pantheon of heroes. The mobility of the family might be representative of other families. Families moved constantly even as the parents of successive generations found a permanent home. The book is also distinguished by its high production values. It is indeed rare to see a book that be filled with snapshots and newspaper clippings that look like professional shots. The clarity of the images is remarkable, and refreshing.

I like the book as well for its wide-ranging approach, its efforts to track down every member of the wider family. We have two exceptional collections at the Trent Valley Archives in which researchers reflect similar instincts. Doug Miller has done the history of the Miller family, and in the process developed about thirty other family trees. John and Mary Young travelled to the places their families had been and returned with remarkable stories, photos and memorabilia. Neither, though, envisioned a book as venturesome as Charles Humber's *Family Sleuthing*.

Simcoe Reformer

cents GST MONDAY, APRIL 2, 2007 www.simco

Left: The **Simcoe Reformer** traces its roots in Norfolk county to 1858. It reviewed **Family Sleuthing** April 2, 2007, page 3.

Humber family history 'a labour of love'

MISSISSAUGA PUBLISHER TAKES GENEALOGICAL WRITING TO ANOTHER LEVEL

CONTRIBUTED PHOTO

The life story *of historian and publisher Charles J. Humber runs directly through the Biddle clan of Port Rowan. At right is Lizzie Biddle – C.J. Humber's grandmother – who lived to the ripe old age of 102. At left is her husband Charles Herbert Humber, who died in 1943 at age 68.*

Monte Sonnenberg
SIMCOE REFORMER

Relatives of Charles Humber better not catch the genealogical bug, for he has well and truly beaten them to the punch.

Humber recently published a striking, hard-cover history of his family. The 440-page book features 650 photos and illustrations, many of them in full colour.

Humber, a retired publisher living in Mississauga, took five years to produce the tome. It was published in a run of 400 volumes late last year. All but 30 have sold.

"To do this book was a labour of love, I can tell you that," Humber said Friday.

Family Sleuthing: Chasing Sunsets and Falling Leaves chronicles the lives of nearly 75 relatives from the early-1800s to the present. The book reads like a social history of Ontario, ranging as it does from one end of the province to the other. Norfolk and Haldimand figure prominently, especially as it regards Humber's connection to the Biddle, Fry and Schweyer families.

Humber, a descendant of United Empire Loyalists, was a history teacher in the early part of his career. As a publisher, he made his mark in 1984 as co-editor of Loyal She Remains, a definitive history of Ontario that coincided with the province's 200th anniversary.

Loyal She Remains was an instant best-seller. It was standard practice for a time to present copies to visiting dignitaries. Recipients included Pope John Paul II, former U.S. president Ronald Reagan and Queen Elizabeth II.

Humber also collaborated with prominent Canadian historians on a seven-volume set called the Canada Heirloom Series. National and international figures wrote introductions to the series, including former prime ministers Brian Mulroney and Jean Chretien, HRH Prince Andrew, economist John Kenneth Galbraith, businessman Charles Bronfman and industrialist Frank Stronach.

Humber's maternal grandmother was Lizzie Biddle of Port Rowan. She died in 1978 at age 102. Through his connection to the Biddle family, Humber spent many summers at the family cottage in Long Point. He also attended for a time the McGaw public school west of Selkirk.

Humber is proud of his family's achievements. Instances include uncle Percy Schweyer, the first and only child born in Cottonwood Mansion north of Selkirk. In 1932, Schweyer won the open championship at the Norfolk Golf & Country Club. Soon after, he turned down an opportunity to serve as the club's pro.

A cousin, June VanFleet of Simcoe, is lauded for winning the amateur novice category at the Norfolk County Fair art show in her inaugural attempt. VanFleet unveiled hitherto unknown painting ability with a stunning portrait of a wolf. A resident of Norfolk Street North, she is pleased with Humber's comprehensive history of her family.

"It's pretty special," VanFleet said. "He found out things that just amazed me. He found out special things I knew nothing about."

A copy of Family Sleuthing is on file in the genealogy department at the Norfolk Heritage Centre in Simcoe. Curator Bill Yeager says ambitious publications like this promise to become more common now that do-it-yourself computer programs have become more accessible and affordable.

Outsourcing printing to low-cost jurisdictions overseas is also reducing the cost of self-publishing. Family Sleuthing was transmitted electronically to a Thomson Publishing printing house in India and flown back to Canada by way of London and New York City. Humber went this route because the publishing house in India was $17,000 less expensive than anyone in Canada.

"That's a lot of kabobs for a guy like me," Humber said.

Monte Sonnenberg
519-426-3528 ext. 150
msonnenberg@bowesnet.com

The County Gazette

Gazette photo by Rick Fralick

Family History – Charlie Humber displays the title page of one of the chapters in his family history, this one dealing with maternal great grandparents William Byron Scott and Mary Ann Farr, for whom the historic Scott's Mill near Milford is named.

Family sleuth's investigation touches County

Ancestors gave name to Scott's Mill, sold property for cheese factory

By Rick Fralick
Gazette Staff

The meticulously researched and lavishly illustrated family history of a retired Toronto-area high school teacher manages to span centuries and borders while illuminating some of Prince Edward County's own past.

But beyond that, Charles Joseph "Charlie" Humber's book is, at heart, a reminder of the fact that the most important thing in the world is, quite simply, family.

Which, no doubt, accounts for its title – *Family Sleuthing: Chasing Sunsets and Falling Leaves.*

With painstaking attention to detail, Humber traces the origins of his own family, from great, great grandparents who lived on the Isle of Wight in the early 19th century, all the way to the present day activities of his own four children.

Along the way, the reader learns of the impact that some of his ancestors had on Prince Edward County, in particular South Marysburgh, where they were responsible for naming the historic Scott's Mill near Milford, and for selling the property on which was built the equally historic, and still very popular, Black River Cheese Company.

Scott's Mill is named for Humber's maternal great grandparents, William Byron Scott and Mary Ann Farr, who returned to Canada from Emporia, Kansas circa 1888-89.

There is a very interesting story how Scott and his family chose to leave Emporia for Milford, Humber explains in his book.

It so happened that Scott was directed to an advertisement in Toronto's The Globe newspaper about a working farm with an operating mill at Milford, Prince Edward County, Ontario.

It was advertised for sale or for trade. Scott wrote to the owners, two brothers with the surname Kirkpatrick. One of them journeyed to Emporia to determine the value of the Scott homestead in Kansas.

A happy transaction was made when Scott agreed to swap his homestead property in Emporia for acreage in Milford that would later become known as Craggy Glen and Scott's Mill.

"No one knows how Scott got his hands on the Toronto paper. One must presume some relative back in Ontario sent it to him...," Humber writes.

Humber's other maternal great grandparents, Samuel Jarvis and Valletta Victoria Blair, homesteaded at Black River Bridge in South Marysburgh Township, where his mother, Evelyn Jarvis was born.

In 1901, the family sold a piece of property which became the site of the cheese factory.

The Jarvises were also prominent supporters of the Black River Bridge Methodist Church, now known as the Black River Memorial Chapel.

Humber writes that his late mother vividly recalled her childhood days at Black River Bridge.

"It was a precious time, when her father took her by the hand on wintery Sunday mornings and led her to the Methodist Church just down the road beyond their farm laneway.

See **Sleuth** page 23

FRIDAY, FEBRUARY 9, 2007 • 23

"Memento finally finished in November of last year

Sleuth from page 1

"Mother affectionately recalled that her father, during the long winter months, customarily made fishing nets in the large family room of their home.

"She reminisced, moreover, that there was at least one ice-house at the back of the house from where large ice blocks were regularly brought to their home to keep certain foods chilled and delightfully fresh during summer months," he writes.

Humber, who lives in Mississauga now, worked full-time for five years on this very personal project, which consists of 440 pages and contains 650 photos and illustrations.

The book – Humber refers to it as a "memento" – was finally finished in November of last year.

"I've had an ongoing love affair with Canada's social history," he says. "Those who neglect the past, don't deserve the future.

"I wrote the book because it was a passion. I hoped that my mother would live to see its completion, but she died in 2005 in her 99th year."

> ***"I wrote the book because it was a passion. I hoped that my mother would live to see its completion, but she died in 2005 in her 99th year."***
> *– Charlie Humber*

Humber, who taught high school English for nearly 20 years before becoming publisher of Heirloom Publishing Inc. in 1985, achieved a certain media profile during the late 1970s and early 1980s by impersonating John Graves Simcoe, the first Lieutenant-Governor of Upper Canada, on public occasions.

He also co-edited *Loyal She Remains*, the history of Ontario that was published in 1984 for the province's bicentennial. Humber presented Her Majesty Queen Elizabeth II with a special edition of the book during a Sept. 27, 1984 ceremony to dedicate the eastern gateway of the Loyalist Parkway at Amherstview.

The library in Picton has a copy of Family Sleuthing and Humber has a few dozen copies of the book for sale. Anyone interested can reach him at *gchumber@sympati-*

The Napanee Beaver

New book offers genealogical inspiration

Charles Humber's Family Sleuthing *takes him through Napanee and area*

By Seth DuChene
Editor

It's no secret that there is a lot of United Empire Loyalist history in the Greater Napanee area, and plenty of family lines can be traced back here. No one knows this better than Charles Humber.

Humber — a former high school teacher and the co-author of *Loyal She Remains: A Pictorial History of Ontario* — has recently published another book which traces his own family roots. And, not surprisingly, some of those roots are planted in Greater Napanee soil.

Humber, who now lives Mississauga, took five years, full-time, to complete *Family Sleuthing: Chasing Sunsets and Falling Leaves*. That included some thorough research, and plenty of time spent at the Lennox and Addington County Archives delving into old family records. What he came up with particular to this area was a great deal of information regarding the background of his great grandmother, Alice Amey, who was born in Napanee to the descendants of Loyalist settlers. A detailed chapter to her and her ancestors is included in the near 450-page book. "Napanee has been an important place in my life," he said.

Humber admits that much of the book — of which only 100 copies were printed — is mainly of interest to his own family, and the product of his own passion for family research and studying history. He advises, however, that it might serve as a good template for individuals who are considering delving into their own family background and recording what they find out. "It will inspire them to want to imitate it with their own family," he said.

A copy of *Family Sleuthing* can be found at the Lennox and Addington County library to be taken out on loan.

Humber says copies have also been donated to other areas of Ontario to which the book relates.

Above left: Produced as a 50-page magazine, the **Heritage Gazette** has been published quarterly since 1997. It reviewed **Family Sleuthing** on pages 39-40 in its August 2007 issue. **Above centre: The Gazette** has been the leading newspaper in Prince Edward County since 1830. It reviewed **Family Sleuthing** on its first page, February 9, 2007. **Right : The Napanee Beaver** is the oldest independently owned newspaper in Canada. The paper reviewed **Family Sleuthing,** February 14, 2007, page 6.

Writers I Have Known

As Co-Editor of **LOYAL SHE REMAINS** (1984) as well as both Publisher and Editor-in-Chief of the seven-volume Canada Heirloom Series, it was most gratifying to interact with many of Canada's most respected writers, scholars, correspondents, journalists, historians, and chroniclers over a twenty-two year period (1984-2006). Most had been cited in the University of Toronto's annual **Canadian Who's Who**. In total, more than 100 Canadian historians were recruited to write at least one chapter in one of Heirloom's seven books. One prominent individual I was unable to recruit was the **Rt. Hon. Pierre Elliot Trudeau.** He was approached to write a chapter for **CANADA From Sea Unto Sea.** This was in 1985 shortly after he completed his second term as Canadian Prime Minister. In an apologetic letter, the former Prime Minister graciously declined my invitation to write a chapter giving attention to "The Silent Revolution" that had socially overwhelmed post-World War II Quebec. Although tempted to partner with us, his decline was simple: there was just not enough spare time to "participate in such a worthwhile project."

Among the literary esquires Heirloom commissioned, six of these licentiates have been profiled in individual chapters elsewhere in this volume. They are Professor J.M.S. Careless, Diplomat John W. Holmes, Major General Richard Rohmer, Lt. Col. Strome Galloway, Aeronautical Engineer Jim Floyd, and Cardiologist Dr. Wilfred Bigelow. Many other personalities have certainly provided me with enduring, long-lasting memories. One of these includes the late **Harry Boyle** who had been Chairman, 1975-77, the Canadian Radio-Television and Telecommunications Commission (CRTC). Harry was a jovial man. He happily accepted Heirloom's invitation to write about the history of Canadian broadcasting in **CANADA from sea unto sea.** He enjoyed conversation and broke bread with me several times, telling me background stories about the Canadian communications industry. Learning how he hired Canada's top-rated news anchor, CTV's Lloyd Robertson, "pretty boy", as Harry called him, was most interesting.

Peter C. Newman was still another salient figure who penned for Heirloom Publishing. Perhaps best known for publications excavating the lives of Prime Ministers John Diefenbaker, Lester Pearson and Brian Mulroney, this former editor of **The Toronto Star** and **Maclean's Magazine** was well-known for his three-volume study saluting the Hudson Bay Company, making him a perfect candidate to write a chapter about this oldest, continuously operating company in North America. When I visited him in his Toronto office, I proposed that he write about the Hudson Bay Company in the forthcoming **CANADA From Sea Unto Sea**. He graciously accepted my invitation, but seemed more inclined to ask about the success of **LOYAL SHE REMAINS**, a volume I co-edited and published by the United Empire Loyalists' Association and that had just sold some 50,000 copies, ten-times a best-seller in Canada. He was impressed!

Most everyone has heard of the famous airplane, the **Beaver,** but hardly anyone knows the name **Richard Hiscocks,** the man mainly responsible for designing the world's most famous bush plane, a workhorse if ever there was one. When I first contacted Dick, he was, at age eighty-two years, living in a condo on the shores of English Bay. Believing he was not long for this world, he happily agreed to write a vignette about the famous DHC 2 **Beaver**, one of the most beloved planes ever to fly over Canada, but only if I accepted the fact he might not live long enough to tell his story. Ironically, I spoke to him in September, 1996. Three months later he passed away, but not before he mailed his wonderful story to me. Dick told me that the condominium where he lived overlooked English Bay in Vancouver and that a beautiful sight was taking place before his eyes while talking to me by phone, namely, that one of "his" **Beaver** planes was flying right by his window. He told me that it was a good omen, meaning that he would indeed live long enough to finalize his story. He kept his promise. The **Beaver**, according to the Canadian Engineering Centennial Board, was voted one of the 20th century's top ten Canadian engineering achievements. Dick's story appears in **Visionaries** (1998), Volume VI of the seven-volume CANADA Heirloom Series.

The Hon. Robert Nixon, who was the Liberal Party's Deputy Premier of Ontario and later, Chairman of Atomic Energy of Canada, accepted my invitation to write a chapter about the rich legacy of Ontario's first nation peoples in **LOYAL SHE REMAINS**, a 1984 bicentennial publication. We became friends after we appeared together on one of CFRB's top radio shows in 1983. When his Liberal Government was defeated in the 1990 provincial election, he called me the next day from his cellphone while travelling along the Queen Elizabeth Way west of Toronto, apologizing that his government order for 1150 copies of **ALLEGIANCE: The Ontario Story** had to be cancelled because he knew that the incoming NDP government would not honor his commitment. That was a devastating phone call as it cancelled some $50,000 in Heirloom Publishing's receivables.

I enjoyed occasional lunches in Simpson's Arcadian Court at Bay and Queen Streets, downtown Toronto, when I was the guest of **Arnold Edinborough**, a Cambridge University graduate. In Canada he was touted as "Man of the Arts". Editor of **Saturday Night** as well as contributing editor of the **Financial Post,** Arnie was dedicated to promoting Canada's artistic world. Over lunch, he agreed to write a chapter in **CANADA From Sea Unto Sea** that would salute and patronize Canadian art. He exposed me to such French-Canadian artists as Jean-Paul Riopelle, Fernand Leduc and Paul-Emile Bourduas. He also introduced me to Canada's leading art dealer, G. Blair Lang. He over-whelmed me with his knowledge of Canada's artistic world, from ballet and symphony, to opera and theatre. He must have been inspirational when he taught at Queen's University or University of British Columbia and the University of Lausanne or the Royal Military College. When Arnold passed on, 2006, Canada lost a dear friend.

Reginald Stackhouse, Ph.D. (Yale University) was Principal of Wycliffe College, University of Toronto, when I got to know him. As a newly elected member of the Conservative Government, he spoke to the Governor Simcoe Branch of the United Empire Loyalists' Association when I was its Branch President. This enabled me to get to know Reg. He also agreed to write a chapter in **CANADA From Sea Unto Sea** that examined Canada's religious foundations and how diversity has made Canada a country that embraces the rights of all religions to practice their respective faiths without fear of prejudice. Reg Stackhouse introduced me to Prime Minister Brian Mulroney in Ottawa, 1985, resulting in the Prime Minister consenting to write the Foreword to **CANADA from sea unto sea.**

Over the years, it has been a distinct privilege to work with a number of intelligentsia, historians like **Michael Bliss**, Professor of History at the University of Toronto for nearly forty years; Professor **Desmond Morton,** former Principal, University of Toronto, Mississauga Campus, and currently (2015) Professor Emeritus, McGill University, Montreal; as well as **Sydney Wise**, Ph. D, former Dean of Graduate Studies, Carleton University, Ottawa. Each of these erudites wrote key chapters for Heirloom Publishing in numerous volumes. They gave Heirloom's books much credibility while encouraging Heirloom to continue publishing its books celebrating Canada's rich heritage, culture and history. Collectively, these distinguished Canadians have provided me with great and fond memories.

The daughter of a very famous Canadian wrote a chapter for Heirloom Publishing celebrating Canada's aboriginal peoples. **Elizabeth McLuhan**'s vignette was published in **CANADA's Native Peoples,** Volume II of the CANADA Heirloom Series. It was special getting to know Elizabeth somewhat because of her father, the world famous Marshall McLuhan, the man who coined such phrases as "the global village" and the "medium is the message" and predicted the Internet thirty years before it was born. But she also implied that it was her father, not Andy Warhol, as so many people have claimed, who ideated the phrase "fifteen minutes of fame."

Donald Blake Webster, born, 1933, was, for nearly thirty years, Curator, Canadiana Department, The Royal Ontario Museum. Many people resented that an American had come to Canada and was responsible for one of the finest collections of Canadiana anywhere. Myself a collector of Canadiana, it was easy for me to befriend Don. In fact we exchanged cottage visits, shared family dinners, and visited with each other to discuss possible purchases he was making for the ROM. Don also illustrated key furnishings that Gay and I had collected in several of his books. When the Royal Ontario Museum staged its Bicentennial Exhibition, 1984, Don induced both Gay and me to loan several pieces from our collection for the fabulous bicentennial exhibition he prepared. Of the list of fifty-four consignors, mainly museums from Great Britain, the United States and Canada, only seven were consigned by individuals, including Her Majesty The Queen. One of the items we loaned was Nicholas Amey's land grant issued by King George III in 1804, twenty years after this U.E. Loyalist ancestor settled on 100 acres just outside Kingston. My son Scott Nicholas Humber is named after this ancestor.

I first met **Marjorie Wilkins Campbell**, thanks to my good friend Hugh MacMillan. This was back in 1985. He urged me to connect with her, an award-winning historian who wrote extensively about the fur trade, especially the Northwest Company. Hugh said she would be perfect to tell the story of this great company in any future book I might publish. Raised in Saskatchewan where so many of the Northwest Company fur traders paddled, I met her when Heirloom decided to profile the Northwest Co. in our upcoming book, **CANADA from sea unto sea**. I simply telephoned her and introduced myself. Since she already had a copy of **LOYAL SHE REMAINS,** she understood the importance of the forthcoming book we were envisioning to publish. She invited me to visit her in her central Toronto apartment. She was very frail but she told me she was most happy and willing to accept my invitation to write a chapter in the forthcoming publication. When I went to pick up her story, she was physically very brittle. She told me that Peter Newman, who was finishing his three-volume tome about the Hudson Bay Company, had been visiting her. Because of the rivalry between the two fur-trading companies, she said that she did not give him everything he wanted, saving some of her knowledge for me. I was thrilled that she was able to complete her assignment. She never saw her story published as she passed away, 1986, prior to the book's publication. Her story was her last salute to paddling, pioneer fur traders who greatly were instrumental in opening the Canadian West.

Wally R. Kent, M.D.

When Gay and I moved from Lansdale, Pennsylvania, to Cooksville, Ontario, June, 1962, we knew where we were teaching the next school year. Gay would teach kindergarten at Cooksville Public School while my first year of teaching secondary school English would be just across the street from her school at T.L. Kennedy Secondary School. We lived at 2340 Park Towers Ave., a new apartment complex that was touted as the most modern of all living quarters in South Peel. Gay's parents were living in California at the time while my parents were living in Pennsylvania. We did not have much in the way of family connections living nearby although I did have two aunts and one uncle, plus my grandmother Mabel Jarvis, living in Meadowvale. As well my aunt Edie and uncle Bill Donaldson were living in Hamilton. In no time, my aunt Edie was introducing Gay and me to Wally and Hope Kent. They lived in Cooksville just down the street from us on Floradale Drive. Wally was a surgeon at the South Peel Memorial Hospital where all four of our children would later be born. Hope was one of my aunt Edie's closest friends. The two had grown up together in Goderich, Ontario. It was inevitable that aunt Edie would arrange for Gay and me to meet Wally and Hope. When we did connect, we struck up a lasting friendship.

Hope and Wally, a veteran who served in the Navy in World War II, had three children: Kevin, Wally and Faith. Gay even tutored Wally. After we moved from Cooksville and settled in the Lawrence Park area of North Toronto, we stayed in contact with the Kent family. Years slipped by, and by the late 1970s, the Board of Directors of the John Graves Simcoe Foundation came up with the idea that Upper Canada's first Governor should throw out the first pitch at a Toronto Blue Jays Baseball game on Simcoe Day, a Toronto holiday celebrated the first Monday of each August. As a Board member, I approached Paul Beeston, President of the Toronto Blue Jays, about this possibility. He thought it was a great idea, especially the one that would have John Graves Simcoe, a.k.a. Charlie Humber, drawn into the stadium aboard an 1893 Brewster-made coach 'n four, formerly owned by Sir Henry Pellatt, builder of Toronto's famous **Casa Loma**. Dr. Wally Kent owned the wonderful coach for years and used it annually at the Royal Agricultural Winter Fair at the Canadian National Exhibition grounds. When the time came, August 3, 1980, Gov. Simcoe, in regal splendor and sitting inside the coach, with His Honour's *aide-de-camp* Terry Poulos at his side, was ushered into the grounds of Exhibition Stadium with Dr. Wally Kent, wearing top hat and all, sitting at the reins of four hackneys. After Simcoe took to the mound and made his "pitch for history" to catcher Ernie Whitt, Wally took the wonderful Brewster coach off the playing grounds and the game commenced, with the Toronto Blue Jays beating the California Angels, 3-1. Afterwards Wally and I chuckled for years over the escapade, wondering how the horses avoided leaving any horse droppings on the playing fields. Wally just said that his horses had "dignity and good manners."

Several years later, I made a telephone call to Wally that was indeed disturbing. I told him that my family doctor had detected a large tumor in my descending colon. As head of surgery at the Mississauga General Hospital, he told me to send the x-rays to him with urgency. Within ten days, I was admitted to the hospital, operated on successfully, and home again. He told me that my tumor was walnut-sized and that I was very lucky to get it removed so quickly. The biopsy indicated the tumor had been caught in time and that I was going to be alright. This occurred in 1986, going on twenty-nine years ago as I write this vignette. Every once in a while I would drop in to see Wally at the house he moved to in the 1990s, near Milton, Ontario. He would say something like, "I was just thinking about you, Charlie, and how lucky you are." I responded, "Wally, I thank the Lord each day how lucky I was to have known you."

Born, 1922, southwestern Ontario, Wally Kent was a gifted surgeon and an excellent horseman. His famous carriage was sold at an Ohio auction prior to his death, January 14, 2006, the same year he was elected into the Hackney Hall of Fame. Wally, a wonderful human being, left me, his family and countless others with many happy memories.

Left: August 3, 1980, in a game at Exhibition Stadium, Toronto, Ontario, Charles J. Humber, a.k.a. John Graves Simcoe, arrives with *aide-de-camp,* former student, Terry Poulos, to throw out the first pitch at a Toronto Blue Jays baseball game. Driving the coach is Dr. Wally Kent.

Bottom: Dr. Wally Kent's 1893 Brewster-made coach 'n four prepares to leave pre-baseball game ceremonies.

KENT HACKNEY STABLES

Wallace R. Kent, M.D.
1570 Britannia Rd. W. R #1.
Milton, Ontario L9T 2X5
Tel: (905) 878-8252

Hackney Horses
Antique Carriages for Weddings,
Show and Pleasure Horses for Sale
Also Breeding Stock.

Dad's Best Memories and Recollections

R. G. LeTourneau

R. G. LeTourneau (1888-1969) is the most dynamic individual I have ever heard in person, including Evangelist Billy Graham. Known as "Dean of Earthmoving," this mover of man and mountains was an entrepreneur whose 300 patents led to the development of unbelievable earth moving equipment, the kind you see today levelling hills, developing mines with their huge bucket shovels and scraping the earth for subdivisions. His garguantuan offshore drilling platforms have been used for drilling oil worldwide for decades. His inventions of the electric wheel, tree crusher, log picker, bull dozer, airplane tow and air crane are legendary. During World War II, seventy percent of all earth moving equipment used by the allies was supplied by R.G. LeTourneau. Much of the machinery carrying soldiers to Normandy was supplied by God's businessman. So when my father, Rev. C.M. Humber, personally reached out to R.G. LeTourneau and got his commitment to preach at Bethany Baptist Church, in Roxbury, Massachusetts, October 1, 1950, it was a special coup as the Evangelistic Association of New England for years had tried to get him to come to Bean Town. Bethany Baptist Church was filled to capacity for the morning service. Ninety-year old Alice Morse even came to hear the famous businessman who had given his life to Christ.

Dubbed "God's businessman," R.G. LeTourneau (1888-1969) was considered the world's greatest inventor of earth-moving equipment. After he spoke at Bethany Baptist Church, (see inset) October 1, 1950, he then spoke the same evening at Tremont Temple Baptist Church, the largest Baptist Church in New England.

The part of the sermon I remember the most occurred when he told a story about his appearance on the nationally syndicated **Ripley's Believe It Or Not** radio show sometime in the early 1940s. He moved back and forth across the pulpit platform as if he was an earth-moving tractor chugging smoke! **Ripley's Believe It Or Not** had been a popular comic strip since about 1920. It evolved into a radio show by 1930. The moderator of the radio show, an over-voice of sorts, began questioning R. G. LeTourneau, wondering what the rewards were for being a faithful follower of the Lord. The millionaire business man responded with a story about what it was like to be in business in Stockton, California, several months after the 1929 crash that was followed by the Great Depression. He emphasized times were tough. He had $500 dollars left to his name and was going to give all of it away to some evangelical cause. This declaration dismayed his partner who exclaimed to R. G. LeTourneau that God, not he, was his partner. R.G. LeTourneau responded "Yes, God is my partner in my business," emphasizing that he gave ninety percent of his yearly profit to his Lord's work and kept only ten percent for himself. The host of the radio show then said matter-of-factly, "And of such is the work of faith -- Believe It Or Not!" I was fifteen at the time and, in my youth, recognized that God surely was this man's best friend....

R. G. LeTourneau, who established the LeTourneau Technical Institute in 1946, and which now enrolls some 3000 students, passed away, 1969, and is buried beside his wife on the campus that both founded four years before he preached at Bethany Baptist Church, October 1, 1950.

Dad's Best Memories and Recollections

Open-Heart Surgery at Ninety-Five Years

Her four children, Anna Rolen (Alexandria, Virginia), Priscilla Hurlbut (Sweetwater, Texas), Paul Humber (Philadelphia, Pennsylvania) and Charles J. Humber (Mississauga, Ontario), were all living, relatively speaking, far away from each other in 2002. Yet we assembled in Philadelphia to be with our mother, Evelyn Audrey (Jarvis) Humber who, in her ninety-fifth year, on February 13, 2002, the day before Valentine's Day, was scheduled for open-heart surgery at the University of Pennsylvania Hospital. Officials had indicated that no one in Pennsylvania had undergone such an operation at her age and survived. So when four siblings, two sisters and two brothers, gathered at brother Paul's home, 327 Green Lane, Philadelphia, before the operation, there was some tension and apprehension, for sure, but we all were trusting that "Mom" would pull through her risky operation. And Mother assured each of her four children that she was in God's hands and that we must accept His will....

Dr. Joseph Bavaria was the operating doctor. Some thirteen years after mother's aortic valve replacement, Dr. Bavaria, today, 2015, is the Vice Chief, Division of Cardiovascular Surgery, at the Hospital of the University of Pennsylvania where he is also the Director of Aortic Thoracic Surgery. There is no question that our mother was not only in the hands of her Maker but in the hands of a very gifted medical doctor. Naturally, we who came together for the big day were apprehensive. Prior to the operation, we laughed together and told stories and reminisced and thoroughly enjoyed the wonderful hospitality that Paul and Prudence provided, especially the scrumptious dinner at their lovely dining room table. Paul's grace at our "last supper" together was wonderful as he thanked the Lord for loaning mother to us for such an extended time (the four of us were all in our sixties!).

When the day of operation came, we, including Jim Rolen, had slept overnight at Penn Towers, the twenty-three storey hotel connected by an elevated walkway to the hospital. We all went down to see mother before she was wheeled by a gurney to the operating room. She was in good spirits emphasizing that she was in God's hands. Her inspiration sustained us spiritually as we waited for the results.

After several very long hours, the lengthy operation was over. Dr. Bavaria emerged and indicated to Paul that everything went well. As far as we all were concerned, the doctor was a magician in the hands of the Lord. After nearly seventy-five days of recovery, about half of which were at the Lankanau Medical Center, mother was home with Paul and Prudence and resting comfortably. She was a major inspiration throughout the ordeal....What a wonderful memory. Her operation gave us nearly four more years of a dear mother before she passed away at ninety-nine years, November 11, Memorial Day, 2005.

Top: Four siblings Paul, Priscilla, Anna and Charlie, pay tribute to their mother, centre, before her open-heart surgery, February 13, 2002.

Middle: Charles J. Humber wishes his mother well before her operation.

Bottom: Two sisters, Priscilla, left, and Anna, right, visit with their mother shortly after her surgery.

Premier E. C. Drury

As Gay and I travel each year to our Muskoka cottage in MacTier, we take Highway 400 to Barrie and sometimes travel past Barrie one exit and take Highway 93 going north so that we can drive through some of the smaller towns like Crown Hill, Dalston and Craighurst. While driving through Crown Hill, and passing the two-and-one-half story farmhouse on the right side of the road, I always draw attention to the bronze Ontario Heritage Plaque. The sign recognizes that it was on this property the Hon. Ernest C. Drury lived, former leader of the United Farmers of Ontario and Ontario's eighth premier. Every time I pass this house I recall the summers of 1958-1960 when I was canvassing this area for the **Toronto Telegram**.

E.C. Drury 1878-1968,
Premier of Ontario 1919-1923.

During one of those summers, I was knocking on doors on the outskirts of Barrie, including the town of Crown Hill. Today, many of the houses in this region have fallen to road development and general progress. But the old Drury house still stands. I believe I was twenty-two when I walked north on Highway 93 and approached the Drury homestead. Of course, at the time, I did not know anything about the Drury family. As I strolled up the laneway to the farmhouse, it was one of those warm sunny days that Ontario experienced in the late 1950s. A big rocking chair sat on the front lawn just off the driveway as if the elderly man sitting in it was waiting for me. The man was E. C. Drury, former Ontario Premier, 1919-1923. He was eighty-one years old at the time. He warmly welcomed me and inquired if I was "local" from Simcoe County. We struck up a friendly conversation that lasted fifteen minutes. He gave me lessons about who he was and how the farmers of Ontario are still the hardest working people. I convinced him to subscribe to the **Toronto Telegram,** primarily because it would be delivered by a local boy whose family Mr. Drury knew. The odd thing was that the former Premier was a devout Liberal yet the **Tely** was very much a Tory paper. He smiled and said to me not to tell anyone after he accepted my offer to a ten-week subscription. We shook hands and it was off to the next sale. Seven years later, at 88 years, he published his autobiography called **Farmer Premier**. In the book is a paragraph that I found very fascinating. The passage refers to my mother's parents, Gilbert and Mabel Jarvis, who lived outside of Picton, Ontario, in 1908, when E. C. Drury was passing through on a very stormy winter's night:

> **After a while we came to a better road with good farmsteads on either side. In one of the houses there was a light in a downstairs window…. The man who answered the knock was fully dressed. His name was Jarvis and he had been to Picton at a Masonic meeting. When he knew who we were, he insisted that we should spend the night with them, for it was now half-past one and we were as far from Picton as when we started. We were happy to accept his hospitality for we were nearly frozen. I think I have never met kinder people than the Jarvises nor seen a more welcome sight than that glowing coal stove. Mrs. Jarvis made sandwiches and tea and we sat and talked until nearly three o'clock – indeed it took us nearly that long get thawed out. Two years later Jarvis was in our vicinity procuring apples and I was happy to return his hospitality. The Jarvises were fine people, typical of farm people across the province worth working for.**

This passage was an amazing discovery for me. The former Ontario Premier I had sold a newspaper subscription to back in the late 1950s had written his memoirs. A passage from the book reports how gracious my maternal grandparents were in 1908 when my mother was one year of age!

Left: Proud mom Gay with her four children, Christmas, 1973.
Above right: Gay wearing her Jonas Brother parka in Fairbanks, Alaska, 1960.
Below right: Voyageur John Graves Simcoe arrives at Big Chute, 1979.

Above: Four Humber siblings, Kristy, Karyn, Scott and Charlie, gather in Chatham, Massachusetts, for July 4th celebrations, 2012.
Right: 1984 bochure promoting best seller LOYAL SHE REMAINS.

INDEX of SURNAMES

Adams, Ducky, 144.
Adcock, Larry, 201.
Aggis, Joan, 209.
Alexander III, 94.
Alexander, Hon. Lincoln, 28.
Alexandrovna, Olga, 94.
Ali, Mohammad, 24.
Amey family, 62.
Amey, Alice A., 164.
Amey, Jonas, 164.
Amey, Nicholas, 136-37, 164.
Amin, Idi, 61.
Anderson, Nell, 195.
Annan, Kofi, 166.
Appel, Gini, 77.
Arthur, Eula, 21.
Armstrong, Neil, 96, 203.
Atkinson, Lucy, 64.
Astaire, Fred, 102.
Atkinson, William, 140.
Autrey, Gene, 146.

Bacon, Roger, 194.
Baker, Gil, 177
Baldwin, Prime Minister Stanley, 186
Ball, Florida, 88.
Ball, Frank, 88.
Ball, Gordon, 67, 88, 156.
Ball, Keith, 88.
Baltimore, Lord, 204.
Barbin, Dana, 184.
Barboza, Joe, 10.
Barker, VC, Billy, 114
Barkley, Murray, 75.
Barnes, Micah, 177.
Barrett, Bob, 121.
Barrett, Ida, 120.
Barrett, Jason, 112, 121.
Barrett, Kaye, 121, 133.
Barrett, Mia, 121.
Barrett, Ray, 57, 120.
Barrett, Stan, 56-57, 112, 120-21, 132-33, 178, 162.
Barron, Ronnie, 135, 185.
Barry, Billy, 36, 130, 135, 159, 160.
Barrymore, John, 101.
Bartlett, Bob, 205.
Battison, Dave, viii.
Bauer, Group Captain A.J., 103, 114-15.
Bavaria, Dr. Joseph, 177
Beeston, Paul, 26.
Bell, Brig. Gen. George G., 106.
Benedict XIII, 135.
Bennett Bros., 134.
Bennett, Tony, 36.
Berczy, William, 66.
Bergman, Ingrid, 101.
Berlin, Irving, 197, 207.
Bethune, Norman, 129.

Biddle, Cornelius, 54-55, 186, 179, 210.
Biddle, David, 55.
Bigelow, Dr. Wilfred, 124-25, 170, 214.
Bigham, Clark, 79.
Billy the Kidd, 211.
Birch, Dee, 20, 41.
Birch, Hon. Margaret, 56, 60, 169, 209.
Birch, Tom, 20, 22, 41.
Bishop, VC, Air Marshall William (Billy) Avery, 114, 115.
Bitter, Beni, 61.
Blalock, Dr. Alfred, 124.
Blanchard, "Doc," 198.
Blayney, Fritz, 201.
Bliss, Michael, 215.
Bloom, Harold, 44.
Bobyan, Vince, 133.
Bonds, Barry, 109.
Borosa, Walter, 59.
Bourduas, Paul-Émile, 215.
Boyd, Charles, 134.
Boyd, Earl, 134-35, 185, 187.
Boyd, Robert, 134.
Boyd, William, 187.
Boyle, Harry, 130, 214.
Boylen, Anne, 187.
Bradford, Robert, 114.
Brant, Chief Joseph, 136.
Breithaupt, Peter, 91.
Breton, Andre, 207.
Brink, Ed, 67.
Bronfman, Charles, 122.
Brown, Dan, 197.
Browning, Lee, 20.
Browning, Wendy, 20.
Buchanan, Premier John M. 49.
Buck, Pearl S., 197.
Buehrle, Mark, 108.
Bulger, James "Whitey," 24, 109, 134.
Burgoyne, General John, 136.
Burke, Elmer "Trigger," 134, 184.
Burleigh, Dr. H.C., 67, 164.
Burns, "Robbie," 101.
Burnside, Elward, 91, 130.
Burton, Richard, 128.
Burwell, Mahlon, 163.
Butler, John, 118, 136.

Cabot, John, 177.
Cadeau, Mitch, 53.
Cahill, Lou, 91, 131.
Callaghan, Katie, 199.
Callaghan, John, 124.
Campbell, Marjorie Wilkins, 215.
Campbell, Sir William, 152
Cantinflas, 21
Cantor, Eddie, 177.
Capone, Al, 29, 109.
Capone, Tullio, viii.

Cappelli, Angela Dea, 107, 125, 153, 209.
Carisse, Jean Marc, 129.
Careless, Prof. J.M.S., 99, 214.
Carnovale, Frank, viii.
Carpentier, George, 24.
Cassels, Aggie, 67, 210.
Cassels, Rod, 210.
Cartier, Jacques, 106, 207.
Chagall, Marc, 61.
Chamberlain, Prime Minister Neville, 186.
Chamberlin, Jim, 96.
Chambers, Prof. A.B., 44, 202.
Chamillard, Albert, 38, 144.
Chamillard, Al Jr., 144.
Chamillard, George, 144.
Champlain, Samuel de, 106, 206.
Chappell, Hillyard G., 153.
Charles I, 178.
Chaucer, Geoffrey, 128.
Cherner, Pam, 138-39.
Chrétien, Prime Minister Jean, 16, 129.
Churchill, Sir Winston, 186.
Clapton, Eric, 178.
Clark family, 62.
Clark, Alexander, 128.
Clark, Angela Dea (Cappelli), 107, 125, 153, 209.
Clark, Prof. Harry Hayden, 202.
Clark, James (Jamie), 153.
Clemens, Roger, 9.
Clinton, President Bill, 108.
Cocker, Joe, 178.
Coleridge, Samuel Taylor, 186, 196.
Colling, Don, 88.
Como, Perry, 36.
Congreve, William, 28.
Connery, Sean, 186.
Conners, Ibra, 67, 164.
Cook, Captain John, 183.
Cookenham, Major Walter, 137.
Cooper, Col. Frank, 165.
Cooper, Gary, 140.
Cooper, Russ, 209.
Cornwallis, Lord, 106.
Coppola, Francis Ford, 100.
Cosby, Bill, 100.
Corrigan, Joe, 148.
Cosens, Don, 163.
Crosby, Bing, 197, 198.
Cromwell, Oliver, 178.
Cromwell, Thomas, 187.
Curley, Mayor Michael, 14

Dark, Alvin, 9.
Davis, Premier William G., 10, 59, 60, 91.
Davis, Glenn, 198.
Dawe, Reg, 209.
de Champlain, Samuel, 106, 206.
Dempsey, Jack, 24.
Deschênes, Benoi, 206.
Dick, Lord Mayor Wilbert, 118.

Dickens, Charles, 186.
Diefenbaker, Prime Minister John G., 90, 96, 129, 214.
Diltz, Bert Case, 154.
Dilworth, Paul, 97.
DiMaggio, Joe, 198.
Dinneen, Joseph R., 141.
Di Palma, Josephine, 135.
Dobson, Barbara, 74, 172.
Dobson, Henry, 74, 172.
Dodds, Jimmie, 198.
Doer, Bobby, 198
Donahue, Wally, 24.
Donaldson, Agnes, 195.
Donaldson, Barb, 195.
Donaldson, Bill, 195
Donaldson, Uncle Bill, 18, 40-41, 42, 116, 188, 192, 202, 216.
Donaldson, Chuck, 18, 119.
Donaldson, Dave, 18, 58, 66, 89, 119, 188, 211.
Donaldson, Aunt Edie (Humber), 18, 40, 119, 188, 192, 202, 216.
Donaldson, Les, 152-53, 194-95.
Donaldson, Nell, 194-95.
Donaldson, Phillip, 18, 58, 119.
Donaldson, Sid, 188.
Donaldson, Ted, 18, 40, 188.
Donne, John, 186.
Dorsey, Tommy, 211.
Doyle, Sir Arthur Conan, 186.
Drew, Evelyn, 165.
Drury, Premier E. C., 220.
Duffie, Paul, 91.
Dulmage, Victor, 83.
Duncan, Dorothy, 91.
Dunn, Prof. Charles W., 128-29.
Duprey, Donalda, 12-13.
Dylan, Bob, 178.

E
Eaman, John, 17.
Eccles, Professor Mark, 44, 202.
Edinborough, Arnold, 214.
Edison, Nancy, 58.
Edison, Samuel, 58.
Edison, Thomas Alva, 58, 66, 161.
Edward VIII, 102.
Egan, Vincent, 91.
Einstein, Albert, 30.
Elizabeth I, 204.
Elizabeth, II, 10, 17, 28, 47, 49, 59, 66, 76, 209.
Elizabeth, The Queen Mother, 118.
Ellerby, Hannah, 162.
Elliot, Charles Adam, 56, 71, 206.
Elliot, Lucille (Jarvis, Longfield), 56, 157, 188-89.
Elliott, Frank, 58.
Elliott, Rev. Fred C., 188.
Elliott, Isaac, 58.
Elliott, William, 58.
Emerson, Al, 29, 153, 202-03.

Emerson, Chris, 202.
Emigh, Nicholas, 67.
Erickson, Arthur, 19.
Euscher Sergeant Marat, 141.
Evans, Gertrude (Reich), 21.
Evans, Ralph, 72.
Everett, Fred, 48.

F
Farr, Ellerby, 162, 210.
Farr, Lambert, 162.
Farr, J.T. "Toat," 162, 210.
Farr, James, 162.
Farr, Mary Ann, 69, 162.
Farr, Thomas, 162.
Farr, William, 69.
Firpo, Luis, 24.
Fisher, Dr. C. Miller, 125, 170.
Fisher, George, 131.
Fisher, "Mr. Canada" John W., 26, 49, 60, 78, 80, 90-91, 95, 101, 130, 168.
Fisher, John Jr., 91, 131.
Fitzgerald, Franny, 36, 135.
Fitzgerald, Joe, 135.
Flaherty, Jackie, 29, 135.
Flaherty, Mikey, 198.
Flaherty, Tommy, 135.
Flemmi, Steve, 134.
Flett, Bernice, 165.
Floyd, James C., 96-97, 214.
Flynn, Mayor Dennis, 209.
Ford, President Gerald, 129.
Ford, Henry, 158, 161, 211.
Forsey, Senator Eugene, 209, 63.
Fox, Myrna, 165.
Fox, Terry, 168.
Francis, Diane, 122.
Fry, Elizabeth, 55.
Frye, H. Northrop, 44, 99, 202.
Fryer, Geoffrey, 209.
Fryer, Mary Beacock, 209.

G
Galbraith, John Kenneth, 122-23.
Gallant, Billy, 134.
Gallie, Dr. William, 125.
Galloway, Col. Strome, 171, 214.
Gareau, France, 13.
Garlatti, Angela, 66.
Garlatti, Joe, 58, 66, 100.
Gatley, Herbert, 144.
George III, 118.
George, Peter, 122.
Getty, Bertha, 132.
Getty, Christopher, 133.
Getty, Fawn, 133.
Getty, Ian, 132.
Getty, Leah, 133.
Getty, Lily, 133.
Getty, Margaret, 132.

Getty, Michael, 133.
Getty, Myrna, 133, 203.
Getty, Norville, 132.
Getty, Nuning, 133.
Getty, Orville, 132.
Getty, Ronald, 132.
Getty, Roogn, 133.
Getty, Sabrina, 133.
Getty, Wayne, 11, 20, 21, 42, 56, 112, 120, 132-33, 203.
Getty, Wayne Jr., 133.
Gielgud, Sir John, 102.
Gilbert, Sir Humphrey, 204
Gill, Jackie, 198.
Gillis, Allan, 48, 135.
Gillis, Angus, 134.
Gillis, Donnie, 36, 48, 134-35, 185.
Gillis, Donnie Jr., 185.
Gillis, Loraine, 134.
Ginsberg, Allan, 100.
Giotta, Giovanni, 100.
Girouard, Gen. Sir Percy, 171.
Giuliani, Mayor Rudy, 9.
Godfrey, Arthur, 30, 182.
Godfrey, Paul, 26.
Goering, Field Marshall Hermann, 17, 61, 168.
Goldie, Naomi, 61, 169.
Goode, Donald (Do Do), 198.
Gore, Al, 167.
Gowdy, Curt, 9, 155.
Graham, Evangelist Billy, 176, 218.
Grant, Doug, 165.
Greenaway, Brig. Gen. Keith, 115.
Greene, Gen. Nathaneal, 184.
Grey, Lady Jane, 187.
Grimshaw, John, 91.
Grobb, Abraham, 172.
Grobb, John, 172

H
Hagan, Rita, 204.
Haleloke, 182.
Hamilton, Roy, 36.
Harle, Don, 98.
Harle, Eleanor, 98.
Harrison, George, 178.
Harrison, Rex, 186.
Harvard, John, 186.
Hastick, Andrea, 13.
Hatfield, Premier Richard, 49.
Hayward, Fred, 165.
Healey, Mike, 41.
Healey, Helen, 41.
Heatter, Gabriel, 71.
Henry II, 204.
Henry VIII, 187.
Hepburn, Premier Mitch, 163.
Herb, Judy, 160.
Herkimer, General Nicholas, 136.
Hill, Dan, 28.
Hiscocks, Richard, 214.

Hirshhorn, Joe, 82.
Hitchcock, Alfred, 120.
Hitler, Adolph, 131.
Hogarth, William, 186.
Holmes, John W., 142-43, 166, 214.
Holmes, Lottie, 119.
Holmes, Tommy, 9.
Hope, Bob, 198.
Hopps, Jack, 124.
Horton, Johnny, 200-201.
Howard, Curly, 197.
Howard, Dr. Michael, 178-79.
Hughes, Howard, 96.
Humber, Dr. Albert Milton, 89, 158, 211.
Humber, Alice (Amey), 192.
Humber, Allan, 68.
Humber, Anna (Lubliner, Rolen), viii, 31, 33, 40, 52, 53, 75, 98, 102, 146, 158, 159-61, 189, 196-97, 201, 203, 219.
Humber, Arthur, 126.
Humber, Austin Nicholas, 110, 111, 185.
Humber, Bruce, 69, 126-127, 210.
Humber, Caroline Emily, viii, 110, 111, 182, 185.
Humber, Charles Austin, 33, 68, 148, 164, 178-79, 192.
Humber, Charles Henry, 109, 110, 161, 182, 184, 197.
Humber, Charles Herbert, 42, 119, 192.
Humber, Rev. Charles M., 18, 32, 52, 53, 84, 98, 119, 127, 132, 140-41, 144, 146, 170, 175, 176, 188-89, 192-93, 196-97, 201, 203, 211, 218.
Humber, Charles W., viii, 9, 17, 18, 20-23, 40, 41, 49-51, 59, 78, 92-93, 100, 103, 108-111, 113, 116-17, 122, 128, 129, 136-37, 146, 152, 158, 161, 170, 177, 181, 182, 184-85, 186-87, 189, 191, 195, 211, 221.
Humber, David Hess, 21, 68, 126, 148, 178.
Humber, Diane, 127.
Humber, Edith, 178.
Humber, Elynor, 158-59.
Humber, Evelyn (Jarvis), 3, 18, 33, 34-35, 40, 52, 75, 92, 98, 102, 108, 119, 146, 188-89, 196-97, 203, 219.
Humber, Frank, 42.
Humber, Gay (Jenkins), viii, 15, 17, 18, 20-23, 28, 33, 36, 40, 52, 59, 66, 67, 77, 84, 85, 92, 108, 113, 116, 121, 146, 152, 156-57, 158-61, 173, 176, 178-79, 181, 182, 186-87, 191, 200-01, 202-03, 204, 206-07, 210-11, 216, 220, 221.
Humber, Gordon, 109-111, 161, 182, 184, 185
Humber, Harold, 178, 210.
Humber, Henry (Hank) Howarth, 69, 104, 148, 175.
Humber, Karyn, viii, 12-13, 17, 18, 20-23, 27, 41, 49-51, 59, 67, 84, 85, 86, 116-17 133, 146, 152, 181, 202-03, 211, 221.

Humber, Kristy (Shennette), viii, 17, 18, 20-23, 27, 38, 41, 48, 59, 67, 84, 85, 86, 108, 116-17, 129, 133, 146, 152, 176, 181, 184, 202-03, 211, 221.
Humber, Leah (Draper), 126, 178.
Humber, Linnie, 148.
Humber, Liz, 108, 182.
Humber, Lizzie (Biddle), 40, 54, 92, 110, 192.
Humber, Madelyn, 110, 111.
Humber, Maitland, 68, 89, 148, 175, 211.
Humber, Maria, 126.
Humber, Maurice, 126-27.
Humber, Molly, (Wroten), 67, 108, 111, 182.
Humber, Oliver, 42.
Humber, Orenzo, 68-69, 148, 210.
Humber, Paul David, 188.
Humber, Paul Gilbert, 31, 33, 41, 51, 53, 58, 71, 75, 92, 108, 146, 188-89, 199, 201, 203, 219.
Humber, Peter, 108, 119, 188.
Humber, Priscilla (Hurlbut), viii, 21-22, 31, 33, 40, 52, 58, 67, 77, 92, 98, 119, 146, 188-89, 196-97, 201, 219.
Humber, Prudence (String), 40, 92, 108, 188, 203, 219.
Humber, Rick, 21, 69, 126-27.
Humber, Ruth, 188.
Humber, Scott Nicholas, viii, 9, 17, 18, 20-23, 40, 41, 49-51, 59, 67, 78, 85, 92-93, 103, 190, 191, 195, 108-11, 113, 116-17, 122, 128, 129, 133, 136-37, 146, 152, 155, 170, 177, 181, 182, 185, 189, 211, 215, 221.
Hurlbut, Beth, 119.
Hurlbut, Chuck, viii, 20-23, 40, 92, 119, 188, 201.
Hurlbut, Jenny, 119, 188.
Hurley, William F, 141.
Hurst, Robert, 130.
Hutchinson, Carl, 152, 172.
Hutchinson, Nancy, 152.

Ignani, Paul, 41, 134.
Irving, James Dargavel, 95.
Irving, James K., 95.
Irving, Kenneth Colin, "KC," 95.

Jackman, Harry, 177.
Jaroensok, Roong, 133.
Jarvis, Gilbert, 162, 188, 220.
Jarvis, Gordon, 56, 188, 211.
Jarvis, John, 77.
Jarvis, Lefa (Prosser), 188.
Jarvis, Mabel (Scott), 56-57, 69, 98, 124, 188, 211, 215, 220.
Jarvis, Marie, 77, 98, 188.
Jarvis, Maude (Wolf), 98.
Jenkins, Alice, 41, 182.
Jenkins, Beatrice "BJ," 20, 21-22, 116-17, 181.
Jenkins, Gayle (Humber), 43, 121, 200.

Jenkins, John, 21, 22, 41, 182.
Jenkins, Ray, 21.
Jeter, Derek, 9.
John, Elton, 178.
Johnson, President Lyndon Baines, 122.
Johnson, Peter, 165.
Johnston, Ada, 67, 164.
Jolson, Al, 20, 102, 197.
Jones, Bobby Jr., 185.
Jorgenson, Christine, 36.
Joubin, Franc, 51, 82-83.
Jouppien, John, 76.
Joyce, Jackie, 198.

Kamehameha I, 183.
Katz, Calvin, 139.
Katz Jason, 139
Katz, Pam, 139.
Keane, Keturah, 210.
Keats, John, 44, 196.
Kemp, William, 186.
Kent, Faith, 216.
Kent, Hope, 216.
Kent, Kevin, 216.
Kent, Dr. Wally, 26, 216-17.
Kent, Wally Jr., 216.
Kennedy, President John F., 36, 92, 122.
Kennedy, Joseph Patrick, 36, 39.
Kennedy, Rose, 36, 39.
Kennedy, Ted, 36.
Keon, Dr. Wilbert Joseph, 125.
Kerouac, Jack, 42, 100.
Key, Jimmy, 26.
King, Rev. Martin Luther Jr., 211.
Kirshenblatt, Rabbi Jacob, 61, 102, 168.
Kitchen, Paul, 91.
Kitchener, Lord Horatio, 171.
Koffler, Murray, 122.
Koene, William, 208.
Kollek, Mayor Teddy, 60.
Komarow, Galina, 94.
Klugoff, Zinaida, 94.
Knowles, Jeremy R., 28

Labbe, Paul, 135, 184.
Laine, Frankie, 29.
Laing, G. Blair, 150-51, 215.
Laskin, Chief Justice, Bora, 20.
Laskin, Mayor Saul, 20.
Law, Prime Minister Bonar, 207.
Leacock, Stephen, 120.
Leduc, Fernand, 215.
Leggett, Dr. Gordon, 17.
Lennon, John, 176.
LeTourneau, R. G., 218.
Lewis, Hon Doug G., 180.
Lindecker, Ethelda (Jarvis), 92.
Lindecker, Joe, 71, 92.

Lombardo, Guy, 163.
Longfield, Lucille (Jarvis, Elliot), 157, 188-89.
Longfield, Stewart, 157, 188.
Longfellow, Henry Wadsworth, 179.
Louis, Joe, 24, 92.
Lubliner, William, 202.
Luckman, Sid, 198.
Lujack, Johnny, 198.
Lunau, John, 66.

Macaulay, Thomas, 132.
MacDonald, Cliff, 84-85.
MacDonald, Wilson Pugsley, 30.
MacKenzie, Gordon, 144.
MacLaughlin, Col. Sam, 67.
MacMillan, George, 47.
MacMillan, Hugh, 90, 101, 128, 181, 215.
MacMillan, Viola, 47, 82.
MacNeil, Christina, 134.
Mahaney, Sidney, 50.
Mahoney, Jimmy (Pucker), 198.
Malone, "Red," 135.
Marcellus, Doris, 17.
Marciano, "Rocky," 124, 135.
Marconi, Guglielmo, 205.
Marlowe, Christopher, 186.
Martemianoff, Constantine, 94.
Mather, Cotton, 30.
Mather, Richard, 30
Matheson, Judge John Ross, 16, 63, 80.
Mayes, Lesa, 13.
Mayzel, Lou, 60-61, 168-69.
Mazzaglia, Peter, 201.
McBride, Robert, 165.
McCallion, Hazel, 207.
McCaugherty, Kaye, 121.
McConachie, Grant, 83.
McConkey, "Skip," 182-83.
McDonald, Nona, 91.
McDonnell, Paul, 134.
McIlaney, Jackie, 198.
McIvor, Bob, 21.
McKinley, President William, 119.
McKinney, Emerson, 79.
McKinney, Ross, 79.
McKitterick, Pat, 79.
McLean, Alastair, 157.
McLuhan, Elizabeth, 215.
McLuhan, Marshall, 44, 99, 215.
McNeil, Bill, 90, 130-31.
McPhee, Howie, 127.
Mencken, H. L., 15.
Mendham, Jeff, 160.
Mendham, Warren, 89, 160.
Melbourne, Phyllis, 107.
Melbourne, William, 107.
Metcalfe, Ralph, 127.
Michener, Edward, 69, 194-15.

Michener, Jacob, 105.
Michener, Joseph, 105.
Michener, Norah, 104
Michener, The Rt. Hon. D. Roland, 26, 69, 104-05, 208-09.
Middleton, General Frederick, 18.
Millard, Carl, 14.
Millard, Dellen, 14.
Millard, Wayne, 14.
Miller, Glenn, 92.
Miller, Bill, 190.
Millson, Jane, 67.
Milton, John, 186.
Minichiello, Ralph, 36, 135.
Mirvish, David, 102.
Mirvish, "Honest Ed," 102.
Mitchell, Betty, 109-10.
Mitchell, Dick (Bunga), 201.
Mitterand, President Francois, 106.
Mix, Tom, 211.
Mize, Johnny, 9.
Molson, John, 99.
Molson, Senator Hartland, 103, 114, 115.
Montgomery, Cal, 21.
Montgomery, Lucy Maud, 207.
Montgomery, Val, 21.
Monroe, Vaughan, 71.
Moore, Henry, 150.
More, Sir Thomas, 87.
Morenz, Howie, 68, 211.
Morrice, James W., 150.
Morris, William, 196.
Morrison, Helen (Scott), 35.
Morrison, Robert, 65.
Morton, Prof. Desmond, 215.
Morse, Alice, 38, 218.
Moulin, Kerry, 109.
Myers, Roger, 38.
Mulroney, Prime Minister Brian, 16, 80, 214-15.
Munch, Delight, 192.
Murphy, Audie, 92.
Murphy, Elmo, 30, 71, 73.
Murphy, Sylvia, 30.

Nash, Frederick, 168.
Nelson, Admiral Lord Nelson, 54, 179, 186.
Netanyahu, Prime Minister Benjamin, 61.
Netanyahu, Commander Yonatan, 61.
Nethercott, Arnold, 165.
Newman, Peter C., 214.
Nicholas II, 94.
Nixon, Hon, Robert, 17, 209, 214.
Noble, William, 203, 176.
Nutting, Wallace, 74.

Obama, President Barack, 202.
O'Brien, Paddy, 135.
O'Keefe, "Specs," 134, 184.

Olivier, Sir Laurence, 31.
O'Neil, Jackie, 198.
O'Neil, William (Wee Wee), 39, 198.
Orgoglio, 110, 161.
Orr, Lee, 127.
Ortiz, David, 108.
Ostrander, Geraldine, 64-65.
Owens, Jesse, 69, 127.

Pain, Howard, 53, 74-75, 88, 172.
Palardy, Jean, 74.
Parks, Frankie, 198.
Pattison, Mrs., 36.
Pattison, Harry, 36.
Patton, General George, 19, 92.
Paul, Bramson, 25.
Pavarotti, Luciano, 100.
Paxton, Tom, 178.
Peacock, "Pinky," 135.
Pearson, Prime Minister Lester B., 99, 214.
Peary, Robert Edwin, 205.
Pecar, Steve, viii.
Pellatt, Sir Henry, 26, 216.
Penfield, Dr. Wilder, 170.
Penn, William, 105.
Pepper, Barry, 153.
Perini, Lou, 9.
Pesky, Johnny, 198.
Peters, "Mr. Speaker" Steve, 163.
Pettitte, Andy, 108.
Piazza, Mike, 108.
Pickford, Mary, 102.
Pinkney, Bill, 88.
Pope John Paul II, 10, 76, 209.
Potter, James (Jim) C., 44, 112-13, 120.
Poulos, Terry, 26, 216-17.
Presley, Elvis, 132.
Prince Andrew, 28.
Prince Charles, 22.
Prince Philip, 28.
Proctor, Martin, 162.
Prosser, Doris, 56.
Prosser, Lefa (Jarvis), 42, 56-57, 64-65, 71, 84, 98, 120, 188.
Prosser, Lester (Levi), 14, 56-57, 64, 71, 82-83, 120.
Provato, Joe, viii.
Punches, Dr. Gilbert, 158-59.
Punches, Grayce (Jarvis), 153.
Putin, President Vladimir, 54.

Quintana, Prof. Ricardo, 44, 202.
Quinton, Jeanette (Mendham), 160.

Rae, Premier Bob, 28.
Ralph, Ed, 163.
Reagan, President Ronald, 106.
Reeves, Charlie, 210.

Reeves, Phineas, 210.
Reichmann, Albert, 60, 186.
Reid, Brian, 88, 156, 190-91.
Reid, Jim, 116.
Reynolds, Col. Jim, 137.
Richards, Keith, 178.
Riel, Louie, 18.
Riopelle, Jean-Paul, 215.
Riva, Calvin, 40-41, 159, 160.
Riva, Carl, 18, 40.
Riva, Wayne, 40.
Rivera, Mariano, 9.
Roberts, Lewis, 205.
Robertson, Lloyd, 214.
Robinette, John Josiah, 153.
Rogers, Johnnie, 198.
Rohmer, Major-General Richard, 19, 214.
Rolen, Lt. Col. James (Jim), viii, 40, 75, 92-93, 158, 188, 219.
Rolen, Linda, 92, 188.
Rollinmud, Elaine, 133.
Romanelli Brothers, 211.
Rooney, Mickey, 25.
Roosevelt, President Franklin D., 122.
Rose, Dickie, 36.
Rosenberg, Ethel, 36.
Rosenberg, Julius, 36.
Ruble, Cynthia, 77, 159.
Ruble, Don 159.
Ruth, Babe, 31.

S

Saguy, Consul Gideon, 168.
Sain, Johnny, 9.
Salinger, J. D., 113.
Salter, Dr. Robert, 125.
Sansone, Giovanni, 135.
Sansone, Salvatore, 134-35, 185.
Santayana, Prof. George, 194.
Schreyer, Gov. Gen. Edward, 49.
Schweyer, Grant, 89, 211.
Schweyer, Fern (Humber), 32, 40, 119, 188.
Schweyer, June (Van Fleet), 89.
Schweyer, Percy, 31, 32, 188.
Scott, Farr L., 211.
Scott, Mary Ann, 162.
Scott, W.B., 69, 210.
Scott, W.T., 42, 64-65.
Scrivener, Leslie, 169.
Sebastian, Dieter, 88, 104.
Seko, Emanuel, 202.
Seko, Mildred, 211.
Shackleton, Phil, 172.
Shadd, Mary Ann, 99.
Shakespeare, William, 162.
Sharkey, Jack, 24.
Shawcross, Prof. John T., 44, 202.
Shoemaker, Beth (Hurlbut), 188.
Shoemaker, Craig, 188.
Shelley, Percy B., 196.

Shennette, Brad, 86, 108, 159.
Shennette, Chris, 86, 93, 108.
Shennette, Erik, 41, 86, 108, 191, 133.
Shennette, Mitchell, 86, 109, 184, 185.
Shore, Dinah, 71.
Sider, Earl, 31.
Sider, Morris, 30-31.
Simcoe, Lt. Gov. John Graves, 22, 26-27, 26, 28, 90, 101, 104, 106, 118, 209, 216-17, 180-81.
Sinatra, Frank, 9.
Sinclair, Helen (Humber), 68, 148.
Sinclair, Ray, 148.
Smith, Dr. Bob, 86.
Smith, Gwendolyn, 165.
Smyth, Prof. D. McCormack, 82-83.
Smythe, Conn, 78.
Soane, Sir John, 186.
Sommerville, Joyce, 79.
Spahn, Warren, 9.
Spencer, Princess of Wales Diana, 22.
Stackhouse, the Hon. Reginald, 80, 215.
Stalin, Joseph, 36.
Stankey. Eddie, 9.
Stanley, Aileen, 197.
Stanley, Lt. Gov. George, 49.
Starr, Ringo, 178.
Stavro, Steve, 78.
Steinbeck, John, 197.
Stevenson, Michael, 91.
Stewart, David Macdonald, 106-07, 208.
Stewart, Don, 74.
Stewart, Liliane, 106-07.
Stickley, Gustav, 196.
Storey, Max, 88, 116, 156-56.
Stronach, Frank, 122.
Strong, Maurice F., 166-67.
Stuart, Okill, 28, 165.
Sullivan, John L., 38.
Sutherland, Donald, 186.
Swayze, John Cameron, 71.
Sweet, Michael, 168.

T

Taft, President William H., 92.
Talbot, Col. Thomas, 163.
Tapley, Nora, 91.
Tennyson, Alfred Lord, 179.
Terry, C. William, 165.
Thome, Jim, 108.
Thomas, Clara, 45.
Thomson, Kenneth, 46-47, 124, 150.
Thomson, Roy, 46-47.
Tong, Edmund, 168.
Thorman, George, 163.
Timbrell, The Hon. Dennis, 106.
Timmins, Brent, 138.
Trainer, Nick, 73.
Trevor, Cliff, 53.
Trevor, Les, 53.

Trew, Bert, 152.
Trudeau, Prime Minister Pierre Elliott, 49, 129, 171, 202, 214.
Truman, President Harry S., 11, 122.
Trump, Donald, 9.
Turco, John, 221.
Turner, Charlie, 198.
Turner, George, 60.
Turner, J. M. W., 186.
Tussaud, Madame Marie, 186-87.
Turner, The Rt. Hon. John, 127.

V

Victoria I, 187, 178, 205.
Van Fleet, June (Schweyer), 119.
VanderWoude, Arny, 144.
Vonnegut, Kurt, 197.
Von Richthofen, "Red Baron" Manfred, 114.

W

Wahlberg, Don Sr., 134.
Wahlberg, Donnie, 134.
Wahlberg, Mark, 134.
Wahlberg, "Tootsie", 134.
Walters, Dr. Allan, 62-63.
Walker, Johnnie, 134.
Warhol, Andy, 215.
Wayne, Mayor Elsie, 49.
Wayne, John, 200.
Webster, Donald Blake, 150, 172, 215.
Weir, Karin, 176.
Weir, Kenneth E., 176-77.
Weir, Mike, 211.
Weir, Shannon, 177.
Weir, Tommy, 177.
Wellesley, Arthur, 1st Duke of Wellington, 186.
Wells, Orson, 102.
Werner, Ed, 76.
Wesley, John, 186.
West, Mae, 102, 205.
Westenburg, Hester, 13.
Whitt, Ernie, 26, 216.
White, Dr. Dudley, 170.
White, Beatrice (Bea), 107
White, the Hon. John H., 90-91, 106, 131.
Wiggins, Doreen (Ormsby), 42, 56, 79, 200.
Willard, Bobby, 198.
Willard, Jess, 24.
Williams, Ted, 9, 155, 198.
Winslow, Edward, 49.
Wise, Prof. Sidney, 215.
Wise, Coach Sue, 13.
Wolf, Cynthia (Ruble), 98.
Wolf, Rev. Don, 77, 98.
Wolf, Rev. Jonathan, 98,
Wolf, Lydia, 98.
Wolf, Rev. Timothy, 98.
Wood, William R., 43.
Wordsworth, William, 196.
Woolsely, Len, 131.
Wren, Sir Christopher, 187.

CPSIA information can be obtained
at www.ICGtesting.com
Printed in the USA
LVOW05s1918210116

471610LV00016B/85/P